ID955609

RACE
TO THE
BOTTOM

RACE
TO THE
BOTTOM

UNCOVERING THE SECRET
FORCES DESTROYING
AMERICAN PUBLIC EDUCATION

LUKE ROSIAK

BROADSIDE
BOOKS

RACE TO THE BOTTOM. Copyright © 2022 by Luke Rosiak. All rights reserved. Printed in the United States of America. No part of this book may be used or reproduced in any manner whatsoever without written permission except in the case of brief quotations embodied in critical articles and reviews. For information, address Harper-Collins Publishers, 195 Broadway, New York, NY 10007.

HarperCollins books may be purchased for educational, business, or sales promotional use. For information, please email the Special Markets Department at SP-sales@harpercollins.com.

Broadside Books™ and the Broadside logo are trademarks of HarperCollins Publishers.

FIRST EDITION

Library of Congress Cataloging-in-Publication Data has been applied for.

ISBN 978-0-06-305672-5

22 23 24 25 26   LSC   10 9 8 7 6 5 4 3 2 1

For my children, and for the accidental activists:
the parents who had no choice but to fight for their kids
when they realized that no one else was.

CONTENTS

FOREWORD

BY PETER SCHWEIZER

As a parent, I was shocked by what you will read in this book. The year 2020 will be remembered for the virus from China that swept across America. Many Americans stayed in their homes for months, but perhaps the most disruptive effect was how schools were closed for much longer—for more than a year in some places, as teachers unions demanded it.

The killing of George Floyd by police in Minneapolis in May set off another viral outbreak of civil unrest in American cities and towns. Racial protests became violent riots when the sun went down. Local businesses that were already struggling because of the effects of the pandemic were looted and burned in the mayhem.

The combination of these two "viruses" exposed the presence of a third virus—in the form of a fringe ideology that attacks not the bodies of our children but their very minds. Masked by rhetoric meant to sound unobjectionable and high-minded, this ideology corrupts Americans' natural sense of fairness and justice, substituting the ideal of equality with the deceptive, loaded word "equity." It deliberately foments dissatisfaction through a Marxist lens, replacing bourgeois and worker with white and black people. It denies successes and instead focuses on omnipresent "systemic racism." This ideology is metastasizing into the curriculum of your son's middle school and your daughter's high school.

Whether you have seen it discussed as "anti-racism" or by its more academic name of "critical race theory" (CRT), the ideas behind it are not new—they have been percolating slowly in academia since the late 1970s. Academics such as Glenn Loury and Shelby Steele have warned for years about its emergence, calling it a toxic stew of racial hatred and Marxist dialectic. Under cover of seeking to redress past injustices, injustices in the present were rationalized and injustices in the future were prescribed. Statistical imbalances in academic performance and test scores became prima facie evidence of racial discrimination. And, along the way, advocates for these ideas also perfected an effective tactic to intimidate and silence their doubters. They simply called anyone who disagreed with them a racist.

In normal times, parents do not hear much of the details of what their children are being taught at school, but the online Zoom classes that came with closed schools gave a firsthand look. They were underwhelmed by the academic rigor, but heard their child's teacher inviting the students to catalog their white privilege, or telling them they are either a racist or an "anti-racist." This was a jolting experience, infuriating to some, and definitely not something mentioned in the class syllabus.

Luke Rosiak's exhaustive work in this book shows that while it might have been parents' first glimpse of such issues, they did not appear in K–12 schools overnight. Through the stories of local school systems in different parts of the country—from inner cities to wealthy suburbs and rural areas—Luke shows readers how, for years, local K–12 school systems have been captured by a variety of special interests whose allegiance is to anything but the "three Rs."

When it comes to the new R—race—Luke goes much farther than the news reports you have seen to explain where this all came from, how it spread so rapidly, who has enabled it, and why they are doing it. For one, grant-giving "philanthropic" foundations have contributed millions of dollars to underwrite the spread of this ideology in K–12 schools, while consultants have profited.

But the reason K–12 schools so eagerly eschewed standards of objectivity and meritocracy for subjective lessons and artificially forced equal outcomes is fascinating. Luke demonstrates convincingly that it is not about race at all, but rather the latest in a series of techniques used by education bureaucrats to hide more fundamental failings around their core mission.

My work as an investigative journalist involves sifting our nation's political class for evidence of corruption. What I have seen over my decades of work is that corruption is most likely to fester where no one is looking. What Luke has found is that some of the same forms of deception, self-dealing, and corruption that I have seen in the halls of power are also occurring behind the friendly-seeming facades of the schools in your town. He identifies systemic rot in an area that is, somehow, simultaneously omnipresent and remarkably underscrutinized.

There are kickbacks to school board members who, wouldn't you know, also run (or have a family member who runs) businesses that do all sorts of educational "consulting" work. There are enormous charitable foundations that gain access through generous grants, only to steer schools to focus on their agendas, which rarely entail better academic outcomes. There are games being played with the statistics to make educators look good without helping students. These are familiar scams to me, but the extent of it is eye-opening.

I also see the parallels with the "public choice economics" theory that large government bureaucracies over time become more concerned with pursuing what is best for the bureaucracies themselves, to the detriment of the people they are supposed to serve. Luke's book presents a strong case against teachers unions and the public school monopoly and will be particularly helpful for those who are considering the merits of policies such as school choice, vouchers, and other alternatives to the public school behemoth.

Among the many things that will strike you is how effectively, over the course of decades, bureaucrats concealed academic problems from parents and activists steered school bureaucracies. Many teachers were too scared or complacent to object, and parents too busy or trusting, so they went along to get along. There are not many stories of heroism here. Perhaps, though, Luke's work will inspire parents to pay more attention to what is happening on their local school boards or, better still, consider running for them. There is not much time left to restore an educational system that once was the envy of the world, and it is essential that American schools produce citizens who not only understand their country's history, warts and all, but are also happy, well-adjusted children who know how to read, write, and perform arithmetic.

RACE
TO THE
BOTTOM

INTRODUCTION

Eight-year-old Lucy lay curled in a fetal position on the floor and rocked back and forth.

It was November 2020, and the little girl had not been to school in almost eight months, since Fairfax County, Virginia, had ordered schools closed in March.

Tracy Compton struggled through tears to type out another email.

"Hi School Board," she wrote. "Have you ever had your kids so upset by school that they hold themselves on the floor and rock? How would that make you feel as a parent?"

In the fall of 2020, life was proceeding for many Americans despite the respiratory virus that had spread from China. They donned cloth face masks to minimize the chance of spread, but otherwise went about their business. Low-paid cashiers showed up for work and handled cash from an endless procession of strangers. Postal workers traveled from house to house. Waiters brought your food in restaurants. Flight attendants cleaned up airsickness bags and navigated the narrow aisles. School sports continued. Heck, even strip clubs were open, albeit with more stringent social distancing required.

Teachers, the highest paid of any of these positions, who interacted with the fewest people during a typical workday, and worked with the age group that posed and faced by far the least risk, refused to return to their classrooms.

Fairfax's schools said they would provide "distance learning" by computer. This turned out to mean roughly an hour of teaching time per day, four days a week. The school day could be over by 9:30 a.m. for elementary school students. The rest of the time was for what the school system called "asynchronous learning," which—translated from jargon—ostensibly meant kids completing homework assignments on the computer, but often just meant parents watching their kids.[1]

No one would think that asking an eight-year-old to use PowerPoint was reasonable. Lucy could not sit in a chair and look at a computer for hours a day. Lucy could not go nearly a full year, or one-eighth of her life, without seeing her friends. So, in frustration, she rocked herself there on the floor.

"You did this to my daughter, Lucy Compton. A sweet energic [*sic*] lovely little girl," Tracy typed in one of her recurring missives to the school board. "She need [*sic*] to go to school. Please help her," she pleaded in another.

Of course, for every teacher who would not do her job, numerous parents had to either quit their jobs or find some way to do both theirs *and* the teacher's. Tracy still had to work or she could not afford to live in Fairfax County. "I HAVE TO WORK. IT IS THE END OF THE MONTH. I HAVE TO SUBMIT BILLS," she wrote in late January 2021.

It did not have to be this way. For months, medical evidence had been clear that children were not drivers of coronavirus transmission. Schools in much of the country were open without incident.[2] In Virginia, by the end of 2020, only one person under the age of twenty who had contracted coronavirus had died.[3] In November, the then head of the Centers for Disease Control and Prevention (CDC), Dr. Robert Redfield, said that "[f]or kids K–12, one of the safest places they can be, from our perspective, is to remain in school." He had been saying the same thing since the summer.[4] Still, in Fairfax County, education—the most basic service of government, the most essential to any family—was being largely withheld.

On October 6, Fairfax County's top health official, Dr. Gloria Addo-Ayensu, said, "Schools can be open now," adding that officials had "squandered a huge opportunity" by not opening sooner. "The entire northern Virginia [area] is currently experiencing low disease burden. Our transmission extent is low, it's been low for a very long time," she pointed out. The school board dismissed her advice, and it was no secret why.[5]

The day after Addo-Ayensu's statement, the teachers union in neighboring Prince William County staged a caravan protest, with child-sized coffins propped on the roofs of their cars. Within two weeks, the Fairfax teachers union formally demanded that the school board "draw and hold the line by keeping Fairfax County Public Schools [FCPS] virtual for the remainder of the 2020–21 school year." They claimed that it was because "Science and Health Safety data support" it.[6]

Similar protests were occurring all over the country, which provided ample evidence that teachers did not actually fear congregating with others. In August 2020 in New York City, teachers held up fake body bags, mock coffins, and signs daubed in fake blood with messages like "We Won't Die for the Department of Education," at a crowded street protest in the middle of America's biggest city. Later that month, they traveled to Washington, D.C., for a political rally at which fifty thousand people packed the National Mall on the fifty-seventh anniversary of Martin Luther King Jr.'s "I Have a Dream" speech. There, Al Sharpton draped his arm across Randi Weingarten, the president of the American Federation of Teachers, who claimed that teachers were "making their wills."[7]

If teachers really believed being in the classroom was a death sentence, it seemed their position was that they did not want to die: they wanted someone *else* to. Fairfax children *could* actually go to public school, if parents were willing to pay extra for the privilege. For as much as $1,472 per month per child, depending on household income, children could sit in school buildings as part of a program called "School Age Child Care," where low-wage county employees with "limited benefits" watched students while they used their laptops to interact with teachers who were at home. For parents with four children, the cost could be as high as $5,152 a month, on top of the taxes they had already paid for the same government service.[8]

Tracy noticed that Lucy's teacher had manicured nails and styled hair, which suggested she was not staying home all the time, but rather going to businesses with close contact. She would disappear for weeks at a time. Fairfax only provided a substitute if the teacher was gone for three or more days.

Kids were becoming suicidal. Debbi Goudreau, a former Fairfax special ed teacher, adopted her two sons out of foster care. The younger was five and had severe emotional problems. The older, his biological brother, was six. She was willing to sacrifice for them. The schools were not. "Within days of the school closing he was sitting in a box threatening to kill himself. And he's only five years old. And the school said 'sorry, this is the best we can do,'" Debbi said. "He goes right back to his trauma response, because this has been what's happened to him throughout his life. He gets attached to someone, and then it gets taken away."

As she watched her son throw chairs and break computers, her friends who were still teachers displayed wild-eyed fear at the most remote chance of contracting the disease. They were so angry that she had broken from their party line of closed schools that most would not talk to her and a guidance counselor unfriended her on social media. Teachers used their access to students to tell them that lives were at stake unless everyone stayed home. Meanwhile, her older son was attending Catholic school five days a week. "Now he [the younger one] is worried that his brother is going to die," Debbi said.

So as Tracy Compton painfully typed her email and Lucy rocked in a fetal position, it was clear that few people in the world had greater power over her family than the Fairfax County, Virginia, school board.

None of its members responded.

* * *

Kimberly Adams, the forty-four-year-old president of the Fairfax Education Association (FEA) teachers union, got a more receptive audience as she addressed the board nearly every meeting, often as its first speaker.

On November 11, the day before Tracy's email, the board had

taken steps to change its public comment policy to guarantee at least three speaking slots at every meeting went to unions. Parents could fight for the remaining slots by registering online early in the morning; they were typically gone within one minute and could also be taken by employees. If a parent did not show up at the meeting, a standby list of speakers would prioritize employees over parents.[9]

A week later, a board panel reaffirmed its commitment to "organizational leave," the policy under which management paid salaries of union representatives who lobbied it. The county had approved nearly $6 million over a three-year period on such salaries. Adams had once been a school librarian and teacher, but now she was a full-time union boss.[10]

Since the summer, Adams had insisted that "a vaccination or a widely available treatment for COVID-19 is necessary before a full return to in-person instruction can be achieved safely." At the time, a vaccine was not expected to be available for at least eight months. She disagreed with Virginia's governor, himself a doctor, who did not believe that a vaccine was necessary to reopen schools for the upcoming school year. The excuse became moot when a vaccine was announced much earlier than expected, in November 2020.[11]

While nationwide mass vaccination schedules were being created, on January 7, 2021, Adams demanded that the board cancel plans to return without a vaccine and "continue virtual learning for all groups at this time . . . lives must be protected. The FEA is asking that you do not put us in further harm's way when we know that a safer return to schools is on the horizon. Vaccinate your staff before you return them to in-person instruction."[12]

The board asked Virginia's governor to give teachers priority to receive the vaccine, which was tightly rationed, and he did—putting them at the same priority level as the elderly. This meant that for every teacher who took a dose, one fewer was available for the one age group that was most vulnerable and faced a significant chance of dying from the disease. On January 14, Adams herself was among the first to receive a shot, even though she did not work in a school. School board members were also in the same group as the elderly. Seventy-five people in their seventies or older in Fairfax died with coronavirus during the four-week period when teachers were getting vaccines.[13]

After teachers had received the shot, the union moved the goalposts with a new demand. "At the last meeting I stood before you to tell you that you needed to vaccinate your staff before returning them to in-person instruction," Adams said on January 21, but now, "please ensure that the fully virtual option remains for all students and staff who feel safest at home."[14]

Adams now told the school board that teachers should "wait for the second dose to be effective" and, even then, not return to work full-time because the *students* had not yet been vaccinated. A vaccine approved for children under sixteen did not exist, and likely was not a priority, since the virus posed very little risk to children without preexisting conditions. This demand meant that even the following school year, parents should not expect their children to go to school more than two days a week. In the intervening days, her union had taken part in a "National Day of Resistance" organized by a group called Demand Safe Schools—a partnership between teachers unions and the Democratic Socialists of America—and now its position, requiring student vaccinations, mirrored theirs verbatim.[15]

In early February, the Fairfax school system unveiled a plan in which, after teachers were vaccinated, students might eventually return to school for two days a week, but thousands of teachers would continue to work from home. The district hired "monitors"—anyone with "any combination of education and experience equivalent to graduation from high school"—to watch students as they sat in classrooms with computers. For fifteen dollars an hour, monitors were willing to do what teachers would not.[16]

The reasoning behind the two-days-a-week schedule was to create two separate cohorts that could spread out more in classrooms and who would not interact with each other, preventing any outbreak in one cohort from spreading to the other. But there was one notable exception: the pre-K to sixth-grade children of FCPS employees would be permitted to attend four days a week.[17]

"Vaccination is not a silver bullet," Adams reiterated on February 4. "We are thankful that nearly 50 percent of the student population will continue to be safe at home."[18]

The school board was meeting in person, but Adams spoke through a video feed. Her head was beamed onto a large screen behind the dais, her voice booming through speakers as she acknowledged the only reason any of this should not seem absurd, if not morally egregious.

"Even after all the targets painted on the backs of those who speak up for what is right, we will continue to make our voices heard, we will protect everyone in our community—because Fairfax County Public Schools is ours," she proclaimed.

* * *

Race to the Bottom is a book about what happens when schools start putting their resources into everything except preparing our children for college or careers.

One side effect of COVID-19, as the illness caused by the coronavirus is known, was to remind Americans just how central K–12 schools are to our lives. For years, we debated everything else—the president, colleges, foreign wars. But the one thing we might realistically have some influence over, that operates in our backyards and has shared custody of our most precious asset, our children? It was more or less on autopilot.

Another side effect was realizing what a mistake this was. As much as parents might respect the people who ran schools, they did not seem to return the favor. It turned out that K–12 schools were at times not benevolent pillars of the community, but deceptive and money-driven entities captured by national politics and special interests.

Throughout the stories in this book, I want to explore two ideas. The first is that racial politics are more than a controversial topic. They can be used as a tool to win administrative battles, distract angry parents, and even cover up inequality. We consistently get these kinds of conflicts wrong. We look too hard at the controversial ideas without asking, what do the powerful have to gain? We misread their decisions. We misinterpret who they are benefiting.

Sometimes well-meaning educators want to make things fairer. More often, the well-meaning become weapons in political and bureaucratic battles.

Parents discovered that the education industry's unyielding primary mission is its own preservation. Fairfax's superintendent, Scott Brabrand, issued a memo assuring all staff that they would receive full pay even if no work needed to be done. To justify the continued employment of bus drivers, he ordered Fairfax's fleet of school buses, which is larger than the fleet of Greyhound, to make their rounds twice a week with no children on board, driving through the quiet neighborhoods and producing a ghostly sight that haunted children who peered out of their living room windows. Bus operations alone cost the district some $167.5 million in fiscal year 2020, which is 5.6 percent of its budget.[19]

By October 2020, thousands of Fairfax teachers had submitted Americans with Disabilities Act (ADA) requests, claiming that they had developed disabilities that legally entitled them to accommodations. As of early 2021, less than 1 percent of requests had been denied. A few months earlier, when high school seniors needed to take the SAT—where by definition there would be almost no movement or contact—the union coached teachers on how to mislead their superiors: "If you are physically ill at the prospect of this work, you must let your administration know that you are sick and cannot help."[20]

Private schools across the country were in session without contributing to community spread.[21] But it was as if the public educational establishment was refusing to work while also demanding that no one find out how others managed to do better. On July 31, Fairfax's neighbor to the north, Maryland's Montgomery County, abruptly banned private schools from opening, and battled the governor, ultimately unsuccessfully, as he overruled the move. Several months later, Montgomery County attempted to give the vaccine to public school teachers who had not been going to work while withholding it from private school teachers who had.[22]

Parents who were able to formed learning "pods," hiring tutors to work with small groups of students in homes. This was a financial burden. But the cost was still only a fraction of the $16,973 per student the Fairfax school system spent.[23]

That could not stand. In August, Fairfax invoked ideological language that amounted to the playground threat *if I can't have it, no one can* to indicate that, if it could, it would have stopped those parents from giving their kids even that chance at an education. "While FCPS doesn't and can't control these private tutoring groups, we do have concerns that they may widen the gap in educational access and equity for all students," it told them.[24]

While educators wanted parents to withhold help from children, presumably to make them equal to those who were floundering, they would not take similar steps when it affected their own children or pocketbooks. As teachers drew a paycheck from schools to stay home on the premise that in-person teaching was too dangerous, some of them double-dipped by tutoring private groups. One offered ten gym classes behind a school for $120.

In nearby Alexandria, Superintendent Gregory Hutchings admonished parents who set up learning pods, saying that this "can cause some inequities if some kids can do things and others can't." Hutchings withdrew his own child from a public school and put him in a Catholic school that was holding some in-person classes. In mid-August, the superintendent of neighboring Falls Church scolded parents for withdrawing their children from a system that was not offering classes. "These actions—that is, disenrolling from FCCPS—have consequences," he lectured. "FCCPS receives funding from the local Government, the State Government, and the Federal Government based on the numbers of students we have enrolled."[25]

But no matter what, public schools never seemed to lose out on money. Before the pandemic, Fairfax had predicted growth of 1,400 students, which it said would require $29 million for additional expenses, including hiring 323 employees. By September 2020, it reported that instead, nearly 5 percent of the student body fled the shuttered system, leading to an enrollment decline of almost nine thousand compared to the prior year. By its own math, that should have meant a savings of $183.5 million and the reduction of 2,044 jobs. Nevertheless, its fiscal 2021 budget was $226.3 million higher than its fiscal 2020 budget, and added 479 more employees.[26]

Fairfax County Public Schools had a fiscal 2020 budget of $3 billion. Fifty-three percent of local taxes in the county went to the schools, meaning whether you had kids in the schools or not, you were paying for them.[27]

Much of this funding came from dual-income households where both parents worked in order to afford Fairfax's hefty cost of living and its taxes. The school system did not seem to care about them. Nazanin Brown and her husband work for U.S. intelligence agencies, and their work never stopped because of coronavirus. Each day they reported to secure facilities where cell phones were not permitted, leaving them out of contact with their four children.

They had stretched to afford their home and chose it specifically because of the schools. Now Nazanin's kindergartner, second grader, fifth grader, and seventh grader were at times home without adult supervision. She had no choice.

She made meatballs at 7 a.m. so their kids would have their next two meals. When possible, her husband went to the office at night, after she came home. Her husband, a scientist with a PhD, saw no medical reason why teachers and children could not go to school buildings. And he saw how ludicrous the teachers' alternative was. "He's trying to get this child to mute, open a tab. . . . It's obvious five-year-olds don't know how to do that. Leila should be playing with blocks. He's trying to get her to 'say hi to your friends.' Those are not her friends. She doesn't know those people," she said. Nazanin had Leila reading at a second-grade level by the time she started kindergarten. After FCPS had its way with her, she was reverting to baby talk and potty accidents.

"I go in and serve my country for eight hours, then I run home and my husband goes to work," she said. "Do you know how hard that is on a family of four kids?" Nazanin contacted school board member Karen Corbett Sanders, who told her that if anyone were allowed back in school, it would be recent immigrants, with her children returning significantly later as part of a staggered queue.

She "told me there are some kids that just got to this country so they need to go first. And I said 'I was born here [Fairfax] and I pay taxes on a $996,000 home and you're telling me I go to the back of the line? Excuse me?'" A "return to school" presentation from the district said that "high needs populations" such as "English learners" might be prioritized, even though the same presentation said that almost 65 percent of Fairfax's coronavirus cases were among Hispanics.[28]

When she heard officials virtue-signaling about identity politics while failing to provide essential services, Nazanin, who is half black and half Middle Eastern, could think only one thing: "Shut up and open the goddamned schools." She finally put her kindergartner in private school, realizing that it cost less than the county-run day care program.

Stories like this present a puzzle we often wave away as a misunderstanding. Why would the people who claim to be the most worried about inequality make decisions that make the problem worse? The answer, so common in ways that we all fail to appreciate, is that once you decide everything is about race, anyone's agenda can be justified as promoting racial equity. Most outsiders are unprepared to fight familiar battles on those terms, widening what bad actors can get away with. In the pages that follow, you are going to see how we keep making these errors now, in ways that have consequences for our children, our communities, and our country.

Educators spent an inordinate amount of time invoking liberal platitudes instead of focusing on reading, math, and science. But even this was little more than a charade. As teachers forced an extended economic shutdown, women's role in the workplace was set back a generation as childcare fell to mothers. More than two million women left the workforce in 2020. In December 2020, women lost 156,000 jobs, while men gained jobs. As Fairfax County sent its empty buses on their pollution-spewing rounds in order to keep drivers employed, the environmentalists on the school board did nothing.[29]

Untold numbers of young children were left home alone day after day in heavily minority neighborhoods of single mothers working blue-collar jobs, but union leaders who constantly invoked racial inequality made their choice. Whether a school system was open or not correlated less with the rate of coronavirus in its area than with the strength of the local teachers union. In right-to-work states, roughly 38 percent of districts offered full-time, in-person class. The figure was around 13 percent in states with progressive laws mandating union membership.[30] Minorities are more likely to live in liberal areas. Chalkbeat, an education nonprofit news organization, lamented in September 2020 that "districts where the vast majority of students are white are more than three times as likely as school districts that enroll mostly students of color to be open," saying it would "exacerbate inequities."[31]

What kind of people would exploit a moment of national vulnerability for their own gain?

And if they would do this, what else had they been doing all these years?

* * *

This leads us to our second, deeper issue. The same qualities that lead us to not worry about school politics—they are local, the elections are small, the politicians and administrators are regular people—actually make them appealing targets for outsiders with money and radical agendas. It is easy to think that kids will learn math and spelling no matter what, and the political fights will be at the margins. That version of the story, the version that most of us live under, is entirely wrong. Once you see it, you will realize how many questions remain unanswered. Who are these outsiders? Why are they so well resourced? How do they become insiders? What are they hoping to do? Let's look at just one of these groups.

After racial protesters highlighted cases of police brutality, many liberals came to believe that police unions operated to the detriment of the rest of society. After the coronavirus pandemic, it was hard to avoid the same conclusion about teachers unions.[32]

Teachers unions' interests were at odds with parents' interests. They seemed to care more about radical politics, money, and power than they did about education. Yet we had given them near-total control over an invaluable bargaining chip: our children.

In Los Angeles in July 2020, the union released a "research paper" calling for schools to be completely shuttered that fall, but its reasons had at least as much to do with politics as with the virus. "The COVID-19 pandemic in the United States underscores the deep equity and justice challenges arising from our profoundly racist, intensely unequal society," it wrote. The union was explicit about the calculation that delaying the return to school would shut down the broader economy of one of the country's largest markets months before a presidential election. Since a president's chances of reelection often hinge on the economy, this would harm President Donald Trump, whom the union opposed. "The Trump administration's attempt to force people to return to work on a large scale depends on restarting physical schools so parents have childcare," the union acknowledged. Los Angeles's top health official, Dr. Barbara Ferrer, underscored the bluntly political message, saying of closed schools: "We're going to be where we are now until we are done with the election."[33]

Your child was their hostage. The ransom they demanded was money and unrelated ideological concessions. Observing that "local policies often set the precedent for more progressive moves at the state and national level," the union set out a list of demands for extreme progressive policies, many of them having nothing to do with schools. These were laid out in the July 2020 "research paper," which would have earned any student a failing grade. The demands begun: "1. Defund Police: Police violence is a leading cause of death and trauma for Black people." It supported this with a footnote pointing to a 2018 paper that said no such thing because it is simply not true.[34]

The Los Angeles teachers union went on to make a series of New Deal–like demands, such as that housing be a "human right," and that undocumented immigrants get welfare. When their demands did relate to schools, they had little to do with children. They called for a moratorium on charter schools, which are viewed favorably by Democrat minority parents as an effective pathway out of poverty, but opposed by the union because if these parents choose them, it could "drain resources" from the district that pays the union members.[35]

By late October 2020 in Chicago, with the schools closed for seven months straight, the Chicago Teachers Union (CTU) refused "to even discuss a return to in-person learning, even as hundreds of private schools in Chicago are open," a school district spokeswoman said. "CTU continues to obstruct and mislead the public."[36] The union was hiding behind children: "Our youngest and most medically vulnerable students deserve safety," the union said. Illinois recorded only a single resident under the age of twenty who had died of the disease by that month: apparently an eighteen-year-old college student home in the state because his college was conducting classes online.

In late December 2020, seventeen Chicago physicians implored the city's schools to open. Among the doctors was the president of the Illinois chapter of the American Academy of Pediatrics. In their open letter to the *Chicago Sun-Times*, these physicians stated: "We cannot understate the serious psychological harm that prolonged virtual school has had on many children. We are seeing an epidemic of serious psychological illness that has reached a crisis point. . . . It is widely agreed upon by the medical community that in-person classroom learning is both optimal and safe."[37]

Chicago's teachers were unmoved. Within days, a member of the union's executive board and a "strike captain," Sarah Chambers, successfully encouraged teachers to defy orders to return to work because it would be "unsafe"—while writing from poolside in Puerto Rico, where she was vacationing. In August 2019, she and other "CTU Strikers" had led a "CTU Delegation to Venezuela," where government officials from the socialist nation gave them a tour, leading Chambers to gush about its merits over the United States in a tweet: "While staying in #Venezuela, we didn't see a single homeless person."[38]

Chicago's teachers knew that despite closing schools to minimize coronavirus spread, young people were still congregating. They did not seem to mind as long as the purpose was more important than education. Political protests raged throughout 2020's coronavirus shutdown, sometimes veering into anarchy and riots. When protesters set up a mock guillotine outside the home of Amazon billionaire Jeff Bezos, the CTU egged them on, writing: "We are completely frightened by, completely impressed by and completely in support of wherever this is headed."[39] The guillotine is a symbol of the French

Revolution, which as history teachers should know, ended in the "Reign of Terror" and a dictatorship.

Before the pandemic, a third of Chicago's kids—nearly 90 percent of whom were minorities—were chronically absent from school. Only about a quarter passed state math exams, 77 percent graduated, and most who went on to college needed remedial courses. In December, CTU said, "The push to reopen schools is rooted in sexism, racism and misogyny."[40]

Teachers had not given students the skills to be successful in the modern economy. But they made them useful pawns for the ideological battles the unions seemed to care about more.

1

CHEATING MATH

Here is the first thing to know about educators: they are failing miserably. The academic performance of American kids is terrible and has been for a long time. Educators apparently do not know how to fix it; nothing they have tried has worked.

As a result, the education industry has settled on finding ways to look good rather than be good. Since most people cannot see what is happening inside classrooms, superintendents and principals live and die on statistics that attempt to gauge a school's quality. They play an Enron-like numbers game, finding ways to juke the stats and mask problems. This helps their careers, but harms kids.

GRADUATION DECEPTION

Weeks before the 2016 election, President Barack Obama announced a significant achievement: the nation's high school graduation rate had reached an all-time high of 83 percent. Ever since the Bush administration ordered states to begin calculating graduation rates in a standardized way in 2008 and this data began being published as of the 2010–11 school year, the rates had risen nicely every year. American education appeared to be on the upswing.[1]

"The high school graduation rate has risen steadily over President Obama's time in office, growing by about four percentage points since the 2010–2011 school year," the White House proclaimed. "This increase reflects important progress schools across the country are making to better prepare students for college and careers after graduation."[2]

Obama made the announcement at Benjamin Banneker Academic High School in Washington, D.C., a city he identified as the poster child for this triumph. "The District of Columbia made the greatest amount of progress in the Nation, improving its graduation rates by seven percentage points," the White House noted, adding that the district had "received support through Race to the Top—the Obama Administration's signature education reform initiative."

At nearby Ballou High School several months after Obama's 2016 speech, every one of the school's 190 seniors was accepted to college—remarkable considering that the previous year only 3 percent of students (including the now-seniors) had managed to pass their citywide English exams, and not a single student met the math standards.[3]

"The class of 2017 at Ballou will go down in history. They are the first class to be accepted, entirely, to college," NPR heralded. "For months and months, staff tracked students' success, often working side by side with them in the school library on college applications. . . . Then there was money. Grants, donations and district funds took students on college tours around the country. The school kept spirits and motivation up with pep rallies, T-shirts and free food."

Student Trayvon McKoy said, "Everyone walks around with their heads high now." He was off to study music production at Bethune-Cookman University, a Florida school that would be put on probation by its accreditor the next year.[4]

The only problem, as NPR realized months after it published its inspirational tale, was that Ballou's success was built entirely on large-scale malfeasance.

In reality, all but eleven of its esteemed graduates were truant so often that the courts should have been notified. Half were truant for more than three months, which, according to district policy, meant they should have failed. Two months before graduation, only fifty-seven students were on track to graduate. One hundred sixty-four walked across the stage two months later.[5] How was this possible?

Teachers said administrators pressured them to change kids' grades and pass no-show students. D.C. also allowed students who failed a class to make it up with something called "credit recovery" courses. Ballou would enroll students in these courses concurrently with the actual class—before they had even failed—indicating that one required far less effort than the other. "They go, 'Oh, I ain't gotta do no work in your class; I can just go over here, do a little PowerPoint, pass and graduate,'" music teacher Monica Brokenborough said. "That's setting that kid up for failure just so you can showboat you got this graduation rate."[6]

When standardized test results were released later, they were little different from previous years: while every Ballou senior may have been accepted to college, not a single one had met the modest math standards necessary to score as "college- and career-ready" on the citywide exam, which was administered just before graduation.[7]

The fact that everyone was admitted to college did little to improve anyone's life. One hundred eighty-three seniors were accepted to the University of the District of Columbia, but only sixteen actually enrolled for the fall semester. One who made it to a four-year college admitted she did not want to be there. "I don't want to. I could care less," she said.[8]

The real scandal was that this was no aberration. As Obama stood in D.C. and lauded the rising graduation rate, similar maneuvers were responsible for increases throughout the country.

That could be seen even without leaving the D.C. area. Prince George's County, Maryland, one of America's wealthiest black-majority counties, showed an 8.5 percent rise in graduation rates over the four years leading up to 2017. Its chief executive paraded with banners and pom-poms to celebrate. But these stats were the result of outright fabrications by administrators.[9]

Two weeks before graduation day, 42 percent of DuVal High

School seniors were set to fail. Counselor Troy Sibila wrote to teachers at 10:30 p.m. on May 10, 2017: "If there is any last-minute, (rub a genie in a bottle), assistance you can [provide to] help our future scholars, please assist." On May 24, nearly 92 percent of seniors walked across the graduation stage. "I did what I was ordered to do," Sibila said later. "It was coming from the CEO's team." Counselor Yvette Thomasson, who, like Sibila, was fired after the scandal came to light, said she should get her job back because "[w]e did what we were told to do, help at-risk kids."[10]

Whistle-blowers presented school board members with evidence that at schools across the county, courses students had never taken were added to their records, and administrators altered grades. Only four of the fourteen school board members chose to act on the evidence. The revelations forced the district to clean up some of its practices, and half of its graduation-rate gains evaporated the next year. The remaining half may be explained by the fact that misconduct still had not stopped. State auditors found that more than 60 percent of 2018 graduates had so many unexcused absences that they should not have qualified for a diploma.[11]

In neighboring Montgomery County, Maryland, similar loopholes were in place. Students who failed state-mandated exams could still graduate by completing a "bridge project." Brian Donlon, a social studies teacher at Richard Montgomery High School, alerted his supervisors that kids were given bridge project worksheets filled out in advance. When the school did nothing, he went to the state. The state did not act, either. Maryland State Board of Education member David Steiner said he feared "an almost total absence of consistent or defensible standards" for so-called bridge projects. Bureaucrats could not tell him whether they had ever declined to rubber-stamp a bridge project with a passing grade.[12]

The gambit to take kids who were illiterate or refused to set foot in school and transform them into glowing statistics for administrators and politicians—without actually improving the kids—also spawned a lucrative industry for for-profit companies. In 2013, Chicago faced a near 62 percent graduation rate. It contracted with the for-profit EdisonLearning to operate special schools, and the rate increased to nearly 79 percent by 2019.[13] In 2011, the company paid basketball legend Magic Johnson to license his name and encouraged youth to "Join Magic's Team." If someone showed interest in one of its schools, call center employees dialed three times a day for forty-five days to get him or her to enroll. In 2017, the company paid students in gift cards for referring others. It paid pastors of African American churches in Chicago's South Side to recruit students. A similar firm, called Accelerated Learning Solutions, told employees to "bring a gift" to Florida high school guidance counselors. They also reminded them of the real gift: by offloading bad students to their for-profit school, their own school's statistics would look better.[14]

What magic were these for-profit companies doing to make up years of learning in just months? To hear them tell it, it was technology. Their students engaged in self-directed learning on computers. In practice that meant this: In a strip mall in Columbus, Ohio, three students sat in a massive computer lab, surrounded by empty seats. The computers presented multiple-choice questions, and students would "keep clicking till they got it right," as graduate Corey Timmons explained. Students often did not even read the questions, but if they did ask for help, teachers would say, "Just google the questions and do the best you can." Though only three students attended the required hours that day, Edison billed taxpayers for educating 171 full-time that month. After a student enrolled, there were no thrice-a-day phone calls begging him to show up.[15]

Did educators really believe that students who had spit in their faces, cut class for months, or struggled to write had suddenly become high achievers? At Brooklyn's John Dewey High School, a credit recovery program that allowed "failing pupils to get passing grades by playing games, doing work online or taking abbreviated programs that critics argue lack academic rigor" was called "Easy pass" by students. Principal Kathleen Elvin had brought the graduation rate from 56 percent in 2009 to 74 percent in 2014, until teachers blew the whistle on a grade-fixing scam in 2015. Hundreds of students had been placed in fake classes, with one teacher purportedly teaching fifty-two classes in a semester. Elvin was not disciplined, perhaps because a disciplinary trial would show that New York City's Department of Education headquarters was complicit. Instead, the headquarters hired her, giving her a $157,000 job in the central office; her salary grew to $184,000 in 2018, her last full year before retiring. City council member Robert Holden said similar activity was happening throughout city schools. "They're doing it to make their bottom line look good. That's the definition of organized crime. That's what the [New York City] DOE has turned into," he said.[16]

SUBJECTIVE GRADING

Similar efforts to show positive outcomes occur through lowering standards. For the 2012–13 school year, 37 percent of Colorado's high school graduates needed remedial courses in college, a sign that a high school diploma did not mean much. But that was for colleges and employers to deal with. To improve their reported high school graduation rate, state officials soon eroded standards further, eliminating science and social studies requirements. In 2015, the Los Angeles school board lowered the "passing" grade for college preparation courses from a C to a D.[17]

In the education world, fads with names like "Social and Emotional Learning (SEL)" and "Standards-Based Assessment (SBA)" are common. These trendy educational "pedagogies" generally have one thing in common: they use subjective measures, result in grade inflation, and sometimes obscure record-keeping that would show whether kids knew basic math, science, and reading.

In wealthy Arlington, Virginia, elementary schools abolished letter grades, complaining that "'ABCDE' grading drives students towards 'A.'" The grades were replaced with three "standards-based assessment" categories: "Approaching Mastery," "Developing Mastery," and "Insufficient Evidence." The worst grade a student could get seemed to condemn the teacher for being obtuse: "The teacher does not have evidence to determine a student's mastery level for this skill." At the high end of this scale, there is no objective way of measuring mastery. "Because every student is unique, SBA accepts any demonstration of skill as valid, so teachers use a wide array of student work examples, artifacts, conferences, and analyses to meaningfully understand each learner." The policy is described as "research-best practices-based." Under "References," it lists an article published in *Slate* titled "The Case Against Grades: They Lower Self-Esteem, Discourage Creativity, and Reinforce the Class Divide."[18]

In San Francisco's school system, an in-house professional development training program called "Grading for Equity with Synergy and Google Classroom" told teachers to grade on an SBA scale of 0–4 instead of 0–100. The trainer explained the benefits: "Mathematically, the idea that it's going to be working a little bit more in the student's favor" for bad students, noting that a student who simply does not complete a third of his work would get the equivalent of a C+. In "the inequitable kind of standard style," he said, he would get an F.

Whether grades were inflated through fraud or "pedagogies," reality threatened to catch up in the form of one pesky thing: state standardized tests. There was often little correlation between a student's grade on his report card and his score on the test that measured the same content. At the Science School for Exploration and Discovery in the Bronx borough of New York City, 94 percent of students passed their math classes in the 2017–18 school year, but only 2 percent passed their standardized math exams. At nearby Harbor Heights Middle School, every student passed their English classes, but only 7 percent passed the state exam. Similar figures abound. A New York school spokeswoman simply shrugged off the "two-day state exam," implying that grades were more accurate.[19]

TEST SCORES DECLINING

There is a dirty secret across the country. Subjectively assigned grades may look good, but objective test scores say different. Few parents pressure officials about this mismatch because when their kid comes home with an A, they are not inclined to argue. Some parents tell themselves their kid is "just bad at test-taking."

As graduation rates rose under the Obama administration, measurements less susceptible to tampering did the opposite. Average

SAT scores fell eight points between 2012 and 2015 (the SAT was redesigned the next year), while the percentage of students taking it remained virtually unchanged. In West Virginia, as its graduation rate rose from 79 percent to 87 percent between 2012 and 2015, its average SAT score fell by 14 points, and the percentage of students taking the test fell as well.[20] National ACT scores have been lower than their 2012 level every year since.

The National Assessment of Educational Progress (NAEP), often called "The Nation's Report Card," is conducted every two years and measures fourth and eighth graders' reading and math skills. For decades, math scores had steadily risen, but after 2013, the momentum reversed. In 2019, the reading and math scores for both grades were all below 2013 levels. In Nevada, as the graduation rate rose from 62 percent to 83 percent between 2011 and 2018, math scores fell from 278 to 274 between 2011 and 2019. In New Mexico, the graduation rate increased from 63 percent to 74 percent, but math scores decreased from 274 to 269. In Rhode Island, the graduation rate rose from 77 percent to 84 percent, while math scores sank from 283 to 276.[21]

Finally, the Program for International Student Assessment (PISA) measures educational aptitude across developed nations, benchmarking Americans against other children who will soon be competing for jobs in a global economy. On the 2018 PISA math exam for fifteen-year-old students, the United States ranked near the bottom of Organisation for Economic Co-operation and Development countries, placing thirtieth of thirty-six. It fell five slots in the rankings since 2009.[22] America's math score fell nine points during that time, while the United Kingdom's went up by nearly the same amount.[23] If math is essential in a modern economy, America is not well positioned against its competitors. In 2018, 27 percent of American students scored at the lowest level of the math exam, which is worse than all but six OECD countries. In the portions of China that took the test, that figure was 2 percent. And when taking all students into account, Russia outperformed the United States by ten points in the PISA math exam.[24]

ANTI-TESTING

Educators faced with irreconcilable disparities between grades and test scores had a solution: get rid of the tests. The idea that there is too much testing in schools, that it is stifling children's creativity, that teachers are forced to "teach to the test," or that they are "high-stakes" has been aggressively promulgated by educators.[25]

None of it, however, is remotely true. The mandatory state tests are designed to measure schools more than students. Students often are not affected in any way by their scores. Tests do not take up more than a few days out of the year, and as anyone can see by looking at sample test questions, they measure the exact topics that students are supposed to have learned. If a test evaluates a third grader's ability to do multiplication, *shouldn't* teachers be "teaching to the test" by teaching multiplication?[26]

These objections are familiar because of an advocacy group called FairTest. Whenever declining test scores are in the news, FairTest's position—that standardized tests themselves are the problem and should be abolished—is likely to be included in the press coverage.[27] In one 2015 case, a *Washington Post* journalist simply turned her column over to the group's executive director.[28] But FairTest is little more than a front group staffed by a part-time PR man. FairTest is funded by the National Education Association, the nation's largest teachers union. Its executive director, Bob Schaeffer, runs a public relations firm and has no training or credentials in education or education research. A prior executive director was billed as an "activist in the Massachusetts Democratic Party."[29] FairTest asks parents to refuse to have their children take the tests—an admission that the tests are not actually high-stakes, because if passing the exam were required to advance to the next grade, no parent could be expected to boycott it. In May 2020, Schaeffer told the *Tampa Bay Times* that tests are not necessary to know where the failures will be, implying that it is obvious that high-poverty minority kids will score poorly (a view an education expert characterized as "cancerous" to individuals who excel despite adversity).[30] In 2013, twenty-four states required twelfth graders to pass an "exit exam" to earn their diplomas; by 2017, FairTest called it a "victory" that the number had dropped to only thirteen. It was elated that "districts across the nation, including locales with many students of color and low-income families, ended their tests."[31]

Of course, standardized tests are the definition of fairness, ensuring that the same criteria objectively measure a broad spectrum of students. FairTest appears to object to every measure of schools or students that produces results that can be reliably compared against others. It faults standardized tests as taking away valuable classroom time and causing teachers to "teach to the test"—yet it also pushes colleges to stop using the SAT, even though neither of these criticisms applies.[32]

FairTest has been remarkably successful in this quest. By 2014, dozens of colleges were abandoning admissions tests each year. In 2020, the University of California system permanently abolished the use of SAT and ACT scores for admissions. Lieutenant Governor Eleni Kounalakis pronounced the tests "very unfair," overriding the faculty senate, whose study found that SAT and ACT scores are highly accurate predictors of success in their university system compared to grade-point average.[33]

Eliminating standardized admissions exams ensured that the grade school stats-rigging con would not be exposed when a child turned eighteen. But when colleges matriculate students who have not demonstrated the ability to succeed in high-level academic environments—an environment that includes taking tests—they are likely to fail or drop out. The SAT's obvious purpose, after all, is to identify which students are likely to benefit from college, and which are not. At four-year colleges with open admissions policies—meaning that they do not use this sorting mechanism—only a third succeed in getting a degree. It is similar for schools that use the SAT but accept people with low scores. At Livingstone College in North Carolina, a quarter of students had reading and math SAT scores of less than 380 (test takers get 200 points per section just for writing their name). Only 28 percent of its students graduate. Wilberforce University, a private college in Ohio, admits students with an average SAT score of 862. Only 10 percent graduate.[34]

Of course, one way to avoid the dropout scandal is for colleges to implement similar standards-lowering, which they have increasingly done. At Michigan State University, nearly one in eight students had to take remedial math, which did not count for college credit and was taught primarily online—until in 2018 the college replaced it with two in-person, nonremedial courses that counted for college credit.[35] Students without a grasp of basic math even included Marqell Mc-Clendon, who was the valedictorian of her Detroit high school. In a bid to increase its college graduation rate, in 2016, MSU removed its requirement that students be able to pass algebra before getting a diploma.[36]

But if unqualified candidates are pushed through college, the house of cards will eventually collapse when employers judge that graduates have not actually learned skills worth paying for. At Livingstone, the college with very low SAT scores, even those who graduate with a bachelor's in business administration—a practical degree—have a median annual starting salary of $25,000. That is in exchange for a degree that costs about $70,000.[37]

The dismantling of test-based standards is often pushed by educators to improve statistics about racial minority achievement, but it comes at a massive cost to young black people. According to a 2017 study, the majority of blacks who graduate with a bachelor's degree do not pay down their student loan principal at all, suggesting that the diploma did not translate into skills with increased earning potential. Twelve years after initial enrollment, with accruing interest, they owe more than they originally borrowed.[38]

This is partly because signals sent by SAT scores are ignored. Of the twenty-five schools with the lowest average SAT scores, most are historically black colleges and universities (HBCUs). More than half of the one hundred schools with the worst three-year student-loan repayment rates are HBCUs—places like Stillman College in Alabama, which its president describes as a college for people "no one else would take." The school has a graduation rate of 38 percent and only a 25 percent student loan repayment rate. Spelman College, an HBCU in Atlanta, is responsible for driving more low-income parents deeply into debt than any other school in the country. It costs about

$41,000 a year to attend, and its most common major is psychology, with graduates earning a median annual salary of $25,500. Others studied fields like drama, leading to an annual salary of less than $16,000.[39]

Educators want to ignore objective tests to manufacture statistics for self-serving and ideological reasons, but their buck-passing game is partly responsible for one of America's biggest financial problems. Saddling young people with tens of thousands of dollars in student loans, which cannot be discharged in bankruptcy—for degrees that they either never attain or which have little value when it comes to marketable skills—amounts to ruining lives. By early 2020, Americans owed $1.6 trillion in student loans, and roughly 11 percent were delinquent or in default. Though this suggests that too many people who will not benefit from college are enrolling, politicians, including Kamala Harris, have advocated masking the mismatch by canceling student debt plus spending $60 billion to subsidize HBCUs.[40]

DISCIPLINE

Discipline is another measure of K–12 schools. The level of violence, disruption, and criminality in them was dealt with in a similar way: by changing measurement systems to cover it up. The Obama administration was disturbed by data showing high levels of infractions by black boys. But its strategy focused more on changing discipline policies to lower the number of punishments than on reducing actual misbehavior. Obama's 2014 initiative on black youth, called My Brother's Keeper (MBK), addressed the "school-to-prison pipeline," a concept that posits that since students who are suspended from school are more likely to get in trouble later in life, it might be the punishment itself that pushes them into a life of crime—not the more straightforward explanation that behaviors that lead to suspensions as a youth also lead to arrests as an adult.[41]

In January 2014, Obama's Department of Education (DOE) sent a letter bearing the intimidating imprimatur of the Department of Justice (DOJ) to every school district asserting that school discipline could violate civil rights laws "if a policy is neutral on its face—meaning that the policy itself does not mention race—and is administered in an evenhanded manner but has a *disparate impact*" (in other words, if "students of one race [are] sanctioned at disproportionately higher rates"). It said school systems whose punishments did not mirror the overall racial makeup of the school could face investigation. If a black boy beat up an Asian boy unprovoked, the school system would be under pressure to suspend both or neither, or risk a years-long investigation and the possibility of being hauled into court.[42]

The effect of the demand for equal outcomes by race was dramatic. California suspensions decreased from about seven hundred thousand in the 2011–12 school year to five hundred thousand in 2013–14, which MBK heralded for "narrowing of the racial discipline gap."[43]

In Los Angeles, suspensions fell from a combined seventy-five thousand days in 2007–08 to five thousand in 2014–15. That looked good on the spreadsheets superintendents sent to Washington. But teachers had to deal with the realities on the ground. "My teachers are at their breaking point," Art Lopez, a teachers union rep, wrote. "Everyone working here is highly aware of how the lack of consequences has affected the site." An eighty-three-year-old administrator found himself in the middle of brawling youths. Teachers fled at such a rate that even ten out of the eleven teachers on the restorative justice committee, which advocated for the "talking circles" that often replaced suspensions, left. "Where is the justice for the students who want to learn?" teacher Michael Lam asked. It also meant that administrators, wary of punishing students themselves, were more likely to call the cops on them. Some Los Angeles students were reportedly ultimately given off-the-books suspensions: free time off school with no mark on their record.[44]

An early adopter of this sort of reform was Broward County, Florida, which had been deploying its own strategies to reduce suspensions and arrests. Two months after Superintendent Robert Runcie implemented one reform, the Obama administration sent out its DOE/DOJ letter, which was so similar that Runcie, who was invited to the White House in 2015 for a "Rethink Discipline" summit, said,

"My staff joke that the Obama administration might have taken our policies and framework and developed them into national guidelines." MBK said that by 2016, forty school districts were "following in the footsteps" of Broward by committing to "reforming discipline policies."[45]

In 2013–14, the first year of a program Runcie called PROMISE, expulsions and suspensions sank by about 60 percent, and arrests by half. But the *South Florida Sun-Sentinel* found that the secret to impressive statistics was a willingness to deceive. For example, the district boasted that PROMISE led to a 90 percent success rate in preventing "re-offending," but that was based on a curious definition of the word in which "students can be considered first-time offenders even if they commit the same offenses year after year."[46]

Less than two years after MBK's praise of Broward County, in February 2018, a nineteen-year-old former student at Marjory Stoneman Douglas High School killed seventeen students and staff and wounded seventeen more in Parkland, Broward County. The shooter, Nikolas Cruz, was able to buy a firearm despite a long record of infractions, in part because he never accrued a criminal record. In fact, even his official school records did not document the vast majority of incidents the school knew about. At least five students had told the school's assistant principal that Cruz threatened to kill and rape people and brought knives and bullets or bullet casings to school. Cruz told a friend that administrators searched his backpack in response and found bullets, but administrators made no official record of this. When Cruz attacked another student, peers tried to show administrators video of the attack.

They told the students to delete the evidence.[47]

2

THE MATHEMATICIAN

GROWTH

To hear Loudoun County, Virginia, educators tell it, Brian Davison is a violent lunatic, a physical threat, someone who should be in jail.

Davison is a ginger-haired forty-eight-year-old who earned two degrees from the Massachusetts Institute of Technology, then spent much of his career in Hawaii as a Navy officer stationed at Pearl Harbor, where he worked on nuclear submarines. He relocated to the semirural outer suburb of D.C. to work for Oracle, and later as a government contractor. By profession, he is a nerd who specializes in "operations research," finding ways to make organizations function more efficiently. Working for the military with a top-secret clearance, he learned to see through acronyms and jargon, finding that they were often deployed as shields by people who did not know what they were talking about. In his free time, he was a gardener who planted flowers not just in his own yard, but around the whole neighborhood. After he had two kids, he figured that his civic engagement efforts might be better spent volunteering his number-crunching skills to help local schools. He began attending school board meetings.[1]

He's not a monster. To teachers, he's something more threatening: a mathematician.

Davison took one look at the way schools measured themselves and realized that they were doing it wrong. Schools reported performance based on the percentage of students who passed state exams. This led to schools in wealthy areas being rated high-performing, and schools in poor neighborhoods appearing to be inferior. Those numbers were reflecting the economic status and parental involvement of the students in the schools, not the schools themselves.

But there was no reason socioeconomic issues had to define schools or prevent assessing them. Focusing on racial "disparities" was a smoke screen, a distraction from what should be obvious: First, the goal should be to make every child smarter this year than he was last year. Second, there were good and bad schools in rich and poor neighborhoods, and good and bad teachers within each school. This could be measured with the same test data that the schools already had. You just needed to look at growth trajectory instead of plain scores: Compare each child's state exam score from last year to his or her score from this year. Had he or she improved a lot, a little, or not at all?

The simple change helped isolate the effect of schools and teachers on a yearly basis, getting rid of outside factors, such as some kids entering kindergarten better prepared than others because of parental involvement. It also addressed another problem: the old statistic encouraged teachers to push everyone toward average. A good student would almost certainly pass the state exams, so teachers had little incentive to press smart kids to do even better because it would not change the overall percentage of students who passed. For the same reason, struggling kids who were unlikely to pass the tests, even with focused attention, could be discarded as lost causes. This different way of looking at the same test results acknowledged the reality that every child was unique and, for reasons outside the control of teachers, not everyone performed at the same level at any one point in time. But it was firm that every child—with the right guidance—could and should improve.

Using a student growth statistic to measure the efficacy of schools and teachers made so much sense that it was odd it was not the standard across the country already. So, it was unsurprising when, in 2009, the Obama administration began requiring it of school districts as a condition for receiving their share of nearly $54 billion in stimulus funding, the best-known component of which was called Race to the Top.[2]

Back in 2001, when reforms associated with the No Child Left Behind Act (NCLB) required school districts to begin publishing their graduation rates in a way that allowed comparisons to other districts, schools responded by lowering standards in order to make their graduation rates seem better. NCLB also required schools to publish statistics broken out by ethnicity, leading to an obsession with race in K–12 education that was similarly statistically flimsy. There was no data warehouse breaking down the test scores based on whether a child had a two-parent household, was frequently truant, or any number of other factors that would likely have a stronger and more direct correlation. There were just ubiquitous spreadsheets that showed that, on average, students of some races did better than others. So, race is what educators dwelled on. And their focus was not so much on whether individuals were learning, but on whether there were "gaps" or "disparities" between groups.[3]

The Obama administration realized the problem.

In 2011, the U.S. Department of Education wrote: "Although NCLB helped . . . shine a bright light on the achievement gap and increased accountability for student subgroups, it inadvertently encouraged some States to set low academic standards, failed to recognize or reward growth in student achievement, and did little to elevate the teaching profession or recognize the most effective teachers."[4] The Race to the Top program required "evaluation systems for teachers and principals that . . . differentiate effectiveness using multiple rating categories that take into account data on student growth."[5]

States responded. Virginia acknowledged that "to receive certain federal funds under the federal American Recovery and Reinvestment Act of 2009, states are required to provide timely data on student growth to teachers in a manner that helps quantify the impact of individual teachers on student achievement." In the ensuing years,

Virginia repeatedly received the money after submitting applications that said that "prior to submitting this request, [schools] provided [to teachers] student growth data on their current students and the students they taught in the previous year." In 2013, Virginia lawmakers wrote this into state law. They specified that teacher performance "evaluations shall include student academic progress as a significant component," following a formula that 40 percent of a teacher's evaluation be based on student performance, and "at least 20 percent of the teacher evaluation (half of the student academic progress measure) is comprised of student growth percentiles."

In 2014, Davison asked for a copy of the growth scores under the Freedom of Information Act. Loudoun County Public Schools (LCPS) told him that it did not have them. In fact, no one in the school system had ever even looked at them. This was remarkable because Loudoun was no backwater. It was a large county with the highest median household income in the nation every year since 2007. Arne Duncan, President Obama's education secretary, lived not far away. "He doesn't know that they were signing these documents and the teachers didn't even have the data?" Davison wondered.[6]

This was not an isolated case. Davison requested the data from other school districts in the state, who told him essentially the same thing. Educators were so opposed to looking at these numbers that they were willing to systematically lie, apparently ignore state law, and put vast sums of federal funding in jeopardy. They were doing it for the same reason the information was so important: it revealed which teachers were good and which were not.

Nothing about the metric was inherently negative to teachers. Good teachers would benefit from a job evaluation rating that bothered to look at their results. And once top performers were identified, underperformers might learn something from them. But teachers unions enjoyed the same standard for their members as the one that they were creating among their students: a world where everyone was average. For the 2013–14 school year, Loudoun County rated 98.3 percent of its teachers as "accomplished" or "proficient."

Growth numbers showed the truth: some teachers let kids down year after year, getting remarkably worse improvement than the teacher in the neighboring classroom. Those teachers remained on the payroll, earning progressively more money, until they retired with a nice pension. Their students headed to a lifetime on the welfare rolls.

And, it seemed, the education industry was willing to do almost anything to keep it that way.

PUBLIC ENEMY NUMBER ONE

Davison's information requests were going nowhere. Almost anyone else might have given up, but the military veteran was determined. In October 2014, he sued the Virginia Department of Education (VDOE) to force it to release the growth data. This was the kind of expense few parents could muster, but he gave himself a legal education and did much of his own legal work.[7]

The battle was not confined to the courtroom. The entire educational apparatus of Loudoun County seemed intent on destroying him. Davison became, as one school board member called him, "enemy #1 of LCPS."

After Davison raised questions at a school board meeting, board member Debra Rose, a lawyer and former congressional staffer for the House Judiciary Committee, requested that a sheriff's deputy remove him. The officer did not. In March 2015, Rose's husband summoned police to their home, where "Ms. Rose advised that Mr. Davison has not made any specific threats directed towards her, but he has made her feel extremely uncomfortable." The police took no action. In May, her husband called police again to tell them that Davison "is posting links on [an internet] forum to [Ms. Rose's] campaign web site which displays herself and her family members including her children." The officer responded, according to his police report, that "this may not be a crime because this certain post is a link of his wife's campaign web site" and that Davison's comments "didn't sound threatening of any illegal or immoral act." Rose herself called Davison's elderly father to tell on him. She also emailed his employer at least five times in a three-day period, potentially jeopardizing his security clearance.[8]

When Davison commented about the school board's ethics on a county council member's Facebook page in early 2016, she blocked him. He sued again—acting as his own attorney—and won in federal court the next year, leading to a legal precedent that later prevented President Donald Trump from blocking people on Twitter. In April 2016, he got his real victory from the 2014 VDOE lawsuit: the court said that he was right about the data. A judge ordered the state to hand it over to Davison and pay him $35,000. The state had provided a shifting series of excuses, claiming it did not have the reports, and that they would invade children's privacy, but a judge found that none of these was true.[9]

But it was not yet over. The teachers union, which was not a part of the lawsuit, sought to intervene and block the release of teachers' names, even appealing twice. The Loudoun school board intervened for the same purpose, claiming that growth data counted as "confidential portions of teachers' personnel files"—even though Davison's whole point was that they had never used it to evaluate teachers, or even downloaded it from the state.

In 2017, Virginia's Supreme Court accepted the board's argument, ordering teachers' names withheld.[10]

NO ONE WATCHING

With anonymized data in hand, Davison plunged in. Teachers often note that test scores correlate highly to the income group of parents. However, student growth numbers completely bust this paradigm, with no correlation to socioeconomic factors. They showed that poor and minority children can and do make improvements all the time—and that some teachers were getting better results than others. For example, in Richmond, Virginia, one teacher had five students in 2014 whose increase in reading put them in the 99th percentile of similarly situated students, eight students who placed nearly as high, and only one student whose growth was below average. Another teacher in the same district had the reverse, with sixteen students in the bottom

3 percent of growth compared to students that started at similar levels, and others faring not much better.[11]

The myopic view of U.S. educators—that the problem is a "gap" between wealthy and impoverished students—distracted parents from seeing whether *anyone* was doing well. Wealthy parents comforted themselves that grim educational statistics were an inner-city problem, that their kid was doing fine—or even that, compared to other kids nearby, he was a genius. They had been deceived. The 2009 Program for International Student Assessment (PISA) test, for example, showed that kids at a Loudoun high school performed worse in math and reading than kids at some comparably wealthy schools in Mexico. Growth scores humbled many wealthy and "desirable" schools: it turned out that they were not actually very good; they just had parents who sent their kids to school well prepared.[12]

The student growth percentile (SGP) metric, also called a value-added metric, was no statistical mirage. Economists who studied eighteen million test scores over twenty-one school years found that even when a teacher transferred to a different school, his or her performance stats remained similar. In Virginia, a teacher ranking in the bottom fifth one year was most likely to be in the bottom fifth again the next year, with only a 3 percent chance of moving to the top fifth.[13]

These increases in test scores had a real-world impact. A 2011 study by economists, including Harvard's Raj Chetty, found that "when a high-value-added teacher enters a school, test scores for students in the grade taught by that teacher rise immediately. . . . And the gains don't stop there: the students who learn from that teacher are more likely to attend college, earn more [as adults], and are less likely to have children as teenagers. Even when new teachers are evaluated with just a few years of data, those who get high value-added ratings produce large gains for their students."[14]

In short, it would be crazy not to use this metric.

But that was not the only crazy thing about how schools were run. Through his research, Davison also discovered that the way teachers are hired and paid is all wrong. In nearly every school district, teachers are paid in a highly unequal fashion based on their years of experience, with elderly teachers making vastly more than young ones. Back-loading pay means that the money is hoarded by people who are already entrenched and unlikely to leave no matter what, while young teachers can rightfully complain that they are under-paid and new talent considering the profession will not perceive it as lucrative. Taxpayers incur all the expense of high pay with none of the rewards. There is no logical basis for this inequality since data shows that older teachers and younger teachers do the same job with largely the same efficacy: The first few years on the job are a learning period, but from year five onward, teachers' performance basically flatlines. Therefore, decades of experience do not mean better results for students.[15]

Moreover, once a teacher is hired, it is almost impossible to fire her. This is a big problem because it is hard to tell who will make a good teacher based on her resume. Districts prefer hiring candidates with master's degrees, paying them extra for the qualification—a premium that costs taxpayers nearly $10 billion a year as of 2019. But there is no evidence that having a master's degree makes them better teachers—some data suggests that it is correlated with *worse* results. It is also hard to improve the performance of bad teachers once they are on the job. Schools dedicate enormous time and money to "professional development" training sessions, but there is little evidence any of them make a difference. Since hiring is a crapshoot and a bad hire is unlikely to improve, a sensible system would hire without much regard for formal credentials, get rid of those who did not perform after the fifth year, and pay young teachers well, but not pay them vastly more as time goes on. In other words, the opposite of what we do now.[16]

Whenever seemingly irrational policies that harmed kids were in place, Davison found that the explanation pointed to financial incentives for the teachers unions. The battle that had pulled him in had nothing to do with unions, but rather his support for an Obama directive. But his experience since convinced him that unions were the real problem. "Schools do not exist to employ teachers. They exist to effectively educate kids," he said.

Schools are clearly immensely important to all residents of a community. For fiscal year 2021, nearly half of Loudoun's budget was allocated to its public schools. But bizarrely, almost no one paying for schools paid attention to how they were actually run. Instead, the employees of those institutions—teachers—held a stranglehold in policy. When it came to school board elections, voters often elected teachers, or at least whomever their union endorsed. They figured that it was a relevant qualification. Really, it was a conflict of interest. In Loudoun's most recently elected board, six out of nine members were either onetime educators or married to one. In 2016, four of nine were married to public school system employees. This meant that when they voted to give pay raises (including across-the-board salary increases), the law required them to make the same disclosure of conflict of interest as if they were awarding a contract to a company in which they held a stake. They never did. "You'd normally have management on one side and labor on the other, and here there's just teachers on both sides," Davison said.[17]

Even as teachers had their exclusive advocacy group in the form of powerful unions, they would not let parents have their own. There was only the Parent Teacher Association (PTA), which made no bones that it placed the desires of teachers and administrators at least as high as those of parents, whose role it seemed to believe was primarily to support them and hold fund-raisers. Teachers union officials even sat on the board of the national PTA.[18]

The Virginia PTA's standard bylaws said that school principals could automatically vote as members of the executive committee of the so-called parents groups. At the PTA chapter for Davison's kids' school, the principal, Tracy Stephens, was a strong presence. After Davison tried to raise testing issues at a PTA meeting in September 2015, Stephens issued a notice that she said made it a crime for him to come to the school for any reason for the rest of the school year. School officials were used to parents advocating to get preferential treatment for their own children, but they were not used to anyone asking bigger questions. "Many of your comments were wholly unrelated to your children. This is frightening to our staff," Stephens wrote.[19]

The day the no-trespassing order was posted to Davison's front door, Stephens called the police on him while he waited off school property to pick up his kids. She refused to allow his children to join him. The police told Stephens that Davison was entitled to pick up his children, but, according to the police report, Stephens demanded, "I want him arrested!" When that did not work, Stephens reported Davison to Child Protective Services as a suspected child abuser. It was not children she was concerned about. The complaint said Davison "exhibits agression [sic] and hostility toward LCPS leadership during public meetings." Stephens faxed sixty-two pages of information to the agency, which has the power to take children away from their parents. They consisted almost entirely of Davison's criticism of school policies or officials' apparent violations of them. At the end, they added two claims that purportedly showed child abuse: one day, his daughter could not play kickball because she was "sent to school in rain boots." Another day, a teacher said she saw Davison's children with him and "both of the kids had straight faces."[20]

Other parents did not agree that Davison's scrutiny of schools was a bad thing. At a March 2016 school board meeting, they cheered for him, leading Rose to snarl from the dais, "You guys are disgusting." In 2018, the county-wide PTA, which held official status with the school system and had its website and meetings hosted by it, apparently elected Davison as its president. The school system refused to accept the election and said the organization would be dissolved.[21] Davison characterized it as "a criminal cartel masquerading as a school district. Their motto should be adults first, kids never."

When people act with the viciousness of Loudoun's officials, it usually means they have something to hide. What began as a lark for Davison turned into a David versus Goliath struggle. He was just a regular dad, but he kept showing up. Each time, it became clearer to him that the entire educational establishment was a house of cards. Davison realized that it was not just growth data that threatened the educrats—it was the idea that anyone was watching at all. They had reason to be so territorial: they had sound bites that sounded okay to people who barely paid attention, but all of them fell apart under scrutiny.

For example, teachers did not just oppose calculating growth from standardized test scores; they opposed all standardized testing, claiming that it took away from instructional time and dampened students' creativity. But Davison discovered that to make scores look higher, Loudoun teachers had kids who failed their state exams retake them after an intense three-week boot camp. This would appear to violate the law, since teachers were not supposed to let anyone know how students did on the exams, yet everyone could see who was pulled out of class. It also demolished the teachers' professed reasons for opposing tests.

TEACHER PAY

The notion that teachers are underpaid was another such sound bite. Teachers frequently claim that they cannot afford to live where they work.[22] But this was numerical nonsense. Loudoun has the highest household income in the country, but "it has high household income because they're two-income households, so it makes no sense to compare one person's salary to the household income," the mathematician argued. "If two teachers get married, they earn more than the median household income of the richest county in America when they are twenty-three." Loudoun's teacher contracts were for 197 days of work per year, compared to 260 for a standard full-time work year, so their income potential increases "because they can work [a side job] in the summertime. Two teachers can earn $300,000 a year and they say they're underpaid," Davison said.[23]

Loudoun also awarded raises nearly every year despite already paying more than the neighboring county and having the lowest vacancy rate in the state. Teachers were beating down the door to work there: five were turned away for every person who was hired.[24] If supply outstripped demand, why did Loudoun continue to raise its salaries?

Pay raises did not seem aimed at attracting more qualified teachers, since the biggest raises went to midcareer teachers, with those with twelve years of experience in 2020 making 35 percent more than they did four years prior, and since the school system never seemed to boast about its high pay. Davison suggested that the school board help fresh college graduates compare the job against private-sector offers by emphasizing the value of the pension and other hidden benefits. Virginia requires the employer to pay about 15 percent of a teacher's salary for his or her pension, and Loudoun pays up to nearly $20,000 a year toward a family health plan with dental and vision benefits. Davison said since the district was investing all that money, it should "advertise that this is what you're really making. It will help attract people," he said. "Would a company understate how much it paid employees when they want to attract candidates? . . . If you told college kids you could make $125,000 a year with summers off, you could get a whole bunch of smart people to go into teaching. The only reason to understate it is so you can keep giving [the existing people] raises without taxpayers saying, 'what is going on?'" When Davison wrote as much on a school board member's Facebook page, the elected official hid the comment and eventually blocked all of Davison's comments.[25]

Nationally, the myth of the underpaid teacher persists, fueled partly by mathematical sleight of hand. During the 2020 presidential campaign, Senator Kamala Harris (D-CA) pledged to spend $315 billion on teacher raises, a highly unusual giveaway since teachers' salaries are generally paid with local, not federal, funds. To justify 23 percent raises, she cited a study by a liberal think tank that claimed public school teachers made 11 percent less than other professionals. This study largely ignored that teachers have almost 25 percent of the year at least partially off. It also misleadingly claimed that it compared teachers to "other college graduates," when it actually compared them primarily to professionals with master's degrees, on the basis that 58 percent of teachers have a master's.[26]

This compared them to people like MBAs, accountants, and engineers, when these groups are not the same: teachers are perhaps the lowest-performing white-collar profession in America. On the Graduate Record Examination (GRE) entrance exams, those seeking graduate degrees in education had the lowest math scores of any field of study. The "verbal reasoning" section of the GRE is highly relevant to many teachers' duties and measures "the ability to understand text (such as the ability to understand the meanings of sentences, to summarize a text or to distinguish major points from irrelevant points in a passage)." Of fifty-one different fields of study, only three had lower verbal reasoning scores than elementary school teachers—and two of those were other education fields. Twenty-four percent of secondary school educators scored a 160 or higher, compared to 42 percent of those going to school for art history.[27]

UNIONS

The National Education Association (NEA) is the largest labor union in the United States, with more than three million members, nearly 1 percent of all Americans. It claims that one in nearly every forty voters lives in an "NEA household." First Lady Jill Biden is an NEA member. "Joe and I will never forget what you did for us," she told the heads of the NEA and the American Federation of Teachers (AFT) shortly after the 2020 election. "Joe and Kamala will not only listen to you, they're going to make sure that your voices are leading this movement. Educators, this is our moment."[28]

Teachers unions stress that job security and pay is their highest priority, and their leverage comes from corralling votes for the Democratic Party. None of this has to do with what is good for children. At the annual NEA conference in July 2019, one of the first actions union delegates took was voting down a motion to "rededicate itself to the pursuit of increased student learning in every public school in America by putting a renewed emphasis on quality education." Instead, it approved motions to "involve educators, students, and communities in the discussions around support for reparations"; to blame the United States for destabilizing Central America, therefore causing a flood of immigrants; and to "incorporate the concept of 'White Fragility' into NEA trainings/staff development."[29]

Teachers unions routinely make demands that Democratic politicians acknowledge are bad policy. When the Obama administration supported factoring student performance into teacher evaluations to "differentiate effectiveness," it was referring to the fact that a performance rating system that deemed 98.3 percent of teachers as effective, like Loudoun County's, is meaningless. Liberal governor Andrew Cuomo of New York wrote in 2015 that "in New York last year, about 99 percent of the teachers were rated effective while only 38 percent of high school graduates are ready for college or careers. How can that be?"[30]

Despite receiving more than $15,000 per student per year,[31] those in charge of American education have done so poorly that few parents actually want their kids in public schools. A 2020 national survey found that just one-third of parents of schoolchildren said they would choose their current district school, rather than a charter or private school, if they had the option. More than three-quarters of those surveyed supported school vouchers, which would take some of the money already earmarked for their child and let parents direct it to a charter or private school if they preferred.[32] This would be a great equalizer, making elite private and parochial schools available to everyone—without increasing public spending at all. It is hard to get three-quarters of Americans to agree on anything, and it necessarily represents a strong bipartisan consensus. It is the kind of issue that might pass if put directly before voters in a referendum.

But no matter how many Americans who consider themselves Democrats might want the life-changing ability to use their own tax money to educate their children as they see fit, the outsize influence that teachers unions have at the party's highest level means that the party will do everything it can to stop it.

Just after Biden's election, the NEA produced a fifty-four-page "policy playbook" outlining its demands for national leaders. Among the first on the list was to "oppose the use of standardized tests for . . . an educator's evaluation." Shortly after was the appeal to "oppose all charter school expansion."[33]

Charter schools are public schools that are independently managed. They tend to produce slightly higher test scores and more student satisfaction for considerably less money. They are also typically not unionized. In 2005, the United Federation of Teachers opened its own charter school in New York, run by union officials. Its purpose, then president Randi Weingarten said, was to "dispel the misguided and simplistic notion that the union contract is an impediment to success." But, as it turns out, she could not have been more mistaken. In less than five years, the school became one of the worst-performing schools in the city, with only 13 percent of eighth graders proficient in math. It also hired a principal who had left the traditional school system after the city and its education department determined that he engaged in sexual harassment.[34]

As for Brian Davison and the growth data he fought to obtain that shows which teachers get results and which do not? Fourteen months after Davison filed his VDOE lawsuit, federal law was changed so that states are no longer required to look at it. A law called the Every Student Succeeds Act, passed in December 2015, bars the federal government from asking states to use student growth data to evaluate teachers. The change came following lobbying by the unions.[35]

SCHOOL BOARD

Fairfax County, Virginia, a suburb just outside Washington, D.C., harbors much of the brain trust that keeps the country safe, as home to the CIA, the Office of the Director of National Intelligence, and the rocket scientists of Northrop Grumman. In 2000, it voted for George W. Bush for president; in 2008, it voted for Barack Obama. Its school system has helped to keep the United States as an economic and intellectual powerhouse with its magnet school, the Thomas Jefferson High School for Science and Technology, whose test scores are the highest in the country.[1]

But by 2019, something was seriously wrong in Fairfax, and in so many of the country's 13,000 school districts.

The elected representatives who shaped the Fairfax school system, a twelve-person school board, were no longer parents puzzling over the best grass for the football fields. Instead, it had become a political power center—with a $3 billion budget, influence over 187,000 impressionable children, and very little scrutiny. None of the ten Democrats on the school board even had children in the schools. The two Republicans did, but in 2019, both were voted out.[2]

Local education, perhaps the most important thing government does at any level, had been taken over by national political interest groups, who were using it to focus on anything but schools' principal mission: providing a rigorous education.

By going in through the back door—as in down-ballot elections that no one was watching—ideologues had quietly amassed extraordinary control, all over the country.

But did residents really love a political agenda more than they loved their children?

KARL FRISCH

Andi Bayer studied education in college, taught school, and raised four kids in Fairfax County, from whose schools she had graduated. For her twelfth birthday, she asked for a subscription to the magazine *Education Week*. For twenty-five years, she watched meetings of the Fairfax County school board. In 2019, she decided to run for the board. She knows every cranny of Fairfax, and insists on giving visitors directions, calculated off the top of her head, from anyplace in the county to wherever an upcoming meeting is. "Pick a topic," she challenged one voter. "Turf wars," came the reply, referring to a debate over the best covering for kids' sports fields. Bayer broke down five sub-issues.

If moms were grateful for her quarter century of civic engagement, it was for the simple reason that it was better her than them. There was nothing fun about attending interminable meetings. After a sleepy, off-year election for the seat representing her little corner of the suburban county, perhaps Bayer would at least get the $32,000 salary for her trouble.[3]

A man named Karl Frisch filed to run for the same position. Frisch had no children and had lived in Fairfax for less than five years. As a child, he had attended private school in California. Nearly two-thirds of Fairfax residents have four-year college degrees and one-third have graduate degrees, but Frisch had neither: he attended a pair of community colleges for a couple of years. Students at his most recent alma mater, College of the Canyons, nicknamed it "College of the Crayons," with one remarking, "this is not a college, it is an institution that babysits those who are too lazy to get a job or go to a real school." Frisch's closest connection to the Fairfax school system was that his partner worked as choir director there.[4]

What Frisch did have was a whopping $183,000 in campaign cash—far more money than anyone on record had ever raised for the position. It was the kind of money that made playing a role in the most local form of government off-limits to any normal person. Most of the money itemized in his campaign finance disclosures came not only from outside the county, but from out of state. The checks were written by national politicos like Joe Trippi, but also by small donors all over the country, people who seemed to have no connection to Fairfax but who were on Democratic fund-raising lists to which Frisch sent mailers about LGBTQ+ rights.

Considering how hard it was to get regular parents even to watch a meeting of the school board, why would a man with no children want to be on it? And why would people in other parts of the country pay so much money to get him there?

Frisch was a political operative who worked for the New Venture Fund, one of the largest and most powerful influence groups in history—one that operates through such a shadowy and complex structure that its name is hardly known. He stood out for his tribalism even within those circles. In 2009, as a senior fellow of Media Matters for America, a David Brock–led nonprofit dedicated to attacking conservatives, Frisch pressed his bosses to pay for an "elaborate" operation that included hiring private investigators to tail employees of Fox News because "simply put, the progressive movement is in need of an enemy."[5]

In his day job with the New Venture Fund, he ran campaigns railing against "pay-to-play" with the goal of "identify[ing] who is influencing public policy debates and why," even as he funded his school board campaign with huge sums of out-of-state cash. He railed against the rich not paying their fair share while the Internal Revenue Service had a lien of about $60,000 against him for unpaid taxes in 2016.[6] None of this mattered: most residents seemed to pay little or no attention to the qualifications or positions of suburban school board candidates. They might as well be running for dog catcher.

But a few people treated it like a major operation. Bayer's campaign sign was stolen from her front yard multiple times per day. Tired of replacing the sign, she installed a video camera and coated the sign in Crisco. Four hours later the next theft occurred. Video showed a male driver pulling up and a female in a hoodie running out. The woman shouted as she struggled to uproot the slippery sign, and finally tossed it into the car. The thefts stopped. With fifteen times as much money as Bayer, Frisch defeated her with 62 percent of the vote.[7] But the real losers may have been the parents who thought that the mission of schools was to help students learn.

SCHOOL BOARD

In this new era, new school board members took their seats to pursue a variety of agendas, few of which had to do with education.

There was Abrar Omeish, elected in 2019 as a twenty-four-year-old with no children and little work history. She lived at home with her dad, Esam Omeish, who as a board member of the Dar al-Hijrah mosque had years earlier hired Anwar al-Awlaki, the imam who later planned terrorism for al-Qaeda before President Obama killed him by drone strike in 2011. The Dar al-Hijrah mosque was attended by two of the 9/11 hijackers and by the shooter in the 2009 attack on Fort Hood, Texas.[8]

Esam was also president of the Muslim American Society (MAS); a 2019 video from a MAS facility showed children being trained to sing, "We will chop off their heads. . . . We will lead the army of Allah."[9]

Esam was determined to implant the most extreme elements of his religion into the power structure of the United States, but his record made a political career of his own impossible. He once declared that Islam must "become the dominant religion of the next century." In 2007, Democratic Virginia governor and eventual Hillary Clinton running mate Tim Kaine booted him off a state immigration board after video of him endorsing jihad emerged.[10] In 2009, he ran for the state legislature, but was rejected by voters after the *Washington Post* reported that he spoke "with great pride and zest to an audience of fellow Muslims about people 'giving up their lives . . . for the sake of the Muslim honor.'"[11]

But in 2019, his daughter, Abrar, won an at-large seat on Fairfax's school board with little scrutiny, meaning she now represents more than 1.1 million people, or about one and a half times as many as the average member of Congress.[12]

In Abrar's late teens, she served as a "Virtual Student Foreign Service Officer" for the U.S. Department of State, where her job was to spread "U.S. ideals" and serve "as a liaison for the U.S. State Department and emerging Libyan leaders." The job was cut short when Libyan militants murdered Ambassador Chris Stevens in Benghazi.[13] Her uncle was a former diplomat on the other side, representing Libya in Kuwait. In June 2011, her father was involved with shaping the United States' policy for the region with the Libyan Council of North America. During her school board run, her father reportedly lobbied the government of Turkey to adopt policies that would send a message to the United States about Libyan affairs.[14]

As a student at Yale and board member of its Muslim Students Association chapter in 2014 (her father is a former president of the National Muslim Students Association of the U.S. and Canada), Abrar sought to stop Ayaan Hirsi Ali, a Somali-born women's rights activist who is critical of Islamic practices such as female genital mutilation, from speaking on campus, according to a *Yale Herald* article titled "Melting Pot Boils Over." Abrar, who went on to study law at her father's alma mater of Georgetown University, told the *Yale Daily News* that "the difference here is that it's hate speech," which "is not protected by the First Amendment." She claimed that criticism of Islam amounted to "slander," an interpretation that would mean a blasphemy law.[15]

As she began her campaign for school board, she was pulled over for running a red light. She refused to show the officer her license. When he asked her to step out of the car, she latched on to the steering wheel and shouted, "A cop is being brutal! Help me!" She later sued the police for allegedly violating her civil rights, represented by lawyers from the Council on American-Islamic Relations (her father is a former board member of the CAIR Foundation). She took the incident to the *Washington Post*, resulting in an article that boosted her name recognition.[16] Her school board campaign raised just under $117,000, or $34,000 more than her highest-grossing opponent. But this support came from a very small portion of the county: at least two-thirds of her reported campaign donors had names with Arabic origins. On the Fourth of July, she pledged to "make changes" to curriculum to "teach our history . . . truthfully."[17]

Also new to the school board was the environmentalist Elaine Tholen. Her interests as they related to schools were "student driven environmental action."[18] Her seat on the school board meant access to a sizeable portfolio of real estate, and she had a plan to install solar panels on schools.[19] When it came to matters of day-to-day learning, she appeared to be less engaged. Previously a Democrat-endorsed member of the county water and soil board, she was drafted by party officials into a school board role only after their first choice for that position dropped out unexpectedly. As the school district was grappling with coronavirus, which purportedly precluded children from going to public places, Tholen traveled to Delaware to watch horseshoe crabs mate. In October 2020, the board took a crucial vote on whether kids should come to school or stay at home; she abstained. Less than a year earlier, Tholen had been on the ballot opposite a woman whose career focused on how schools should respond to emergencies such as epidemics. Voters chose Tholen, who had the Democratic endorsement.[20]

There was the black activist Karen Keys-Gamarra. Keys-Gamarra lived in an upscale neighborhood with a median income of $250,000 where, according to the census, there were no other blacks. Her contribution was injecting race into seemingly every aspect of education. Typical was her objecting to a policy that noted that a school resource officer's "primary role in schools is as a law enforcement officer," demanding that the language "shall be revised to recognize that students from marginalized communities . . . may not readily accept this characterization."[21]

And there was Frisch, the warrior for gay identity politics. Few would object to a gay school board member. But for Frisch, his sexual orientation was intertwined with politics. He began his ca-reer working on Republican John McCain's unsuccessful presidential campaign in 2000, before coming out of the closet as both gay and liberal at the same time. As a *Huffington Post* contributor in 2012, he predicted that a President Mitt Romney would modify the U.S. Constitution and force gays to leave the country. A June 2020 fund-raising event for his school board campaign advertised an appearance by a drag performer.[22] His Twitter account, which is filled mostly with school board content and political bromides, follows accounts dedicated to tweeting hard-core pornography.

THE CASE OF THE MONDAYS

Elizabeth Schultz, a mom from Clifton, Fairfax's last remaining ru-ral corner, had tried to warn voters that K–12 schools had forgotten their basic, but critical, mission. She won a seat on the school board in 2011 after the board shut down Clifton Elementary School based on a series of dubious and ever-shifting premises culminating with the false claim that its water well was contaminated. The closure left forty square miles, one-tenth of the county, without an elementary school.[23]

As each excuse fell apart, no one could explain why the school was actually being closed. When a parent requested information under the Freedom of Information Act to get to the bottom of it, the school system attempted to charge $624,000 to produce the records.[24] But Schultz eventually found a document that provided a clue.

On April 27, 2010, the district said that "[a]s part of Fairfax County Public Schools' (FCPS) major commitment to closing the achieve-ment gap, the district will identify a specific number of schools which will be deemed Priority Schools." Every elementary school was given a ranking, with the schools with the most students who failed tests and the biggest racial achievement gaps ranked higher in terms of priority. Fairfax already gave elementary schools with many immi-grants or impoverished students extra resources to compensate for what it called the "added instructional burden." But it did not seem to work, so under this plan, schools where there were too many English speakers, schools that had many minorities but where the minorities performed well, and schools where minorities and whites had similar scores—even if that score was barely passing—would be further deprioritized.[25]

Clifton Elementary, because it had good test scores and no evidence of racial inequality, ranked near last on the list, at 136th out of 137 elementary schools. On July 6, the "Priority Schools" plan was presented to the school board. Two days later, the board voted to close the school. Schultz could conclude only one thing: it was shuttered because it served as a ruler against which Fairfax's other (that is, the higher-priority) schools looked bad. They had to destroy Clifton to lower the bar.[26]

While the rest of Fairfax had turned into urban sprawl, lined with townhouses and apartment complexes, Clifton remained a historic village of two-parent households in single-family homes on multiple acres, one where the previous mayor had doubled as the proprietor of the ice cream shop on Main Street.[27] Schultz's infant had just gotten out of the intensive care unit, so she had no desire to run for office. But when she saw how school officials were willing to lie and tear the fabric of a pleasant community, seemingly for having the audacity to perform well, she felt she had no choice.

On the board, she established that the county was not meeting state minimum requirements for instruction time because its elementary schools had half days every Monday. The teachers union was furious, but few could argue she was wrong, and the district reinstituted a standard five-day week.[28]

The school board seemed to have little focus on whether or not children were learning, and more focus on identity politics. It spent hours debating what it called "menstrual equity"—a quest to restore free tampons to elementary school bathrooms, after the facilities department moved them to the nurse's office because they were being used largely for pranks.

In 2015, it rushed through a policy about transgender students despite citizen feedback that overwhelmingly opposed the policy, and even though its sponsor acknowledged that the board "has never received a concern regarding a bathroom incident." Schultz voted no, and a woman named Laura Jane Cohen, a liberal activist whose child had severe cognitive difficulties and was also transgender, ran against her, running a campaign fueled by national ideological interests.[29]

It was the schools' mission to provide basic education, and ancillary culture-war issues hardly seemed to warrant a school board seat anywhere—particularly in rural Clifton, whose representative on the county board of supervisors is Republican. But outside activists descended on the town, taking advantage of the fact that most people did not pay any attention to school board races. The gay pride club of George Mason University made the trek to the district to run Cohen's campaign and knock on doors. Unions and Moms Demand Action, a national anti-gun group funded by billionaire Michael Bloomberg, provided an army and a campaign infrastructure.[30]

Cohen watched the results come in with Bloomberg's national gun group. She won. She said that her stance on gun issues—which had little to do with school policy making—"resonated" with voters.[31]

Reflecting on her loss the same night, Schultz said that the school board was more focused on "pushing a social agenda" than on education, and that "I feel sad for Fairfax County residents that they are not paying attention to the local issues."

Within a year, residents began to realize that they had made a serious mistake.

But, as you will see, the teachers got back their Mondays off.

TIMELINE

Cohen bawled as she was sworn into the school board in December 2019, while another member, Rachna Sizemore Heizer, carried a copy of radical anti-American historian Howard Zinn's book *A People's History of the United States*.[32]

On February 20, 2020, the school board voted unanimously to support increasing the power of the teachers union.[33] The Virginia School Boards Association had cautioned the board not to, as it amounted to popularly elected representatives willingly relinquishing power. But Frisch told the association, "Sorry, folks. I stand with teachers." Cohen said the association did "not speak for this School Board Member."[34]

The next month, schools were ordered closed due to the coronavirus pandemic.[35] Parents had no choice but to pay attention to the school system. And it was hard not to see it for what it had become: incompetent, self-serving, and political.

For a month after the governor ordered schools closed, Fairfax did not offer any online classes. Then when it finally attempted to begin online learning, it lost another two weeks because, despite having a $2.6 million contract with online learning provider Blackboard, it had neglected to run software upgrades.[36] As engineers scrambled to get a basic remote-learning system running, Cohen and another board member threw sand in the gears, pointing out that they had not structured the software to have two name fields—one for official records, and one for transgender children's preferred names.[37]

The head of information technology resigned, and a new one was not hired for months.[38] The district was also operating without a chief academic officer, because it had replaced the position with that of "chief equity officer." As the schools failed to offer a meaningful learning experience for children, the board's meetings showed that its members had other priorities.

On March 27, the district said it would offer virtual school only four days a week. This meant that it was again at odds with requirements to receive full state funding. Cohen later schemed workarounds. "Is there any thought given to . . . where we could add in like an asynchronous hour so we are meeting our state requirements but we get kids home earlier or asynchronous hour plus recess?" she asked about elementary schools. The day off was Monday for middle and high school students. Though there were no classes, administrators' workaround was having students log in to take "attendance," for no other reason than to count it as a school day.[39]

On April 20, the board considered buying electric buses to replace the diesel-powered ones that were not currently taking children to school.

On May 21, Cohen led a proclamation about Gun Violence Awareness Day. Tholen, the environmentalist, "recognized the teachers, staff, and students in FCPS schools who have earned awards by improving the sustainability of their schools." Omeish promoted a "High School Voter Registration Challenge" aimed at using schools to get more young people to vote.

In the meantime, children were not even attending school.

On June 25, 2020, the meeting opened with an "urgent matter with budgetary implications." It was not about how to deal with a pandemic, but about how to use the school curriculum to combat "racism and implicit bias." Next, Frisch introduced a resolution commemorating the fifty-first anniversary of the gay rights Stonewall riots.[40]

But the board had no plan to return to school full-time in the fall.

Officials took advantage of Americans' obsession with national politics and tribalism, and of their inattention to the details of how schools worked. In July, Fox News host Laura Ingraham singled out Fairfax for not to returning to school full-time in the fall despite the fact that "kids under the age of 18 . . . basically have a 0 percent chance of becoming seriously ill. . . . So, what are parents who work outside the home, what are they supposed to do?"[41]

She played a clip of its superintendent, Scott Brabrand, addressing the question: "I really hope that we can have our communities of faith and our nonprofits find ways to help support these families," he said.

Ingraham asked, "It's too dangerous for kids to congregate in class and learn and interact with each other, but it's okay for them to congregate in church basements?"

To school board member Sizemore Heizer, the fact that a Republican did not want children to languish was a good reason to take the opposite position. "The best evidence I have that I'm doing something right is getting called stupid by Laura Ingraham on Fox News," she said.[42]

Board members seemed to count on residents being unfamiliar with down-ballot elections and, if they voted at all, simply selecting whoever the Democratic nominee was. That meant board members had little reason to care what residents thought. "Someone just angrily wrote to me that they will not be voting for me in November if I don't put kids back in school 5 days a week in the Fall," Cohen said on July 20. She saw that he did not even know when school board elections occurred. "I hope he knows he's going to need to hold onto that feeling until 2023."[43]

She lectured parents who pleaded with her to do something. "Do not tell me that kids can't get sick and quote an 'article' that someone wrote online in their parents' basement," Cohen wrote. "Do not ask me where we will be sending your direct deposit because now that you are expected to 'teach' your child at home, you expect FCPS to give you [three-fifths] of a teacher's salary. . . . Do not compare teachers to grocery store clerks, doctors, or nurses. Full stop."[44] Schools would remain closed, though Cohen co-owned a store of the most nonessential variety—a trinket shop selling the likes of loose tea leaves and gold candelabras—that was open for business.[45]

On July 23, the board voted to rename a high school, considering the names Barack Obama and Cesar Chavez before settling on Congressman John Lewis, who had just passed away the previous week. It also voted to rename Columbus Day "Indigenous People's Day," and to ban students from wearing Confederate flags on their clothes.[46]

In August, the school system paid $20,000 for "anti-racism" author Ibram X. Kendi to give a one-hour speech, from his computer, to administrators and staff.[47]

It still had no plan to return to school.

On September 3, the school board honored Hispanic Heritage Month (though there were more Hispanics than blacks in the county, there were none on the board because they had run as Republicans) and promoted initiatives to get high school students to register to vote.[48]

On September 11, with a new school year beginning, students could not log on to their online classes. The day before, hackers had announced that they had infiltrated the school system's computers and were holding its data for ransom, but the school system had neglected to tell anyone.[49]

On September 15, the board discussed white privilege and sought to change the curriculum to train children "to recognize injustice in systems and institutions." On September 29, it discussed the racial achievement gap.

Children did not go to school.

On October 8, it honored October as LGBT History Month and re-named a school, Mosby Woods, because of its connection to the Con-federacy. On October 13, it discussed disparities in honors classes. It had paid a consultant $71,000 to write a report on "Equity" in "Advanced Academic Programs." The consultant's findings did not support the premise of systemic racism, and instead found that ra-cial bean counting was already rendering the honors program some-what meaningless. Black students were nearly six times *more* likely to be put in honors classes compared to whites with similar scores. But teachers told the consultant that some students in honors classes were "not reading even on grade level, making it 'a waste of time to assign'" advanced work. The consultant said that it was "aware, around the country, of central administrators' general hostility to-ward the concept of advanced education, but even we were surprised at the depth of that feeling among some FCPS central administrators and some principals."[50]

Children did not go to school.

On November 4, the board learned that county-wide student en-rollment had shrunk by almost nine thousand students, or 5 percent, as parents were fleeing the shuttered system. But it was a good day for school board members: it was the day after the general election, and Frisch soon tweeted a picture of himself with President-elect Joe Biden. The board approved a proposal from Frisch to reissue high school diplomas and transcripts to past graduates who are transgen-der to avoid "deadnaming" them.[51]

On November 16, it introduced a new chief equity officer.

Children did not go to school.

In December, it lowered standards at Thomas Jefferson High School for Science and Technology, a math and science magnet school and the nation's top high school in 2020, in order to be more "equita-ble," following concerns that there were too many Asians. To close out 2020, the board renewed the superintendent's contract at nearly

$312,000, not including a $7,200 annual car allowance and other perks.[52]

Children did not go to school.

MONEY

The district received tens of millions of dollars in coronavirus emergency funds to assist in reopening schools. On January 11, 2021, the board spent almost three hours discussing the federal money, which amounted to $84 million. Though the money was billed as being for urgent necessities for dealing with coronavirus, the board was sure about only one thing: that it should go to pay raises for teachers, even if they had to use moves that seemed to border on money laundering.[53]

"What are the ways that we're looking at getting money into the pockets of these teachers?" said Frisch, who would benefit from such a raise since his partner is a teacher.[54]

Superintendent Brabrand replied, "It needs to be tied to the pandemic, but I think there may be ways that we can make that happen."

"What I'm trying to do is figure out a creative way of getting there," Frisch said.

A member of Brabrand's leadership team interjected: "But I have never seen compensation be [an allowable use]. And you should also know that the CARES Act . . . says that funds generally will not be used for bonus, merit pay, or similar expenditures unless related to disruptions or closures resulting from COVID-19."

Frisch pressed Brabrand, suggesting he lobby to have the rules changed. Brabrand replied, "But I think there may be ways to skillfully look at how we can replace onetime money that we've got now and free up operating dollars that could be legitimately used for anything, and that 'anything' could be compensation for our employees, but it's going to take a skillful review of the budget."

"I don't have to tell you that we're all eager to see the result of that 'skillful review,'" Frisch said with a grin. Brabrand laughed.

Two days later at a virtual meeting with constituents, Frisch claimed that he was not sure how much coronavirus money there was. Also, he did not know how much money was spent and specifically what it would be spent on without consulting his notes.

"I am a mother . . . I am also a community pediatrician and curious as to why when the CDC [Centers for Disease Control and Prevention], the AAP [American Academy of Pediatrics], and the Virginia AAP have strongly endorsed a return to school . . . why the school board continues to delay back-to-school?" one resident asked. "So, what's the holdup? You've gotten COVID money. How much?"

Frisch responded, "The first batch was sixty. . . . I don't remember the exact figure, sixty something million."

The physician asked how much was spent, and Frisch said that he did not know. "And what has that been used for to date, if not mitigation factors?" she retorted.

Another meeting participant's voice began to crack as she spoke. Carin Lomax, a mother of two teenage boys, one who is a special ed student and another who has ADHD, delivered an emotion-filled, forty-three-second segment that captured the feelings of many American parents during the coronavirus pandemic: "Not once have I heard one school board member . . . ask what is in the best interest of our children. Not once, not one board member. It is shameful . . . and this virtual learning environment is horrific for both of them, horrific."

Three days after that, on January 16, Frisch and Cohen raised money for their reelection campaigns by holding an event to "Celebrate the Long-Overdue Retirement of Betsy DeVos," mocking the outgoing U.S. secretary of education, whom these Fairfax leaders vaguely blamed for their problems. DeVos had steered $68 billion in coronavirus money to school districts. Only $4.4 billion had been spent.[55]

Teachers simply repeated the notion that schools were "underfunded," and counted on Americans never looking into the matter. A day after a staff member told Fairfax's school board that the district had so much personal protective equipment (PPE), like masks, that "in fact, some of the issues we had were trying to find storage of some of the quantities that we have provided outside of the warehouse,"

Fairfax's teachers union wrote on Twitter, "Want in-person schools? Then fund #PPE."[56]

CDC

On January 20, Joe Biden was inaugurated as president. And a multibillion-dollar shakedown began.

On February 3, Dr. Rochelle Walensky, whom Biden appointed to lead the CDC, said, "There is increasing data to suggest that schools can safely reopen and that safe reopening does not suggest that teachers need to be vaccinated." Hours later, White House press secretary Jen Psaki sought to walk back the comments, stating that they were not "official guidance."[57]

By February 12, Walensky was twisting herself into knots in a press conference alongside Donna Harris-Aikens, whom Biden appointed senior advisor for policy and planning at the U.S. Department of Education. Harris-Aikens was a longtime NEA official, though she said "my presence here is not a message to anyone."[58]

Walensky said, "What we are finding from the science-based literature is that there is more spread that is happening in the community when schools are *not* open than when schools are open." Transmission among students is rare, and if teachers get the virus, it is more often from other adults who fail to wear masks correctly or even at all, she said. Yet in the same call, she unveiled guidance that, if followed, would have the effect of closing most schools, even those that had long been open without issue.[59]

Walensky said, "The decision on when and how to begin in-person learning is one that must be based on a thorough review of what the science tells us works and an understanding of the lived experiences, challenges, and perspective of teachers and school staff, parents, and students." In between the about-face, the CDC had been lobbied by the AFT, with Walensky taking a call from its president, Randi Weingarten. Emails showed that the science agency modified its recommendations to incorporate some of the union's proposed language almost verbatim.[60]

Walensky pressed states to "prioritize teachers and other school staff to get vaccinated." Since she had just acknowledged that there was nothing about their job that put them at high risk—coronavirus spreads mostly through adults, and few workplaces had less adult-to-adult contact than teaching—she said that this was to keep them "from getting COVID-19 in places outside of schools where they might be at higher risk."[61]

Even vaccines would change nothing about the other requirements for reopening schools. Those requirements were, in a word: money. "President Biden is calling on Congress to provide funding in the American Rescue Plan to provide the critical resources that are needed to safely reopen schools," Harris-Aikens said.

"There are, certainly, equity issues at play, and have been for quite some time. And we look forward to the American Rescue Plan being passed so that schools, states, and local districts have the resources they need to make their schools safer so we can actually get all students back to school safely, and as soon as possible," she added.

The plan included "$128.6 billion for the Elementary and Secondary School Emergency Relief Fund for preparation for, prevention of, and response to the coronavirus pandemic *or for other uses allowed by other federal education programs.*" Five percent of the money would actually be spent in 2021; the rest would be paid through 2028, making it doubtful that it was only about the coronavirus.[62]

By February 14, Walensky was on board with the message, saying, "I think we need a lot more resources," billed as addressing unrelated issues like "asthma" and "exposure to mold."[63]

Dan Domenech, executive director of the School Superintendents Association, said that teachers would go back "only if this bill is passed, only if the dollars get to the school districts in time for them to be able to do the work that they need to do." Though parents were outraged, Democrat strategists were preparing to blame Republicans who voted against the billions for shuttering schools.[64]

By then, Fairfax County schools seemed to have all but given up on educating children. On February 18, the district canceled classes because of snow—even though classes were online.[65]

RIOTS

The year 2020 was defined not only by the economic shutdowns of the coronavirus pandemic, but by race riots in multiple American cities that descended into anarchy.

Schools shared blame in this, too.

The epicenters of the carnage were Minneapolis–St. Paul, where estimates of the physical damage exceeded $500 million, and Seattle, where anarchists created an "autonomous zone" off-limits to law enforcement. In contrast to perhaps any race riot in history, the perpetrators who burned things in the name of black lives were often white young people who grew up in affluent suburbs.[1]

The riots followed the death of a black man named George Floyd at the hands of Minneapolis police. But Minnesota and Washington would appear to be unlikely hot spots for this sort of looting or rioting. Among states with the most fatal police shootings per capita, Washington ranked twentieth and Minnesota ranked thirty-eighth. Seattle has one of the lowest poverty rates among the top one hundred U.S. cities, and an urban population that is 63 percent white and only 7 percent black—making it less black than Des Moines, Iowa.[2]

Though it is not possible to know how direct the connection is, they *were*, on the other hand, the places whose public schools had most aggressively inculcated a generation of young people to see oppression everywhere—in the parlance of their state departments of education, to see life through a "lens" of race and equity, or the opposite of rose-colored glasses.[3]

One thing in particular connected the two powder kegs: their school systems' thorough embrace of a man named Glenn Singleton, an Ivy League–educated consultant and businessman.

Singleton owns a consulting company called Pacific Educational Group (PEG), which has made millions of dollars implanting radical ideas into K–12 schools through his trademarked "Courageous Conversation." Thanks to consultants like him, the rhetoric spouted by thousands of rioters in 2020 had been mainstreamed in K–12 schools for decades. By 2008, Singleton was training teachers across the country about "white privilege," demanding that they enter a "zone of productive distress," and exhorting them to become "anti-racist leaders," which may result in their becoming "physically, intellectually and emotionally exhausted." He had attendees separate into racially segregated groups where white people must confess "in what way(s) am I White?" and then, for each, develop a plan to "challenge my whiteness."[4]

Singleton's methods at times appeared to border on child abuse. In 2009, he hired actors who took children from their classroom in the overwhelmingly white town of Eden Prairie, Minnesota, chained them together, blindfolded them and drove them to a park, then ran after them angrily as they fled. When the actors caught them, they had the children write down the things they loved, then took the paper away. The ordeal was purportedly to teach "tolerance." Parents were not asked to sign permission slips authorizing the activity. "Some kids got really emotional right away," a history teacher said. She said this was because they "felt that cultural empathy." Taxpayers paid Singleton $31,000 for the event.[5]

Singleton, who is black, educated the educators that white people believe in "fostering independence and individual achievement," whereas black people have an "aversion to formality" and "a concern with style more than with being correct or efficient." He trained them that white people believe in "individual thinking" and "private property," whereas black culture is based on "group consensus" and belief in "shared property."[6] Thousands of teachers across the country absorbed these outlandish and obviously untrue statements for decades. Not one appears to have publicly refused. They internalized the lessons and passed them on to their impressionable students. Singleton sat atop a pyramid he called "train-the-trainers," through which his destructive philosophy embedded in school systems.[7] It was an effective way for a tiny group to push their beliefs on huge numbers of people.

But it only seemed to make things worse.

SINGLETON

Glenn Singleton was born in Baltimore in 1964. His family was not poor and his mother was a federal employee. He received a bachelor's degree in communications from the University of Pennsylvania, where he pledged the fraternity Sigma Chi, and was quickly hired by a New York City advertising agency. When his Ivy League credentials did not guarantee him "a fast-track journey to an executive-level position" in less than a year, as he expected, he quit in disgust and went to work as an admissions officer for his alma mater. In 1990, the school relocated him to Los Angeles to oversee its West Coast recruitment office, and he lived a few blocks from Beverly Hills and the Sunset Strip for most of 1991. After five years at that job, he enrolled in a master's degree in higher education program at Stanford University, in white, liberal Palo Alto, before setting up his successful multimillion-dollar business. He bought a house in San Francisco, which he later sold for $1.25 million, in a neighborhood that was 53 percent white and 5 percent black.[8] He never married or had kids.

On the surface, his was a life of privilege, full of opportunity and success. But he was dogged by an identity crisis, by "a painful question that has nagged me and literally stopped me in my tracks since middle school: Am I, Glenn Singleton, Black enough?"[9]

It was one he would spend the next four decades working out on hundreds of thousands of children.

From seventh to twelfth grade, Singleton had attended the Park School, an exclusive, mostly Jewish prep school in the Baltimore suburbs. There, he directed the horseback riding program and "received the highest award for my contribution to life on campus."[10]

He also experienced the unease common to many adolescents. While he felt "called" toward singing and dancing in the theater program at Park, he had "feelings of alienation" from his family and the black kids in his neighborhood, and "long-lasting self-hatred." At Park, "White students would not date me" and "sometimes would not invite me to their parties." He remembered a simpler time: his days in an all-black Baltimore public elementary school, where "never did I question whether my teachers understood me, my family, or our Black culture, as this was a shared experience."

While the all-black Baltimore public school enabled a culturally relevant education that Singleton found valuable, he could not understand why his Jewish day school did not help him to develop his blackness. At the "Jewish, suburban day school . . . I was never allowed to 'unpack' my racial identity," he lamented. Instead, "the educators at Park School prided themselves on being race neutral." At the same time, he complained when they did encourage him to consider his blackness. "How often I recall, in my own schooling at the elite Park School in Baltimore, not being able to focus on the lesson at hand for fear that one of my White classmates (or the teacher for that matter) might ask me to offer 'the Black perspective' on an issue," he wrote.[11]

He blamed his unease on the Jewish school. "The forced process of racial assimilation also prevented me from being fully a part of my family and my larger Black Baltimorean and American community," he wrote. If this was true, his response was overcompensating. "My Black friends and members of my own family would chastise me for even bringing up the topic. 'Oh, there he goes again . . . young Malcolm X!' they would say, referencing me as a Black radical, racial separatist, or, oddly enough, as racist," he recalled.[12]

Singleton never got over it. When he launched Pacific Education

Group in 1992, its sole mission was changing private schools like Park. He worked with elite private schools like Marin Academy near San Francisco, and New York's Spence School and Dalton School. By early 2021, Dalton parents feared to write to the headmaster except anonymously to assert that the school to which they paid $54,000 a year had traded a vibrant, well-rounded education for an innocence-destroying monotony. "Not once this semester have any of us heard . . . mentioned the joy of reading, of learning, of independent thinking, of curiosity, of discovering math and science, of human cultures. What we have heard is a pessimistic and age-inappropriate litany of grievances in EVERY class. We fear that rote learning of political concepts that must be accepted as gospel is not a nutritious educational experience," they wrote.[13]

The truth is that Park was a progressive school. In Singleton's first years as a racial equity consultant, its principal, who was black, actually hired his firm. When Singleton gave his usual presentation about how poorly minorities were treated at fancy private schools, however, there was one problem: unlike the people at other schools who hired him and who accepted his claims as gospel, among the people he was speaking to were Singleton's own former teachers, coaches, and advisors, and they could challenge his specifics. "Revered educators callously invalidated my narrative and requested that such conversations cease immediately," offering evidence that Singleton called "token examples." When Singleton complained that Park counselors had encouraged him to enroll in an Ivy League school instead of a historically black college or university, they deemed him "ungrateful."[14]

"The large cultural price that I personally paid to experience academic success in an independent school continues to haunt me today," he said.[15]

Singleton, who laid the groundwork for the rhetoric that now dominates a large portion of American school districts, is prototypical of figures who have picked up the banner since. From Ibram X. Kendi, the self-styled racial expert who is the son of tax accountant Larry Rogers and business analyst Carol Rogers, to "1619 Project" author Nikole Hannah-Jones, who was raised in Iowa by a white mother and black father, they are privileged people with limited connections to inner-city culture.[16] As if grappling with some adolescent worry that this meant they were somehow not authentically black, they developed a fixation on race in an attempt to prove otherwise.

There could hardly be a perspective less relevant to solving the significant issues of schools. Of all the problems facing poor black children whose underperformance is the impetus for educators' concerns about race, feeling insufficiently black is not one of them. While inner-city children, by Singleton's own account, were the first to recognize that he was not like them, white progressive educators seemed to accept him as expertly speaking on their behalf. And they were willing to pay for that expertise.

After Singleton's awkward return to Park as a consultant, he swore off working for private schools for several years and turned his business to public school districts. "It was at the predominantly White and Jewish Park School where my foundational and conscious work as a racial equity leader commenced," he wrote. "As a child, however, I simply could not envision how significant a leader for racial equity I was to become."[17]

This was not merely hubris. Though PEG once held a summit with a keynote speech addressing "Social Transformation Through a Marxist Lens," the Ivy League graduate has turned the idea that blacks cannot succeed into a multimillion-dollar empire. Of the thirteen thousand school districts in the United States, Singleton has been hired by more than five hundred. At least fifteen of the nation's largest one hundred school districts have retained him in recent years, from Dallas and Fort Worth, Texas, to Omaha, Nebraska. Between 2017 and 2020, New York City paid him nearly $900,000. Baltimore County paid him nearly half a million dollars from 2014 to 2017, and the city of Baltimore, whose long-standing black city leadership and sizeable black student body (76 percent for the 2020–21 school year) made white supremacy an unlikely cause of the city's ills, paid him as well. According to Singleton, many more school districts use his materials without paying a formal retainer.[18]

Singleton developed technical-sounding slogans like the PEG Cycle of Inquiry ("ready, fire, aim"), which he pitched to schools as best practices, with no scholarly evidence of their efficacy. He ran exercises such as the Color Line, in which participants are physically ranked by their "white privilege," and declared that "you will come to recognize that race impacts every aspect of your life 100% of the time."[19]

Singleton's trainings were expensive, but as K–12 education fell under the thrall of equity nationwide, sacrifices would be made. "Providing brand new school buildings or purchasing an adequate number of up-to-date multicultural textbooks for all the children in that school is no proxy for a cadre of Courageous Conversation–trained, racially conscious teachers," Singleton said. The superintendent of one large school district laid off some teachers to pay Singleton, declaring, "I am choosing to invest in racial equity professional development rather than retaining personnel."[20]

While other blacks were busy simply being themselves and working to make ends meet, Singleton had a lot of time to think. Looking for motivation to write a manuscript, he once traveled to a cabin in Tahoe National Forest and "entertained [himself] with one-sided conversations on topics such as the virtual absence of people of color in the forest and why enjoying the outdoors is so often depicted as a White cultural norm and not as something people of color typically do." A typical anecdote from Singleton's training sessions comes when he recalls flying first-class. A flight attendant comes to take meal requests and apologizes that there is only one omelet left. She offers it to him. His seatmate, who is white, complains that he will have to settle for the fruit plate. Though Singleton was treated better than the white man, he stewed about it for years: his seatmate was being "typically White" by complaining. The flight attendant might have engaged in "reverse discrimination" by serving the black man first. Of course, if she had served the white man first, Singleton's verdict of racism would be similar.[21]

Singleton's material stresses the slogan "Beyond Diversity," because his call is not so much for integration but for an apartheid power struggle. When it comes to Hispanics, the largest minority population in America, he is not interested so much in kinship (he "simply [has] not made it a priority to be multilingual") but in stopping what he perceived while in Los Angeles: that Hispanics often did not even view "Latino" as a particularly meaningful identity, that their opinions on the severity of racism in America were far closer to those of whites' than blacks', and that many Latinos embraced the English language, apparently simply considering themselves American. He faults "the 'colonization' of the Latino mind" and points to "the need for constant vigilance to address the allure of Whiteness and the abandonment of Latino cultural affinity as Latinos rapidly attain numerical dominance in the United States and potentially gain access to societal leadership and its privileges."[22] The struggle must continue.

EQUITY INC.

Hiring PEG meant a school district would be turning over a significant degree of control. In one Minnesota suburb, a principal hollered in a meeting, "Damn it, I'm the principal of this building, not Glenn Singleton!" and soon retired—leaving Singleton behind.[23]

As Singleton explained, "partnering with PEG essentially means that school system personnel at all levels must address their underlying fears and/or their disbeliefs about the existence and effects of systemic racism in their midst and courageously commit to implementing equity programming as the solution for meeting the needs of all the children in their schools." Although Singleton's politics are clearly on the left, school districts in areas blue, purple, and red gave him the keys to the kingdom. When the Topeka (Kansas) Public Schools set out to hire a director of equity in 2014, one job requirement was: "Willingness to attend training and complete Affiliate Certification with Pacific Education Group at the first available opportunity."

With tens of millions of dollars on the table, consulting businesses proliferated—many of them borrowing from Singleton, who in turn often lifted content for his training worksheets directly from 1990s college academics. The philosophy thoroughly swept the K–12 industry. Corwin, a leading textbook and teaching manual company, has published 265 books on "Equity & Diversity," compared to 326 on "Literacy, K–12" and 352 on "Curriculum & Content." That includes three by Singleton. Corwin has deployed a "Deep Equity" program in unlikely places such as rural Fauquier County, Virginia, and West Des Moines, Iowa. The Chandler Unified School District, outside Phoenix, paid the company around $420,000 for the training, while asking voters to approve a major bond package because it was strapped for cash to handle student growth, upgrades, and repairs. Corwin's Deep Equity product even includes a built-in defense mechanism, ordering teachers to "explicitly reject and resist" those parents who oppose it.[24]

But it was in Seattle where Singleton's ideas had been driven into the minds of young people harder and longer than anywhere else. Seattle was perhaps the first school system in America to put equity on par with or above education as one of its defining missions. It hired Singleton in 2002. Under his guidance, the school system deemed "future time orientation"—the ability to plan ahead—and "emphasizing individualism as opposed to a more collective ideology" as attributes of "Whiteness," and thus improper to expect from students. This kind of conduct in Seattle led to a 2007 U.S. Supreme Court case in which the use of race to determine where students go to school—in other words, busing—was struck down. Justices expressed shock at Singleton's ideas, with Clarence Thomas writing, "The racial theories endorsed by the Seattle school board should cause the dissenters to question whether local school boards should be entrusted with the power to make decisions on the basis of race." But that setback did not slow down Singleton's career. That year, Greenwich, Connecticut, one of the wealthiest towns in America, hired him.[25]

ST. PAUL

In the Obama years, St. Paul, Minnesota's, schools were a war zone. High schoolers carried out classroom invasions to exact violent revenge for drug deals gone bad. Police reported melees involving fifty people. When students tired of class, they simply got up and left. Fourth-grade aide Sean Kelly said, "I've been punched and kicked and spit on."[26]

To Superintendent Valeria Silva, the problem was not that this was going on. It was that it was not properly statistically distributed. St. Paul's were not typical inner-city schools. They were predominantly Asian, at 31 percent, followed by 28 percent black, and 24 percent white. However, in the first school year of Silva's tenure, black students were suspended roughly fifteen times more than Asian students. This she blamed on "white privilege." She may have been strongly influenced by Singleton's PEG, who received about $1.8 million from St. Paul over several years beginning in 2010. Silva demanded that the rate of black suspensions be no greater than double that of Asians, no matter who did what.[27] This was called Equity.

And that's when things got really bad.

A classroom of gifted and talented fourth graders learned little for an entire year because of a single disruptive classmate, teacher David McGill complained. The student was black, and under Equity, he could no longer be disciplined. Reported assaults on staff tripled in 2015 and teachers often went home in tears. "Please, don't give us more staff development on racism or . . . how to deescalate a student altercation," one said. "We teachers feel as if we are drowning." Asian, black, and white community leaders all publicly called for Silva's firing. Teachers threatened to strike. Aaron Benner, a black teacher, begged the school board to break free of Equity, saying, "I believe we are crippling our black children by not holding them to the same expectations as other students." St. Paul students "are being used in some sort of social experiment," he said—and it was not working.

But it was as if the school system were controlled by some outside force. Not Silva, but Benner was soon out of his job. K–12 education had become a cult around the word *Equity*, and when people whose lives were getting worse pointed out the obvious, all school bureaucrats felt the need to do was to say the magic word. Roy Magnuson, a social studies teacher and union official, said, "There is an intense digging in of heels to say there is no mistake . . . that people like me have issues with racial equity and that is the reason we are challenging them. That makes for a very convenient way of barring the reality of the situation."[28]

As St. Paul's schools descended into anarchy, the Asian families who had comprised the district's largest group moved to where they might stand a chance of getting an education. People left St. Paul for the suburbs because their children's lives were being destroyed—and it was not because district officials had been unable to stop it, but because they were making it worse.

But the forces that seemed to take St. Paul's schools away from their own residents were everywhere, lying in wait.

EDINA

Edina, a suburb southwest of the Twin Cities, was just the place a family might move if they wanted to trade dysfunction for academic rigor. Edina is a Norman Rockwell–esque town of about twenty-two thousand households with a median household income of $104,000, thanks in part to the draw of its historically well-performing schools.[29]

But Singleton had already found a customer in numerous Minneapolis suburbs. Edina hired him even before St. Paul, in 2009. In 2013, Edina school leaders committed themselves to a radical vision of what public education is about. Reading and mathematics were deemphasized in favor of a new focus: under the district's "All for All" plan, Edina reoriented "all 'teaching and learning experiences' through the lens of racial 'equity.'" Bus drivers were hauled into seminars where they were told that "the core of our work as white folks" was not driving students from point A to point B, but rather "dismantl[ing] white privilege" that would "requir[e] a major paradigm shift in the thinking of white people."[30]

The school system's priority became not the highest test scores possible, but the most equal ones. "Educational Equity" was defined bluntly as "promoting equality of educational results." This was a surprising goal for a school. Most bizarre was that the district was turning itself upside down on the purported behalf of a constituency that virtually did not exist: the town of Edina is 84 percent white, 8 percent Asian, 3 percent Hispanic, and 3 percent black.[31]

Even those who accepted these predicates had reason to doubt what was going on when an initiative aimed at equal educational outcomes led instead to the opposite. Shortly after the experiment began, 31 percent of black eleventh graders were proficient in math. By 2017, the figure was less than half that. Administrators only doubled down on the same techniques. It was as if fixing that gap was never their aim at all.[32]

The goal of these suburban bureaucrats seemed to have less to do with academic achievement, or even race, than with shaping children into ideologues. This, it turned out, came not on top of traditional instruction, but instead of it. Previously, Edina's youngest children focused on learning the alphabet, discovering that C represented the familiar sound of *cookie*, and giggling as they thought of Cookie Monster's trademark *nom nom nom!* Now the ABCs book pushed on them by school officials explained the letter C by saying it stood *for Creative Counter to Corporate Vultures. T* stood for *Trans*, and A stood for *Activist*. These were words they could not possibly understand, much less form a reasoned and independent opinion about. Worse, they did nothing to help a child learn her letters.

At one point, the course description for eleventh-grade "Blended" U.S. Literature and Composition read, "By the end of the year, you will have . . . learned how to apply marxist [*sic*], feminist, postcolonial . . . lenses to literature." By 2012, tenth-grade pre-AP English became not an exercise in learning how to write, but a pretext for studying tracts on "Colonization" and "Immigration." In fact, they did not even do that: the "Colonization" section of the syllabus lists just one text, but five films. The texts for the course were written at about a fifth-grade level. Only the most paranoid or nosy parents would have picked up on these changes. A course description sent to parents offered vague and arguably false platitudes, saying changes had been made "to ensure that *all* students get the high-quality curriculum and instruction they need," claiming that the changes were to comply with Common Core (an unrelated national initiative that was new and in the news at the time), and implying that the class would function at an honors level.[33]

Besides having no academic benefit, the shift also had no nonacademic benefit for minorities. Orlando Flores, a Hispanic immigrant, pulled his children from the school, saying, "Relentlessly obsessing about [race and racism] and pretending that race is the only thing that matters is counterproductive and harmful to everyone."[34]

This negativity did not seem to be an accident, but rather its essential feature.

Jackie Roehl, a white tenth-grade English teacher in Edina, contributed an essay to one of Singleton's books. She was more open with his readers than with parents. She wrote that the hours-long training sessions taxpayers purchased from Singleton had succeeded in reforming her thinking. "Teachers must understand that equity is not equality," she wrote. "Before working with PEG, teacher conversations around classroom observations were staid and focused on the positives." Not anymore. Previously, "my English classroom focused on whole-class discussions about literature. . . . Although I called these discussions Socratic and believed I was teaching my students critical thinking skills, I realized that mostly my White students were reflecting my White Culture back to me." What they should have been doing in class, she wrote, was "active social justice work."[35]

Roehl was named Minnesota's "Teacher of the Year" in 2012, which coincided with her contribution to Singleton's book.[36]

When English Department officials recognized that none of these dramatic efforts had worked, their solution was doing more of the same. "Equity could not be achieved as long as we had systemic curricular gaps between [honors] and regular classes," Roehl concluded.[37] Even though there were few black students in *any* class because less than 3 percent of Edina students were black, black students were less likely to be in honors classes. Therefore, there would be no more honors classes. Everyone would operate at the same level. The district claimed that this would be equivalent to the honors level. If true, this would *lower* the grades of students previously in regular classes, the opposite of the stated goal.

Roehl seemed to grasp that few wanted any part of this counter-intuitive logic. "When the school district made a Commitment to ensure racial equity for all Edina Public School students, some parents, students, and even employees questioned that decision," she wrote. But convincing governmental bodies to dismiss the wishes of their constituents is what makes Singleton's conversations so "courageous." With all the complaints, "parent-teacher conference days are draining," she wrote. But "because of my PEG training, I was able to stay centered on the compass."[38]

Roehl's admission of a strategic initiative that was unpopular, reduced academic performance, and was not on track to achieve its stated goals was a natural topic for scrutiny for any elected school board. Shocked by Roehl's essay, the board's vice chair, Sarah Patzloff, encouraged residents to read it themselves and linked to it on a Facebook post, where she called it "frightening." But Singleton generally refuses to work in districts unless elected board members themselves undergo his training. After her social media post, Patzloff was dragged behind closed doors for a five-hour "disciplinary meeting." When she emerged after midnight, she issued an apology. In exchange, the board chair said, "no form of disciplinary action will be taken against Ms. Patzloff and the district will consider this matter to be closed."[39]

If this was the treatment faced by an elected leader—nominally in charge of the "district," not subject to "discipline" by it—for calling attention to a teacher's own published words, it is not hard to imagine the experience of students, who are trained to accept what teachers say as truth and are subject to their authority. After some black students were disruptive during a Veterans Day assembly in 2017, a club of conservative students criticized their behavior as disrespectful to those who had given their lives. In response, mobs of up to thirty surrounded the critics and threatened to "injure them if they did not change their political views," according to a lawsuit. The principal, the suit alleged, responded by telling them they had "brought it upon themselves."[40]

What was happening in places like Edina back in 2013 had become widespread in schools across the country by later that decade, and American culture at large by 2021.

But if there was a goal besides discontent, it did not seem to have been realized.

American high schoolers were coming out less academically accomplished than before. Less happy, too. A large-scale study found an "epidemic of anguish" among young people between 2009 and

2017. Depression rose 69 percent among sixteen- and seventeen-year-olds, and one in five twelve- to seventeen-year-old girls experienced major depression by 2017.[41]

And in the Twin Cities, after a decade of a "major paradigm shift" in the instruction that children were given by authority figures, one that was supposed to lead to racial harmony and equality, young adults were setting fire to their towns, tormented by a sense of agonizing oppression.

Did this happen because the Equity agenda did not work, or because it did?

DIVERSITY, EQUITY, AND IGNORANCE

In August 2020, well after the Floyd riots, the death of another black man in Minneapolis triggered a new round of looting and vandalism—even though the man had committed suicide on video after authorities determined that he was a murder suspect. In San Francisco, young people toppled a statue of former president and general Ulysses S. Grant, who led the Union army that ended slavery. In Washington, D.C., young people accosted Senator Rand Paul (R-KY), demanding he "say her name," referring to a black woman killed by police. They seemed unaware that Paul is the country's most famous libertarian and often critical of police overreach. Paul had written a police reform law named after the woman.[42]

Such ignorance should not be surprising because the Equity agenda has subsumed and displaced perhaps the majority of all discourse around K–12 education. Offered in place of reading, science, and arithmetic is overt political activism whose standards for quality are almost nil. A St. Paul school system's Equity "Digital Suitcase" document on civil rights manages to misspell Emmett Till's name, along with that of "Malcom [sic] X." A lesson plan on Rosa Parks says she worked in the congressional office of Michigan representative "Coyner's," referring to civil rights leader John Conyers Jr. It inexplicably links Parks to what it calls "Row [sic] vs. Wade—women have the right to safe legal abortions."[43]

"Right [*sic*] a narrative of what life might look like from day to day during the struggle," it instructs students. "Who are the social outcast [*sic*] today in America's society/culture?" Teachers are instructed to say, "Class, I ask you today, 'What is your blueprint for life and influencing social justice?'" If the intent of St. Paul's Equity curriculum is to turn students into effective political activists, it fails to do even that, as it has basic misunderstandings about our system of government. It refers to "Lyndon B. Johnson's Affirmative Action Laws," which was actually a 1965 executive order, and elsewhere describes the legislative process as "a law is being recommended."[44]

Though the casual observer might assume such sessions promote multiculturalism, the industry of Equity consultants that has sprung up around Singleton focuses almost entirely on black victimhood and progressive policies unrelated to race. In St. Paul's cultural curriculum repository in 2020, Hispanics, the county's largest minority group, were a caricatured afterthought, with a list of twenty-four items including siesta, piñata, and maraca. It referred to Hispanics as "Latinx," a criticism of the "gendered" nature of Spanish, despite the fact that only 2 percent of Hispanics nationwide use the term to describe their ethnicity. It used this to pivot to a group with more influence in activist circles: "Latinx helps me remember my commitment to being disruptive in my gender expression. Identifying as a Trans*gressive genderqueer Latinx, I embrace living on the border," it said. A section on Asians, the largest racial group in the district, was the sparsest of all.[45]

NEEDLESS NEGATIVITY

Objectively speaking, the early twenty-first century was a great time to be alive and in America.

Math and science advances put more computing power in the hands of the poorest resident than the spacecraft that took Americans to the moon in 1969. Technological breakthroughs allowed someone at the poverty line in modern America to live better than kings a hundred years ago.

In 2019, the poverty rates for blacks and Hispanics were the lowest on record, at less than 19 percent and 16 percent, respectively.[46] The black unemployment rate was also at its lowest rate ever, below 6 percent, as was Hispanic unemployment, under 4 percent.[47] In late 2018, President Trump signed a criminal justice reform law called the First Step Act, and the black incarceration rate was also at its lowest in three decades.[48] Violent crime had been trending downward nearly every year since the early 1990s, with the exception of a slight uptick after 2014. That uptick is sometimes attributed to the "Ferguson effect" because it came after racially fueled anger stemming from the police shooting of Michael Brown.[49] (Singleton had a contract with the Ferguson school district.[50])

Shootings by police were also at historic lows. In 1971, New York City cops shot 314 suspects. In 2017, it was nineteen. In 1975, Chicago cops shot 148 people. In 2019, it was ten. Out of nearly 330 million Americans, twenty-six unarmed white people and twelve unarmed black people were shot and killed by police in 2019.[51]

In other words, while nothing is ever perfect, things were very good. These things can be measured, and they are objective facts. Metrics that affect everyone's lives were getting dramatically better. Police shootings, while devastating to the decedents' families, amounted to statistical noise, and were certainly too few to draw any conclusions of racial bias.

So why were America's young people so angry? Why were rates of depression and suicide going up?[52] Why did they report increasingly negative views of their country, and increasingly feel like victims of "systemic" oppression?[53]

The first answer is that America's young were taught to be angry and preoccupied with race. The second, as you will see, is that they were not being taught math.

5

DON QUIXOTE

TRACY CASTRO-GILL

In June 1997, a thirty-six-year-old child molester named Brian Gill was released from a Washington state prison after serving time for repeatedly abusing his eight-year-old cousin. Unemployed and without prospects, Gill spent his days immersed in a computer game called Second Life, where players create idealized images of themselves—and interact with others' false personas in a massive alternate universe. There, Gill met a woman named Tracy, who was fourteen years his junior. Tracy's avatar became the "submissive" to Brian's "dominant" in violence-tinged online sex games.[1]

In real life, Tracy Hammond was a classic California housewife, a stay-at-home mother of three whose husband provided for her. Some part of her had always been a rebel in search of a cause: in junior high school, she had gravitated toward "goth" culture. She had the usual teenage tension with her father, Rick, who she felt was too strict. But her life from birth until middle age was "Mayberry," her father said. "It wasn't until the Second Life stuff that she started really changing." Glued to the game for the better portion of entire days, she did not even notice when her son came home from school.

Ron Hammond, a handyman, struggled to understand what was happening. Ron and Tracy were high school sweethearts who had been together since they were sixteen. One night at 3 a.m., he woke up and found her sitting in front of her computer, entranced by the game. "You're the only man that ever earned my respect," he watched her type to Brian. Soon after, Tracy told Ron she was going to Vegas for the weekend with a girlfriend. Then that friend called Ron looking for her. By Monday, Ron had filed for divorce.

Tracy wanted to take their four-year-old daughter and move to Seattle to live with Brian. The judge overseeing the custody case barred the girl's move and ordered that the minor have no contact with Brian. Tracy said she was going anyway: she would leave her only daughter behind. It was one of the only times Ron has ever cried. "No one will ever understand when you're sitting in a courtroom and you are praying that somehow the mother of your kids snaps out of it," he recalled. "'Court adjourned, father takes custody' . . . I walked out of the courtroom with tears in my eyes—not of joy, but of disappointment and disgust."[2]

SECOND LIFE

In Seattle, Tracy received a master's degree in education in 2013 and became a substitute teacher that year. She increasingly inhabited a Second Life–style parallel universe. The Seattle area is one of the most progressive and wealthiest in America, but in Tracy's version, "white supremacy" was omnipresent. The reason she was "so angry all of the time" was that "our students are dying from violence, because they are dismissed regularly in their classrooms." She was tired, but "I think I figured out why. I am under attack. All women, but especially womxn of color, are under attack."[3]

She had a new name, a colorful world of villains, and an explanation for a lifetime of perceived slights and unhappiness. "My name is Tracy Castro-Gill," she proclaimed. "I am Xicana, chingona, and pissed off." In this world, she was the hero. Teachers gravitated toward her as she laid out an inspiring story.[4]

"I'm angry, because when I was in high school, I wasn't encouraged to succeed," she said. The school, in fact, placed her in honors classes, but she withdrew. This, she now declared, was "not because I couldn't do the work, but because it was all Shakespeare and Whiteness."[5]

In this telling of her life story, Castro-Gill grew up in poverty and was homeless. Her father, she said, was a Hispanic who betrayed his identity by being what she called a "U.S. nationalist," which made their home "intolerable." To avoid "assimilation" and show that she was authentically Hispanic, her new history went, Castro-Gill joined a gang and began using drugs.[6]

None of this was real, her father, Rick Castro later said. In fact, he said, he and his wife, Rita, had provided for Tracy a conventional, stable middle-class upbringing in California's cowboy country. Rick eventually earned a six-figure income as a prison guard, and Rita was a stay-at-home mom. "Everything since [Tracy] moved to Seattle has been one big lie," Rick said. "It hurts to be the subject of a complete fabrication. . . . She never said a word about any of this racial stuff back then. If anything, she was racist because she hated the Mexican girls . . . her best friend was a bipolar schizophrenic. I don't know if it rubbed off, or we missed something raising her."[7]

Rick, who is half Hispanic, said Tracy's closest connection to Spanish culture may be her similarity to Don Quixote, who attacked windmills believing he was doing battle with ferocious giants. "My mom was white . . . my dad was born here in Long Beach," Rick said. "You've seen pictures of her, she's basically white. How are they racist against you? She can't speak Spanish. She's got a last name of Gill. . . . Remember Rachel Dolezal, that lady a few years ago who pretended to be black? That's exactly what this is," he said, referring to a white woman who became an NAACP official while identifying as black, also in Washington State.

Like Dolezal, Castro-Gill turned this persona into a job—and in Castro-Gill's case, a position of genuine influence. Seattle's school system named her to a district-wide, central-office position called Ethnic Studies Program Manager, paying her $93,000 a year to convey to children the pervasiveness of racism.[8] She described herself as a "radical atheist and consider myself a far-left anarchist."[9]

Castro-Gill's racialized version of education mirrored her self-proclaimed history of joining a gang and using drugs to avoid "assimilation." Under her leadership, the Seattle school system—located in an area with two of America's largest high-tech companies, Amazon and Microsoft—decided to partially replace the math curriculum of every grade with "math ethnic studies." To pass, students must explain how math is "used to oppress and marginalize people and communities of color." They must "explain how math dictates economic oppression," and answer "Why/how does [sic] data-driven processes prevent liberation?"[10]

She was contending that using variables in algorithms was not for minorities, while enormous companies just miles away paid legions of computer programmers six-figure salaries to do just that. Then she was cultivating their despair over the racial income gap.

In spring 2018, the math ethnic studies program was piloted in six schools. The school board had approved the pilot program hoping that it would decrease the achievement gap, writing, "1. We affirm our belief that the integration and addition of ethnic studies into the education of Seattle Public Schools' students can have a positive impact on eliminating opportunity gaps. 2. We direct that the Superintendent incorporate ethnic studies . . . as a high-leverage gap eliminating strategy."[11]

On the next state math exam, the performance of black students at those schools plummeted. At one pilot school, John Muir Elementary, black achievement had been rising steadily every year, but all those gains and more were wiped out, with the black passing rate dropping from 28 percent to under 18 percent the next school year. At another pilot school, 69 percent white and with only seven black students, the white students' pass rates also plunged, from 60 percent to 36 percent.[12]

Confronted with these results, Castro-Gill replied that she never had any intention of narrowing the achievement gap. Gaps, she believed, are a *good* thing, because they ensure that we focus on race.

"Closing 'Achievement/Opportunity' gaps is a Western way of think-ing about education," she said. "We should never 'close' that gap be-cause it provides space for reflection and growth."[13] It also justified jobs like hers.

Despite the failure of the pilot program, the district said it would "prioritize ethnic studies . . . [and] help integrate ethnic studies into all curriculum, content areas, and grade levels."[14] An option to skip a requirement to take Algebra II, a staple for those planning to go to college, and replace it with a course covering "power & oppression," became enormously popular.[15]

CHILD ABUSE

In 2014, when her daughter was nine, Castro-Gill went back to court to seek custody and won. She moved her daughter in with her and Brian, the convicted child molester, at his 750-square-foot house. She enrolled the daughter in the Seattle schools. Castro-Gill at times re-ferred to herself as the nongendered "they" instead of "she." By sev-enth grade, she was pushing literature about transgenderism on her daughter, who had been diagnosed to have a "serious emotional dis-turbance" and "extremely low" social skills. Her daughter decided she was "nonbinary" and, according to Castro-Gill, began dating a transgender person.[16]

Ron said Castro-Gill became "obsessed" with the child's sexual-ity, seemingly in order to cultivate the currency of victimhood sta-tus. "Her daughter is white with blue eyes, so what are you gonna say? 'She's not black or Mexican, but she's gay!'" he said. Ron told his daughter her identity did not come from a category. "I don't care what you are, I love you with all my heart, as long as you're happy. I've said don't live your life to please me, or your mother . . . just be you and be happy. There's nothing wrong with just being you."[17]

Rick, Castro-Gill's father, said his sister is gay and he gladly ac-cepts it, but "my granddaughter is not transgender, it's wishful thinking on the part of Tracy."[18]

Castro-Gill had alienated much of her family with her determination to find negativity everywhere and her loose connection with the truth. She steamrolled over anyone in her way. They saw her less and less often. When her older son had a child of his own, Castro-Gill interrupted a game of cops-and-robbers to accuse her five-year-old grandson of wanting to kill her because she's a poor Latina woman, Ron said. Castro-Gill's son asked her to leave. "Those that are trying to inject poison, your best bet is to distance yourself from them," Ron said.

But one group of people could neither distance from her nor question her beliefs: the fifty-four thousand children of the Seattle public schools, where Castro-Gill held a high-level central office position. She made no bones about what that meant for those children. She posed for a picture with someone wearing a shirt that said, "Marxist Ringleader," adding on social media: "Next step is matching 'IN-DOCTRINATED' t-shirts!"[19]

The state named her Regional Teacher of the Year for 2018–19.[20]

The rise of Castro-Gill and of ethnic studies in the Seattle schools is in part because a large part of what students learned in ethnic studies was how to demand more ethnic studies. Castro-Gill's underage acolytes packed school board meetings and pressed officials to "mandate ethnic studies, Pre-K to 12th, and fully-staff [sic] ethnic studies departments" and "mandate thorough and frequent staff racial equity trainings."[21]

While she was employed by the school system, Castro-Gill also led an activist group called Washington Ethnic Studies Now, which attempts to change school policies. A handful of Seattle students associated with this organization created the NAACP Youth Coalition, and school board members encouraged them to show up at school board meetings to advocate. Yet the teenagers did not actually seem to believe they faced racism dire enough to take time out of their days to engage in activism, and club membership declined. "If you are facing multiple, interlocking systems of oppression, who has the time or ability to keep showing up to pressure school board directors?" one coalition member explained.[22]

The group's fortunes improved after government money was used to pay them to lobby the government. Rita Green, an NAACP official who nominated Castro-Gill as teacher of the year, applied for a "Best Starts for Kids" grant from King County, which was used to "pay the youth for their antiracism efforts. . . . No longer do adult coordinators have to ask students to volunteer their time to make change." The local NAACP received an $877,000 grant to "improve school culture and climate for all students. In partnership with Seattle Council PTSA, and Seattle Public Schools District."[23] The tiny group of compensated activists could pack a meeting, allowing board members to say they were just being responsive to popular demand.

Castro-Gill's tactic of expanding ethnic studies programs in this way was helped by another tactic: bullying. In her old life, she might have seen this as a personality flaw to overcome. But her new persona was full of righteous indignation to eradicate hidden racism, which justified any form of aggression or scheming. As a sympathetic journalist described it, "she admits to having little time to dither or speak 'Seattle polite' to people who either didn't understand or recognize the issue: Children of Color had been drowning in educational 'whiteness' for centuries and even learning to swim meant assimilating, meant subverting their identities. If you were too daft to understand the curricular overhaul necessary to stem this chronic tide of whiteness, after having a little fun at your expense, Castro-Gill was ready to get back to work."[24]

The advocates simply built a footing within the bureaucracy, then began treating everyone else—parents, taxpayers, even colleagues—as the enemy. When the media began asking about the curriculum, Castro-Gill's bosses asked her to give interviews. It was a chance to bring her important message to a mass audience. She resisted, saying that public backlash to the framework amounted to "emotional, racialized trauma." A resident complained to a curriculum manager about the "math ethnic studies" tenets: "Despite being a staunch liberal, I desperately hope this document does not represent what we are teaching in our schools, in either math class or social studies. . . . My hope is that some well-intentioned but naive individual created this document, and the larger group brought common sense to the situation."[25]

The resident pleaded for a reply. The manager simply forwarded it to Castro-Gill with the note, "No worries, Tracy. I didn't respond."

Even as her power grew, Castro-Gill routinely accused colleagues and superiors of racism. When she wanted to put materials on the school system's website in early 2019, IT employees noted that the web pages did not comply with the Americans with Disabilities Act's accommodations for the blind, and Castro-Gill reported the IT guys for racism. In May 2019, when a female teacher called the police to document that an eleven-year-old male student threatened to "fucking beat your face," Castro-Gill worked with a member of the school's Racial Justice Team to "gain social justice" for the student, who was black. Castro-Gill sought out audio of the call and the police report and shared them, leading to an online mob that alleged the teacher "wielded her white fragility and racial bias like a weapon." The teacher (who noted that she had previously experienced trauma) filed a complaint against Castro-Gill for bullying. Castro-Gill lied to internal investigators that she had not requested the files from the police. In contrast, her supervisor gave her a glowing performance evaluation in July 2019, calling her "a strong moral compass" who "has had a very successful year."[26]

As 2019 went on, more colleagues filed complaints against Castro-Gill, but "retracted their complaints for fear of more public shaming and further retaliation," according to an internal report. The school administration continued to give Castro-Gill's work a large platform. In October, Lindsey Berger, who played a lead role in the school system's important Strategic Plan, considered elevating Castro-Gill's teacher trainings to an even more prominent role. Castro-Gill responded by accusing her of "appropriation."[27]

TOXIC

While racial activism may have temporarily given Castro-Gill a sense of purpose, it also took its toll on her. The work was never done. "How can I be so angry all of the time and not have toxic stress?"

she wondered. "I'm so angry all of the time as a result of working on racial equity in my district," she said. "Today I cried in my boss's office. The level of toxic whiteness in that building is unreal. . . . I wish we didn't have to cry because we are doing the jobs we were hired to do."[28]

By the end of 2019, Castro-Gill and at least three others of the system's racial justice professionals sought and got paid medical leave because of the "stress" of working in what they viewed as a cripplingly racist and oppressive atmosphere—the unionized public school system of a progressive city that paid them to focus on racism.[29] If there were any doubt about whether ethnic studies would help develop students into resilient adults prepared to thrive in their future endeavors, that seemed to provide the answer.

Two months later, Castro-Gill returned just in time to provide advice to a state education official from Massachusetts who hoped to replicate her work there and to bill the school system for four days of travel to a "youth organizing conference."[30]

On January 24, 2020, a staff member at Olympic View Elementary School sent out a survey about Valentine's Day. Usana Jordan, a teacher who was part of Castro-Gill's racial posse, forwarded it to Castro-Gill and other racial equity staff demanding that they "call out the whiteness." Castro-Gill fired off an email to the principal, claiming his school was "in violation of the Equity Policy #0030" due to "explicit acts of Whiteness," which "jeopardizes your fulfillment of the Strategic Plan for the school and the district."

She signed the letter using the names of high-level executives. Those leaders said they had not approved the language. One of them, Dr. Laura Schneider, manager of Professional Development Services, told investigators, "I was not in agreement that the version of the letter as it [was] sent out was complete or reflected my input." She had tried to collaborate on revisions, she told investigators, but "the response [from Castro-Gill] is, you're just a white person at the central office, so everything that you say is racist. It's like there's nowhere—I don't know how to work with that."

Castro-Gill is "a bully," Schneider said. "I thought she might hurt me."

As a result of the misrepresentation, Castro-Gill was placed back on paid leave, this time for "alleged misconduct," on January 31. In May 2020, the superintendent determined that "[y]ou engaged in unprofessional behavior. . . . Being trustworthy, having integrity, collaborating with staff and families, and communicating in ways that allow inclusivity and voices/opinions that are different than your own, are essential and critical job functions for the Manager position. Your inability to exercise these skills on a regular basis impacts our staff, students, and families, plus it stalls the important Ethnic Studies work that must move forward."

There was only one thing to do: "I conclude that it is in the best interest of the District that you get placed back into . . . a teaching position."

NO RESULTS

Of all her outlandish actions, only this one crossed the line; she had besmirched the reputations of top education bureaucrats by tying them to an email that caused embarrassment. This is the education industry in a nutshell: focused above all else on presenting a positive public image for top officials, even if it makes things worse for children.

Equity "initiatives" are little different. They make for pleasant press releases for school board members and superintendents. They temporarily placate a tiny but insatiable band of activists who demand them, but bring neuroticism, anger, ignorance, suspicion, and dysfunction for everyone in the end. Seattle's experience proves such equity initiatives do not solve the problems used to justify them. The city has embraced every conceivable equity program for decades. As of 2017, it had one of the worst black-white achievement gaps in the nation.[31]

In 1986, a Seattle "task force" recommended a goal "for the elimination of disproportionality in academic achievement and discipline by the end of the 1989–90 school year." In 2013, the school board aspired to "closing the opportunity gaps" by 2018. But the gap was only getting worse. In 2016, black students were the equivalent of 3.5 grades behind white students, meaning the average black eighth grader might perform as well as the average white fifth grader. By 2017, it had widened to 3.7 grades. Progressive racial activists might be surprised by the states with the smallest black-white achievement gap when it comes to high school graduation rate, as measured during the 2016–17 school year. Those states are West Virginia, Oklahoma, South Carolina, Maine, Wyoming, Alabama, North Carolina, and Georgia. Chris Stewart, a black, liberal former Minneapolis school board member and CEO of education think tank Brightbeam, crunched the numbers and reluctantly found one solid correlation: the more progressive the city, the worse the "achievement gap."[32]

"We tried to explain it away" by controlling for population size, percentage of white students, spending, income inequality, and poverty rate, "but we couldn't," Brightbeam's 2020 report *The Secret Shame* admitted. "Leaders of progressive cities often frame their policy proposals in terms of what's best for those with the least opportunity and the greatest obstacles—those who have been 'left out and left behind,' as the Democratic party states. But, in education, we found the opposite." The average gap between the percentage of blacks and whites proficient in math is forty-one in progressive cities and twenty-six in conservative ones. The Latino-white gap is thirty-four in progressive cities and nineteen in conservative ones. In San Francisco, 70 percent of white students are proficient in math compared with 12 percent of blacks.[33]

"Shouldn't an incredibly wealthy place like San Francisco be the most likely to have used their considerable resources, political will, and community support for helping black and Latino children succeed in school? Shouldn't this be where we see the smallest educational disparities between white students and their black and brown peers? It should be, but it's not," Stewart said.

Conservative cities like Virginia Beach, Anaheim, and Fort Worth had virtually no racial achievement gap in at least one academic category. In Oklahoma City, children of color did *better* than whites on high school graduation rates. That occurred even though conservative cities spent less money per pupil, and even though the conservative cities had similar income inequality to progressive cities. Yet fueled by a sizeable industry of consultants and activist groups, "inequitable" cities are not seeking to replicate the success of places that do work. Closing the gap, as Castro-Gill acknowledged, does not actually seem to be their goal.

Instead, the most remarkable successes in the nation have begun emulating the failures. In 2020, the Virginia Beach school system passed an "equity policy" and began training teachers using consultant Glenn Singleton's "Courageous Conversation" materials. Nowhere did it note that Virginia Beach was actually a shining success story. Instead, the listed resources featured an Equity consultant with a master's degree in English education who offered a diagnosis in 2015, asserting that teachers' "amygdala has been unconsciously programmed" to make them racist.[34]

Castro-Gill's methods have cowed the educational establishment from wealthy purple hamlets to military towns and the rural Midwest. Almost every large school system—most of them suburban—has created a high-ranking "equity" czar position. Across the country, more and more Tracy Castro-Gills are creating lasting damage in the areas that they are being hired to fix.

LAKE FOREST

Lake Forest, Illinois, is a posh waterfront village of nineteen thousand north of Chicago, known for its country clubs and love of polo. Its closest brush with trauma, known locally as the "Lake Forest Chainsaw Massacre," happened in the 1980s when a Hollywood actor cut down a hundred trees on his mansion estate to mitigate his allergies, angering his nature-loving neighbors. In 2020, less than 1 percent of Lake Forest High School's students were low-income, and just over 1 percent were black. In 2015, the school hired a new principal: Chala Holland, the head of a racial equity consulting firm, Holland Educational Consulting Group, that branded itself on a 2014 Facebook post with a memorable Malcolm X quote: "Only a fool would let his enemy teach his children."[35]

In 2008, Holland was working for the Evanston, Illinois, school district, and after she joined a "committee on race and privilege," the district contracted with Glenn Singleton's Pacific Educational Group (PEG). The next year, PEG gave Holland an award. Evanston's high school is racially mixed, with 46 percent white, 26 percent black, and 19 percent Hispanic. There was little evidence that minorities were systematically mistreated there. It spends about $22,000 per student and has an average class size of seventeen. Its campus is a castle with Gothic spires, two swimming pools, a robotics lab, a planetarium, even an urban farm. Following PEG's hire, black students' math scores went down, and the black-white achievement gap at the school widened. In late 2013, a school board member found that "there is no concrete evidence that PEG's programs have helped narrow the achievement gap" and "I can attest from my own experiences in four PEG workshops that they don't want to talk about homophobia, poverty, misogyny, anti-Semitism and the like. Those are outside PEG's ideological paradigm." The district had told the school board member in 2011 that it would cease involvement with the company, but it had not.[36]

In July 2011, Holland moved to Oak Park and River Forest High School, which was roughly half white and a quarter black. The next month, it paid more than $50,000 to become a "PEG Affiliate," with the principal noting Holland's connection to the firm. By 2013, the eleventh-grade black-white achievement gap in math and science had increased by 11 and 14 percent, respectively, compared to the 2010 figures. In 2015, Holland quit after bursting into tears claiming that Oak Park, which is significantly more diverse than Illinois as a whole, was grounded in "white cultural norms."[37] She then took the top job in Lake Forest, which is almost entirely white. While Lake Forest's pride and joy was its rigorous honors program, Holland called honors classes the "New (Educational) Jim Crow" and "beacons of racial inequities disguised by a false notion of meritocracy." She wrote: "It's not a matter of 'if racism' is operating in the schools, it's a matter of knowing that it is there and working constantly [sic] uncover it." In 2018, Holland received another award from Singleton.[38]

The payoff for suburban schools whose leaders court Equity activists is venom, increased accusations of racism, and declining performance. They travel from town to town, lining their pockets at each stop. They deflect scrutiny from their records with charges of racism, and bully residents who dare get involved in the affairs of their own local governments.

In 2012, Dennis Carpenter and his wife, LaQuanda, were working for the Newton County, Georgia, school system, where he was deputy superintendent and she was principal of Alcovy High School. After a teacher, Kevin Dockery, "brought up some issues" with testing procedures at Alcovy, he said he was targeted by LaQuanda.[39] When residents posted negative comments about the principal in the comments section of a local news site, she sued the anonymous internet commenters, complaining that her school had been forced to "divert resources" to rebut the criticism, and attempting to force the newspaper to reveal the identities of the citizens.[40] After a school board member, Jeff Meadors, expressed concerns about Dennis and LaQuanda, LaQuanda sued him. Meadors said that "she filed a frivolous suit aimed at smoking out her husband's critics, and when skeletons marched out of litigation discovery she refused deposition and dismissed her suit. . . . I have no idea why she pretends to be victimized."[41]

Nevertheless, in 2013 the school board paid both Carpenters $70,000 to simply go away. "It is in the best interest of the school system and the Carpenters to sever the current employment relationship," it said. This buyout was pure profit because Dennis had already accepted the superintendent's job in Hickman Mills, a troubled urban district outside Kansas City, Missouri.

There, LaQuanda became principal of a charter school that was soon shut down after state inspectors and auditors found "irregularities." The school reported a 99.5 percent average daily attendance rate, but when the inspectors stopped by, only 174 out of 636 students were there. The school gave academic credit to high schoolers for their experiences learning about the four seasons of the year, babysitting, and hair braiding, and had the state pay it for doing so. When it came to tests, fewer than 20 percent of students were proficient in English and math.[42] Meanwhile, with Dennis at the helm of Hickman Mills, statistics went up dramatically by 2014. "One year after Carpenter arrived in Hickman Mills, the district's annual performance report increased by 18.9 percent, the largest increase of any K–12 urban or suburban school district in the state," local media reported.[43]

Dennis, a black man whose career has been defined by racial and political advocacy, did not stick around. In early 2017, he leveraged those statistics into a new job where his background did not seem applicable: the wealthy and predominantly white suburban district of Lee's Summit, where virtually everyone already passed their tests.[44] In 2018, he demanded that the school board pay Glenn Singleton $7,000. The district abandoned the idea, citing parents' concerns about cost and Singleton's divisive and almost entirely black-focused approach to "diversity."[45]

After he heard secondhand in early 2019 that a Lee's Summit parent had said he was "running our school district into the ground" and that a home shopper should only buy there "as long as we can get rid of our superintendent," he claimed he was the victim of threats and secured a police detail, even though the police department found the allegation "unfounded."[46] He threatened to slash basic academic programs and quit if the board did not award a $97,000 contract to an Equity consultant.[47] Dennis quit in mid-2019, but not before stalling long enough to sign a contract extension. The school board paid him an astonishing $750,000 to buy him out.[48]

For more than a year after, he played the victim. "A black superintendent doesn't = the absence of racism. In fact, white backlash & closed group social media plotting/lynching is a racist response to having a black superintendent," he wrote on Twitter, where his handle was @EquitySupt1.[49] He started a racial equity consulting business, and when a local business association withdrew an offer to hire him to give a $1,500 speech, he sued the Lee's Summit Economic Development Council, claiming "it's not OK to interfere with any individuals [sic] right to make a living."[50] "Dear Black People: The more successful you are, the more racism you experience. The only thing that changes is your willingness or unwillingness to see it and acknowledge it," he wrote.[51]

This was the same lesson he taught children, straight from the Singleton playbook. The primary focus of every aspect of life should be on racism at all times. Hard work, success, and good intentions will never alleviate the oppression.

As for Tracy Castro-Gill? After being removed from her job for misconduct, she began offering professional development training, at costs ranging up to $70,000, through her nonprofit.[52] Within a few months, she had contracts with twelve area schools.[53] In March 2021, the Washington State Board of Education voted unanimously to require its own members and staff to take eighteen hours of training from Castro-Gill, with the intent of making ethnic studies a required course statewide.[54]

6

CRITICAL RACE THEORY

Loudoun County, Virginia, has the highest median income in the country. In 2015, every member of its county board was Republican. The county's eastern half is filled with high-end housing developments less than twenty years old, brimming with residents working well-paying jobs in government and the technology sector. The western half is rural. Black families in Loudoun, proportionally fewer than both Asians and Hispanics, had an estimated median income of $112,000 in 2019.[1]

Yet even here, by 2020, Loudoun's school superintendent, Eric Williams, was using the schools to get "all students, staff, families, and other members of our community to engage in the disruption and dismantling of white supremacy."[2]

In 2019, the school system had hired the Equity Collaborative, LLC, a for-profit California-based consulting firm owned by a one-time employee of Glenn Singleton named Jamie Almanzán. Williams approved a $242,000 contract that included paying three employees of the firm $5,000 per day each for a "Systemic Equity Assessment." The firm taught the "5 tenets of critical race theory."[3]

"Critical race theory" (CRT) is a byzantine logical framework developed in academic writings by black feminist professors in the

1980s and 1990s. The theory was fringe among academics of the time and its creators never expected it would escape the lab and become an accepted way of governing American schools. A 1998 paper by Gloria Ladson-Billings, one of the first to apply it to children, said, "I doubt if it will go very far into the mainstream. Rather, CRT in education is likely to become the 'darling' of the radical left, continue to generate scholarly papers and debate, and never penetrate the classrooms."[4]

In 2002, data reporting requirements introduced by the No Child Left Behind Act highlighted racial disparities in test performance, sending superintendents grasping for some way to address them.[5] For-profit consultants and philanthropic foundations began offering CRT as a solution, repackaging it as "equity." The theory is, perhaps intentionally, difficult to understand. It is packed with jargon, and sometimes redefines common, innocuous words to take on specific new and radical meanings. Principals are not always familiar enough with CRT to recognize it when they have invited it into their schools. But these equity programs are, in general, a direct application of CRT.

A May 2020 presentation offered by Almanzán's firm, titled "Introduction to Critical Race Theory" and defining CRT's five tenets, was clearer than most.

Permanence of racism, the presentation explained, means that "racism controls the political, social, and economic realms of U.S. society. In CRT, racism is seen as an inherent part of American civilization."[6] Critical race theory is not a tool for solving problems: as the name implies, it is a predetermined conclusion that racism lurks in *every* situation. The theory is put into practice by identifying, then criticizing, how racial power dynamics lurk in even the simplest situations, even if this requires huge leaps of logic. It is, to put it simply, a hammer looking for nails.

Whiteness as property is a concept borrowed from the title of a 1993 academic paper that suggested that "the question was not so much 'who is white,' but 'who may be considered white.'" Outsiders of different ethnic origins who accepted "Anglo-American norms" could be considered white. Conversely, even a black person might not be "politically black" unless they subscribe to the right ideology.[7]

Counter-storytelling is the practice of considering people's subjective perceptions ("lived experiences"), or even inventing "composite" stories, in lieu of verifiable facts, specifically to propagate CRT. "Counter-stories are a *resource* that both expose and critique the dominant (male, White, heterosexual) ideology," as Almanzán's presentation puts it.[8] This storytelling concept comes from a 2002 academic paper that explained that, like other postmodern philosophies, CRT rejects objective reality itself, in favor of "situated realities." CRT "questions dominant claims of objectivity, meritocracy, and individuality in United States society," the paper continued.[9]

CRT thus argues that all of society is white supremacist but defines "whiteness" as not simply a skin color but anything that is "dominant" or accepted as the "norm." Commonly accepted "practices, standards and discourses," such as the scientific method, are "dominant" within the world of education. Therefore, the logic goes, they are part of white supremacist society. According to this premise, traditional educational virtues, such as the "high value society places on the . . . 'hard sciences,'" ignore and exclude "the knowledge, practices, beliefs, norms, and values that are derived from culturally specific lessons within the home space and local communities of people who have been subordinated by dominant society."[10]

Oddly, proponents of this logic rarely give specific examples of these closely held cultural customs supposedly excluded by Western norms. This is not surprising because CRT is the domain of highly educated, well-off black consultants and scholars who wield it to find ways (invisible to most of us) in which they have been oppressed. Most have little in common with the inner cities, where efforts to resolve disparities might be more useful.

Not only is CRT *not* a method for solving problems, it is a method for *discovering* them where no one had perceived them before. The 2002 paper promoting "situated realities" over objective "reality" was cowritten by a female assistant professor in Utah. Her paper's focus was reasoning through why an imagined ("composite") assistant professor with a background strikingly similar to her own had an unsatisfactory meeting with the tenure review committee. The paper concluded that it was because Western systems of thinking had caused the committee to unfairly believe her work was not as good as those of other candidates.[11]

The implications of this tenet for education are pessimistic. Because the dominant culture relies on the scientific method and empirical research to determine and discuss truth, and those experiencing oppression purportedly operate by a different set of rules, this creates an "apartheid of knowledge," the paper says. It is therefore unlikely that the two groups will ever be on the same page.[12]

Interest convergence is "the notion that whites will allow and support racial justice/progress to the extent that there is something positive in it for them," Almanzán's presentation explained.[13] In other words, whites will only entertain equity initiatives out of their own selfishness. The effect is that no matter how much well-meaning officials indulge and pay the critical race theorists, the criticism will never end. If a white person successfully manages to follow critical race theory, then he/she must be doing it to feel good about himself/herself, thus inevitably demonstrating white supremacy.

Finally, the *critique of liberalism* refers to the fact that critical race theory opposes traditional liberal values—including, as the Equity Collaborative explains, liberalism's belief in "ideas of colorblindness, the neutrality of the law, incremental change, and equal opportunity for all."[14]

The legal system of liberal Western democracies relies on the ability to arbitrate truth among competing claims but, according to CRT, that does not work when there are multiple, subjective realities. The scales of justice under law are supposed to give each party equal weight, equal opportunity. However, critical race theory evaluates fairness based on *outcomes*. Liberal justice systems grant a presumption of innocence, where the core premise of CRT is that people with the property of whiteness are innately oppressive. Liberalism in its broadest sense therefore conflicts with CRT in irreconcilable ways. Liberalism cannot be simply improved, but must be torn down, because "incremental change" is not enough. Equity advocates, the presentation explained, believe that "the powerful maintain power and only relinquish portions of it when they have nothing to lose."[15]

Loudoun County was becoming a more "liberal" place politically, casting a majority of its votes for Democrats in 2020.[16] CRT conflicted with and expressly opposed long-standing liberal beliefs. Yet it took only a handful of activists, working alongside a for-profit consulting firm, to turn the school system of America's richest county on its head. They followed the same playbook that was used at schools across the country.

COUNTER-STORY

Leading the charge in Loudoun was Michelle Thomas, a woman in her late forties who became president of the county NAACP branch in November 2018.[17]

A brief biography of her says, "Pastor Michelle C. Thomas is widely known and revered as a 21st century leader. Her proven track record as a revolutionary thinker, business innovator, prolific communicator and prophetic voice has established her as a leader of leaders. . . . After graduating Magna Cum Laude from the prestigious Duke University School of Engineering, she shattered the corporate glass ceiling and started her own IT Consulting Firm, moving from IBM employee to IBM partner. Retiring at the age of 27, Pastor Michelle has partnered with fortune [sic] 500 companies, the Federal government, politicians, churches, and heads of state for more than 20 years."[18]

In 2006, Thomas founded a church, Holy & Whole Life Changing Ministries, International, and became its pastor. She took to wearing a clerical collar at political rallies. In 2017, she incorporated a nonprofit called the Loudoun Freedom Center, of which she was the sole board member, and after litigation with a real estate developer, got the developer to donate a nearly three-acre historic slave burial ground. When her sixteen-year-old son drowned while swimming with his friends near the Potomac River in June 2020, she had him buried among slaves, and she plans to be buried there as well.[19]

All of this was a counter-story.

Thomas was not a corporate wunderkind. In 1997, when she was twenty-five—two years before she purportedly retired—Florida authorities issued a warrant for her arrest on felony charges for passing a "worthless" check. According to public records, she had moved out of state by 1998, with no indication that she was ever taken into custody. The arrest warrant was withdrawn in 2017 when the statute of limitations expired.[20]

There is no indication that she had theological training; her church was "nondenominational."[21]

Nor did she have any direct connection to American slavery, as she is the daughter of Jamaican immigrants.[22]

Her race was an asset to her under existing U.S. policies. She created computer businesses that received money from government contractors (which are required to subcontract some of their work to minority-owned businesses), then subcontracted out work to others.[23]

In 2003, Thomas's company, MCA Computer Group, began working as a subcontractor for Unisys, which after the September 11, 2001, terrorist attacks was awarded a contract to manage the Transportation Security Administration's information technology. Though it was an IT-related business, MCA's (now-archived) website was comically primitive.[24] In 2006, auditors found that under Unisys, "many airports were operating with archaic telephone systems, dial-up internet, . . . and [law enforcement] radios" that did not get reception.[25]

Pastor Thomas lived opulently, but the blessings did not extend to others with whom she interacted. Despite earning money from several federal government clients, even from the Internal Revenue Service itself, MCA did not pay its taxes. In 2006, it had a $66,000 federal tax lien levied against it. By 2007, she lived in a million-dollar house and owned a Jaguar, a Land Rover, and a 1948 Plymouth, but had unpaid taxes in four jurisdictions. She declared bankruptcy that year to avoid paying creditors, including her landscaper, home theater installation company, and satellite TV provider. She kept the house and the cars. In 2015, she filed for bankruptcy again, listing numerous unpaid debts related to a beach resort property.

DISRUPT

The Loudoun County Public Schools (LCPS) superintendent was Eric Williams, a genial white man in his midfifties with a degree from Harvard and a long record of enthusiastically supporting liberal diversity and inclusion initiatives. Its schools were ranked among the best in the state.[26]

But the goal of critical race theory is, in its own terminology, to "disrupt." At least twenty-eight thousand academic papers have been written about how to use the theory to disrupt different aspects of life.[27]

In Loudoun, the disruption began with a shoddy report by one woman, Kenya Savage, who led a quasi-official group within the school system called the Minority Student Achievement Advisory Committee (MSAAC). "The District has a profound job to educated [sic] our children and must be held accountable for the preparation of future leaders, Doctors, Engineers, Teachers/Educators, Journalist [sic], Scientist [sic], Mathematician [sic], Business Owner [sic]," it said. "Why is the on-time graduation rate for Hispanics and students with disabilities or our ELL [English Language Learner] students nearly a 30% gaps [sic] from their White and Asian peers?"

Savage, a black woman who was not an English language learner, continued, "Their gap [sic] exist because of the limited academic instruction to support their gifted and talented intellect. As a result, these students [sic] experience [sic] are not challenged or stretched to their fullest potential." Her report went on to lament the "Schools To Prison Pipeline," a reference to racial disparities in school suspensions.[28]

This was essentially creating a moral panic. The simple reason English language learners took longer to graduate was that they did not speak English proficiently. And as the school district's own internal January 2019 report showed, "The difference in suspension rates between African American and White students in LCPS is the *lowest* among comparable divisions." Only 2 percent of black students were suspended during the 2017–18 school year, compared to slightly less than 1 percent of white students.[29]

Nonetheless, the shaming in the MSAAC report forced Williams to consider whether or not the school system that he had presided over since 2014 was, despite his intentions, racist. To get an outside opinion from a seeming expert in the topic, in 2019, Williams paid $242,000 to Almanzán's Equity Collaborative to conduct a number of services, including the "Systemic Equity Assessment."[30]

To help answer the question, the consultant interviewed the MSAAC and members of Thomas's local NAACP.[31] It also gathered a group of minority students and questioned them. The consultant acknowledged that black students were "performing well academically," but offered up the counter-story: they "do not feel that they are supported in developing a sense of cultural or academic identity."[32]

The Equity Collaborative's report then claimed that shocking incidents had occurred. "Some participants in school communities shared experiences of extreme racially motivated acts of intimidation, including nooses hanging from trees . . . and school sites being visited by members of the KKK," it said. It claimed a teacher told a class, "All Arabs are terrorists." There was no evidence offered that such dramatic, awful events occurred—in fact, the attention given to far less serious events virtually assures that they did not. The same section of Almanzán's report lamented that a teacher once mentioned police, which stood out to students because it was "not in a mean way." When a white fifteen-year-old Loudoun student sent a friend a video exclaiming, "I can drive, nigga!" after she got her learner's permit in 2016, it was so remarkable that students circulated the three-second video and held on to it for years. Eventually, a vindictive student posted it publicly and the story ended up on the front page of the *New York Times*.[33]

The consultant also asked the children what should be done to solve the schools' problems. The children asked for what any child would: more fun. Schools should offer more programs like "Wiggle Room Wednesdays," instead of where "a teacher stands there and tells you a bunch of things over and over again." One of the real solutions offered to solve these purported problems, of course, was to hire the Equity Collaborative for more work. The $242,000 Loudoun contract eventually swelled to some $500,000 in payments.[34]

The schools, the report said, should "[e]stablish student affinity groups at all levels to support the social and cultural identities of students of color," which is important because it "provides a vehicle for outside community or business partners to disseminate important information about educational opportunities or to provide mentoring and encouragement to students of color." In other words, the schools should create racially segregated clubs so that nonprofits can train students to see CRT as an inherent part of their race, and plausibly speak on behalf of an entire race—even though, contrary to CRT's questioning of "individuality," members of the same race might not all share those beliefs.[35]

In February 2019, the school board created an equity committee, consisting of school board members and citizens chosen by MSAAC, the NAACP, and other groups. Unlike other meetings of the elected school board, its meetings were "facilitated" by the Equity Collaborative, with the firm's logo appearing on its meeting agendas. The committee was supposed to be temporary, but was eventually extended indefinitely.[36]

All school staff were required to take "Equity in the Center," a training designed by the school system and initially "cofacilitated" by the Equity Collaborative. In January 2020, the committee unanimously recommended that training extend to parents, too.[37] The racial pronouncements came not from people with particular records of oppression, but from some of the most privileged people imaginable.

By that time, committee member Katrecia Nolen was chair of the MSAAC. Nolen runs a government contracting company headquartered in her home that is eligible for contracts reserved for people from disadvantaged groups. Her company received around $400,000 in government contracts in fiscal 2019. She suggested "a webinar of some type that the parents would have to review" before they could access ParentVue, the website parents must use to see their children's report cards.[38]

Their goals seemed to be engaging in a power struggle, spreading CRT, and punishing or purging those who disagreed. One equity committee member, Wendy Caudle Hodge, a black professional oboe player, accused the committee itself of oppression after it did not allow her to speak for longer than others. "Having a bell cut off committee members is a supremacist act," she scolded.[39]

Committee member Lara Profitt, a white woman who works as a teacher, enjoys yoga, and owns four cats, demanded "enforcement" of the new equity regime's actions. "Will the system be able to withstand the discomfort that will definitely come from this type of change AND will leadership be able to stay on track and enforce these changes within schools? . . . are we ready to let go of teachers and administrators who don't buy-in?" she asked.[40]

Another member, Zerell Johnson-Welch, a black woman who is an attorney admitted to practice before the Supreme Court and a competitive tennis player, added, "Folks who need this change in mindset will not voluntarily feel they need to [do it]. . . . How are we ensuring that [human resources] is identifying future LCPS educators that possess the same ideology we are trying to create?"[41]

In August 2020, the district proposed forbidding teachers from expressing concerns about equity policies, even in their private conversations outside of work. "Employees are expected to support the school division's commitment to action-oriented equity practices through the performance of their job duties, as the Division engages in the disruption and dismantling of white supremacy. . . . Behavior that will not be tolerated includes . . . undermining the views, positions, goals, policies or public statements of the Loudoun County School Board or its Superintendent," a proposed policy revision said.[42]

"An employee's First Amendment right to engage in protected speech . . . may be outweighed by the school division's interest in . . . [protecting] class equity, racial equity, and the goal to root out systemic racism," the policy draft continued. "Actions that are not in alignment with the school division's commitment to action-oriented equity practices" include "off-campus speech, social media posts, and any other telephonic or electronic communication." Any employees who "have witnessed such conduct, should notify their supervisor immediately." The idea was eventually withdrawn after withering criticism by local news media.[43]

Williams also put forward a "Detailed Plan to Combat Systemic Racism" that contemplated subjecting individual school board members—who are popularly elected and to whom he reports—to "pre and post tests to determine individual School Board members' and cabinet members' racial literacy and consciousness."[44]

The superintendent seemed to believe that the school system was inherently racist. By then, he had led it for more than six years, so it was hard to see how this did not implicate him more than anyone. But he also seemed to believe that draconian measures imposed by him, from the top to bottom, might be the solution.

WHITENESS AS PROPERTY

CRT views "whiteness" as "anti-black," and positions other minorities along a spectrum based on how willing they are to stand against anti-blackness by embracing CRT. This makes it an outdated approach for racial issues in modern K–12 American schools. In 2017, there were nearly twice as many Hispanic students in public schools as there were black. Asian students are the fastest-growing group.[45]

This was also the case in Loudoun County. Blacks make up only about 8 percent of the county's population, but represent one-third of the county board of supervisors, including its chair. There were no Hispanic or Asian members on the board, though both groups vastly outnumbered blacks in the county. Yet most of the racial discussion centered upon how poorly blacks were treated in Loudoun. In a typical equity committee meeting, nine of seventeen members present were black.[46]

After Williams had spent hundreds of thousands of dollars in taxpayer money paying the Equity Collaborative from 2018 to 2020 in an honest effort to address activists' concerns, the NAACP used the consultant's Systemic Equity Assessment report against him. "It is quantifiable evidence that racism and discrimination continue in a systemic way," Pastor Thomas said.[47]

In May 2019, Thomas's NAACP filed a civil rights complaint with the Virginia attorney general's Division of Human Rights, saying that an independent report had found "pervasive inequities division wide" in LCPS, including "racial insults, slurs, or racially motivated violent actions toward Black/African American, Latinx, and Muslim students." The complaint used the Equity Collaborative's general allegations as evidence that racism was behind disproportionate racial figures at the county's math and science magnet school, the Academies of Loudoun (AOL).[48]

This was an odd target for demands of major reforms. The academy was brand-new and served fewer than two thousand of the more than eighty-one thousand students in the school system. In the 2020–21 school year, the Academies of Loudoun was 5 percent black, compared to about 7 percent of the school system overall. But there was a simple reason, it turned out, for the complaint: the son of the NAACP's education chair did not get in.[49]

If this was such a big problem, it was hard to see it as white supremacy or anti-black. The black makeup of AOL was the most closely proportionate of any race. Asians made up 23 percent of high schoolers in Loudoun, but nearly 47 percent of AOL students, double their representation in the county. Whites, meanwhile, were underrepresented by 12 percent, making up only 36 percent of AOL in a county that is 55 percent white. Hispanics made up less than 10 percent of AOL, a 7 percent underrepresentation.[50]

The focus flummoxed even the CRT apostles at the Equity Collaborative. "The controversies surrounding the Academies of Loudoun is [sic] among a small number of people. This issue was not identified as a major theme (i.e., top concern) in the Equity Assessment," it told the attorney general's office in an August 2020 telephone interview.[51]

There seemed to be little interest among black students in even attending the school. In 2018–19, the first year the school was open, twenty times more Asians than black students applied for admission. Was it because of white supremacy that Asian students applied for, and gained entry to, a math and science school, displacing whites as the largest bloc?

Only under the warped lens of critical race theory was this possible. Asians' success in the mainstream subjects of math and science demonstrated, according to the CRT framework, that they had the property of whiteness. Under CRT, blacks' underrepresentation at a school dedicated to the hard sciences proved racism, even as CRT also claimed that blacks did not and should not share the "high value society places on the . . . 'hard sciences.'" This assured the most important tenet of CRT: the permanence of racism.

CRITIQUE OF LIBERALISM AND THE NEUTRALITY OF LAW

If the complaint were a lawsuit, Williams and LCPS could confidently present ample evidence of nondiscrimination in court and proceed with the important work of providing a rigorous, math-based education. But the Democratic attorney general's Division of Human Rights was a quasi-judicial body that, like CRT, seemed to operate with disregard for the liberal tradition of neutrality before the law and the careful, rational weighing of evidence.

The NAACP provided the division with the email addresses of eighteen individuals "who agreed to serve as witnesses," and investigators from the office emailed most of them. The division printed "a select group of pertinent narratives" from these exchanges. Typical was a secondhand account of unspecified "treatment of two black [kids]" at the hands of a teacher. Another parent complained that her biracial child had been suspended, while acknowledging that "it's very subjective if [his] disparate discipline was due to his race."

A substitute teacher complained that out of a group of thirty new hires, only three were black, with no mention on record by the division that this meant blacks were actually *overrepresented*. The parent of a student who came home with bad grades wrote, "My son . . . has told me repeatedly that all the brown kids receive Fs and the white kids receive As," a statement that could be easily checked against Loudoun school records.

There is no indication that Williams saw their full allegations, knew the names of the witnesses, or was even allowed to respond to their claims, as the division cited "apparent witness concerns surrounding confidentiality and retaliation." Nor is there any indication that the division sought to verify any of them. This violated essentially every element of legal due process.[52]

Following this "investigation," the division ruled in favor of the

NAACP in November 2020. "Having found reasonable cause to believe that LCPS's policies and practices resulted in a discriminatory impact on Black/African American and Latinx/Hispanic students, the Division of Human Rights requests that the [NAACP] and [LCPS] engage in a post-determination conciliation process in an effort to resolve this matter," it said.[53]

Pastor Michelle Thomas donned her clerical collar and read from the division's order in soaring tones. Then she invoked "lived experiences," the CRT term for the use of anecdotal stories as "realities" that are used to undermine society's usual reliance on facts and objectivity. "We must understand the historic nature of this finding, not just in a sense that it is another piece of documentation that we have of the lived and shared experience of being discriminated against at the hands of LCPS," she orated.[54]

PERMANENCE

Williams, whose school system was the target of the NAACP complaint, appeared to be as committed to equity and anti-racism as anyone. When the complaint was filed in May 2019, the magnet school was only in its first year of operation and still working out its processes. Well before the division's determination, Williams had already taken strong action to respond to the racial concerns. AOL's admissions standards had removed geometry as a prerequisite, replaced the multiple tests used for admission, such as the PSAT, with one billed as "culturally sensitive and inclusive," changed the essay portion to evaluate the "applicant's motivation, perseverance, and creativity" instead of writing ability, and agreed to consider "the principle of geography/socio-economic equity in the selection process."[55]

The district had created special programs for minority or low-income middle and elementary schoolers who showed promise and interest in STEM subjects, but were not yet fully qualified for honors courses, in order to create a pipeline to the magnet high school. It generated a list of every black and Hispanic eighth grader enrolled in algebra or geometry, had staff personally encourage each of them to pursue applying to the magnet school, and waived the application fee for them.[56]

On August 11, 2020, the school board had given in to an NAACP demand that the magnet school accept students with a "C average or better," even though not a single resident who spoke at the board meeting supported the change.[57]

All of this would seem to make the pseudo-legal challenge unnecessary. Instead, the activists used Williams's efforts against him. The NAACP complained that "LCPS pulled Black/African American and Latinx/Hispanic students out of their class and encouraged these students to fill out an application, without prior notification to students or parents." Of the elementary and middle school pipeline programs, it lamented that "LCPS maintains two separate tracks of gifted and talented programs."[58]

What, at this point, did Thomas's NAACP really want? The answer appeared to be money, power, and the ability to further propagate critical race theory. It complained that "LCPS refuses to include NAACP to be part of the solution" and made nineteen demands, called "Terms of Conciliation," which were incorporated into the division's determination. At least twelve of them involved steering money, influence, or both to one of Thomas's two groups, the NAACP and the Loudoun Freedom Center.[59]

The school system must, they said, "develop and implement an annual equity training program to be provided to all students two times a year (September and January), through a collaborative effort between NAACP Loudoun Branch, Loudoun Freedom Center, and LCPS." It must also "implement an African American history course developed by organizations such as Loudoun Freedom Center." LCPS must partner with the NAACP and the Loudoun Freedom Center "to provide racial literacy training initiatives for LCPS employees," specifically including even its bus drivers. The NAACP did not explain what role bus drivers played in preventing black students from applying to or attending the magnet school.[60]

The "Terms of Conciliation" went on. LCPS must "develop a STEM based elementary after-school and summer program with a focus on African American studies. Develop this program in partnership with Black/African American studies experts from local academic institutions and organizations, such as Loudoun Freedom Center." In this request, Thomas did not explain why a program intended to increase math abilities would actually focus on "African American studies."[61]

LCPS must also "negotiate monetary payment to compensate for time, resources, and costs associated with NAACP Loudoun Branch's efforts" in filing the complaint.[62]

As for admissions requirements, not only did the NAACP want to "eliminate 'high stakes' testing," it even wanted to "eliminate letters of recommendation as they can be biased."[63] The most demanding and rigorous high school in the wealthiest county in America would be composed not of students who demonstrated the desire and ability to succeed in advanced math and science, but of a random assortment of C students.

INTEREST CONVERGENCE

On September 25, 2020, Superintendent Williams, the school board, and the county board issued an "apology to the Black community of Loudoun County" for segregation in the 1950s. "There are many examples and instances in which systemic racism, inequitable treatment, and disproportionality began and have persisted since," it said. These included "a lack of diversity among applied and admitted students to the Academies of Loudoun" and "disproportionate discipline of Black students." It thanked "the Loudoun Branch of the NAACP, the Loudoun Freedom Center, Loudoun Diversity Council, Excellent Options, and other organizations whose continued advocacy has led to this apology and an intentional focus on racial equity in LCPS."[64]

Unmoved, Thomas called the apology "self-serving."[65]

Williams was met with only acrimony and more demands, despite having done virtually everything the equity advocates had asked. In the process, he attracted significant ire from other parents, who charged that he was neglecting the schools' basic duty to educate in favor of never-ending racial ideology.[66]

Finally, in late 2020, besieged from all sides, Williams abruptly moved across the country for a job at a school district in Texas that is half the size and came with no pay increase. A big longevity bonus from Loudoun, soon due if he had stuck around, was not enough to keep him there.[67] He had forgotten a central tenet of critical race theory: interest convergence, the belief that when a white "ally" like Williams does everything a CRT practitioner could be expected to, he must be doing so only out of self-interest, thereby demonstrating his continued racism.

In the end, critical race theory exists simply to "disrupt" systems. In Loudoun County, it certainly did.

7

RACE TO THE BOTTOM

Educrats wanted to eliminate anything that could function as an objective assessment of the scholastic competence of American children—and, therefore, their own job performance. Fringe racial activist consultants offered them a convenient political tool. Superintendents began paying big bucks to racial equity "consultants" to make the argument that basic performance standards and units of measurement were inherently racist. What these entrepreneurial consultants talked about was not diversity, nor how to help minority students excel. It was nihilism: that nothing was real and nothing mattered.

Under the standard preached by these consultants, any "system" that highlights racially unequal results is inherently "systemically racist." This included grades, rules, test scores, and any other way of objectively assessing accomplishment. Therefore, every indicator of the massive failures of America's public schools was illegitimate. This was like a doctor claiming he cured your fever by breaking the thermometer.

New York City paid race consultant Glenn Singleton nearly $900,000 and instructed teachers in 2019 that "perfectionism," "worship of the written word," "individualism," and "objectivity" were aspects of "white supremacy culture." The idea that *reading* was white supremacist, and therefore undesirable, undercut one of the most basic missions of teachers. But for educrats, it was convenient, since in some minority-heavy schools in the city, only 5 percent of kids were proficient in reading during certain school years.[1]

Beginning with a handful of consultants like Singleton, these theories spread upstream into how teachers are trained. Such ideas were adopted by virtually every professional association in the education sector. These groups, and an army of "coalitions," "partnerships," and "networks" that purported to "bring people together" around equity, pushed them to their members. After Seattle began teaching that math is "used to oppress and marginalize people and communities of color," the president of the National Council of Teachers of Mathematics, Robert Q. Berry III, was excited to use his group's influence to bring the idea everywhere. "Seattle is definitely on the forefront with this," he said. "What they're doing follows the line of work we hope we can move forward."[2]

The Association for Supervision and Curriculum Development (ASCD) is an $80 million organization that sets standards and trains teachers. A publication on its website encouraged "antiracist grading." This, it explained, would allow a principal to report that everything was excellent in a school where 98 percent of students could not tell you that two plus two is four. "The term 'fall behind' is a social construct," it claimed. "There are multiple ways a kid can express their knowing. And so, if you know 2+2=4, one way you can express your knowing is by writing it." But another "way is by performing a play . . . There might be 100 kids in the school who know 2+2=4, but if only two of those kids can write it, then only two of those kids will receive As. That is profoundly discriminatory."[3]

Teachers accepted these pronouncements like commandments from on high. In San Diego, "students will no longer be docked in their academic grades for turning work in late or other factors related to work habits." This is "more equitable" because "Black students received D or F grades 20 percent of the time and Hispanic students received them 23 percent of the time, while White students received them 7 percent of the time and Asian students received them 6 percent of the time." The policy on cheating was similarly changed to reduce "disparities" without changing behavior.[4]

To the equity activists, the problem with grades is that they are based on equality: students' grades tended to correlate tightly with the amount of effort they put in. This was not *equity*. According to the American Time Use Survey, on average, Asian students spend about two hours a night on homework, while whites spend just under one hour, and Hispanics slightly less. Blacks spend an average of nearly half an hour. (The liberal Brookings Institution, which crunched the numbers, wondered if this could be because impoverished students had to spend time working or taking care of relatives, but found that time that did not go to homework went to leisure.)[5]

Was it bad that Asians got higher grades when they spent two to four times as long on their homework compared to other racial groups? Only if you do not believe that success comes from hard work. So that, too, was on the chopping block.

Grit is the education world's lingo for hard work and determination. By 2015, many teachers were against it. Capturing the view that year at EduCon, a "progressive education-technology conference," *Education Week* wrote, "Is 'Grit' Racist?" Pamela Moran, the superintendent of rural Albemarle County, Virginia, said, "We have to think about our own cultural biases, why grit appeals to us, and why we want to focus on it in our schools." Instead, students need "slack."[6] This was a popular view. "Could Grit Thinking Drive Inequality?" *Inside Higher Ed* asked in 2016.[7]

It was almost enough to make one forget that the "system" in question was teachers encouraging students to do their homework—or at least accepting that not doing so might mean a lower grade. But school districts paid consultants to reinforce the point. For-profit consultant Crescendo Education Group suggested that even grading based on effort, let alone assignment completeness or correctness, was racist. "The problem is that homework completion is more often a reflection of a student's income, language and family, and this grading approach places underprivileged students at a huge disadvantage," it said. The group was open in sharing the purpose of this policy: "Fewer students fail classes and fewer students receive A's, because students are no longer rewarded or penalized for compliance or perceived 'effort.'"[8]

Not even charter schools were safe. The KIPP chain of charter schools serves more than one hundred thousand students (it stands for Knowledge Is Power Program) and is known for doing for poor black kids what traditional public schools did not: helping them succeed. KIPP had a no-nonsense atmosphere, and it showed. In New York City, 74 percent of KIPP students in grades three to eight scored "at or above proficiency" on state math exams in 2019, compared to 46 percent citywide. This apparently did not please the racial activists who purported to be motivated by concern about the "achievement gap." In July 2020, KIPP retired "Work hard. Be nice" as its national slogan, explaining that it "places value on being compliant and submissive [and] supports the illusion of meritocracy."[9] It was official: broad swaths of the entire educational establishment had come out against hard work and being nice, the antithesis of equity and pessimism-fueled activism.

The same went for expecting students to be attentive and curious. The Sarasota, Florida, school district awarded a $115,000 contract to equity consultant Sharroky Hollie to give teachers seven presentations about race relations. In an August 2020 livestream, Hollie told teachers to "consider whether students' behavior is cultural," which he said would include students shouting "This is boring!" in the middle of a lesson. If a student did this, the teacher should "thank" the student for the "honesty" of this cultural behavior, instead of "chastising" him. (The superintendent pulled the contract after embarrassing media coverage.)[10]

This parallels what Singleton has been telling teachers for more than twenty years. He has long instructed that black culture differs from white culture in that whites believe in "self-reliance," "hard work," and being "polite." Whites place an "emphasis on [the] scientific method" and "objective, rational, linear thinking." They believe in "plan[ning] for [the] future" and the "nuclear family."[11] Schools that assign tasks that promote or rely on these traits are therefore being culturally insensitive to blacks.

In other words, he peddles the most demeaning and vile anti-black stereotypes. This is so obvious that after Singleton tells white school officials how to be "anti-racist," they cannot do it without being accused of racism by other blacks. California hired Singleton to try to address the high rates of suspensions of black students, and its white state superintendent, Jack O'Connell, repeated an idea from Singleton that it was simply part of black culture to "speak loudly and be a bit raucous," saying that the children learned it in church. The comment caused a "mini-tempest" of criticism against O'Connell in 2007, and an NAACP official demanded "a statement of clarification or an apology" from the superintendent for the "big put-down."[12]

But as often as school districts got burned, there was always another in line. The Illinois Mathematics and Science Academy (IMSA), ranked the top public high school in Illinois, began teaching in early 2020 that "like Whiteness, Math operates as an unearned privilege. . . . Who gets credit for doing and developing mathematics, who is capable in mathematics and who is seen as part of the mathematical community is generally viewed as white."[13]

"Math was never neutral," IMSA said, and suggested replacing the entire field with "Mathematx," which would take "into account Indigenous Knowledge." Mathematx, it continued, "acknowledges that all persons will seek, acknowledge, and create patterns differently in order to solve problems and experience joy. Multiple knowledges are valued and sought. Mathematx allows for a variety of expressions without suggesting one is 'normal,' superior, or the reference point for erasing other epistemologies."[14]

IMSA's strategy for racial harmony involved having students say the "N" word in order to fulfill one of Singleton's "Four Agreements of Courageous Conversations," the need to "experience discomfort." A lesson plan says: "Using the 'N' word in a discussion will make some of the group uncomfortable and it may be controversial. Because of this, you should say the 'N' word and participants should say the 'N' word." It has them watch a video in which a diversity consultant seems to convince black students that their classmates might be thinking it at any time. "Just because you don't say N***er (say the 'N' word), doesn't mean you don't believe N***er (say the 'N' word)," it says.[15]

IMSA also drew from Dr. Muhammad Khalifa, an equity consultant who travels the country telling suburban superintendents that eradicating "Christian Privilege" requires rethinking the "purpose of education, and even sources of and what counts as knowledge."[16] His 2018 book, *Culturally Responsive School Leadership*, widely studied by school administrators, states that "the CIA facilitated the entrance and distribution of massive amounts of crack cocaine and heroin into Black and Latinx communities to quell the rage and protest exemplified by oppressed Blacks." The footnote providing the evidence for that wild assertion says it is "accepted as truth in many US Black communities."[17] In other words, it's false—but that depends on "what counts as knowledge."

Citing Khalifa, IMSA explained that critical race theory "attempts to understand American education and reform, acknowledging the unique perspective and voice of people of color as victims of oppression in racial matters and valuing their story telling [*sic*] as a legitimate way to convey knowledge."[18] That is, racial minorities intrinsically have "different" ways of doing things like math, which cannot be viewed as worse than regular math even if they never arrive at the correct answer. Their "lived experience," or "storytelling," supersedes the scientific method.

Of course, none of this nonsense can withstand the barest scrutiny. The numerals used in math are famously Arabic. "Indigenous people" did not discover the theorems that make modern life possible, and there was no evidence that Native American children were demanding to hear about "indigenous knowledge" from public school teachers in a math class. Almost every finalist in a 2020 American student math competition was of Asian descent.[19] None of that mattered. It served a function to educrats: it said that they were not actually failing minority children—they had simply forgotten to take into account their subjective "ways of knowing." It turned out that the educators (and illiterate children) were doing great after all. This was the foundation of the educator/critical-race-theory alliance. After decades of trying—and failing—to improve minority academic achievement, by the late 2000s, America's schools settled on a shocking new strategy: giving up on them.

It was not only young minorities who would suffer. It was everyone. Mathematicians engineer the bridges that we drive across. They calculate the distance at which a train must begin slowing down. They program computers that keep nuclear reactors humming. These are not the wild assertions of a few crackpots to be laughed at: they pose an imminent threat to modern medicine, national security, technological advances, and to civilization itself.

CRSE

These ideas, plainly at odds with what most people of every race believe, nevertheless spread largely unnoticed by parents for several reasons.

One is that no one believes that entire government bodies would be crazy enough to adopt them. If parents hear about these ideas at all, they presume that they must be hearing exaggerations, statements taken out of context, or the cherry-picked ideas of a few zealots, or assume that they are limited to inner-city schools. This is a fatal mistake. It is *everywhere* in the world of children's education, and has been for years.

Another reason is the education industry's use of acronyms and euphemisms to dress up simple or poorly thought out concepts in impressive-sounding language. Finding the truth can only be accomplished by plunging through a world of jargon that most parents will be either bored with or overwhelmed by.

In 2019, the New York City Department of Education decreed that every child in the state would receive "culturally responsive-sustaining education," known as CRSE. Officials told the media that CRSE simply meant "high expectations for all" and avoiding the use of sailing examples for city children in tests. A few of the most engaged parents might get a little further: the New York State Education Department produced a sixty-four-page paper explaining that CRSE would empower students "as agents of positive social change." Policy makers would "use differentiated approaches to instruction based on need and culture." Leaders should support "multiple forms of assessment that consider personalized student needs." It offered only a few concrete examples, such as instructing leaders to "post high-quality work in the physical environment that is not limited to the display of correct answers."[20]

If you actually wanted to know what the policy *was*, the only paragraph that mattered was buried on page thirteen: "The State Education Department worked closely with various academic experts, renowned in their respective fields, to draft a NYSED definition of culturally responsive-sustaining education. New York University Metropolitan Center for Research on Equity and the Transformation of Schools (Metro Center) used these conversations to draft a robust guidance document from which this framework was created."

Few parents would follow the trail of footnotes to that "robust guidance" where the New York University (NYU) experts—David E. Kirkland, Pamela D'Andrea Montalbano, and Evan M. Johnston—spelled out what New York's new state policy meant. While media reports suggested that CRSE meant teachers could, for example, use rap songs to help inner-city kids learn science,[21] the architects of the state policy specifically deemed this "racist" because such teachers would be trying to fix the "achievement gap" by having black children learn academic content. "Their inclusion of hip-hop does not sustain their students' cultures, it uses a surface-level part of culture to further a white-centric paradigm of education," they explained. A central tenet of CRSE is that there *is* no achievement gap: teachers are just measuring the wrong things by asking minorities to demonstrate competencies like the ability to add. Anytime schools teach minority children skills required of productive members of society, they "serve to indoctrinate minorities into the dominant culture so they can further serve the reproduction of their current roles in society through entering the workforce," the document underlying New York State's official education policy says.[22]

Lest this language be too clear, the academics provide two examples, with "Teacher A" and "Teacher B." In Teacher A's classroom, the academics reiterate that though students would "likely enjoy their hop-hop math lesson," and it could help them "succeed,"[23] it should not be done because it would "facilitate their assimilation by dominant systems and ideologies which centered Anglo-European-Christian-Judeo-cis-hetero-male whiteness as the normative reference point to which all other cultures and categories were expected to conform."[24]

According to CRSE, the correct approach is the one promoted by Teacher B. Under this scenario, students spend their classroom time rapping for its own sake. "Because hip-hop in this classroom is not tokenized, but treated as a vehicle for and the object of learning, we can walk into the classroom (which is no longer [the teacher's], but the classroom of the cultures of their students) on any given day and see hip-hop culture authentically represented," the architects of the official policy of America's fourth-largest state wrote.[25] CRSE scholarship calls schools a "site of trauma" whose remedy is "not to trust in the sites of oppression but rather in the very bodies that have been historically robbed of their rightful voice."[26] In other words, put the kids in charge. To most people, black kids are like any other kids: happily enjoying popular music and other hobbies in their free time. Academics like Johnston (who is not black), on the other hand, appear to see them as exotic specimens practicing an ancient tradition—a popular forty-year-old music genre—that faces extinction if the entire apparatus of public education is not replaced by it.

Critical race theory offers bottomless criticism, not coherent solutions. So, equity activists routinely simultaneously excoriate schools for opposite reasons. If officials granted all the demands of one equity campaign, they would still be called racist by another. CRSE's position that the achievement gap does not exist negated the vast majority of other equity strategies, which were justified by the gravity of the gap. Equity advocates also accused New York schools of being "segregated" and demanded "integration," even as CRSE opposes moving students to create racially balanced schools. Spending school days rapping in order to "sustain" a student's culture is only possible if all the students are of the same race. "How does the culturally responsive teacher respond to multiple cultures in a room without essentializing or privileging any of them? This is delicate work that, perhaps, gets ahead of where the current terrain of theory and research is," the NYU experts shrug.[27]

This sort of mealy-mouthed academic-speak is used by professional activists and consultants to exclude parents and students. But parents' confusion is not because they lack sophistication, but because these policies are incoherent. Even the foremost scholar of culturally responsive education (CRE) admits that he has no idea why schools should do it. "Is CRE the end goal of policy, or a means to some other end or ends? If the latter, what is its purpose?" Kirkland's document concludes: "Have we answered these essential questions of policy and practice? The truth is that it appears the goals of CRE are still being decided."[28]

TEACHER CREDENTIALS

Teachers' unions have used the same rhetoric, attacking standards and other evaluation methods as being racist in order to remove already-minimal qualifications for their jobs. Most states use a suite of tests called Praxis to credential their teachers. Praxis Core (previously known, in a slightly different incarnation, as Praxis I) measures whether teachers can pass grade school themselves. "All of the content and skills in the three Praxis I tests . . . cover skills that do not exceed a high school level," the test's creator explained. Another Praxis exam tests their knowledge in the subject they intend to teach. For example, to teach elementary school English, teachers must pass a multiple-choice quiz similar to ones they would give fifth graders. A typical question on that test asks whether "fair and fare" are homophones, antonyms, or homophobes.[29]

The percentage of black would-be teachers who passed this elementary school–level English test was thirty-five points lower than the percentage of whites, according to a 2011 study cowritten by the NEA. On average, 62 percent of would-be black teachers—many of them recently educated in public schools implementing the policies you have read about—fail these basic tests, according to a 2019 study. The NEA used these disparities to make demands that exhibited its own difficulty with English: "Praxis and other licensure tests can create barriers to entering the profession. This is particularly true for candidates of color. It has been largely documented that standardized test [*sic*] are culturally biased," its website says.[30]

The actual 2011 study, in fact, showed no such evidence of bias. Instead, it found that the Praxis standardized test results mirror other measurements. Pass rates were well predicted by undergraduate grade point averages (GPAs), and black test takers tended to have lower GPAs. Nonetheless, as of 2017, twelve states had adopted a more subjective evaluation method, called edTPA, in which candidates submit portfolios and videos of themselves teaching. In New York State, black prospective teachers failed the edTPA at nearly twice the rate of whites and Hispanics.[31]

Whatever the scores on Praxis tests or the edTPA, the vast majority of states already had loopholes that allowed teachers to be certified even if they failed. Minority teachers used this option twice as often as whites. Despite this, in 2019, Washington State eliminated its "cut-off score requirement for the entry exam to teaching colleges" entirely. In 2020, California's state assembly voted to stop requiring teachers to pass the California Basic Educational Skills Test, which measures whether teachers can read at an eighth-grade level. In 2017, New York State scrapped its requirement that teachers must pass a literacy test "because just 46 percent of Hispanic test takers and 41 percent of black test takers passed it on the first try, compared with 64 percent of white candidates." It did so even though a couple of years earlier a judge had ruled that the test was not discriminatory.[32]

Prioritizing the economic interests of a few adults over the needs of thousands of students had dire consequences. In California, 68 percent of fourth graders were not proficient in reading in 2019. In twenty-one New York City schools, only 10 percent or fewer of fifth graders, even excluding immigrants who were still learning English, passed English language arts exams in 2019. Being taught to read by teachers who themselves cannot read is unlikely to correct this devastating statistic. Educators who push for lowering standards to increase the number of minority teachers claim that research shows that having a teacher of the same race improves educational outcomes. Besides amounting to arguing for segregated classrooms, here, educators' ineptitude at math is apparent. A large study often cited as showing a correlation between having a teacher of the same race and better test scores, based on a long-term analysis of black and white students in Florida, found that the improvement was 0.004 to 0.005 standard deviations for reading. Statistically, that means the effect is virtually meaningless.[33]

As with students, the real issue with teachers was not racial gaps but poor performance all around. College students intending to major in education have SAT scores that are among the lowest of any group. Their average score of 1021 is lower than the score for gender studies students, better only than those studying topics like "parks, recreation and leisure studies" and "personal and culinary services," according to the College Board. These same students go on to receive higher college GPAs than any other major, according to a 2011 university study. In some cases, the study argues, A's are awarded so freely in teachers' colleges that students have little incentive to exert effort and it is impossible to tell a good prospective teacher from one who is not cut out for the job. This carries over into principals who routinely give the majority of teachers positive ratings.[34] And it likely informs their expectations for children, too.

Education colleges are so bad at their only function—producing good teachers—that the NEA's 2011 study showed that majoring in education in college correlated statistically with doing *worse* on teaching exams. On average, undergraduate education majors scored consistently worse on Praxis I exams than those who majored in anything else.[35]

If education programs are not providing practical training, what are they doing? The American Educational Research Association (AERA) is the leading group of education college professors and other academics, with more than twenty-five thousand members in the United States and overseas.[36] At its 2019 conference, "Social Justice" was the third-most frequent topic discussed, with 265 mentions. "Equity" appeared 211 times, "Race" 186 times, "Critical Race Theory" 131 times, and "Critical Theory" 122 times, according to AERA's index. "Student Behavior/Attitude," on the other hand, was discussed 64 times, "Accountability" only 58, and "Reading" just 57 times.[37]

8

FUNDING

Thirteen of Baltimore's thirty-nine high schools did not have a single student who was proficient in math in 2017, according to state test scores. In six other high schools, only 1 percent of students tested proficient. All in all, this accounted for nearly half of the city's high schools, where only 14 out of more than 3,800 students were math proficient.[1]

In 2020, then senator Kamala Harris (D-CA) had an explanation for fiascos like this: "Over the last many decades, we have essentially been defunding public schools," she said. As a presidential candidate the year before, Harris stated, "It is completely upside down that we currently have a system where the funding of a school district is based on the tax base of that community. It's just basic math. The community that has the lowest tax base is going to receive the fewest resources, and by the way probably [has] the highest need."[2]

Another presidential candidate, Senator Elizabeth Warren (D-MA), claimed, "Funding for public K–12 education is both inadequate and inequitable," resulting in "many students from low-income back-grounds receiving less funding than other students on a per-student basis."[3]

And a third presidential candidate, Senator Bernie Sanders (I-VT), demanded "equitable funding for public schools," alleging that "over the past decade, states all over America have made savage cuts to education."[4]

This is a lie. But it was repeated until it was accepted as true: that America's schools are "underfunded"; that funding has declined; and that inner-city schools are particularly underfunded, leading to their students' poor performance. Every element of this is false, but politicians and educators push it to line their pockets and excuse their failures.

In fiscal year 2018, Baltimore schools received $19,063 per K–12 student, or nearly enough to pay for room, board, and student services fees at Harvard University. For a family with two children, the cost to educate them in Baltimore exceeds the city's 2019 per capita income.[5]

Although it is one of the poorest cities in America, Baltimore's per-student expense exceeded all but five of the largest one hundred school districts. In 2018, a Baltimore public school system spokesman conceded that when measured against all of the nation's thirteen thousand school districts, including small, wealthy towns, Baltimore outspent four out of five of them. This is typical. According to a nationwide study, school districts grappling with poverty have historically spent *more* money per student compared to districts with wealthier students, not less.[6]

And *within* school districts across the United States, the liberal Brookings Institution found in 2017 that, on average, poor and minority students enjoy the benefit of having more money spent on their education than their neighbors who are white and not poor. Since 1965, a federal program called Title I has given extra funding to schools with a large number of low-income students. And contrary to the notion that school funding corresponds to local property taxes, since the 1970s states have chipped in as much as local governments, and state funding usually gives more to poor districts.[7]

If there is a racial implication behind this, it does not demonstrate discrimination against minorities. A 2008 study published by the Urban Institute found that from 1982 to 2002, "spending per pupil for nonwhite students was slightly higher than for white students in most states and in the United States as a whole."[8]

Even more extra money is spent on immigrants, who are largely Hispanic. In Montgomery County, Maryland, taxpayers spent nearly $22,000 per year to educate students who were not proficient in English in 2015, compared to $14,000 for all other students. In Alexandria, Virginia, almost half of the schools' budget went to teaching non-English-speaking students, who constituted 29.5 percent of total enrollment. Such high percentages of children who still cannot speak English suggest that teachers either have little to show for this money or are in no rush to turn the kids into fluent English speakers and lose the justification for higher budgets. According to cognitive scientists, childhood is a "critical period" in which children can rapidly absorb languages like a sponge. During the 2014–15 school year, Alexandria's schools were 33 percent Hispanic.[9] Was it really possible that nearly all of those had arrived in this country so recently that they had not had time to pick up English?

No student in America can claim to have less money spent on his education compared to decades past. Spending has risen dramatically. Using inflation-adjusted dollars and excluding administrative and pension-related costs, K–12 public education spending per child has nearly doubled since 1980 and almost quadrupled since 1960. In 1950, America spent the modern equivalent of $2,784 per child on education; in 2017, it was $15,424. Yet history is not littered with tales of one-room schoolhouses where zero students could do math.[10]

At the 2017 average spending level, a class of twenty would be funded at $308,480. The average teacher in the United States made nearly $62,000 during the 2018–19 school year. Where did the rest of the money go? Between 1950 and 2015, the number of students in American public schools rose by 100 percent, while the number of teachers rose by 243 percent. Yet, the largest growth occurred in schools' administrative bureaucracy, such as the people who process statistics and come up with equity programs: administrators and other nonteaching staff grew by 709 percent.[11]

If Baltimore's schools were abysmal despite receiving $19,000 per student, was a lack of money really the problem? In late 2019,

Maryland legislators' answer was to propose spending an extra $4 billion on schools over ten years with the hope of improving the performance of places like Baltimore. Teachers and politicians mobilized children to agitate for the proposal, known as the Kirwan Commission's plan, which would require massive tax increases. "I believe it is the duty of adults to lead in a way that young people can actually focus on learning," said Baltimore city schools CEO Sonja Santelises. A city councilman said, "Our children don't just deserve Kirwan, but demand Kirwan." One teacher, a former NFL player, stood alongside his students and told WJZ, Baltimore's CBS affiliate, that the city's schools were "underfunded."[12]

Now Baltimore's youth were not just uneducated, but angry, too.

How would extra money increase Baltimore youth's focus on academics? By giving raises to teachers. "They need funding in the schools. I see teachers not having proper salaries," the former football player added. Such raises might only bolster the complaints of "inequity": virtually all teachers' earnings already exceed the median household income in Baltimore of $50,177. In 2018, most teachers in Baltimore made $75,000 or more, and some made as much as $187,000. That kind of money goes far in a city where the median owner-occupied house costs $179,100.[13]

Did anyone really believe that giving raises to teachers would make juvenile delinquents pay better attention in class? It seemed unlikely. But the two biggest Maryland State House lobbying campaigns for the six-month period ending on April 30, 2020, by far, were from a group set up to advocate for Kirwan and the state's main teachers union. These campaigns cost more than half a million dollars each, or three times what major lobbyists representing bankers and Realtors spent on each of their respective industries. The teachers union money, on the other hand, comes from taxpayers.[14]

If $19,000 per student was not enough, what was? Beginning in 1985, a federal judge named Russell Clark tried to find out what would happen if money was no obstacle. He ordered a massive spending program that infused billions of extra dollars over twelve years into the decaying city schools of Kansas City, Missouri. This made Kansas City the highest-spending large school district in the country, adjusted for cost of living. It outspent similar districts around the country by two or three times. Clark said that he "allowed the district planners to dream."[15]

The district constructed laboratories, a planetarium, and an Olympic swimming pool, and it provided kids with computers, foreign language programs, and field trips to Senegal and Mexico. It added all-day kindergarten and aftercare, and every elementary school classroom had $25,000 of toys in it. It had a teacher-student ratio of one to twelve or thirteen and gave teachers 40 percent raises. Clark anticipated that Kansas City students' achievement would match the national average within five years.

By 1995, the dropout rate had not decreased and test performance showed "no measurable improvement." Over four years of high school, the average black student's reading skills increased by only 1.1 grade equivalents. As Gary Orfield, head of the Harvard Project on School Desegregation, whose testimony helped spur the bonanza, later admitted, "They had as much money as any school district will ever get. It didn't do very much."

Most people would interpret the statements of politicians to mean that low-income students have less money spent on their education than their middle-class colleagues. This is because they do not understand the power of the word *equity* to distort reality. Only through such a word can people say that getting the most money for the worst results proves that they are oppressed.

"There's a big difference between equality and equity," Kamala Harris explained. "Equitable treatment means we all end up at the same place."[16] But in reality, equity means writing bigger and bigger checks to the bureaucrats who run inner-city schools, until equal outcomes by students are achieved—even though there is little evidence that money will ever cause that to happen.

Educrats are assisted by a small but influential industry of activist "social scientists" who create pseudo-academic papers that advance the fiction. Journalists and policy makers, apparently not considering that anyone could torture numbers to this extent, simply repeat them.

"School districts with large numbers of black and Hispanic students need more money to help students succeed but get less," the

Washington Post stated as fact in 2020. The article was the result of a study by the Century Foundation, an equity think tank frequently relied upon by school officials as the basis for policy changes.[17]

Incredibly, nowhere does the Century report on school funding ever say how much districts actually spend. It simply declares that, for example, the Wagon Mound Public Schools in New Mexico has a "funding gap" of $20,184 per pupil. This egregious omission is by necessity, because no informed person could agree with its argument. The truth is that Wagon Mound already spends an astonishing $35,182 per pupil. The Century Foundation's study called it a "gap" because it thought that the district should spend $55,366 per student—more than the 2019 median household income for New Mexico, an impossible sum for any society to sustain. This extra $20,000, the study implied, would put this small New Mexico school district on the path to equity.[18]

But even that would not be enough. Since equity is defined not by helping people but by forcibly making everyone the same, it was also necessary to bring others down. In the same state, Los Alamos Public Schools spent $10,804 per student, less than a third of Wagon Mound. Despite that, its students perform well—after all, Los Alamos's largest employer is the national laboratory that developed the atomic bomb. The residents of Los Alamos were already subsidizing Wagon Mound, and their children's performance was not achieved by spending highly on their own schools. Yet the study recommended that the children of atomic physicists should have their funding slashed to $8,000 per student, or roughly one-seventh the amount of money it thought Wagon Mound needed to compensate for having "minority and low-income children."[19]

That equity means forcing everyone to be the same by deliberately dragging down success stories rather than seeking to emulate them, without even having a proven plan to improve real performance of underachievers, is explicit in Century's methodology. It states the purpose of the exercise: adjusting funding to enable poor-performing school districts "to achieve national average outcomes on reading and math assessments." It does not take a PhD in educational research to see that this is not about helping poor children, but rather about creating metrics that help bureaucrats and politicians. Basic math says that it is essentially impossible for every poor-performing district to achieve the national average simply by doing better, because if poor-performing districts improve their results, that in itself would cause the national average to go up significantly—moving the goalpost and ensuring continued jealousy and more laments for funding. There is only one way to ensure that everyone is average: to force everyone to be merely average.[20]

Of course, no parent would willingly subject her child to a situation like that. That, perhaps, is why nothing threatens the educational establishment more than charter schools, which teachers unions like the Massachusetts Teachers Association claim "steal" money from public education.[21] If a child chooses to attend a public charter school instead of a traditional public school, the traditional school system gets less money. But this also reduces its costs, so it is unclear how there is any harm—unless the purpose of public schools is to simply grow the rolls of union member teachers and pay the salaries of administrators.

In some cases, teachers unions have gone to enormous lengths to ensure that parents could not redirect the money already being spent on their children's education to a voucher for a public, independently run charter school, never mind a private school[22]—even though private schools, on average, cost less than public ones.[23]

That viciousness should not be surprising, because what is at stake is enormous, and on the merits, educators' hold on that money would clearly be precarious. The money currently funneled to public schools that churn kids into lives of poverty is so generous that, if spent in virtually any other way than being fed into the educational bureaucracy, it could eliminate poverty in America overnight.

Washington, D.C., spent $29,906 per student during the 2017–18 school year.[24] In 2019, 23 percent of the city's eighth graders were proficient in reading.[25] For the typical single mother with four kids making $20,000 a year in southeast Washington, the government spends nearly $120,000 on educating her children each year. But she likely doesn't realize it, because she is certainly not getting her money's worth. If that amount were given to her outright, she could hire a PhD student to come to her house every day and provide personal, one-on-four instruction from morning until night, while still having enough money left over to take her from poverty to six figures.[26] Instead, the money goes to a D.C. school system that is likely to leave her children perpetuating the cycle of poverty.

Indeed, while public schools are filled with activists who constantly talk about "inequitable" outcomes in terms of race and income, such outcomes seem to happen more in their own schools than anywhere else. At Higher Ground Academy, a charter school in St. Paul, nearly the entire student body is composed of low-income Somali, Ethiopian, and Kenyan immigrant students. This was never what school founder Bill Wilson expected, but these families chose to send their children there, and he gladly accepted them. He set high standards, and Higher Ground's academic performance is on par with state averages. Nearly twice as many students there read at grade level as compared to black children in St. Paul's public schools.[27]

"Why can't people go to the schools they want to? Why take that choice away?" Wilson said. "There's an interest in closing down schools like this. We bust a myth," that poor and minority students cannot excel in school.

Worse, charter schools are a threat to something almost unfathomable: a captive market that receives the better part of a trillion dollars each year, despite performing so poorly that few would participate if they had a choice.[28]

No one who took the time to look at the actual expenditures could think that American schools were starved for cash. But ironically, their incompetence helps to sell their lie. What casual observer would guess that someone managed to spend $15,000 per student with so little to show for it?

9

BRAINWASHED

In the boys' bathroom of a Wake County, North Carolina, high school, a massive mural of child climate activist Greta Thunberg, who has autism and takes literally the assertion that the world will soon end unless carbon emissions are brought to zero, hangs on a wall and features her quote: "I don't want you to be hopeful. I want you to panic . . . and act as if the house was on fire."[1]

Wake County, surrounding the state capital, Raleigh, has the fourteenth-largest school system in the United States.[2] On a Saturday in February 2020, Wake teachers and equity activists huddled in a magnet school to do just that. They approached the problem that brought them together as if it were the end of the world: "whiteness," they said, was present in the suburban school district.[3]

"White" cultural values, teachers were told, included traits such as "efficiency," "perfection," and being "polite." Meeting minutes show that educators were concerned about this "white standard," and learned to use "applied critical race theory" to rid the school of whiteness.[4]

In favor of what? The educators received similar instruction about minorities through studying the "Five Pillars of Hip Hop Culture," which a provided "resource" taught them includes "graffiti" and "bboying," which it defined as "a style of street dance." Parents would resist the changes being called for, the minutes warned, but "you can't let parents deter you."

This was a confidently delivered call for dramatic action that would change education in one of America's largest school systems forever. Where did the facts and research underlying it come from? Conference organizers did not really know. Their notes appeared cobbled together from various presentations by consultants and online sources. A primary source was worksheets created by Debby Irving, a racial equity consultant who travels the country giving such insights, for a fee, at multiple schools and community venues per week.[5]

On the topic of "whiteness," the sixty-one-year-old white woman's credentials were sterling. After a childhood spent at country clubs, yacht clubs, and private school, Irving now lives in Cambridge, Massachusetts, in a neighborhood where 4 percent of the population is black.[6] She escapes the stress of Cambridge by retreating to her second home in Maine, where in the surrounding 194 square miles, there are only sixteen black people[7] and she can take her seventeen-foot boat out on the lake. But Irving had been trained as a racial expert by the People's Institute for Survival and Beyond and had absorbed the teachings of Glenn Singleton and Peggy McIntosh, whose 1988 essay on "white privilege" spawned an entire industry of people like her, most notably the education professor Robin DiAngelo.[8]

Wake's teachers unquestioningly accepted her expertise. They decided that they must function as "change agents" and "knowingly make people uncomfortable" by having "courageous conversations." They should walk a "fine line between expressing feelings and overstepping boundaries that may jeopardize employment." They would have to circumvent parents, principals, and, most especially, the "resisters," their term for teachers who expressed doubts about all this.[9]

The Wake teachers' strategy was simple: repetition and militancy that would make it impossible for anyone who did not accept these ideas to work in taxpayer-funded schools. "Lean into the discomfort. Resistant teachers will eventually fall off," they said. Administrators, who could not be dislodged so easily, would have to undergo "cognitive coaching."[10] The best way to make the schools comfortable for the political activists working in America's most common government job, they determined, was through the hiring process. "What questions are we asking WHITE TEACHERS in interviews?! Make sure they are anti-racist & culuturally [sic] responsive" teachers, the minutes said.

They also discussed why "real history"—such as a version holding that African Americans are "decended [sic] from kings and queens"—was not being taught. The reason, they concluded, was "fear" of "parent backlash." "What do we do with parent push back? White parent's [sic] children are benefiting from the system," meeting minutes said. The solution was to be "afraid of nothing" and to coordinate with like-minded "networks," just as they were doing that day.[11] They were quite clear about what networks they meant. It was the same handful of groups that have implanted identical ideas in many, if not most, of the nation's thirteen thousand school districts:[12] the Southern Poverty Law Center's (SPLC) Learning for Justice (formerly Teaching Tolerance); Glenn Singleton's Courageous Conversation; a group pushing the *New York Times'* 1619 Project revisionist history; one tied to the late anti-American historian Howard Zinn; and the teachers unions.

LEARNING FOR JUSTICE

More than any other network group, SPLC is why schools across the country have become intent on teaching children that they are victims.

SPLC otherwise has no background in education; it is an unapologetic activist group with a reputation for tagging as "racist" anyone or any group that disagrees with it.[13] But it discovered that teachers could not resist the lure of free, prepackaged lesson plans that did their work for them. SPLC began producing these lessons in huge quantities for a program it calls "Learning for Justice." Its "Teaching Tolerance Magazine" is sent, for free, to more than four hundred thousand teachers and reaches nearly every school in the United States.[14]

Few organizations could match this scale. But money is no problem for SPLC. Founded in 1971 by mail-order salesman Morris Dees, it has for decades raised money by soliciting everyday people who want to help weed out "hate groups" like the Ku Klux Klan.[15] The good news was that virtually everyone in America agreed with this premise, which caused money to roll in. The bad news, from a business standpoint, was that most such racist groups have almost completely vanished. Nevertheless, SPLC kept the gravy train rolling by calling an increasingly broad list of things hate-related. According to its 2018 tax forms and financial statements, SPLC has kept huge portions of this money, stashing away more than half a billion dollars, over 20 percent of which is cached in offshore tax havens like the Cayman Islands.[16] Not only can it afford to provide free lessons to teachers, it even began awarding teachers grants of up to $5,000 to "support [K–12] educators who embrace and embed anti-bias principles throughout their schools."[17]

Perhaps its most important boost came in 2010, when the first of forty-one states, the District of Columbia, and U.S. territories began signing on to an Obama initiative known as Common Core.[18] Some feared that having Washington bureaucrats implement a single national educational standard was part of a federal takeover of children's minds. The reality was not so simple. Teachers had to figure out how to comply with a slew of specific new directives, most of which were apolitical. But they were confused and did not seem to want to put in the work. Enter the SPLC. Common Core was like a catalog listing what everyone needed to buy. All that Dees's group had to do was to provide it.

SPLC packaged and marketed the Learning for Justice program as fulfilling items on the Common Core checklist. It was able to do this so quickly in part because it simply shoehorned in ideological tracts. Purportedly giving teachers a way to fulfill "CCSS.ELA-LITERACY. RF.3.4," the Common Core directive to teach third graders to "read with sufficient accuracy and fluency to support comprehension," Learning for Justice asks the question, "How convenient is Capitalism [sic] for me?" and then has the children watch a video on "poverty and homelessness" and review two graphics from the left-wing magazine *Mother Jones* described as depicting "income inequality in the United States." Another lesson, which Learning for Justice says fulfills a Common Core requirement for citing "specific textual evidence to support analysis of primary and secondary sources," tells students "the belief that a person in the United States who works hard, assumes personal responsibility and maintains a strong moral center can accomplish anything" is a "myth."[19]

Its lesson plans seek to mold children into people who think of themselves primarily as members of a particular race. They lecture kindergartners about slavery and tell them that "the responsibility for eliminating institutional racism lies with those of us who control the institutions. That is white people." Behind the Common Core standards, it developed its own Social Justice Standards. "Students will develop positive social identities based on their membership in multiple groups in society," one says. Its version of civics amounts to training students to become activists. "Students will plan and carry out collective action against bias and injustice in the world and will evaluate what strategies are most effective," says another. The NEA endorsed these standards in late 2015, and they became widespread in K–12, absorbed even by the Indiana Department of Education in mid-2020. This largely happened without parents knowing. In Portland, Oregon, parents can view a website that provides an overview of what their fourth-grade children are learning and how students are evaluated, based on Common Core standards. But a version of the same site visible only to teachers overlays Learning for Justice's Social Justice Standards.[20]

Some "lessons" are no more than commands for which position young children should take in contemporary political debates, such as instructing that "a wall along the border with Mexico would not 'stop' undocumented immigrants from coming to the United States."[21] Learning for Justice tells teachers to put signs in classrooms reading "Migration Is Beautiful." It reduces complex policy debates to matters of fact to be imparted onto the impressionable, having teachers instruct students that it is a "myth" that illegal immigrants do not pay taxes, because "immigrants who are undocumented pay taxes every time they buy taxable goods." Children do not know the difference between income tax and sales tax, so this is not an attempt at fostering debate. But if students do attempt to poke holes in Learning for Justice's claims, teachers are instructed to find out if that's because "that's what my parents say," and to respond: "That sounds like it might be an opinion, not a fact."[22]

SPLC content is injected into schools on the premise that it is addressing race relations. But a large portion of Learning for Justice's lessons has nothing to do with race, discrimination, or tolerance at all. It simply pushes a political ideology so far left that it would not be supported by most Democrat-leaning parents. Learning for Justice says that its standards are based on the work of Louise Derman-Sparks, a former member of the Socialist Community School Committee. Race is, in fact, secondary to this ideology. In 2014, SPLC condemned Ben Carson, a black brain surgeon who is conservative, as an "extremist." On the other hand, Learning for Justice heaped praise on Bill Ayers in 1998. Ayers, the white founder and former leader of the Weather Underground terrorist group, was then a college professor and was described as a "highly respected figure" who believes that "reforming inner-city schools is as much about fighting for social justice as about improving the quality of teaching and learning."[23]

BURROWING

The ubiquity of ideological indoctrination in public schools is remarkable because if one political faction were allowed to use the vast resources of government—in this case, access to impressionable children in compulsory schools—to propagate itself, that would amount to a virtually insurmountable tactic to retain power. It would be the stuff of third world dictatorships. U.S. laws guard against this sort of thing in other spheres: politicians must be careful to separate their campaign and office funds, and rank-and-file federal employees are averse to anything approaching political activity because it could violate a law known as the Hatch Act. Entities that receive grants or payments from the federal government may not use the money for lobbying.[24]

Yet in K–12 schools, a slew of organizations freely focus inordinate resources on crafting opinionated lesson plans and pushing them out across the country, and teachers on the government payroll promote them. One well-funded umbrella group alone, the Partnership for the Future of Learning, boasts "education and social justice field leaders from 300+ organizations," including the two major teachers unions, the SPLC, and a parent group of the Zinn Education Project.[25] The politicization of education should be objectionable to anyone who wants to secure the legitimacy of our education system, regardless of the particular slant. But making it even more remarkable, essentially all groups pushing ideology in schools to any meaningful extent are far left. And they are doing it in school districts that are located in left, right, and center areas, notably without apparent regard for the desires of local parents and the electorate.

Successful equity groups jump from spending money to influence government to embedding inside it, where they can steer taxpayer dollars to more of the same. In 2013, under pressure from the Obama administration because of racially disproportionate suspension rates, the Wake County schools created an Office of Equity Affairs. It hired former Learning for Justice official Lauryn Mascareñaz.[26]

In 2019, it paid Glenn Singleton to train teachers with his "Courageous Conversations," and Wake's "professional development" had teachers take a "deep dive into questions about whiteness." Tenth graders in an honors English class were given charts demanding that they document the races of their friends, doctor, neighbors, and classmates in a "diversity inventory." Though the equity office was created by the school board, it was open about its intent: to use its taxpayer-funded budget to lobby the government to implement more of its favored policies. This is not the role of a government agency. But it had a way around that: it directed teachers use an "action-oriented mindset"—in other words, teaching children to be lobbyists. Then it would "leverage student voices," trotting them out as sympathetic spokesmen to advocate for policies.[27]

One example of this puppet show played out in July 2020. James Ford is a member of North Carolina's state board of education, but he simultaneously works as an equity consultant. A foundation-funded equity group had paid him to write a "statewide study of equity in our schools." In May 2020, Ford had visited the class of a Wake County teacher, Matt Scialdone, who was named Wake's Teacher of the Year in 2015–16, to share materials from his activist group, Center for Racial Equity in Education (CREED). Scialdone then brought students to lobby the state board in July to add "hard truths" about America to its social studies standards. The speaking slot was approved by Ford. The students parroted the rhetoric of equity consultants back to Ford's colleagues. One former student, Abby Rogers, recognized Scialdone for making her "'better prepared' to be an advocate." She essentially had to accept whatever she was told about racial issues as fact, because "my privilege . . . comes from a place of basically never being able to understand the Black experience and what it means to be Black in America."[28]

The second hallmark of the juggernaut that might be called Equity Inc. is using multiple front groups, all linked to the same people, to hide their influence and cross legal boundaries. In expanding equity initiatives to ever more radical positions, Wake's equity office bureaucrats said they were simply responding to the demands of citizens. Among the most vocal groups making such demands was Equity4Wake, which bills itself as a "grassroots collective of passionate interrupters" that proudly refers to its volunteers as "disruptors."[29]

Although the Saturday meeting of teachers plotting to eradicate "whiteness" in February 2020 took place in a school facility, the event was officially a project of this private group, which rented space from the school.[30]

But there was nothing grassroots or citizen-led about Equity4Wake. It was formed by an Office of Equity Affairs staffer named Christina Spears. Each and every one of the people behind Equity4Wake was paid by the school system, while also running a professional activism campaign aimed at their own employer.[31]

Even more bizarrely, though the meeting had the tenor of a coup, it was anything but. The district's top officials, including its superintendent, were in attendance. In fact, Equity4Wake is so fully a creature of the school system that when reporter A. P. Dillon filed a Freedom of Information Act request with the school system for Equity4Wake documents, it apparently forgot the pretense that it was an outside activist group—which would not be subject to public records laws—and provided them.[32]

The groupthink mentality of teachers, and their penchant for taking advantage of opportunities to offload the work of creating lesson plans to others, has allowed a handful of activist groups to dominate the lesson plans that teachers draw from, turning even curriculum repositories with no obvious ideological bias into propaganda warehouses. In North Carolina, it is common for teachers to take lesson plans from a database of more than four hundred plans provided by the University of North Carolina at Chapel Hill that are certified to meet standards set by the state. But the people creating those lesson plans often appeared to simply take the free lessons from the activist groups and shoehorn them into the specific topics that North Carolina teachers are required to cover. UNC's contribution often appeared to be adding spelling and grammatical errors.[33]

For example, in North Carolina, a state where Republicans hold most congressional seats, state standards require schools to teach about terrorism, such as the September 11, 2001, attacks. UNC helps teachers meet this mandate—and perhaps subvert its intent—by drawing from Learning for Justice. A UNC-provided K–12 lesson plan instructs students to think of the Islamic State of Iraq and Syria (ISIS) as "pirates." It says, "the word 'jihad' means struggling or striving," and instructs students to come up with their own examples of jihad. Then it explains that "the main terrorist threat in the United States is not from violent Muslim extremists, but from right-wing extremists." As proof, it directs students to an article in the *Huffington Post*.[34]

It is not just civics lessons that have this monotone spin. A lesson that is supposed to be about the country of Tunisia involves providing a handout called "The Overblown Islamist Threat." Then it has the teacher say that Ronald Reagan once called the United States a "beacon of freedom" and instruct: "Can you think of times when the United States did not live up to the ideals expressed in this quote or when people were denied freedom? Students should answer 'yes.' Using the United States as an example, you can refer to slavery." While there may be religious extremists in countries like Tunisia, it adds, this is similar to how "there are some conservative Christians in the United States that would like to change our laws to conform to their religious views."

A lesson on the Holocaust says that "when many people study the Holocaust, they focus on the mass killings of Jewish people," but steers students to instead focus on non-Jews. It emphasizes that "African-Germans" and other groups "deemed undesirable by [Adolf] Hitler" were persecuted and/or killed and asks students "in what ways are themes that were present during the Holocaust still at play in our society today?" It directs students to Learning for Justice.[35]

A lesson on "The American Dream" emphasizes that "currently," some groups have "limited access to 'The American Dream.'" A UNC lesson's summary of the Constitution—"The U.S. Constitution endorsed slavery and favored the interests of the owning classes. What kind of Constitution would have resulted from founders who were more representative of the entire country—including enslaved people, workers, and farmers?"—comes directly from the Zinn Education Project.[36]

ZINN

Howard Zinn was the author of an opinionated 1980 history book called *A People's History of the United States*. Zinn readily admitted that his history book was deliberately biased and explained why he focused on influencing students: a political idea, he said, "coming from the apparent objectivity of the scholar, is accepted more easily than when it comes from politicians."[37]

Zinn received his PhD in American history from Columbia University, and, according to his FBI file, taught a class in Marxism at the Communist Party headquarters in Brooklyn. In 1956, he began teaching at Spelman College, a historically black women's college in Atlanta, figuring that "since our radicalism was expressed mostly in our views on race relations, well, that fitted in with the black community quite well." Spelman was a Christian college, but Zinn labored to change it from a school where students "talked properly, went to church every Sunday, poured tea elegantly and, in general, had all the attributes of the product of a fine finishing school" into a "school for protest." In 1963, he was fired and compared the black president to a "colonial administrator."[38]

Zinn scorned America's Founding Fathers as "rich white slave-holders, merchants, bondholders, fearful of lower-class rebellion, or, as James Madison put it, of 'an equal division of property.' Our military heroes—Andrew Jackson, Theodore Roosevelt—were racists, Indian-killers, war-lovers, imperialists. Our most liberal presidents—Jefferson, Lincoln, Wilson, Roosevelt, Kennedy—were more concerned with political power and national aggrandizement than with the rights of nonwhite people." His book drew young people to over-the-top conclusions with passages like "With the defeat of the Axis, were fascism's 'essential elements—militarism, racism, imperialism—now gone? Or were they absorbed into the already poisoned bones of the victors?'"[39]

Zinn died in 2010, but his ideas—originally written as a provocative counterpoint—are entrenched and even accepted as the default perspective in education today. The Zinn Education Project, an activist group that carries on his legacy by producing hundreds of teaching materials, says that more than one hundred thousand teachers have signed up. A company called Newsela, which produces content used in 90 percent of American schools, also draws from these materials. It is not just public schools that use its lesson plans, but private and parochial schools, too.[40]

All this, despite the fact that the material is overtly partisan. "Teaching more civics will not save us from Trump," the Zinn Education Project says, adding that "the white supremacist, nativist, misogynist language we have heard spill from the lips of Donald Trump resonates with the 39 percent who steadfastly support him precisely because it has deep roots in U.S. history and politics."[41]

Its teaching materials alternate between highlighting America's ills and promoting communism. Following the coronavirus pandemic, a Zinn lesson plan encouraged children to dole out sentences for mass murder. "This people's tribunal begins with the premise that a heinous crime is being committed as tens of millions of people's lives are in danger due to the outbreak of the novel coronavirus—COVID-19. But who—and/or what—was responsible for this crime? Who should be held accountable for the spread of the virus and its devastating impact? . . . list the names of all the 'defendants' on a slide: Mother Nature, Gen Z/millennials, the Healthcare Industry [*sic*], Racism [*sic*], the Chinese Government [*sic*], the U.S. Government [*sic*], and the Capitalist System [*sic*]," it says. Its author, Caneisha Mills, added, "I shared textbook and encyclopedia definitions of capitalism with [students] that we read prior to our departure, but I also reminded them of the real-life definition of capitalism that they saw in videos on the profits of Amazon, harm to workers in Amazon factories, and quotations from Michael Moore's film *Capitalism: A Love Story* and Matthew Desmond's 'American Capitalism Is Brutal,' a piece in the 1619 Project."[42]

The "tribunal" is not an exercise in seeing different perspectives or understanding the legal process. "I allowed my students to choose who or what they wanted to defend. Naturally, many students were reluctant to choose capitalism," Mills wrote. If the students conclude that communist China, rather than the United States, holds even partial responsibility for the virus that originated there, Mills would then correct them: "I plan to ask whether they still consider the Chinese government partially guilty, despite the evidence. Students, like adults, suffer from cognitive dissonance. They know the Chinese government built hospitals in days. They know the Chinese government alerted the World Health Organization of the pending global pandemic. But they refuse to not blame the Chinese government."

In the end, the students reached the verdict that Mills apparently hoped for: "In my students' minds, the U.S. government was the culprit, and they wanted time to discuss it and how to alter or abolish the government. . . . They wanted to put Donald Trump, Mike Pence, and all members of the federal government in jail," Mills wrote. One of the students' suggestions to prevent the coronavirus from happening again was to "[e]nd, or lower the amount of, capitalism so no secrets are present."

Mills teaches eighth-grade U.S. history at Washington, D.C.'s,

Hardy Middle School. In 2017, only 42 percent of the students at that school were "on track for the next grade level" in terms of literacy, and only 17 percent when it came to math. She was deliberately taking advantage of unsophisticated, impressionable thirteen-year-olds to convince them to try to overthrow a capitalist system that they had only heard about days earlier, because of a disease that came from a communist one. She did it by having them watch movies instead of learning to read. The AFT described Mills as a "hero."[43]

1619

It is a straight line from Howard Zinn to the most infamous example of politicization of the K–12 curriculum. *New York Times* reporter Nikole Hannah-Jones's "1619 Project" argues that every aspect of America is defined by racism. The true founding of America, she claims, was not in 1776, when the Declaration of Independence was signed, but in 1619, when the first African slaves were transported to the New World.

Hannah-Jones is a forty-five-year-old woman from Iowa with one white parent and one black parent. Her radicalism was first evident in 1995 at Notre Dame University, for whose school paper she wrote that "the white race is the biggest murderer, rapist, pillager, and thief of the modern world." Echoing Zinn, she wrote that "Columbus and those like him were no different then [*sic*] Hitler." She added: "Even today, the descendants of these savage people pump drugs and guns into the Balck [*sic*] community, pack Black people into the squalor of segregated urban ghettos, and continue ot [*sic*] be bloodsuckers in our communites [*sic*]."[44]

Hannah-Jones's *Times* series argued that America's Founding Fathers declared independence from Britain "in order to ensure slavery would continue." As leading historians wrote in 2019 to the *Times*, "If supportable, the allegation would be astounding—yet every statement offered by the project to validate it is false. . . . These errors . . . suggest a displacement of historical understanding by ideology." The *Times* said that historians had been consulted as part of prepublication fact-checking. But one of those wrote an article headlined "I Helped Fact-Check the 1619 Project. The *Times* Ignored Me." Partisanship of critics could not be blamed, with some of the earliest coming from the left-leaning World Socialist Web Site.[45]

But Hannah-Jones's aims went beyond facts. "When my editor asks me, like, what's your ultimate goal for the project, my ultimate goal is that there'll be a reparations bill passed," she explained. This is a compromise because "it feels more realistic than, like, can we get white Americans to stop being white?"[46]

There was one important group that did not particularly care that this version of our country's most basic history was written by someone with no historical training, who got a central premise wrong, and who admitted she was motivated by politics: the teachers of young children across America. Lessons based on the articles fast became part of the permanent curriculum in 3,500 K–12 classrooms across America, reaching "tens of thousands of students in all 50 states." By September 2019, just a month after it appeared as a piece of journalism in a magazine, the Chicago school system was incorporating it as history. A few months later, the Buffalo, New York, school system "infused" it into its core curriculum for nearly every grade level in middle and high school.[47]

The *New York Times* ultimately walked back the project's central claim that slavery was the "true founding" of America, erasing it from its own online materials. Hannah-Jones falsely claimed she had never said such a thing. She deleted most of her social media history, which included many such statements. Even then, school curricula continued to teach kids that very claim.[48]

The 1619 grade school curricula were the product of a nonprofit called the Pulitzer Center on Crisis Reporting, which paid teachers up to $5,000 each to create lesson plans based on the series, and pushed them out into school districts nationwide. This group is not affiliated with the Pulitzer journalism awards, but rather is a nonprofit helmed by executive director Jon Sawyer, who in addition to drawing a $219,000 salary, employs his wife, son-in-law, and nephew. With a 2018 annual income in excess of $14 million, the group has a dramatic effect on what children learn, shipping out copies of the *New York Times Magazine*, along with free lesson plans, to school districts.[49]

The group worked similarly to SPLC. Numerous lesson plans were provided, ready-made for teachers, allowing them to avoid having to do their own daily preparations. They were marketed as fulfilling particular requirements of Common Core. In these lessons, young children are asked to provide any "evidence" they see about how "some might argue that this nation was founded not as a democracy but as a slavocracy."[50] Many are not real lessons at all, designed to expand a child's knowledge, but instead are exhortations to become political activists. "How can you see the racial inequity described in the article you read in your own community? What do you think should be done to address this inequity?" asks one lesson plan. None of the plans provides children the option of disputing the premise that America was founded to prevent Britain from abolishing slavery there, the answer that would put them in line with essentially all serious historians.[51]

Instead, 1619 Project–based lesson plans included encouraging students to cross out parts of the Declaration of Independence to "reclaim and reshape the idea of America and its founding." A Chicago teacher and Learning for Justice advisor assigned this task and published her favorites in October 2020. One crossed out almost every word until America's founding document read simply: "We are the evils to the world." Another had students write a poem in which each letter of "America" stands for something. The teacher highlighted one that began, "A land of false freedoms / Mass genocide & slavery hold the world's support beams / Environment is dying, and the animals are crying / Racism stokes the fires of violence & oppression."[52] And so on.

BLM/NEA

Teachers unions have a direct line to school districts across the nation and use it to influence curricula. The NEA is a hard-core leftist organization whose website once recommended Saul Alinsky's "theories

& materials," including his book *Rules for Radicals*, specifically noting his admonitions that a radical will "fight conservatives" and that "[i]f you have a vast organization, parade it before the enemy, openly show your power." In 2021, its delegates voted to approve a resolution to join with the Zinn Education Project on more advocacy, to "oppose attempts to ban critical race theory and/or The 1619 Project," and to provide a study that "critiques . . . capitalism . . . and other forms of power and oppression." When parents noticed, it hid the vote from its website.[53]

NEA's activism arm, EdJustice, is closely tied to a curriculum called Black Lives Matter at School. Those behind the curriculum make four "demands," which they say will "insure [*sic*] safety and equity in our schools," including mandatory ethnic studies courses in grades K–12. In 2019, NEA delegates voted to support the "demands" and to "promote" them in schools. Local unions helped to spread the message across the country.[54]

The banner quote on Black Lives Matter at School's website comes from Assata Shakur, an escaped cop killer who was granted political asylum in communist Cuba, where she called Fidel Castro a "hero of the oppressed" and referred to herself as a "20th century escaped slave."[55] The quote says, "It is our duty to fight for our freedom."[56]

Black Lives Matter at School provides lesson plans for teachers. Much of the content has little to do with race relations, and more to do with socialism. One lesson plan has teachers ask students, "When the [Black] Panthers denounce 'robbery by the capitalist' and say that the government should 'give every man employment or a guaranteed income' or else give back the 'means of production' to the community, what political philosophy/system of government comes to mind?" It continues, "According to the Black Panthers, what conditions might justify violence?"[57]

The middle school lesson plan also instructs, "We are committed to disrupting the Western-prescribed nuclear family structure requirement."[58]

Teachers unions profess to be enormously concerned about the "achievement gap," but an analysis of test results from the international PISA exam, which asks detailed questions about test takers' backgrounds, showed that the presence of two parents is perhaps its biggest determinant. From 2000 to 2012, the percentage of students with intact families who passed their exams was 27 percent higher than those with only one parent, amounting to the difference of an entire year of learning.[59]

In September 2020, the adult Black Lives Matter movement deleted a statement opposing the nuclear family from its website following widespread ridicule. The version targeted to children, however, still includes it.[60]

10

CHILD ACTIVISTS

The caliber of America's young will determine, in the near future, not only the country's economic viability but also its civic and political reality.

Teachers should be deeply ashamed of, and all Americans gravely concerned by, their record when it comes to cultivating competent citizens. There are some fifty-six million students in U.S. elementary, middle, and high schools, most of whom will be of voting age within a decade. This is nearly as high as the total number of votes garnered by winning presidential candidates. Yet according to the 2019 National Assessment of Educational Progress (NAEP) exam, only 11 percent of twelfth graders in public schools were proficient in U.S. history, by far the worst result of any subject. The subject with the second-worst result was geography, where only 19 percent were proficient. The fourth-worst was civics, where only 23 percent were proficient. Many of those twelfth graders were old enough to vote that same year.[1]

Teachers were not ashamed. They decided that instead of *learning* civics, children would *do* civics—becoming advocates who lobbied governments on the same topics they had not managed to grasp academically. This would be easier to give top marks in: if students complied and became activists, they would pass. As is the education industry's wont, it dressed this up in fancy terminology: it was New Civics, Action Civics, Civic Engagement, or Project-Based Civics.[2]

The National Action Civics Collaborative, a foundation-funded group that is one of many that successfully pushed this transformation, wrote in 2010 that "Action Civics, an authentic, experiential approach in which students address problems through real-world experiences that apply to their lives, can be a powerful motivating experience setting them on a path towards lifelong civic and political engagement. In practice, Action Civics is an iterative process typically comprised of issue identification, research, constituency building, action, and reflection."[3]

Arne Duncan, who served as President Obama's secretary of education, added in 2012 that unlike your "grandmother's civics," action civics is "more ambitious and participatory." There was also another difference: the grandmother knew civics and the child did not. A 2018 survey found that only 19 percent of people under the age of forty-five could pass the citizenship test required of immigrants, and which immigrants overwhelmingly pass. The figure was 74 percent among those sixty-five or older.[4]

Wouldn't it be dangerous for authority figures to instruct a group with such an objectively abysmal record of understanding policy issues and America's founding ideals to become little lobbyists, like putting unlicensed drivers on the road? Perhaps, but youth's activism was also predictable. It would almost always be for leftist causes.[5] More specifically, it frequently mirrored the parochial interests of teachers unions.

In March 2021, Rhode Island legislators responded to parents' concerns about children being subjected to emotionally fraught content, seemingly to turn them into political weapons, by introducing a bill titled "prohibition of teaching divisive concepts." It defined the term as instructing that one race or sex is inherently superior, that an "individual's moral character is necessarily determined by their race or sex," that "an individual should feel discomfort, guilt, anguish, or any other form of psychological distress on account of their race or sex," or several similar transgressions. In all, the bill's text reads like a 1960s civil rights bill—simply reiterating that the government may not take a position that some races are inherently worse or better than others.[6]

Yet teachers apparently found this an impediment. And instead of getting the message that they were hired help, paid to perform a service for taxpaying parents, they used government resources—including their students—to try to shape their own jobs. One sent an email to her class: "I have just learned that H6070 is in committee in the RI House of Representatives." The bill "essentially states that there should be no discussion of race or gender in classrooms," she told the students. She offered extra credit to anyone who testified to the state legislature based on this false summary: "You will receive 5 points on your next unit test if you decide to testify and provide me with your written testimony." Another teacher sought to submit testimony against the bill and wrote that "I would like to be able to include student voices." Whose voices she was interested in depended on what they had to say. "Please feel free to share with me what you believe is the benefit of potentially 'divisive concepts' such as Race and Gender," she wrote.[7]

Across the country, in Oakland, California, teachers went on strike in 2019. Children were there at the picket line, practicing action civics. "Students, students, what do you see?" teachers called out. "I see my teachers standing up for me," children responded in singsong.[8] On the surface, these children were advocating against their own interest in getting back in school. Was this a decision based on some more nuanced economic analysis they had performed? Had they reviewed the collective bargaining agreement and found its provisions unfairly tilted in favor of management? Or were they simply being used, cynically exploited for financial gain?

Adult partisans hungrily see children as their ticket to passing policies that would otherwise be rejected as plainly self-interested, poorly thought out, or extreme. Children put a sympathetic face on the cause. Their emotions naturally run high. Their natural innocence is supposed to, in some people's telling, give them insight into complex policy questions that adults lacked.

Of course, this is nonsense: how many parents would allow their teenager to run their household budget or set the rules at home? Nevertheless, activists increasingly position them as the ultimate authorities on matters of major public policy. Their recipe is simple: tell children what to think; then when they respond accordingly, use them under the guise that they are simply "empowering" youth voices. When anyone points out problems with the proposals, the children are used as human shields, deemed off-limits to criticism because of their age.[9]

DAVID HOGG

Perhaps the best known of a new breed of teen activists is David Hogg, the outspoken survivor of the February 2018 Parkland school shooting. To Hogg, the gun issue was not one of competing interests, varied lifestyles in a geographically large country, and a constitutional dilemma. Rather, it was no different from "when your old-ass parent is like, 'I don't know how to send an iMessage.'" The problem was that adults "don't know how to use a fucking democracy."[10]

He, on the other hand, had it all figured out. Hogg claimed that the "gun violence prevention movement [was] started centuries ago" by "lgbtq [sic] women and non binary [sic] people that never got on the news or in most history books." When he stuck to safer forays, proclaiming, "Lincoln was a really good president," he managed to reverse his position within hours. "I was not aware of the scope of how detrimental he was so [sic] many native american [sic] populations. He was not a really good president," he corrected.[11]

Hogg's claim to fame was organizing the March for Our Lives, held in Washington, D.C., in March 2018. Though it was billed in the media as a massive student rally for gun control, a survey found that only 12 percent were there to support firearms restrictions. The others were there for a free concert from performers like Ariana Grande or to oppose President Trump.[12] Outfits like Planned Parenthood and the AFT helped organize the event. A group funded by billionaire Michael Bloomberg, Everytown for Gun Safety, helped fund it. Though March for Our Lives said it was "for kids and by kids," the average age of attendees was forty-nine.[13]

This was not for lack of trying. The groups were battling mightily to capture children. Everytown earmarked millions of dollars to promote the organization of student chapters and local marches across the country.[14]

In Montgomery County, Maryland, a club called MoCo Students for Gun Control, later renamed MoCo Students for Change (MCS), formed. One of its cofounders, Matt Post, took the stage at the rally and bemoaned "the insatiable greed of a few," saying "our nation's politics are sick with soullessness, but make no mistake, we are the cure."[15]

The cure was simple: vote for Democrats. In Virginia's 2019 election, which flipped legislative control to Democrats for the first time in decades, Everytown spent $2.5 million, making it the largest outside spender in the state. MCS members traveled across the state line to knock on doors with Bloomberg's group.[16]

Government officials facilitated these students' political activism. Montgomery County's school board "partnered" with MCS to hold voter registration drives in high schools. This partnership with a government body occurred even though MCS is a partisan organization that endorsed candidates (all Democrats) in those elections. The county's teachers union and the school system's "MCPS Equity Initiatives Unit" were among the "sponsors and founders" of a program called Youth Creating Change, which paid for students "to kickstart their social justice projects" and bankrolled MCS.[17]

But adults' empowerment of youth went only as far as they were useful to a particular partisan quest for power. D. A. Osorio, the head of advocacy for Montgomery County's PTA and a former teacher who ran for school board, made this clear during the 2020 Republican National Convention when he tweeted about Nicholas Sandmann. In January 2019, Sandmann gained notoriety as the MAGA hat–wearing, "smirking" teenager who stood silently on the steps of the Lincoln Memorial while a Native American activist banged on a drum inches away from his face and a group of Black Israelites hurled racial epithets at him, his fellow students, and Native Americans. Nineteen months later, Sandmann was in the spotlight again to deliver a speech at the convention. This may have been too much for Osorio, who tweeted that Sandmann deserved "a great radical beating."[18]

For ideologically compliant youngsters, premature immersion in the world of politics could also come at an emotional cost. Some of Montgomery's prominent child politicos were taught or mentored by Maxwell Bero, a social studies teacher who announced a run for Congress in 2019, challenging a Democratic incumbent from the left. In August 2020, Bero was arrested for, and later pleaded guilty to, sexual abuse of a minor. "The defendant has shown he is willing to engage minors in surreptitious communication to groom them for abuse," a prosecutor said.[19]

A female high school student who served as Bero's campaign manager went on to intern and work part-time for the county council. A twenty-five-year-old legislative aide there was openly the eighteen-year-old's "boyfriend," apparently to no one's consternation. She also ran for a slot on the school board that was reserved for a student, coming in second. Through that slot, as you will see, adults had set the stage for using children to impact local politics years before David Hogg's rise to fame.

BUSING

Few school districts in America have done more to implement equity, or done it for longer, than Montgomery County. More than a decade ago, consultant Glenn Singleton had convinced Montgomery to adopt an "equity framework." Superintendent Jerry Weast, who ran the system from 1999 to 2011, drew a red line around poorer, minority-heavy neighborhoods, and a green line around others, and steered dramatically more money to red schools than to green ones. To do this, the schools' annual budget ballooned from about

$1 billion to nearly $1.6 billion over the course of six years. Elementary schools with impoverished students eventually had a teacher-to-student ratio that was 41 percent better than other schools. In 2009, Harvard experts heralded Montgomery as a beacon for the nation when it comes to equity.[20]

But by 2018, black and Hispanic children were still underperforming, and the gap was getting worse in more academic areas than where it was getting better.[21] One school board member and outspoken equity advocate, Jill Ortman-Fouse, began demanding the opposite tack: redrawing school boundaries so that each school had a similar racial makeup. This would make it impossible to target extra funding to poor and minority students, the very thing that activists had previously demanded as equity. But would exposing minorities to more white children do what billions of dollars and decades of concerted equity initiatives had not?

The school district knew from the outset that it would not. It paid a consultant $540,000 to prepare a 152-page report on the impact of demographics at the county's schools, with foundations such as the Kellogg Foundation chipping in for almost half the cost. The report did not find what they may have been hoping for: it showed decisively that when impoverished students were surrounded by wealthier ones, their academic outcomes did not improve at all. Across the school system, black students who received free or reduced-price lunches had almost the exact same proficiency rate whether their school was 10 percent poor or 90 percent poor.[22]

Even as being near wealthier students did not help impoverished students, the performance of middle-class students plummeted when they were put in higher-poverty schools. At Francis Scott Key Middle, which has the county's fourth-highest rate of students who qualify for free or reduced priced lunch, only 21 percent of impoverished students were "proficient." That was nearly identical to poor kids at the school with the fourth-*lowest* poverty rate, Westland Middle. The difference was what happened to everyone else: 76 percent of wealthier students were succeeding at Westland, while at Key fewer than 40 percent of wealthier students were proficient.[23]

Nonetheless, the latest definition of equity sought to distribute students so that every school had the same poverty rate. In Montgomery, that meant every school should have the same rate as the system as a whole: 35 percent. Montgomery's data suggested that was the last thing anyone should want. The three schools that were closest to a 35 percent poverty rate (Montgomery Blair High, Roberto W. Clemente Middle, and Colonel Zadok Magruder High) already had the second-, fourth-, and seventh-*worst* achievement gaps in the county, respectively.[24]

If busing would not help poor children, would hurt wealthier ones, and would make it impossible to target extra funding to the needy, then why do it?

For policy makers, the likely answer is statistical manipulation. If poor kids frequently do badly in school, then jurisdictions must either find a way to make their population less poor, or find ways to help poor children learn. Montgomery's officials seemed uninterested in or unable to do either. But having poor children attend schools near their neighborhoods made the problem too conspicuous. By rearranging children, the number of schools with abysmal averages would go down on paper, even if the number of failed children remained the same.

For equity activists, the answer is because that is what they do: continuously criticize the status quo and claim that success would be right around the corner only if everyone would listen to them and do something else—even if they have repeated this cycle so many times that they were going in circles.

Weast's famous plan to direct money to disadvantaged students was recent history to adult residents. The alternate approach, busing, had also been explored on a smaller scale in more recent years, only to be called off when minorities said they had no interest in such a thing. An official survey of residents' desires on the newest busing initiative would later, predictably, find similar results: 79 percent thought it was "extremely important" to minimize boundary changes, while only 4 percent thought it was not important if it meant attaining racial balance.[25]

How could a plan so at odds with public opinion and clear-cut data on efficacy come to pass? In Montgomery, the answer was that insiders didn't need you to agree.

They already had your children.

STUDENT MEMBER OF THE BOARD

Back in March 2016, Maryland state lawmakers held a hearing in a capitol committee room to make a student a full voting member of Montgomery's eight-person school board. Seventeen-year-olds cannot sign legal contracts or vote in U.S. elections and most have likely never seen more than a hundred dollars, but now one would be a fiduciary steward of a $2.5 billion budget.[26]

In April 2017, Matt Post, the MCS cofounder, became that student board member. A year later, on April 12, 2018, the board made some revisions to its policy for drawing school boundaries while maintaining its long-standing policy of equally weighing proximity, stability for students, overcrowding, and diversity.[27]

Ortman-Fouse wanted an amendment to elevate the latter above all else—even the commonsense factor of whether a school had the capacity or not. The policy would obligate staff to "especially, and in particular," focus on "diversity." Even in hyperliberal Montgomery County, this was not likely to pass. But Ortman-Fouse had a plan: have the kid do it.

"Matt had made the motion instead of me at the board meeting because he had more pull with Board leadership. I was hoping that would get us the votes we needed," she later disclosed to an activist in a private email. Post had introduced the amendment as his own five months earlier. He told his adult colleagues that race should be the "priority, and then we can talk about next steps in ensuring quality education."[28]

The board rejected the motion, and Post departed to attend Yale University. The otherwise mundane revisions were advertised for public comment, as required so that citizens know what is happening and can have their say. As soon as the comment period closed in September, the substance of Post's amendment was stealthily re-incorporated. The change, undoing twenty-five years of precedent and approving something that voters believed had been rejected, was passed.[29]

The sleight of hand again came down to child activists. An Indian American student named Ananya Tadikonda succeeded Post on the school board. The seventeen-year-old chaired her own committee and comprised one-fourth of the committee that oversaw school boundary policy. At 3:00 p.m. on September 13, 2018, the day after the public comment period ended, that committee met. Ordinary parents were at work, and besides the four members and staff, only three people were visible in the audience.

Ortman-Fouse said, "I'm going to try one more time for this language change that Matt had recommended before and I had seconded. I don't know that we'll have a different outcome." She said that white students would benefit because the culture of "competition" at their schools would be reduced if there were more minorities.[30]

Ortman-Fouse had been browsing the websites of activist education groups. "I just looked up the benefits of diverse schools on the internet and came up with so many articles and studies," she said. She named one of her Google results, but got the name wrong, calling it the "Southern Poverty Leadership Center," referring to the Southern Poverty Law Center, the group behind Learning for Justice.

Patricia O'Neill, the committee chair, made clear they would not be passing the already-rejected amendment. "I don't particularly like that language . . . I had told Matt that in the spring," she said. It did not seem like the public had "coalesced" around such a position, she noted.

Ortman-Fouse dismissed the public. "We have to at some point take a stand that aligns with our values regardless," she said.

There was only one thing to do if an adult's half-baked reasoning was not persuasive enough: put it in the mouth of someone younger. The seventeen-year-old Tadikonda came to her aid. "I think Ms. Ortman-Fouse has presented some excellent data to support her proposal," she said.

But it turned out a seventeen-year-old was not qualified to single-handedly shape the financial future of a multibillion-dollar school system: it would need to be someone even younger. Tadikonda continued, "I was just talking to a group of about five kids and they were ten or eleven years old, and they asked me two questions. They asked me: Why there weren't any Caucasian students sitting with them at lunch. And why the kids living in the houses across the street from the school that are valued at about a billion dollars—and I was surprised that these kids actually knew that—why those kids don't go to school with them."

Judith Docca, a gray-haired woman who was the board's longest-serving member, was forceful in her opposition. She was a former NAACP officer and the president of the Montgomery County Alliance of Black School Educators. "We tried to integrate the schools in the '70s . . . we were willing to move people [in poverty, and they] said they wanted to stay in the neighborhood," she said. "Our schools are 72 percent black, Hispanic, and Asian . . . we need to be grounded in reality."[31]

Ortman-Fouse interjected—over Docca's protestation of "wait, I wasn't finished"—that it was "my understanding" that there was a failing school where boundaries had been gerrymandered to spare a wealthy neighborhood.

"Well, your understanding is not right, it really is not," Docca said flatly.

"So it doesn't move forward here," Ortman-Fouse conceded. "But I will be bringing it back" at the full board hearing anyway. Except she would not let it go. She continued to badger the other committee members, who were used to more dispassionate affairs. The meeting could not move on.

Docca sighed. "You just can't convince me."

Tadikonda could not believe that the prepubescent-home-appraisers gambit did not work. "I just have to say that it's not OK for ten- and eleven-year-olds to be able to recognize that they are distinctly segregated by socioeconomic status from their neighbors across the street to different middle schools," she repeated.

Ortman-Fouse, for her part, had to settle for the ghost of a Yale freshman. "As Matt said, I think, very eloquently, it just gives it a tiny bit more weight. It's not robust, full-throated, I think was the word he used that he would have preferred . . . and that was giving up a lot."

"So that doesn't pass," the chair said.

At issue was a several-word change in an obscure policy document that would have the effect of requiring Montgomery to draw school boundaries primarily around race. The phrase "especially and in particular" changed diversity from just one among a handful of equal factors to the mandatory, overriding one. It was the kind of thing that could easily slip past busy parents, but insiders knew its significance.

"What about 'especially' as opposed to 'especially and in particular'?" Ortman-Fouse prodded. She had worn the chair down. O'Neill capitulated to the semantic change, which had the same meaning as the one she repeatedly stated would make for bad policy. That meant the amendment passed in the committee.

Docca furrowed her brow. "I just want us to be realistic about what we are able to do, that's it. And where the kids are, we need to provide the very best programs for them."

REASONABLE

Eleven days later, the policy went to the full board for a final vote. Parents had no idea the rejected amendment had risen from the dead. But student activists had been tipped off by Ortman-Fouse, and they packed the room and lined up to make three-minute speeches in support.[32]

"Thank you specifically to Jill Ortman-Fouse for continuing this fight on behalf of us students," said Brian Kramer, the white, seventeen-year-old "executive director of the Association for the Advancement of Maryland Public Schools," a former student of Maxwell Bero's who told members it would be "criminal" not to vote for the measure.

An Eritrean immigrant from Tadikonda's Richard Montgomery High School lamented that one high school, Wheaton, had less than 13 percent Asians. That was in contrast to the school system as a whole, which had about 14 percent. As for the benefit of diversity, she offered that it allowed her to segregate among others like her. "I met

Leah, an Ethiopian girl who I'm good friends with to this day. Our similar backgrounds brought us together."[33]

A self-described "sixteen-year-old South Asian Muslim" followed by conceding that in her middle school program, there had been enough Asians—but not enough South Asians.

Next, Giovanni Gutierrez said he emigrated from Peru, where "there was one common culture that was accepted and endorsed, while any others were put down." He seemed to want the same thing in his new country. "As a student of color attending a primarily white school, it's difficult for me to assimilate into their culture. School is supposed to enrich me, not gentrify me," he later claimed.[34]

He attended Rockville High School, which is 41 percent Hispanic and 31 percent white. Apparently, that was too many whites, as the school system overall is 28 percent white. Rockville, statistics on exam scores reveal, has the smallest "achievement gap"—the difference in academic performance between the advantaged and disadvantaged—in the county. Closing that gap is one of the equity activists' stated goals. But not only did that not make him happy; he also did not even seem to be aware that he was in the promised land. "We, your students, want equity," he demanded.[35]

Activists made contradictory arguments for the same policy. Some argued that "research" proved that diversity would raise the test scores of all groups, while others lamented the fact that the county's most homogeneous schools had higher test scores than the others.

Ortman-Fouse had described her "ideal" school, one that did not seem to include any Asians or Arabs. "My children's elementary school . . . was about a third white students, about a third African American students, and about a third Hispanic students . . . and I truly feel like that's the ideal scenario," she said. Of course, Gutierrez objected to the demographics of Rockville High School, which were almost exactly that.[36]

A white student in a "high-poverty, 93 percent-minority school" had "the best experience," her mother said, because she learned so much about other cultures. But her sole example belied a humorous unfamiliarity, as black basketball fans would be the first to tell you:

she purportedly learned that, in contrast to materialistic whites, other cultures were not obsessed with the nicest footwear.[37]

What they lacked in coherence, student activists made up for in endearing naiveté. "And I listen to these students, and I hear their powerful voices," Lynne Harris, the president of the countywide PTA, testified, breaking down in tears. "And I don't think this is the time for us to try to be reasonable and flexible."

When it was time for board members to speak, Ortman-Fouse (who is white) and the seventeen-year-old student board member (who as an Indian American belongs to the richest ethnicity in the country) went to war against Shebra Evans, a black woman who was the school board's vice president. The strategy of packing sleepy board meetings with children tied to a few radical organizers did not elude Evans. "We've got seventy-eight comments; we have 163-plus thousand students. I want to hear from more people. You didn't hear from my next-door neighbor 'cause they're working," Evans said. "I don't know that we're thinking about the psychological impacts, the family factors" of separating students from their friends and putting miles between parents and their children.

Docca, the former NAACP official, agreed. "'Especially strive' I think is too strong. . . . I feel upset that people were lecturing to me about desegregation, but I'm not sure that they really understand the implication of it, and they have to understand that in order to make this program go forward." Ortman-Fouse responded by quoting the white Paul Gorski of the Equity Literacy Institute on "privileged people."

Anyone who was alive in the 1970s, or had a knowledge of American history, knew what busing resulted in. Race-based social engineering had been tried decades ago, and abandoned for a reason. Parents would find it hard to be involved with their children's schools. It would be unpopular, and lead to resentment, with all racial groups. The children who were brought to a new school were likely to stick together rather than integrate. People who could afford to were likely to move out of the county altogether.[38]

Jack Smith, the normally reserved superintendent, warned that "there will be unintended outcomes [from the proposed change], and we will all live with them." The board president agreed, while O'Neill, the committee chair, pointed out that the policy would expose the district to lawsuits. Board member Rebecca Smondrowski reminded them, "When we did take the time to go door to door in our last discussion of this issue, [poor minorities] didn't want to change."

But thanks to the existence of a student member of the school board, the boundary policy passed by one vote. In the face of the intense badgering by one adult member and her army of children, Docca, who initially said she could not support the measure, had resigned herself to going along with it.

SHAKEDOWN

MCS and Tadikonda made quick work of pushing the board to hire a consultant to conduct a full-scale review of the county's school boundaries. This would have more impact on families and taxpayers than anything else a school board does, but Tadikonda fought to block allowing community input.[39]

At a March 2019 press conference, she mixed the hyperbolic angst of a teenager with the buzzwords of the equity industry. "It is exhausting to go to school in a place where you walk into an honors class and people don't think you belong there," she complained.[40] That Indian Americans are underrepresented in advanced academics is laughable. Further, she was a student at Richard Montgomery High School, which reported an Asian population of 24.6 percent, compared to a white population of 29.1 percent as of September 30, 2019.[41]

But it was personal, pleading, and coming from a child. Who could object?

The rest of the public process was a charade. In April 2019, the school system held a listening session for about fifty people on school boundaries and equity. No school board members attended. When parents started expressing their opinions—an Asian parent asked if they would change the rules of basketball so that more Asians could grab rebounds—a school system staffer walked out.[42]

A politician would risk being voted out if they introduced such a widely detested initiative. On the other hand, by the time the next election rolled around, Tadikonda would be firmly ensconced in college, where this kind of activism looked stellar on an application. She chose the University of North Carolina, which had more than twice the proportion of whites as her high school. Just as Tadikonda succeeded Post as "Student Member of the Board," Nate Tinbite followed Tadikonda for the 2019–20 school year. He continued the busing push. A primary position of Tinbite, who is black, was concern about racial equity. In reality, in a county that is 19 percent black, the school board was 50 percent black. It had no Hispanic or Asian members, despite those groups having nearly twice as many county residents.[43]

Like Post, Tinbite was also a cofounder of MCS. At the Student Rally on Gun Violence in March 2018, Tinbite compared the United States unfavorably to Ethiopia, from which his parents had immigrated. In Ethiopia, people only get eight to nine years of schooling. But the endgame of the busing proponents' plan might be consistent with the African nation. As the CIA's *World Factbook* puts it, Ethiopia is a "one-party state with a planned economy" that can boast "the lowest level of income-inequality in Africa"—because nearly everyone is dirt-poor.[44]

Everyone except the politicians, of course. Tinbite insisted on being paid the same $50,000 salary as adult board members, implying that because he had managed to push through a busing policy that they had been reluctant to, he was doing more than the rest. As he described himself in his salary pitch, according to board minutes, he is "an extraordinary young man" whose duties include "national events" and who is "going above and beyond what other Board members are doing," some of whom are merely "stay at home moms."[45]

It seemed like a shakedown: a payoff for providing cover to adult politicians who wanted to betray their constituents.

11

FOUNDATIONS

Pierce Delahunt is a trust-fund baby with an inheritance in the millions, generated from a chain of successful outlet malls. By thirty-two, Delahunt took "nongendered pronouns" like "their," was a self-styled anarchist and communist, and was directing the inheritance to nonprofit groups that advanced those causes. Their parents were socially liberal and Delahunt often heard things like "be kind to all, and mindful of those less fortunate." But after learning "social justice throughout high school," Delahunt realized that was not equity. They expressed distaste for concepts like "NeoLiberalism (an intentionally repackaged Capitalism), 'Classical Liberalism' (similarly repackaged Conservatism), Liberalism itself (as opposed to Leftism) . . . and other liberation-washed practices of oppression."[1]

With time and money at their disposal, Delahunt "put a lot of energy into critiquing this country. I enjoy problematizing in general." Though outlet malls provide name-brand goods at deeply discounted prices, allowing lower-income earners to enjoy the same luxuries as the rich, Delahunt was ashamed of the source of their wealth, saying, "When I think about outlet malls, I think about intersectional oppression." They decided to donate their inheritance to anticapitalist groups that "tackle the externalities of discount shopping."[2]

Delahunt now has a master's degree in education and gives speeches to children, such as one geared toward middle and high schoolers called "Vegan Praxis in a Political Context of White Supremacy." As a professional biography says: "Their research was a study of activist-education programs throughout the country. They grew up in occupied Lenape territories of New York and New Jersey, and . . . teach social emotional learning, activism, social justice, and Leftist economics."[3]

Key to Delahunt's activities was a group called Resource Generation, a group funded by the Ford Foundation and the W. K. Kellogg Foundation to coax guilt-ridden young scions of millionaires into steering their families' funds to activist groups that oppose capitalism. Delahunt is one of a thousand or so dues-paying members of Resource Generation, a network that stands to influence a combined $22 billion in inheritance. The group held "workshops on family dynamics" to train young inheritors how to siphon off their parents' money on the premise that capitalism is based on "stolen land, stolen labor, and stolen lives."[4]

This is typical of how philanthropic foundations like Ford and Kellogg work. Elite, well-heeled foundation executives use the billions from their endowments—amassed through capitalism—to create various associations and activist groups. Those nonprofits radicalize youth by associating racism with America, and America with capitalism. The foundation money serves as seed money that is eventually leveraged by another source. The foundations have created their own mouthpieces, and gotten others to pay for it.

There are hundreds of such activist groups, local and national, pushing complaints about "systemic racism," equity, and the evils of capitalism to public schools and children. It is a veritable industry, breathtaking in its volume and complexity.

But like the Hydra of Greek mythology—the immortal, multi-headed snake monster that, if someone cut off a head, would grow two more in its place—these activist groups are all parts of one machine. Pick any one of them, and its funding is likely to tie back to the foundations, primarily Ford; Gates; W. K. Kellogg; Annie E. Casey; MacArthur; and Surdna. There is also the New Venture Fund, a group that pools money from all of these foundations and then distributes it.

The Ford Foundation spent $665 million on "racial equity" between 2011 and 2020. But foundations do not simply subsidize existing, independent nonprofits. They decide what they want to allocate their focus and money to, then a crowd of activist groups lines up with grant proposals promising to do just that, even if it means diverting from what those groups would have otherwise done. In October 2020, Ford announced $180 million in new funding for racial equity, with a focus on litigation—perhaps suing over racism and fighting for the likes of racial quotas in the courts. In making this decision, Darren Walker, the gay black former securities trader who leads the foundation, was like a coach calling the play, sending his players out into position, and setting the course of American activism.[5]

Equity grantee groups are professional outfits, but many operate in largely esoteric areas such as school board policy making and curriculum development, where the "other team" is simply regular parents, who rarely have the time or know-how to resist, or even notice these efforts. The obscurity of their work makes them harder to challenge.

In 2016, Hillary Clinton spent more than half a billion dollars on her presidential campaign. By comparison, the Ford, Kellogg, and MacArthur foundations alone commanded assets of nearly $27 billion and, between them, doled out more than one billion dollars in 2015.[6] Imagine having the resources of two presidential political campaigns without having to worry about expensive advertising, because the arena they were influencing was, to the average citizen, so small and arcane.

Then imagine that in this presidential campaign, there was no opposing candidate—essentially no organized faction presenting a competing choice.

Then imagine that the views being pushed by this campaign were far more extreme than a mainstream candidate like Clinton—ideas that, if Americans had been paying attention, most would oppose, regardless of political party.

Now imagine that the people behind this campaign were among the wealthiest, most powerful people in America, working in close coordination, and that their arena was the nation's K–12 schools. This is how this game is actually being played.

In this framework, the foundations seek to transform America in ways few Americans would want, and to do it, they seek to transform your children, by influencing the largest and most intimate thing government does: operating America's public schools. For some reason, this *is* viewed as an obscure policy arena by most people, who spend more time paying attention to things like presidential politics. But it shouldn't be. And the philanthropic foundations should not be thought of as merely the rich families who paid for some art museums or public television programming. These rogue foundations are perhaps the most radical, powerful, and least understood force in American politics. And their aspirations go far beyond the outcome of an election.

FOUNDATIONS ARE BEHIND ALL EQUITY INITIATIVES

Much of what you have read about in the preceding chapters happened in no small part because of these foundations.

The 1619 Project, Nikole Hannah-Jones's 2019 *New York Times* series turned grade school curriculum, might never have seen the light of day if not for the MacArthur Foundation. In 2014, MacArthur awarded a $1 million, three-year grant to ProPublica, a liberal nonprofit news outlet for which Hannah-Jones wrote about race issues. She joined the *Times* the following year. In 2017, MacArthur awarded Hannah-Jones, whom it described as an "investigative journalist chronicling the persistence of racial segregation in American society, particularly in education," a "$625,000, no-strings-attached grant for individuals who have shown exceptional creativity in their work and the promise to do more." In "How the 1619 Project Came Together," the *Times* explained that Hannah-Jones consulted with "Kellie Jones, a Columbia University art historian and 2016 MacArthur Fellow." Matthew Desmond, who contributed an article about the "brutality of American capitalism" to the series, was a 2015 MacArthur fellow. The Pulitzer Center, the nonprofit that pushed curricula based on the series into school districts across the country, is also funded by the MacArthur Foundation.[7]

In 2021, MacArthur secured a position for Hannah-Jones as a professor at Howard University, where she would teach her racial ideas and continue the 1619 Project, by donating $5 million to the school.[8]

The Zinn Education Project, which has inroads in the majority of school districts and relentlessly criticizes capitalism and America, is a project of the activist groups Rethinking Schools and Teaching for Change, the latter of which is funded by the Kellogg Foundation and the New Venture Fund.[9]

David E. Kirkland, the architect of New York State's radical culturally responsive-sustaining education strategy—who said asking black children to learn basic skills would "serve to indoctrinate minorities into the dominant culture"—received $500,000 from the Kellogg Foundation to push racial equity in public schools, and $1 million from the Gates Foundation to promote "racial identity formation" in schools. Both grants were awarded a couple of weeks apart in late 2020.[10]

A group called FairTest, which has successfully pushed to limit standardized tests, is funded not only by the NEA union but also by the Ford, MacArthur, and Soros foundations. FairTest's former vice chair, Judith Browne Dianis, is prone to lashing out against "white supremacy and capitalism." Dianis is also the executive director of the Advancement Project, a black advocacy group that is funded by Ford, Kellogg, and the New Venture Fund.[11]

President Obama's My Brother's Keeper initiative, which threatened schools over "disproportionate" suspensions of black boys whether or not the suspensions were justified, is a still-active partnership between Obama and a "who's who" of foundations that pledged $200 million over five years. The Kellogg Foundation spent $15 million to persuade local school systems to relax disciplinary policies.[12] After two large federally funded studies showed that "restorative justice," the practice of schools having violent assailants "talk things out" with their victims instead of suspending them, did not work out as hoped, George Soros's foundation offered Baltimore schools $1.2 million to do it anyway. More than 3,500 teachers were trained to use restorative justice.[13] In cases of "student/staff physical conflict," a "trained, neutral conference facilitator" would give the student assailants "the opportunity to share their perspectives on the situation."[14]

It is philanthropic foundations who have injected critical race theory into society. Casey Foundation executives incubated a group called Equity in the Center that says it works with "coconspirators" to develop strategies to help critical race theory colonize organizations. Its "Woke @ Work" blog preaches that whites are "born into and conditioned by a toxic culture" and need "healing from white supremacy." Society must "reckon with how white supremacy has dehumanized us."[15]

A presentation authored in August 2020 capitalized on the coronavirus pandemic, advising that "[c]risis creates opportunity to take radical actions." It said that to get away from "white dominant norms," employers should "[m]ove away from perfectionism to being okay with 'good enough.'" Organizations should "[r]elease ideas around 'objectivity'—create space for people to share how emotions, identities and lived experience connect to their viewpoints" and "[b]reak down silos and move away from indivualism [*sic*] to collectivism." Employees may be "shocked," "angry," and "sad" by the dramatic change in their organization, but after "critical psychological realignments," they will come to accept it.[16]

EDUCATION

The world of K–12 education policy has long been dominated by philanthropic foundations. It was the Bill and Melinda Gates Foundation that pushed for Common Core, the national education standards that, perhaps inadvertently, allowed activist groups like Learning for Justice to invade American schools. Common Core was conceived of largely by Gene Wilhoit and David Coleman. Wilhoit was executive director of the Council of Chief State School Officers, a convening of government officials whose largest funder is Gates, with the Carnegie, MacArthur, and Ford foundations also chipping in. Coleman, a former textbook executive, cofounded Student Achievement Partners, a prominent education group that is funded by Gates, Carnegie, and the NEA union, with Gates its largest funder by far.[17]

Common Core became a reality thanks to an influence campaign by Gates topping $170 million and aimed at getting states to agree to essentially give up control of their own standards. For example, more than $15 million was spent lobbying state lawmakers in Kentucky. One group in North Carolina, the Hunt Institute, received $5 million to manufacture grassroots activism, often known as "astroturfing," by providing "sample letters to the editor" and "op-ed pieces that could be tailored to individuals." Forty-six states ultimately signed on.[18]

Groups that have used the imprimatur of teachers to turn core classes like English into forums for racial activism, such as the National Council of Teachers of English—whose 2021 convention was titled "Equity, Justice, and Antiracist Teaching"—are funded by the Gates and MacArthur foundations. Even groups that serve to get education officials and elected representatives on the same page, such as the American Association of School Administrations; the National Association of School Boards; the National Association of Secondary School Principals; and the National Association of State Boards of Education, are funded by Gates's foundation and on a smaller scale by others like the Carnegie, Ford, Kellogg, and Soros foundations.[19]

If regular people want to follow the ins and outs of education, they are likely to get their information from news outlets set up to cover K–12 that also are funded by foundations, and do so with a slant that views racial and statistical equalizing as a primary mission of schools. These include the *Hechinger Report*, which is funded by Carnegie, Kellogg, and Gates and has syndication agreements with the *Washington Post*, NPR, and CNN. "We cover inequality and innovation in education," its mission says. A typical "opinion" headline: "Youth of Color and Young Women Use Social Media the Most, so Why Are Most Digital Technology Developers White Men?"[20]

Another such publisher is *The 74*, a "non-profit, non-partisan news site covering education in America" funded by the Gates and Carnegie foundations that has published more than one thousand articles about "equity." Then there is *Education Post*, funded by foundations including Gates's and Michael Bloomberg's. One mid-2020 column said, "I'm tired of White people taking their violent culture, standards and metrics into Black spaces and telling Black children that they don't measure up. . . . [I]f you really want to make a difference in Black lives—and not have to protest this shit again—*go reform white kids*. Because that's where the problem is."[21]

Foundations also set the narrative by funding reams of social science "research" that make claims about race and education, and whose findings can quickly make their way into the national discourse. The Spencer Foundation pays academics to create racial research on education. In 2018, it paid one roughly $50,000 for a paper titled "Leading While Black (and Female): Exploring Microaggressions in the Lived Experiences of Black, Female School Leaders." It also awards journalists $82,500 fellowships to publicize such studies.[22]

YOUTH ACTIVISM

The foundations' goals are political, and schools give them easy access to society's most impressionable. But foundations relentlessly seek to shape children's politics both inside and outside of the classroom.

The Ford, MacArthur, New Venture Fund, and Soros's Open Society Foundations are among the top funders of the Alliance for Youth Organizing (AYO), which bills itself as "America's premier youth organizing network." Its website proclaims, "We entice millions of young voters into our sweet democracy." Between 2018 and 2020, Ford gave AYO over $6.5 million. AYO and several other activist groups put voter registration stations in high school proms. If you have not heard of AYO, that may be because it operates through dozens of local affiliated fronts for it, such as Chicago Votes and Minnesota Youth Collective. Its New York affiliate aims to lower the voting age to seventeen.[23]

Some AYO affiliates look to use children to make conservative areas into progressive ones, like Forward Montana, which is aimed at "passing policies that are representative of the needs and vision of their generation."[24]

Others have names designed to appear nonpartisan, such as the Ohio Student Association, which AYO acknowledges is actually an "intergenerational movement for racial, social, economic and educational justice. OSA's leaders are between 18 and 35, some are not students." Foundations frequently help establish such forums, which purport to speak on behalf of broad constituencies, but instead funnel people with legitimate, nonpartisan interests into groups that are actually controlled by liberal ideologues. Though equity policies often harm Asians, such as changing the rules for admission to magnet schools when too many Asians score highly on tests, an innocuous-sounding group in Nevada called the Asian Community Development Council is actually an AYO affiliate.[25]

The Ford Foundation also funds the Sunrise Movement, a climate activist group whose members carry signs with slogans like "The Youth Are Coming for You." Activists are whisked to a retreat where they are trained in shaping "public narrative." When a trainee asked whether they should be in favor of nuclear power, the reply was that "Sunrise's role is not to be super caught up in the details. . . . We're 18-, 19-, 20-, 21-year-olds who don't really know policy." On the other hand, when one trainee, playing the role of a news interviewer, asked whether Sunrise wanted to "drag this country into socialism," her counterpart was more certain, replying, "Yes, that actually sounds great!"[26]

These activist groups understand the potency of using young children as props. In one noteworthy scene, adults in Sunrise Movement T-shirts brought young children and teens to the office of Democratic senator Dianne Feinstein to demand that she support the Green New Deal in early 2019. "There's no way to pay for it," Feinstein told them.[27]

"Yes, there is," a child directed.

A teenager added, "Our earth is dying, literally. And it is going to be a pricey and ambitious plan."

"That resolution will not pass the Senate, and you can take that back to whoever sent you here," Feinstein replied.

Moments later, an adult in a yellow Sunrise Movement shirt interrupted. "You're looking at the faces of the people who are going to be living with these consequences . . . and we're asking you to be brave," she lectured the senator, who in 1978 discovered the slain body of Harvey Milk and who once had the windows of her house shot out by revolutionaries.[28]

As Feinstein and an aide told them they had to go, a girl with pigtails, who looked to be about ten years old, put both hands out and children began repeating the talking points imprinted upon them by adults. "Of course, saving our world is a pricey and ambitious project . . ."

Ford also funds groups like Law for Black Lives, which "provides legal and policy support to youth-led campaigns to redirect funds from criminal justice systems to education and social services in black communities." It is involved in paying bail to release black criminal suspects from jail, including those accused of violent crimes, and arranges for them to receive "cigarettes" and "burner phones" when they get out. It also describes itself as "the Black femme led legal arm of the Black Liberation movement." And, along with five other activist groups, it created an educational curriculum where students are asked to agree or disagree with statements like "we must end incarceration in the U.S." and "I see bail reform as a steppingstone to abolition."[29]

FOUNDATIONS ARE TWO STEPS AHEAD OF THE DEMOCRATIC ESTABLISHMENT

The Ford Foundation harbors a sort of shadow government. Kamala Harris's sister and closest political confidante, Maya Harris, was a Ford Foundation vice president, after previously working for PolicyLink, a key equity activist group and Ford grantee. Joe Biden's senior campaign advisor, Cristóbal Alex, was its program director during the Obama years. Ford's chief of staff, Taara Rangarajan, was President Obama's national security advisor for about three years. Even Obama's mother worked for the Ford Foundation at one point.[30]

Ford has also shown a knack for steering the Democratic Party to the left. It does this by funding groups that operate at local levels that are more radical than national mainstream politics would accommodate. Once the time is right, they are elevated to national roles.

For example, between 2013 and 2020, Ford gave a Florida-based group called Dream Defenders $1.1 million to "build a young people's movement to end mass incarceration" and other "youth-led civic engagement organizing." As the group explained in 2018, "we believe that our liberation necessitates the destruction of the political and economic systems of Capitalism. . . . We want an immediate end to the police state and murder of Black people. . . . We want free, fully-funded public education for all that teaches us our true history and our role in present day society. We want community control of land, bread, housing, education, justice, peace and technology." Dream Defenders is involved in county-level races for state attorneys, backing candidates for prosecutors who align with their mission of "a world without prisons, policing, surveillance and punishment." It is run by Philip Agnew, whose fringe racial beliefs, the Anti-Defamation League said, posed harm to "the State of Israel and the American Jewish Community." In March 2020, Bernie Sanders's presidential campaign tapped Agnew as a senior advisor on matters of race and inequity.[31]

On the day when Joe Biden assumed the presidency, the North Star Fund—which the Ford Foundation funded to the tune of nearly $1 million from 2016 to 2019, with the Rockefeller, Surdna, and Soros foundations chipping in as well—bemoaned, "The administration may have changed but white supremacy and capitalism are still here."[32]

LOCAL MATTERS

K–12 schools are run by thirteen thousand independent school districts, but foundations have also perfected the art of implementing national political agendas through local government.

Financially, this is a brilliant plan. For the same amount political actors might spend influencing one congressional election, they could elect an entire slate of school board candidates or county council members in a large jurisdiction. Unlike a back-bench congressman, these school board or council members would enjoy complete control. It is not just money, but the lack of attention that makes these efforts especially potent. In fact, it is easy to elect far-left candidates in center-left jurisdictions, because if the far-left candidate can squeak through in a primary where just 5 percent of voters participate, a majority Democrat county is likely to blindly support him in the general election, with no real idea who he or she is.[33]

This goes doubly for the suburbs. Suburbs are crucial to those seeking to transform American politics because they are among the only "purple" areas left. Generally speaking, U.S. cities are blue, and rural areas are red. Therefore, as go the suburbs, so goes America. Suburban residents often pay little attention to municipal elections, and newspapers have been forced to cut back severely on local coverage. But some populous suburban counties have upward of one million people—more than the population of six states.[34] Savvy political operatives realized that this offered them a remarkable opportunity.

A large portion of what might appear to be grassroots local activism, particularly concerning education issues, can be traced directly to the foundations.

One of the counties with more than one million residents is Wake County, North Carolina. There, a group called the Youth Organizing Institute pays children $100 to attend a "Freedom School" that trains them to become activists on topics like "environmental racism," the "school to prison pipeline," "Indigenous land reclamation," and "reproductive justice."[35]

There is no paperwork about this group because it is an arm of another nonprofit, called the Southern Vision Alliance, whose other tentacles include the Community Alliance for Public Education; Comite de Accion Popular (whose motto is "Fuck La Migra," or "fuck the immigration police"); and Durham Beyond Policing, whose goal is to get "police out of our neighborhoods!" Southern Vision Alliance is funded by the Ford Foundation and the New Venture Fund.[36]

12

ARABELLA INC.

In the early twentieth century, a handful of "robber barons" consolidated extraordinary wealth and power. John D. Rockefeller controlled the oil industry. Henry Ford dominated the new automobile market. Andrew Carnegie held a vertical monopoly on steel. The Kellogg brothers created a breakfast cereal empire. And James E. Casey of Seattle founded the company that later became UPS, which conquered the world with its package delivery service.

President Teddy Roosevelt, the great "trust buster," won acclaim for his efforts to break up the concentrations of power these industrialists enjoyed.[1] But while some of the corporate names no longer exist, the fortunes of these families remained intact, and some of the same families have only increased their influence one hundred years later.

When Henry Ford died in 1947, the estate taxes owed were enormous. To satisfy the obligation, his heirs would have to sell off so many shares of the automobile company that they would no longer control it. By donating it to existing charities they could lower their tax bill, but would be giving away all of that wealth. They devised a loophole: they could instead donate it to a charity they controlled and avoid paying Uncle Sam, all while retaining control of both the company and the money. It was called a foundation.[2]

The Ford Foundation's holdings were so vast that the interest alone yielded massive sums each year, and it was from these dividends that it would make its donations, to be selected by the Ford family's appointees. This meant that the foundation would preserve the bulk of Ford's wealth in perpetuity. When the Rockefellers had done similar, the federal government objected to this "immortal" status, but the Rockefellers found a state, New York, that would permit it. Teddy Roosevelt is long dead, but New York has become the home of many other similar foundations, preserving the fortunes of the robber barons—forever.[3]

The problem with the monopolies of the 1900s was not that what they were doing—selling goods and services that Americans wanted—was inherently bad. The issue was their size and ability to collude that allowed a handful of elites to dominate crucial parts of American life. Decades later, the foundations created from this wealth exert similar control. Only their aims are social rather than economic. Having conquered industry, they pursue the only challenge left for people with endless ambition and billions of dollars: social engineering. The Ford Foundation came to see itself as the "research and development arm of society."[4]

From its beginnings, the foundation movement was a politically progressive one, fueled by a belief in the power of science to improve lives, and the idea that the wealth of the elite obligated them to pursue big ideas that could make the world a better place.[5] It was also defined by a fixation with race.

From 1910 to 1939, the "Carnegie Institution of Washington Station for Experimental Evolution" operated a Eugenics Record Office that cataloged Americans' genetic traits on "pedigree charts," warehousing them at an eighty-acre parcel on Long Island. Its director lobbied to "restrict immigration and sterilize 'defectives,' educating the public on eugenic health, and disseminating eugenic ideas widely." Cereal magnate John Harvey Kellogg was happy to join in. In 1914, the nation's leading philanthropists met with the Carnegie program's director and other scientists at Kellogg's Battle Creek, Michigan, compound to plot the way forward.[6]

By the 1920s, one of the Rockefeller Foundation's first grants funded the American Eugenics Society (AES). In 1937, a foundation executive recounted a meeting at the Hotel Delmonico in New York: "The first paper on a eugenics program in operation was read by Miss Marie Kopp, Ph.D., and dealt with the German program. . . . Everyone agreed that it had been most stimulating and interesting."[7]

In 1952, the Ford and Rockefeller foundations partnered to create the Population Council, dedicated to reducing the reproduction of undesirables because "modern civilization had reduced the operation of natural selection by saving more 'weak' lives and enabling them to reproduce." By the mid-1960s, a study revealed that roughly a third of all women of childbearing age in the U.S. territory of Puerto Rico had been sterilized.[8]

The problems with the industrialists' reincarnation became apparent to some in Congress, which established a select committee in the 1950s "to investigate tax-exempt foundations and comparable organizations," noting that because foundations and their donors received massive tax breaks, the government was in effect subsidizing them.[9] The peril of the Ford Foundation using American society as its plaything is that "its errors can be huge errors, gigantic in impact," said Rene A. Wormser in 1958. Wormser had been a staff attorney for the select committee and was not concerned just by Ford, but by the concentration of effort possible when multiple foundations act together. "A more tight and monopolistic control of great wealth would be hard to find in any other segment of American economy," he wrote. "Unlike the power of corporate management, it is unchecked by stockholders; unlike the power of government, it is unchecked by the people. . . . [Americans] are not likely to be pleased to find a quasi-monopoly operating in intellectual areas which are not mere 'ivory tower' but influence our society very materially." Wormser's words have proven prophetic in many ways.

NEW RACE

By the late 1960s, the Ford Foundation began using the familiar language of modern civil rights. But beneath the veneer, its version of progressivism was hard to tell from its earlier worldview. It now believed that the best path to racial integration was an indeterminate period of racial separation in which blacks could develop. As historian Karen Ferguson recounted in an in-depth study of the foundation, "African Americans, in its staffers' minds, required time alone to build community and catch up socially, culturally, and politically with whites."[10]

To do this, the Ford Foundation pushed a plan to turn New York schools over to "community control" in three black neighborhoods. To decide who would speak on behalf of the "community," the foundation paid radical black separatists to oversee quasi-official community elections, which they also ran in and, naturally, won. Ford deliberately picked groups who were "the most militant, the most alienated, the most mistrustful, the most volatile." The separatists did not generally represent the views of most in the community, but the elections were low-turnout affairs. In the Two Bridges neighborhood of the Lower East Side, even the most militant group had no desire to push for independent schools until Ford encouraged them with the promise of money. Few parents were involved. As Ferguson put it, "A small minority of administrators and largely nonparent school activists called the shots."[11]

The racialists were not on the same side as teachers; in fact, teachers were the villains. In the Ocean Hill–Brownsville neighborhood, the radicals' position was that New York's largely Jewish teachers were to blame for the abysmal performance of students. "Hey Jew boy, with the yarmulke on your head / You pale-faced Jew boy—I wish you were dead," a key figure in the new semiautonomous district said in a radio interview attacking the head of the United Federation of Teachers. He was reading a poem reportedly written by a student.[12]

In 1968, the new district fired nineteen unionized educators, eighteen of them white, without due process, setting off a citywide teachers' strike, and tried to install as principal a black nationalist who was under indictment for allegedly conspiring to assassinate the leaders of the NAACP and the Urban League. The move failed when the Board of Education refused the appointment, but another district "used [Ford] Foundation money to hire him as a paid consultant."[13]

All of this was the result of the Ford Foundation identifying and steering a small group of radicals, positioning them to speak for a large group that was not homogeneous, then using schools to take such beliefs from the fringes to the mainstream. An arm's-length survey showed the desire of black parents for "order and discipline in a traditional classroom setting." But once the schools were taken over in the name of racial autonomy, they did not implement what most blacks wanted, but rather trendy ideas from progressive education colleges. A "behavioral research laboratory" in California offered a free curriculum for "self-directed, ungraded, programmed" learning, which Ocean Hill–Brownsville schools implemented, claiming that under this "radically new approach," students would choose to become "engrossed in the pages of *Ulysses* by James Joyce." That, suffice it to say, did not happen.[14]

By every measure, this experiment failed. In its assessment, the Ford Foundation largely blamed the Chinese for the poor results in one of the neighborhoods. It quoted one black mother saying that "most of the Chinese are a drag." The failure meant that, by the foundation's measure, blacks were still not ready for integration.[15]

By 1991, one of the Rockefeller Foundation's favored means of improving society as it relates to blacks was aborting them. It functioned as an umbrella group for an array of groups, including the National Black Women's Health Project, the National Council of Negro Women, and the National Latina Health Organization. In exchange for funding, these groups ceded control to the foundation for "unified communications strategies." Through this, the wealthy white men in the Manhattan executive suites of the foundation purported to speak for various minority groups.[16]

Professional foundation executives became some of the most power-ful men in America, without enduring the scrutiny that comes with having a famous surname. They frequently jumped from one foun-dation to another, taking their priorities and methods with them and further crossbreeding the foundations. As the business of giving away other people's money became an industry in itself, virtually all foun-dation money was sucked into this orbit, regardless of the intention of the deceased.

John Andrus was a Republican congressman who had made his fortune in chemical manufacturing. In 1917, he created the Surdna Foundation, and one of his first goals was to found an orphanage, which he established within a few years to ensure that his legacy lived on. That "Surdna" is Andrus spelled backward is an apt metaphor for how the trustees carried out their duties after his death.[17]

In 2018, Surdna hired a former Ford Foundation executive, Don Chen, who decided that the foundation would be entirely dedicated to racial and social justice. It did this by sending its money to groups like the Democracy Collaborative, which argues that "the excep-tional period of capitalist prosperity following World War II was just that: an exception," calls for "fundamentally reorienting the econ-omy towards community," and advocates for "public ownership" of major industries. When descendants of John Andrus pointed out that his stated desire was to support hospitals, orphanages, schools, and churches—alleging that the trustees were "hijacking" his group—the chair of the board, Peter Benedict II, simply retorted that the foun-dation was not legally bound to use Andrus's money for "causes he personally supported."[18]

Under Chen, Ford had focused on "Just Cities and Regions." In 2009, Surdna began using eerily similar language, dedicating itself to "fostering the development of just and sustainable communities across the United States." In 2020, the Andrew W. Mellon Founda-tion made an identical switch. It had previously been mostly dedi-cated to the arts and humanities. Now it shifted its focus to "social justice" and "building just communities." The pivot came after the appointment as president of Elizabeth Alexander, who had been hired from the Ford Foundation, where she turned an arts program into "Art for Justice."[19]

The story of the Annie E. Casey Foundation is little different. The desire of James E. Casey, the founder of the company that eventually became UPS, was to help orphans. In fact, he expressed so little interest in politics that no one knew if he was liberal or conservative.[20] To ensure that his foundation reflected his values and focus, Casey decided to have UPS employees serve on the board, such as George Lamb, a UPS CEO who was instrumental in running the charity. In 1990, the board was searching for a new president.

Lamb was himself a conservative, but he chose as president of the foundation Douglas W. Nelson, who had run the Center for the Study of Social Policy. During his interview Nelson assured Lamb that, if chosen, he would lead the foundation in a nonpartisan manner. Gary MacDougal, another board member who agreed to hire Nelson, later said that Nelson was a "chameleon," adept at telling the board one thing while actually running the foundation as a far-left activist. When presenting grants to the board, Nelson would describe them using jargon that obscured their nature. When the board caught on to his tactic, it added a former Reagan administration official, Constance Horner. Horner said that the trustees were "mainstream Republican bordering on libertarian," but that they needed a translator to figure out what Nelson and other liberal-leaning executives were actually doing.[21]

The one thing known about James E. Casey—that he yearned to provide foster care for orphaned children—could have easily and productively spent the entire budget and transformed the lives of thousands of children. But by 2012, the Casey Foundation was no longer providing foster care at all. It retained its focus on children, but became a primary source of leftist activism aimed at schools. Instead of providing the direct, unglamorous, but essential services for individual children, it spent much of its time on what it called "convenings," where others in the foundations and social science world would get together and coordinate.

ARABELLA

By 2020, about a dozen of these big-money foundations were bent on transforming America by remaking what and how American children learn. Because there are several of them, they might seem immune to the charge of monopoly, except that even with the vast resources they each have at their disposal, these foundations routinely embark on joint projects with each other. Another way that their interests align is by coming together through jointly funded middleman entities, such as the Social Science Research Council, which is funded by the MacArthur, Carnegie, Mellon, Ford, Gates, and Rockefeller foundations.[22]

But one hundred years after the dawn of the foundation era, it reached a new level.

In 2006, Eric Kessler, a former environmental advisor to Bill Clinton, incorporated a nonprofit called the Arabella Legacy Fund, telling the Internal Revenue Service (IRS) that its purpose was to warn of the environmental damage from off-road vehicles such as ATVs and snowmobiles. This nonprofit said that it would focus on evangelical Christians, and its application paperwork included Bible verses. "At this time, the Organization does not anticipate compensating [future] employees more than $50,000 per year," it wrote. It acknowledged that the nonprofit would pay a for-profit company owned by Kessler, Arabella Philanthropic Investment Advisors Inc. (which later became Arabella Advisors, LLC). When the IRS expressed several concerns, including the lack of a competitive bid and a potential conflict of interest, the Arabella Legacy Fund replied that the agreement "only has a one-year term. As soon after this period as the Organization has adequate funding, it will no longer require the services of the Advisors."[23]

In 2009, the nonprofit changed its name to the New Venture Fund, and within a decade, New Venture and Arabella Advisors became among the largest and most powerful political machines in history—operating through such a shadowy and complex structure that their names are hardly known.[24] The New Venture Fund was a clearinghouse for the major foundations. It was as if billion-dollar organizations decided that they did not have enough money or power on their own and decided to consolidate.

In late 2015, the Wyss Foundation convened its board to approve what it called a "communications hub" that "will dramatically increase our ability to win policy campaigns." Illustrating the way that virtually every billion-dollar leftist advocacy group was merging into one, the Wyss Foundation was creating a project that would actually operate at an entirely different nonprofit. Though the Wyss board would "review the top priority campaigns annually," the board was told, "the hub would be housed at the New Venture Fund."[25]

The hub was called "The Hub Project" and its major funders were the Wyss Foundation, the AFT union, and Seattle venture capitalist and civic activist Nick Hanauer. "It essentially creates a place to have a shared strategy on issues with groups that might seem disparate," Randi Weingarten, head of the teachers union, explained.[26]

This consolidated the high-dollar progressive movement to such a surprising extent that it led to embarrassment for its own director, Arkadi Gerney, before he was even hired. Not wanting his existing employer, the Center for American Progress (CAP), to discover that he was job hunting, Gerney insisted that the Hub Project keep his application top secret. Soon after, the Wyss Foundation's president sent an email to start the hiring process. In an odd twist, Gerney discovered that his current boss, CAP chair John Podesta, would be conducting the job interview.[27]

In 2017, New Venture Fund employees were paid salaries as high as $530,000. In 2018, the organization reported total revenue in excess of $400 million, and a staff of 623. And—notwithstanding its earlier pledge to the IRS—New Venture Fund paid Arabella Advisors almost $19 million in compensation that year. Between 2014 and 2020, the Gates, Ford, Rockefeller, Kellogg, MacArthur, and Open Society foundations gave the New Venture Fund more than $565 million, making it one of their top ten recipients behind groups like the World Health Organization and UNICEF USA.[28]

But New Venture is not the full extent of the Arabella corporate ecosystem. It has three sister groups that also consolidate the foundations' money and funnel much of it to the for-profit Arabella. These include the Hopewell Fund and the Windward Fund, but most significant is the Sixteen Thirty Fund, which as a 501(c)(4) is permitted to engage in outright political activism. Sixteen Thirty was started in 2009 with seed money from the Association of Community Organizations for Reform Now (ACORN). Between 2015 and 2019, the four Arabella groups raised an astonishing $2.7 billion in all.[29]

New Venture Fund and its three sister groups pay the for-profit Arabella Advisors to "manage" them, but in effect, they do not exist; they are run out of Arabella's offices. Their real function is to create a third layer—hundreds of "pop-up" activist groups—that operate as "projects" of the parent group. Overnight, groups with names like "Allied Progress" can be created from nothing, and through Arabella's political expertise and resources will appear to represent a major coalition. In reality, they are "astroturf" front groups.[30]

This structure ensures that the public-facing groups are not incorporated in any way, limiting their financial disclosure. The four shell funds "managed by Arabella Advisors" provide a convenient loophole around restrictions on political activity: when aspects of a front group's work cross the line into undeniable politicking, the New Venture hat comes off and the Sixteen Thirty hat comes on.

Kessler's creation was rolling in so much dough that in 2020, not only did New Venture and Sixteen Thirty spend more than $1 million each on lobbying Congress—their in-house lobbyist also won $1 million off a scratch-off lottery ticket.[31]

MEDIA

Arabella embraced the caricature of dark-money boogeyman. Invoking the tendency of political groups to name themselves using opaque acronyms, it created one group that was called simply "Acronym." Beneath Acronym it created a group called Shadow Inc. Acronym was used to create another firm, Courier Newsroom, which set up would-be news websites to meddle in local politics across America.[32]

When people in, say, North Dakota started hearing about local politics, they were reading from a deliberately slanted news outlet called *That's Just North Dakota*, which was one of dozens of online "news" outlets spawned by Arabella's digital media empire. Over a two-year period, Acronym affiliates spent nearly $10 million on digital ads to place articles in the social media feeds of people in the regions targeted. They included purported news sites like *Sounds Like Tennessee*, *Colorado Chronicle*, and *Nevada News Now*.[33]

These sites exploited the void in local journalism created by the collapse of the traditional newspaper model. While none of these sites was especially high-traffic, they were sometimes among the *only* online sources of information about local political races. In Montgomery County, Maryland, a father named Stephen Austin decided to run for school board in 2020 to stop the busing plan being pushed by activist groups. A Facebook group he started quickly amassed eight thousand supporters. But the momentum reversed course when a website called *Maryland Matters* ran a piece written by activists demonizing Austin, a college art major who is married to an immigrant and grew up on food stamps, as a right-wing extremist.[34]

As if an invisible trigger were pulled, higher-level politicians, such as the majority leader of the Maryland House of Delegates, began blasting out links to the site, and other officials who opposed Austin penned a letter published by the site. Austin lost the election. *Maryland Matters* is yet another part of the Arabella network, organized under a group called "States Newsroom" that was seeded with $1 million from the Wyss Foundation in 2019.[35]

GOVERNMENT

Many of the teachers who worked to make race a constant focus of children, you will recall, received "Teacher of the Year" awards for their efforts. The National Network of State Teachers of the Year was a project of the New Venture Fund, funded with millions of dollars from the Gates Foundation. Katherine Bassett, until recently the network's executive director, was a New Venture Fund employee as well as a board member of the National Association of State Directors of Teacher Education & Certification.[36]

One of the teacher of the year group's main missions is pushing the work of race consultant Glenn Singleton, whose "Courageous Conversations" sessions are behind much of the takeover of schools. The program directs teachers to read Singleton's materials and has a video series titled "Courageous Conversations About Race in Schools." In one of the videos, "2015 Minnesota State Teacher of the Year Tom Rademacher shares a dream that he hopes every school he works in has a culture where it is more uncomfortable not to talk about race than to talk about race," it says. The group asks viewers to discuss: "What is 'whiteness' doing to our schools?"[37]

New Venture Fund has the money and connections to buy government. It paid for the federal government to create an official body called the "Equity and Excellence Commission," which the Department of Education said would "examine the disparities in meaningful educational opportunities that give rise to the achievement gap, with a focus on systems of finance, and recommend appropriate ways in which Federal policies could address such disparities." The commission was authorized thanks to U.S. representative Chaka Fattah (D-PA), who was later sentenced to ten years in prison for an unrelated scheme in which he directed federal money to a fake nonprofit, stole from an education nonprofit, used campaign funds to pay for his jailed son's college debts, and accepted bribes.[38]

The Equity and Excellence Commission pushed the federal government to exert power over local school districts to promote a return to busing. "The commission recommends that the federal government do the following: Develop policies that give states and school districts incentives to pursue legal and feasible means to promote racially and socioeconomically diverse schools," it said. More significantly, it sought to consolidate local governments into larger metropolitan entities. "Regionalization can broaden districts' tax bases and support funding equity, leading to higher student achievement. . . . [O]ur traditional localism remains so strong that it is now, on balance, an obstacle to efficient, equitable, excellent education."[39]

COLLUSION

Most people seeking influence would strive for one large group, with as much name recognition as possible, not hundreds of seemingly disconnected, smaller ones. But the foundations have deployed this technique before in order to hide their outsize power and manufacture the illusion of organic consensus around an issue where there was none.

In the lead-up and follow-up to the McCain-Feingold Act of 2002, which reformed campaign finance law—an area most Americans do not particularly pay attention to—almost $140 million was spent on lobbying over a ten-year period, and nearly 90 percent of that total came from eight foundations. These included Carnegie, Soros, and Ford. Coordinating the effort was the Pew Charitable Trusts. Pew paid experts, propped up fake affinity groups, and flooded the media though a mind-numbingly complex array of entities. After it was over, a former Pew official, Sean Treglia, was caught on video describing the plot.[40]

"Now that I'm several months away from Pew and we have campaign finance reform, I can tell this story," he said. "The idea was to create an impression that a mass movement was afoot—that everywhere they looked, in academic institutions, in the business community, in religious groups, in ethnic groups, everywhere, people were talking about reform." The various nonprofits that received funds were instructed never to mention Pew. "If any reporter wanted to know, they could have sat down and connected the dots," Treglia boasted. "But they didn't."

It was not just the particular methods of foundations that have remained the same over many years.

In the early 1900s, John Harvey Kellogg wrote that "the intellectual inferiority of the negro male to the European male is universally acknowledged," and that he was also concerned with restraining the achievements of Asians, saying, "If we don't deal with this, we're going to be ruled by 'orientals' in the future."[41]

As you will see, more than a hundred years later, the substance of their beliefs appeared similar, too.

GENIUS

For nearly half of the twentieth century, the country was gripped by an epidemic. By the late 1940s, poliovirus had disabled or paralyzed more than thirty-five thousand Americans a year, especially targeting children. It struck each summer, forcing movie theaters to close, playgrounds to empty, and quarantines to be enforced. All of this changed when, in 1955, Dr. Jonas Salk developed a vaccine that nearly eradicated the disease worldwide.[1]

Salk, the son of Russian immigrants, got his start at Townsend Harris High School, a school for the gifted in New York City that his biographer called "a launching pad for the talented sons of immigrant parents who lacked the money—and pedigree—to attend a top private school." It was not for everyone: its motto was "study, study, study," and most dropped or flunked out.[2] Luckily for the world, Salk was a genius, and the school pushed him to his potential. The same could be said for most of the advances that have made modern life comfortable for the average person: they came about thanks to a handful of people who were anything but average.

New York City's genius incubators had changed little since Salk's day. Stuyvesant High School, the city's most famous magnet school, produced alumni who pioneered string theory, along with former attorney general Eric Holder.[3] Magnet schools offered a free, top-flight education to the city's most promising students, whether they came from the Upper East Side or the Bronx. But to be accepted, a student had to demonstrate the aptitude to succeed there, and be the rare teenager who wanted to study around the clock in a high-pressure, competitive atmosphere.

Aptitude was measured in a similarly egalitarian way: via the Specialized High School Admissions Test (SHSAT). The straightforward, objective measure ensured that parents with elite society connections, who craved the prestige of having a child admitted, could not do so by invoking political favors.

It worked. Stuyvesant was nothing like New York's expensive private academies. In 2018, more than 80 percent of its students were either immigrants or the children of immigrants, from more than fifty countries. More lived in Queens than in Manhattan. Based on 2018–19 school year enrollment, 44 percent were "economically disadvantaged," and only 19 percent were white. Forty-two students were, in an incredible testament to the human spirit, homeless.[4]

Here was a school in which merit could trump privilege. That contradicted what the equity industrial complex was teaching to children.

So it had to be destroyed.

In June 2018, the city's Democratic mayor, Bill de Blasio, announced a plan to eliminate the SHSAT. "For thousands and thousands of students and neighborhoods all over New York City, the message has been these specialized schools aren't for you," he said. "So, the solution is simple: the test has to go."[5]

The problem was that nearly three-quarters of Stuyvesant students were classified as Asian or Pacific Islanders, including the children of people who came to this country with nothing but the audacity to succeed through hard work. "I just don't buy into the narrative that any one ethnic group owns admission to these schools," de Blasio's schools chancellor, Richard Carranza, said a few days later.[6]

The mayor's alternative plan would guarantee admission to the top 7 percent of students from every middle school in the city—even though at forty-eight schools less than that percentage were even "proficient," or at grade level, based on the standard statewide eighth-grade math exam. In fact, fourteen city middle schools did not have a single student who was proficient in math. The data also revealed that in 165 schools less than 7 percent of students were able to "excel," even by the standards of the relatively easy grade-level competency exam.[7] Either these students would fail out, leading to more cries of unfairness, or the school would become Stuyvesant in name only.

De Blasio and Carranza seemed determined to destroy this beacon of meritocracy and objectivity at all costs. For years, the refrain was that minorities could not make it to take the SHSAT on a weekend. But when the city began to loosen several requirements to increase diversity in 2016, including offering the test during the week, even fewer black students took it.[8]

They also claimed that Asians were buying their way in with expensive test-prep courses. But, as it turns out, Asians had the highest poverty rate in New York City in 2017, and both the city and nonprofit organizations offered free test preparation. Moreover, the test simply measured skills that students were supposed to have learned in middle school.[9] If it was possible to learn how to solve math problems in a few weekend courses, how come schools couldn't do the same during months of classes?

Next was the claim that standardized testing inherently favored some races over others. Kirkland, the NYU professor, was appointed to a city task force on school diversity and said that it was "culturally biased." For the SHSAT, the math section consisted of questions like "Mr. Jones has 550 goats, which is 10% more than Mr. King has. How many more goats does Mr. Jones have than Mr. King?" A typical question in the reading section asked students where the comma should go in the sentence: "In 1962 the agile athletic Wilt Chamberlain became the first and only professional basketball player in the United States to score 100 points in a single game."[10] Neither Dr. Kirkland nor any other standardized testing detractor could explain how a test on English comprehension was biased in favor of people whose native tongues were Asian languages, or how asking children to do multiplication was an unfair way to determine whether they were good at math.

The purported bias did not prevent New York's top officials from choosing the schools for their own kids, nor did it keep the kids from getting in. Carranza's daughter, who is Hispanic, had attended the prestigious Lowell High School, San Francisco's version of Stuyvesant. De Blasio's son, whose mother is black, went to Brooklyn Tech, an SHSAT school. The SHSAT's long history also proved inconvenient. In the 1970s and 1980s, blacks and Hispanics took the same test and comprised a much larger share of specialized schools' student bodies than today.[11] So if racism is the cause of low SHSAT scores, is society more racist now than it was forty or fifty years ago?

Carranza made a new excuse in 2018: the exam "is not necessarily valid or reliable in terms of identifying student competencies to be successful in the specialized high school environment." This was a lie. The city had paid for and received a major study to answer that exact question in 2013, but concealed the report for more than five years when it did not like the findings. The study analyzed the subsequent academic careers of students who had taken the SHSAT and found a "strong positive [predictive] relationship" with long-term grades and other test scores, even after controlling for various factors. In other words, those who did not score well on the SHSAT were unlikely to have succeeded at a specialized school.[12]

Not even the fact that killing the SHSAT would be illegal seemed to especially trouble Carranza. State law specified that "admissions to The Bronx High School of Science, Stuyvesant High School and Brooklyn Technical High School and such similar further special high schools which may be established shall be solely and exclusively by taking a competitive, objective and scholastic achievement examination."[13]

ASIANS

In the United States, more than a quarter of Asian American children who grew up in a household with an income in the bottom fifth rose to the top fifth by adulthood. This realization of the American dream was not limited to those of one skin color: in 2019, Americans with ancestry from Ghana had an estimated median household income of $69,000, which was nearly the same as white households. Women with ancestry from Nigeria who worked full-time had an estimated median income of about $52,000, compared to $45,600 for white women.[14] Was it possible that racists were holding back black Americans but exempting African females and other immigrants? This seemed to be the position of the nation's largest school district. To press its point, it mobilized against the parents who funded it.

Carranza paid about $400,000 to a Kellogg Foundation–backed activist group called the Center for Racial Justice in Education, which gave a presentation to parents in 2019 that drew a racial hierarchy with blacks at the bottom and whites at the top. Hispanics were apparently in the middle. Asians were omitted entirely, but when questioned, a presenter explained they had "proximity to white privilege." In October 2018, parents at an education forum in Queens used public input time to support the test. When the group's leader, Lucy Accardo, stepped out to use the restroom, a de Blasio official blocked her from returning to the stage, ordering, "End it. We don't need to hear no more comments." When the school system held a meeting on related issues in Chinatown in July 2019, it provided a Spanish translator, but not a Chinese one. In February 2020, several Asians and whites were blocked from entering a town hall with Carranza. Video showed blacks being allowed in, while Asians and whites were restrained by a police officer as a white man shouted, "We have a right to this meeting!"[15]

Carranza and de Blasio were not wrong to see a race issue in the New York City schools. There were eight "specialized schools" like Stuyvesant, and in 2019, only about 11 percent of admissions offers went to black and Hispanic students. But New York's public schools housed more than one million students. The fewer than sixteen thousand students in specialized schools were a statistical blip.[16]

What made the racial makeup of Stuyvesant and the other specialty schools under an objective system intolerable to the mayor and his schools chancellor was that it spotlighted a much vaster problem.

For grades three to eight in 2018, only a quarter of black New York-ers were proficient in math, and nearly sixty-seven thousand Hispanics received the lowest possible score of Level One in math—or more than any other level by a margin of over twenty thousand students. In fact, the majority of all students were not proficient in math or English.

Carranza's bureaucracy had spent almost $28,000 per student in 2016.[17] Would he try to find a way to actually educate hundreds of thousands of the most at-risk students? Or would elite, well-paid lib-eral policy makers give up on them, concealing them behind a thin veneer of a tiny number of decent-performing tokens?

De Blasio appointed a School Diversity Advisory Group (SDAG), cochaired by Maya Wiley, who made $290,000 in 2017 as senior vice president for social justice at the New School. Wiley's connection to the underclass in New York's inner-city schools was tenuous. She has one white parent and one black parent, owns a $3 million home in a neighborhood patrolled by private security, married a white man, and sent her daughter to private school. To empathize with her mi-nority audiences, she reached back more than thirty years to her time at Columbia Law School, when she was once pulled over by a police officer for a cracked taillight. She felt "panicked" because it was a white cop, she said. He gave her a warning, not a ticket.[18]

As cochair of the diversity panel, Wiley oversaw its roughly forty members, most connected to activist groups, such as Matt Gonzales, who referred to Asians as "white adjacent." In August 2019, this advi-sory group wrote, "There are low-income communities, especially in New York City, where families make significant sacrifices to fund test prep and children spend large amounts of time preparing and sacri-ficing other developmentally appropriate activities to gain admission and do so at an unnecessary cost. This is not equitable even if it is effective for some."[19]

MAYA WILEY

Of the radical activists of the 1960s and early 1970s, the most effec-tive might have been the little-known George Alvin Wiley. As head of the National Welfare Rights Organization (NWRO), he pushed as many people as he could to storm government offices and sign up for government assistance. Wiley organized "mass demonstrations of several thousand welfare recipients," occasionally leading to "rock throwing, smashed glass doors, overturned desks, scattered papers and ripped-out phones," according to the *New York Times*.[20]

Wiley was a black man who grew up middle class in Rhode Island before earning a PhD in organic chemistry from Cornell University. He was radicalized by his wife, a white woman who picked up her political leanings in college, and he began sporting a dashiki and speaking on behalf of poor single mothers. "I think most activists basically come out of middle-class backgrounds . . . and were oriented toward people having to work, and that we have to get as many people as possible off the welfare rolls," he said. Instead, Wiley wanted more people on welfare.[21]

At the time, New York's liberal mayor, John Lindsay, tried to appease Wiley's group, and was met with further demands. After a woman yelled at him, "It's my job to have kids, Mr. Mayor, and your job to take care of them," Lindsay appointed as welfare commissioner a Columbia University dean with close ties to welfare rights activists. The commissioner loosened fraud screenings, and annual welfare expenditures more than doubled to $1 billion, which overloaded the city and led to its insolvency in 1975.[22]

This was not a setback for Wiley. His goal was laid out by two others involved with the NWRO, white Columbia professors Richard Cloward and Frances Piven. In a 1966 article in the *Nation*, they wrote that activists could use the ensuing "profound financial and political crisis" to trigger "major economic reforms at the national level." Therefore, the plan was not to help the needy, but to adopt a "flood-the-rolls, bankrupt-the-cities strategy."[23]

Several strategies were critical to Wiley's agenda. The first was that he managed to get the government to fund activism against itself. Federal programs, such as one known as Volunteers In Service To America (VISTA), gave grants for community organizing in impoverished areas, which essentially meant paying activists to lobby the local government for leftist programs. Second, such lobbying was not just aimed at persuading local governments, but at embedding activists inside them, where they could use taxpayer dollars to continue the campaign. Third, Wiley forced national change through the local level with a franchise structure similar to McDonald's, in which regional activist groups would spawn across the country following a common template. By 1970, one hundred thousand families who received welfare from the government sent a portion of their checks to one of three hundred local NWRO affiliates, which in turn sent money to the parent group.[24]

Wiley was ultimately unable to control the monster he had created. Increasingly radical members turned against him for his middle-class background. He quit and later perished in a sailing accident.[25]

Before he quit, Wiley hired a white college dropout from Arkansas named Wade Rathke, who applied Wiley's model to a new group, called ACORN. ACORN's U.S. operations were forced to shut down in 2010 after a criminal voter fraud investigation. But by then, its activists had mastered the art of dressing up their demands in vague and innocuous-sounding language and crossing into the mainstream. A dozen years after Rathke stormed the Citibank headquarters in 1992 by busting past security, Citibank was voluntarily giving ACORN contracts.[26]

Speaking for the impoverished was big business. Rathke's brother embezzled at least $1 million from ACORN, but remained on the payroll even after the organization knew of his theft. And Rathke cofounded the Tides Foundation, which received money from billionaires and forwarded it to radical groups at their behest through a system of "donor-advised funds." The intermediary "funds" obscured the paper trail connecting these billionaires to funding specific radical groups. This also positioned the Tides Foundation at the center of a constellation of nonprofits. Oftentimes, it let them serve as unincorporated "projects," essentially borrowing its 501(c)(3) IRS designation. It developed expertise in creating or grooming smaller organizations. And it took a cut of the money it handled.[27]

George Wiley's daughter, Maya Wiley, inherited a commanding role in this empire, where she wore many hats. From 1997 to 1999, George Soros, a major Tides donor, employed the younger Wiley as senior advisor of race and poverty at his Open Society Institute. By 2006, she served on the board of the Tides Center, which oversaw Tides "projects" and was chaired by Rathke. By 2011, she was chair and director of the board of the Tides Network, an umbrella group over its labyrinthine operations. That same year, the Tides Foundation and the Tides Center spent about $100 million each. In 2014, she was appointed counsel to Mayor de Blasio, triggering the *New York Times* headline "De Blasio Picks More Liberal Activists Than Managers for City Posts."[28]

In its August 2019 report, Wiley's SDAG panel concluded that the city's "screened" schools—schools less selective than "specialized" schools that nonetheless had admission requirements to cohort students so they could be taught content appropriate to their skill level and interests—should no longer admit students based on test scores or grades. In fact, they could not even consider truancy or discipline problems. For elementary schools, her panel advised to "[i]nstitute a moratorium on new Gifted & Talented programs, while phasing out existing programs." For middle schools, screens such as "grades, test scores, auditions, performance in interviews, behavior, lateness, and attendance" were frowned upon. Anything else would likely be considered racist.[29]

Few New Yorkers agreed with any of this logic, based on the results of a May 2020 survey of about one thousand parents from all five New York City boroughs. But as Maya Wiley sought to transform the way that New York City's 1.1 million schoolchildren were educated, she found that her father's old tricks still worked.[30]

GOVERNMENT-FUNDED LOBBYING

VISTA, the federal grants program that paid far-left activists during George Wiley's heyday, was still playing the same role fifty years later, only now under the name AmeriCorps VISTA.[31] It paid for Carranza's school system to hire adults to recruit children to agitate for changes mirroring those in Wiley's proposal. "VISTA will work hand in hand with inspiring youth leaders and their adult allies to support and build on two dynamic youth-led programs, Students and Educators for Equity (SEE) and Youth Restorative Justice (YRJ)," a job ad said.

One recruit wrote in 2020, "My name is Melody Castillo and I am a SEE Adult Partner and AmeriCorps VISTA. To me educational equity means dismantling oppressive institutions." At times, the "equity" they demanded seemed synonymous with Democratic partisanship. The children and adults mailed postcards through a group tied to Hillary Clinton that encouraged residents in swing states such as Georgia to vote in the 2020 election. SEE grew out of, and worked with, NYU's Metropolitan Center for Research on Equity and the Transformation of Schools, which employed activists on Wiley's panel.[32]

SEE appeared less interested in finding out students' opinions than in telling them what to think. It conducted a survey that asked: "Research tells us that disproportionality (black and brown children are more likely to be disciplined than their counterparts) and glaring opportunity gaps exists [sic] in New York City schools and nationwide. Knowing this, what does it feel like to be *you* in school? Consider what it means to be YOU, in other words, your race." The group's website states, "Disproportionality is the outcome of institutionalized racism and bias that result in discriminatory beliefs, policies, and practices." Children, steered by activist adults, went on to become a large and vocal contingent supporting the abolition of the SHSAT.[33]

Activists also embedded into the offices that controlled curriculum and teacher training. Under Mayor de Blasio, the cost of the school district's midlevel bureaucracy had more than doubled to $351 million by 2020. This consisted of people like Jeremy Chan-Kraushar and Toni Gold, directors of implicit bias and culturally responsive education, and Dru Collins, a director for educational equity. Normally, staff simply implements policies approved by boards and leaders. But equity staff functions differently: it pushes its bosses to embrace increasingly radical policies. In June 2020, Chan-Kraushar wondered about how to "demand [that individuals] with the most power craft policy that entirely reimagines a system that so blatantly caters to those with privilege and means."[34]

In essence, government was lobbying the people. A July 2018 column appeared in the newspaper *Crain's New York Business* under the byline of nine Asian American graduates of specialized schools, urging Asian Americans not to oppose SHSAT reform. It parroted the language of the school system's equity bureaucracy almost verbatim, faulting "implicit bias, stereotypes, inequitable school funding, culturally irrelevant curricula and disciplinary disparities." An editor's note acknowledged that Chan-Kraushar, who was not listed as an author, had made "contributions" to the piece.[35]

The activists inside government were coordinating with activist groups outside it. In May 2020, Carranza wrote to parents regarding the proposal to do away with screened schools: "We have not yet made any decisions on this policy, and will not do so without hearing first from you." But these opportunities for officials to weigh the sentiments of regular people were merely a charade.[36]

Miriam Nunberg, cochair of the activist group New York City Alliance for School Integration and Desegregation, let slip in an email that Carranza's Department of Education was steering groups like hers to drown out dissenting parents. A few minutes later she sent a second email asking "not to forward the full text of the email I sent, since it has come to my attention that it might be problematic for word to get out that the [New York City] DOE is encouraging folks to make noise," she wrote. "We don't want this to backfire on us." Nunberg is a white lawyer who makes her living as an "educational equity" consultant. Her own son attends a selective screened school.[37]

Inside the bureaucracy, equity staff purged colleagues who did not comply. While Carranza was telling the public in 2019 that he wanted "Equity and Excellence," Leslie Chislett, a sixty-year-old white woman who oversaw the district's advanced academics program, said that all DOE employees were subjected to racial training sessions where they were taught that "excellence" is actually a by-product of "white supremacy." Officials with the DOE's Office of Equity and Access stood up one by one to excoriate Chislett, saying that they were protecting children from people like her, according to a lawsuit. This logic did not improve the productivity of the workplace. When Chislett asked a subordinate why she missed a meeting, the employee allegedly replied, "How dare you approach me out of your white privilege."[38]

Yet this kind of thing had become more important than educating. Days after Carranza told the city council that if he had to trim the budget, he would increase class sizes and postpone treating schools for rats, Paul Forbes, the executive director for educational equity, anti-bias, and diversity, revealed that mandatory "Implicit Bias" training for teachers would continue, at a cost of $23 million. "The work won't stop . . . can't stop!" he wrote.[39]

Implicit bias is a favorite concept of consultants because it is unfalsifiable. Even if observable racism is on the decline, and even if the accused were liberal New Yorkers who chose to dedicate their lives to helping urban youth, invisible racism could be revealed by a modern-day Ouija board. In schools, the premise appeared to be that black children were already well behaved and well educated, but teachers, because of racism, made them out to seem worse than they were—even though this would amount to teachers making themselves look worse at their job.

Implicit bias was made famous by Harvard academic Mahzarin Banaji and psychologist Anthony Greenwald, who created a test they said could show it. In a bestselling 2013 mass-market book, they wrote that their method "has been shown, reliably and repeatedly, to predict discriminatory behavior." Deep in academic journals, meanwhile, they had conceded to their peers in 2009 that, at best, the connection between their implicit bias scores and discriminatory behavior was only 5.5 percent. On top of that, some of the test's leading critics argued that the research relied on questionable methods.[40]

On these tests, if a white person got a score that suggested he favored whites, this was a sign of racism. But if his score suggested that he favored blacks, that counted as anti-black implicit bias, too, on the suspicion that he must be overcompensating. A 2012 study found that taking the test actually stoked racial tensions in minorities.

Patrick Forscher, a scientist who conducted a major review of literature on the topic alongside one of Banaji's own Harvard colleagues, assessed, "We cannot claim that implicit bias is a useful target of intervention . . . the desire to do something, anything, to solve problems related to race has led some people to jump to conclusions."

As Carranza and Forbes prioritized junk science over small class sizes and rat-free schools, in December 2019, the deputy chief of staff responsible for spearheading Carranza's equity agenda at the highest level, David Hay, was charged with soliciting sex from a minor. There were red flags in his past, but the city had not completed a full background check before hiring him.[41]

NEVER LET A CRISIS GO TO WASTE

When the coronavirus hit in early 2020, it struck America's most densely populated large city hard. By the end of May, nearly eighteen thousand New Yorkers had been confirmed dead.[42] And Wiley saw the missing ingredient in her father's recipe for radical transformation of society: a crisis.

School chancellor Carranza noticed, too. "Never waste a good crisis to transform a system," he said. "We see this as an opportunity to finally push and move and be very strategic in a very aggressive way [for] what we know is the equity agenda for our kids."[43]

Because of the coronavirus, the city closed schools to in-person learning in March, asking students to log onto computers from home for online instruction. Many of the city's most vulnerable students simply dropped off the grid. Attendance for remote learning was as low as 18 percent. Academic mastery was abysmal. At one Brooklyn high school, up to 71 percent were failing.[44]

New Yorkers knew who remote learning would harm most: poor and minority children who in some cases had only one parent and many siblings.[45] They wondered what was so "equitable" about this.

But that is because they were confusing equity with fairness or equality. Equity, a term essentially cooked up by educators, has a specific meaning: statistically equal outcomes by race on paper—without changing the behavior of any actual students. It means lowering standards and tampering with measurements to make educators look better, and replacing rigorous education with political ideas.

And under coronavirus, the equity agenda could be implemented at scale.

Many New York students, especially minorities, had always been failing, but now that the failure rate climbed even higher under coronavirus, administrators could excise their worst statistics from the books. They used the opportunity to implement "standards-based assessments," the grading scheme long favored by progressive educators. Elementary and middle schoolers would no longer get letter grades, but rather marks like "meets standards" or "needs improvement." High school students were given the option to convert grades of D or higher to simply "pass."[46]

The state exams that, before the pandemic, showed that 90 percent of students in some schools had not mastered basic content were out the window—the outcome that teachers unions favored long before the coronavirus emerged.[47]

"My students can get away with doing virtually nothing," one teacher said. Administrators cheerfully called it "Operation Graduation."[48]

Attendance was eventually eliminated as a performance metric, solving the truancy problem.[49]

With no hallways to fight in, there would be no racial discipline disparity.

And, of course, gifted and talented programs could not screen students based on grades or test scores because those measures were gone, and the SHSAT test that was the legally required admissions criterion for specialized high schools was postponed indefinitely by the city's DOE.[50]

Philanthropic foundations funded hubs through which district administrators coordinated. Carranza sits on the board of a Gates Foundation–funded group called Council of the Great City Schools, through which urban school administrators share policies. Soon, cities like San Francisco, whose superintendent was also part of this group, were doing away with the test for their prestigious magnet schools.[51]

In San Francisco, where the Lowell magnet high school was one of the few bright spots in a bleak academic landscape, parent Todd

David remarked, "They're using the pandemic as a catalyst to do this. . . . This is the beginning of the end of Lowell High School as we know it."[52]

A school board member there, Alison Collins, said via Twitter in October 2020 that "admissions changes are being considered based on logistics (SFUSD doesn't have grades or tests [sic] scores as we did in previous years due to COVID-19)." But in the same thread minutes later, she let the truth slip. "'Merit' is an inherently racist construct designed and centered on white supremacist framing," she wrote.[53]

Once you realized that the changes educators claimed were necessary because of coronavirus were the same ones that they had already wanted to ram through, it was clear that they intended them to be permanent.

"We are just not going to bring New York City back to the status quo," de Blasio said. "We're going to try to create a series of changes that bring equity."[54]

Equity meant the same thing it had always meant. Not a world that embraced diversity, but one in which everyone was identical: equally failing. As New York's large cohort of students who could not read or do basic math fell even further behind, there would be no paper trail to document it. On the spreadsheets by which educrats were judged, everyone would be indistinguishable.

CENTER FOR POPULAR DEMOCRACY

As the 2019–20 school year ended, Wiley's agenda remained unpopular with parents. The May 2020 survey of about one thousand parents from all five New York City boroughs found that 92 percent of parents were reluctant to embrace the changes justified by the coronavirus, believing that these were being used as "cover" to create a "less fair" system. Meanwhile, evidence accumulated that schools did not appear to spread coronavirus, that people were still congregating for higher-risk activities, and that "remote learning" was an utter failure. Pressure mounted to open schools.[55]

New York's screened schools had not yet been permanently abolished.

The "crisis" that activists intended to capitalize on had apparently still not reached its boiling point. But through Wiley's network of franchised nonprofits across the country, she had the infrastructure to turn up the heat.

In August, teachers nationwide spilled into the streets with militant rhetoric in a "National Day of Resistance," insisting that schools would not open in the fall unless their aggressive demands were met. The protests were organized by a group called Demand Safe Schools, which said it was an umbrella organization that brought together the Democratic Socialists of America and local teachers unions from twenty cities and states ranging from Los Angeles to the state of Massachusetts to Little Rock, Arkansas. Though their name seemed to invoke the coronavirus, their concerns about "safety" were largely unrelated. One demand was for "Police-Free Schools." Another one sounded like a threat: "Equity Or Else."[56]

Demand Safe Schools' website pictured large numbers of kids attending its protests, some without face masks, and pumping their fists. The picture was accompanied by a petition and the following text: "Trump Uses Excessive Force to Re-Open Schools: Parents, Communities and Teachers RESIST!"[57]

Under "Demands" the group wrote, "No reopening until the scientific data supports it," even though the Centers for Disease Control had already said that the data supported it. Overall, the message was merely a smoke screen for its real demands: a "moratorium on new charter or voucher programs and standardized testing" to please the teachers, and "taxing the billionaires and Wall Street" to make the socialists happy. They eventually extended this to "Cancel rent and foreclosures."[58]

By bolting on generic far-left causes to what was otherwise a teachers union job negotiation, the movement had real people advocating for something other than their own self-interest. The teachers unions, in turn, provided the socialists with an organized machine. Providing emotional resonance was the constituency that the teachers themselves had created: students whom they had subjected to daily lectures about oppression, who eagerly turned out to support the demands for equity.

In the name of "democratic socialism," teachers were willing to do what they would not for the cause of education: gather with students. At the same time, teachers used their students as both hostages and props.

As it turns out, there was no nonprofit by the name "Demand Safe Schools." It was effectively a front for the Center for Popular Democracy (CPD), a group that previously counted Maya Wiley and Randi Weingarten, the powerful president of the AFT, as directors. CPD's co-executive director is Brian Kettenring, a former employee of ACORN. Some ACORN chapters orphaned by the group's dissolution as it pleaded guilty to felony voter fraud were adopted by CPD, which also partners with labor unions, who have their own local affiliates.[59]

There are two national teachers unions in America, and their 2020 membership numbers were strong: the NEA, with just under 3 million members, and the AFT, with 1.7 million. Through their involvement with CPD, they converged. Each union has contributed millions of dollars to CPD since 2010.[60]

More came from the foundations that orbited Wiley's world. In recent years, CPD and its "action fund" have received nearly $18 million from the Ford Foundation, more than $5 million from George Soros, and additional money from the Surdna and Kellogg foundations, at least two Tides Foundation groups, and Arabella's Sixteen Thirty Fund.[61]

In 2018 it raised $37 million, but even this understates it. Separately drawing from the same funding sources were local CPD affiliates across the country. For example, there were Make the Road New Jersey, Make the Road Pennsylvania, Make the Road New York, and Make the Road Connecticut. There was the New Florida Majority and an accompanying "Education Fund," and nearly identical structured groups with the word *Virginia* instead of *Florida*. While CPD officials worked against the interests of Asian Americans in New York, the New Virginia Majority or its Education Fund received millions of dollars from Arabella's New Venture Fund, the

Ford Foundation, CPD, and Soros, much of it aimed at getting Asian Americans to vote for "the progressive transformation of Virginia."[62]

That was only the beginning of a dizzying array of pressure groups in which the same players wore multiple hats. In 2002, Soros and Tides incubated a Wiley-led group called the Center for Social Inclusion.[63] Like CPD, it operated through unincorporated public-facing fronts called "projects." Its most public face was the Government Alliance on Race and Equity (GARE), which, as you will see, managed to bring the radical policies of New York City to leafy suburbs across the country.

14

ONE FAIRFAX

In 2014, at a conference on equity in Portland, Oregon, representatives of Maya Wiley's Government Alliance on Race and Equity (GARE) approached Karla Bruce, a midlevel bureaucrat from affluent Fairfax County, Virginia, who was in attendance. GARE taught Bruce how to cajole her mostly center-left elected bosses into enacting far-left policies. Years later, she recalled how the concept of government policies based on "disproportionality" would have been "politically difficult" to sell. Bruce had learned, following her GARE collaboration, that calling the concept "equity" made it easier to get "elected officials on board."[1]

This was not just offhand advice, but the result of psychological experiments done by GARE's parent nonprofit in how to manipulate language to "garner support for progressive policy." The Ford, Soros, and Kellogg foundations paid to hire corporate research firms Westen Strategies, the Analyst Institute, Lake Research Partners, and Pacific Market Research to discover how to mask radical agendas for moderate audiences. Study participants turned a dial up and down to record their reactions to different phrases and words.

This showed them that repeating the word *equity*, which few listeners could define but which sounded innocent enough, worked.

Bruce not only got officials "on board," but also talked them into creating an entirely new and higher-paid job for herself: chief equity officer. From there, many more of GARE's ideas could be deployed, with the full resources of the government behind them. Bruce would implement GARE-influenced policies that racialized every aspect of government and pulled it far to the left, without constituents even realizing it.[2]

Average citizens who approached local government officials with a suggestion or request would be lucky to get a thoughtful reply. Yet a partisan, out-of-state group had managed to transform the entire apparatus to do its bidding.[3] This did not happen by accident. Fairfax was the deliberate target of an aggressive, multiyear operation by massively well-funded and savvy outside activists.

Ever since 2012, the Center for the Study of Social Policy (CSSP), which is funded by the Ford and Casey foundations, had carefully analyzed the power structures of Fairfax, studying both how to influence county decision makers and how to repeat the same playbook in other counties.[4]

Its 2018 write-up of what it learned told the story: "[A Fairfax manager], Bruce, and others returned from the GARE Conference with the idea for establishing visible leadership, perhaps through a resolution or policy." There was only one pesky afterthought left for the unelected staffers to accomplish: "Now they had to build popular and official support."[5]

PolicyLink, a partisan activist group that pushes policies such as a federal job guarantee and slavery reparations and which is a "partner" of GARE, got to work strategically taking over nodes of influence. In 2015, Karen Cleveland, the CEO of a nonprofit called Leadership Fairfax that trains people to lead local community groups like civic associations and charities, signed and began to push a seventy-three-page report written by PolicyLink and the University of Southern California.[6]

By influencing Leadership Fairfax, PolicyLink and GARE tapped into a force multiplier that cascaded their influence to its numerous trainees, who were the type of people likely to speak to county officials, as well as to the groups they led. GARE later gave a grant to Leadership Fairfax.[7]

Cleveland presented the report to county officials, giving it an organic feel. It was not every day that a major university did an entire study on one county, so this was surely valuable data. "PolicyLink and . . . the University of Southern California studied the economic impact of inequity in Fairfax County," county officials gushed. "[The study] found that the county's gross domestic product would have been $26.2 billion higher in 2012 if its racial gaps in income were closed."[8]

After relying on the study's findings and engaging in "work behind the scenes," GARE and PolicyLink helped push through a policy called "One Fairfax" by November 2017. It was the most far-reaching policy measure ever passed in the county—not only covering both the county government and its separate school system, but controlling every subsequent policy that each passed. Every other policy, however unrelated, would have to be seen through "an equity lens." The policy is four pages long and uses the words *race(s)/racial/racism* a total of twelve times and *equity* twenty-four times. A "racial and social equity resolution" that preceded the policy reads as follows: "'One Fairfax' can only be realized with an intentional racial and social equity policy at its core for all publicly delivered services." This was another highly effective power play. Most things that took place in government were limited to a single department. But this gave Bruce's new bureaucracy power over the actions of *every* department.[9]

Though influence peddlers like Cleveland were powerful in the sleepy world of county politics, they were not household names. Few Fairfax residents knew or cared who they were or what they were doing, and the policy passed with little public input or interest. After the adoption of the resolution in July 2016, a local newspaper editorial—in one of the few examples of contemporaneous coverage— scoffed at One Fairfax not as dangerous, but as meaningless feel-good language, calling the measure "completely over the top with buzzwords, jargon and platitudes." Noting that it mandated "strategic actions to advance opportunities and achieve equity that includes intentional collective leadership, community engagement, equity tools and infrastructure to support and sustain systemic changes, and shared accountability," the paper asked: "Is that in English, or Klingon?"[10]

Once it was passed, the county had an obligation to enforce those buzzwords and platitudes. The problem was—no one knew what they meant. Almost no one, at least. PolicyLink seemed expert at interpreting them, and helpfully "began advising the county in formulating a vision for how best to enact the One Fairfax policy, and making the critical shift from policy adoption to implementation."

There are just a few problems with the way this played out. For one, all of these groups are generally composed of the same people. The study came from a USC-branded program called the Program for Environmental and Regional Equity (PERE, now called the Equity Research Institute), which is a research-for-hire activist group controlled by Manuel Pastor, who was at the time also a PolicyLink board member.[11]

The irresistible premise of the study—that the county's GDP would have been $26 billion higher in 2012 if no racial income gaps had existed—would not pass even as a high schooler's term paper. This conclusion appeared to merely assert the tautology that if all white people continued to earn the same amount of money, while racial groups who earn less began earning the same amount as whites, the county's economy would be that much larger.[12]

Though Fairfax parroted that "a racial and social equity policy provides both the direction and means to eliminate disparities," the paper had no suggestions for how to cause everyone in the county to begin earning white-collar wages, much less how to run a functional economy with no blue-collar workers, such as waiters or truck drivers. An economist with the Independent Institute, Richard Vedder, observed, "If this approach is valid, why don't we just say we want to triple the incomes of the minorities instead of double, and raise the GDP even more?"[13]

After Pastor's USC group had used the veneer of academic rigor to create a government requirement to do something, it fell to his radical partisan group, PolicyLink, to define for the bedazzled county government what that *something* was. The confusing language that Fairfax County officials had passed in 2017 was "Klingon" for something radical indeed. But with a bureaucracy under Bruce dedicated to implementing it and explaining it to them, they were unlikely to see it in those terms.

While Bruce may have completed the latter half of the task set out for her by CSSP—"Now they had to build popular and official support"—there still remained the issue of selling all this to the voters. Democrats on the school board insisted that One Fairfax required them to draw school boundaries based on the racial makeup of students, leading to results like busing. Given the county's expensive housing market, a change in school assignment could plunge a home's value by massive sums, taking out a family's life savings with it. And the county's own data showed that this would not produce the equal outcomes demanded by One Fairfax: in fact, the academic outcomes of disadvantaged students were constant at Fairfax schools of all demographic mixtures.[14]

None of this mattered, however, because the county had locked itself into a policy that it did not write, and which tied its hands on all other policies. "One Fairfax happened, and I'm superintendent, and I don't believe we've had a One Fairfax lens for the boundary process," Superintendent Scott Brabrand said in explaining why neither parents nor officials had any choice in this regard.

Outraged voters had only one option: replacing board members who enacted One Fairfax with ones who would repeal it. But because local media paid so little attention to the story, that was prevented easily enough with a less sophisticated strategy: a few easy lies.

In 2018, Jane Strauss, a school board member who represented areas most likely to face plummeting home values from the policy, such as a high school near the CIA compound called Langley, told her colleagues: "I've warned Langley, sorry"—she clucked and grinned—"a big chunk is going to get re-boundaried. I've already told them that." A colleague said: "If we don't make very clear that . . . equity and integration are a big part of what we do . . ." Strauss replied, "Right." If any Langley parents had been watching the meeting, they would have known she'd done no such thing. As the 2019 election neared, she lectured angry voters that "no one is pushing anyone out of the Langley [High] School area."[15]

Just a few weeks before the election, Superintendent Brabrand used the school system's mailing list to email every parent a video backing the Democratic school board members' latest message: that it was crazy to think they were planning on changing school boundaries based on demographics.[16] As easy as this was to disprove with other video clips of the same man's words, opponents had no access to the list of email addresses to correct the record. Here you can see the sleight of hand in the strategy used by equity practitioners: what begins as a handful of advocates lobbying government ends with the government spending taxpayer money to lobby its constituents.

Democrats swept the school board in 2019 by denying the effects of One Fairfax, but gloated on election night that the results signaled a mandate to double down on exactly that. With the nuisance of an election now past, the self-perpetuating operation could resume. Erika Bernabei, a former PolicyLink staffer and GARE trainer, had spun off her own for-profit consultancy, and in April 2020, Fairfax steered her an $87,000 contract for "county-wide equitable policy development under the One Fairfax initiative."[17]

Bernabei's contract was for ten months and her compensation included a two-day, in-person session at a cost of $4,000 per day, of which $2,000 were for training and the remaining $2,000 were paid for merely being on the road. In addition, Fairfax authorized at least $650 in travel expenses per trip. Once all of these costs were added up, they were multiplied by the number of hours assigned to the session. Therefore, the two-day trip with a total of two hours of training resulted in a payday of more than $17,000. Also, the contract called for a one-day trip with a more intense training schedule (six total hours). In this case, Bernabei's price tag for the trip ballooned to almost $40,000.

"We will co-develop performance frameworks for cross-agency Opportunity [sic] Communities of Opportunity efforts that roll up into a the [sic] larger strategic plan," her proposal said. "Using an understanding and role [sic] and impact to make sure that the agencies makes [*sic*] a difference in the lives of People of Color," Bernabei, who is white, continued.

That may have been Klingon for "give me some cash." But what her proposal lacked in substance and coherence it made up for with an endorsement from GARE, which described her as a "key partner." To avoid having to consider other bidders, Fairfax took the unusual move of making it a "rider" to a contract Bernabei already had with a school system across the country: King County in Washington State, whose county seat is Seattle.[18]

Bernabei said her work promotes the "anti-racist" principles of the People's Institute for Survival and Beyond, a group that "challeng[es] the urgent nature of capitalism," supports lessons and models "inspired by Saul Alinsky," and has trademarked the term "undoing racism."[19] One of these principles, which the group calls "Gatekeeping," calls for taking over institutions by targeting obscure levers of power.

"Persons who work in institutions often function as gatekeepers to ensure that the institution perpetuates itself," it says. "The gatekeeper becomes an agent of institutional transformation by operating with anti-racist values and networking with those who share those values and maintain accountability in the community."[20]

It was what GARE had done to Fairfax with Bruce.

THE MACHINE

This well-oiled machine, of course, did not invest this much time and energy to target just one suburban county. Fairfax County was a domino in a long line that GARE, PolicyLink, and their foundation backers were systematically knocking over across the country. "GARE gave Fairfax templates of what other municipalities had done; in a nice symmetry, Fairfax's policy is now used to help other cities develop their own policies," as CSSP put it.[21]

School districts are much like teenagers in that they incessantly copy each other. Small districts watch large, well-resourced ones and assume—often wrongly—that if they did something, it must have been for a good reason. Consultants advertise what other districts do as "best practices," based not on whether the policies worked but simply the fact that others are doing them. Fairfax and other similarly situated districts targeted by GARE were "bell cows"—a salesmen's term for the idea that if you sell an item to a prominent customer, others will buy it, too. The phrase is a metaphor for the way bovine dumbly follow each other around in a field and assume that whichever cow is wearing a bell is the leader.[22]

Even without counting secondhand victims, GARE's tentacles reached directly into an astonishing portion of America's local governments and trained them to implement radical policies. Since it has perfected the art of embedding in local governments regardless of the desires of constituents, no town is safe. GARE's conquests include Peoria, Illinois; the self-described "largely conservative, rural" county of Shasta, California; South Bend, Indiana; the city of Lawrence, Kansas; and the town of Brookline, Massachusetts, which is only 3 percent black.[23]

One PolicyLink initiative alone, called "All-In Cities," says that it is active in thirty-three areas with a combined population of more than twenty-eight million, or nearly one in twelve Americans.[24] As Fairfax created One Fairfax, Atlanta unveiled One Atlanta in 2018.[25] Milwaukee established the One Milwaukee Task Force in early 2020.[26] In Florida, Unite Pinellas went on a quest for the $3.6 billion that income inequality was costing the county, based on a PolicyLink report's findings.[27] In the Southwest, there was One Albuquerque, citing that "Albuquerque's economy would be [$11.1 billion] stronger with equity."[28] In the South, PolicyLink and the Casey Foundation created Southern Cities for Economic Inclusion in 2015, which focused on bringing similar policies to deep red states by operating at the local level.[29] And on and on throughout the nation.

Where this machine cannot identify nodes of influence, it creates them, funding new local-seeming boards that gain buy-in by offering prestigious seats to local officials. As PolicyLink named Buffalo one of its "All-In Cities," the Kellogg Foundation funded a nonprofit there, the Greater Buffalo Racial Equity Roundtable, whose members included philanthropists but also the mayor, a state lawmaker, a magistrate judge, and eventually the superintendent of schools.[30]

In 2018, it put out a report called "The Racial Equity Dividend: Buffalo's Great Opportunity." It was clear that it was not something Buffalo's mayor had come up with. The report cited PolicyLink and PERE and said, "Racial diversity has been shown to lead to better business performance . . . the region would be an estimated $12 billion wealthier." The report led to the city hiring a chief diversity officer who "sees part of her new job as incorporating the [Racial Equity Dividend] report's recommendations."[31]

MANUEL PASTOR

None of these eerie commonalities happened by accident. They are the dark-arts application of political science deployed with the goal of the partisan transformation of America by Manuel Pastor, the USC professor.

Pastor says bluntly that the recipe for influencing governments and obtaining the desired results is a single group simultaneously doing research, activism, and networking. "From region to region, organization to organization, we began to notice that the successful examples evidenced common themes of power analysis, leadership development, and community organizing," as he explained in his 2009 book, *This Could Be the Start of Something Big: How Social Movements for Regional Equity Are Reshaping Metropolitan America.*[32]

He said that political scientists refer to these actors as "policy entrepreneurs," and acknowledges that the latter push "policy solutions [that] are frequently a bit ahead of the research that might actually back them up."

A tenured full professor at a private university, Pastor is the kind of guy who boasted that he still paid his maid despite the coronavirus lockdown. He is also always plotting. In the early days of the coronavirus pandemic, he cowrote an article with another professor in which they concluded that the lockdown is "a once-in-a-generation moment to refashion our economic rules."[33]

Pastor represents the social science arm of the philanthropic foundations, laundering ideology into pseudo-academic papers, where they become the basis for legislation and policy. He has a staff of twenty working full-time toward this. "Our work will advance an understanding of, dialogue about, and funding towards building power among historically excluded communities by developing data-driven frameworks and tools for key learning and strategizing opportunities," he said.[34]

Pastor has received a fellowship from the Kellogg Foundation and grants from the Irvine, Rockefeller, Ford, and MacArthur foundations. He advises that it is "key for foundations and nonprofits to recognize that while good ideas, well-told stories, and solid research can contribute to change, the ultimate lever is power."[35] Everything he does is carefully calibrated toward that end.

In June 2020, Pastor recalled the day after Donald Trump won the 2016 election and tweeted: "I met with my devastated staff. I suspect that they were hoping for inspiration—but what I said was 'I think it will be worse than you think.'"[36] He had written numerous reports purporting to quantify various benefits of increased immigration, but as President Trump was about to take office, Pastor let slip what was perhaps his underlying motivation: Democrat votes.

"Every electoral season brings the high hope that this will be the year when Latinos will finally make a difference," he wrote. "The term 'sleeping giant' gets bandied around, with the hope that the wake-up occurs and that the results will be overwhelming for the good guys. . . . Applications for naturalization in the first half of 2016—which had historically been enough lead time to ensure citizenship and registration by November—were up about 30 percent above the first half of 2015."[37]

Though his work is funded by foundations, he is clear that the foundations' billions are not enough to transform America. The goal is to use it as seed money.[38] That is what happens when the groups persuade government to create their own equity departments, which in turn are filled by operatives from a remarkably tight network.

Under GARE's and PolicyLink's tutelage, Asheville, North Carolina, created a city office to apply an "equity lens to City departments." In July 2017, Asheville hired Kimberlee Archie as its "first
racial equity and inclusion leader." Archie made her living selling
equity consulting to governments, higher learning institutions, and
other groups. After studying community organizing in college, she
trained at the People's Institute for Survival and Beyond, worked for
the city of Seattle, and drew funding from the Casey Foundation.
The new office enables activists to spend their time influencing the
government of the small city, while taxpayers pay for it. Given the time,
money, and insider knowledge they had, this ensured that the activism
of those inside the government could easily overpower actions taken by
ordinary citizens. In July 2020, Asheville's city council unanimously
passed a "Resolution Supporting Community Reparations for Black
Asheville," egged on by its own staff.[39]

15

SOCIAL ENGINEERS

When Carol Silver needed groceries, she strapped her baby into his stroller, stepped out of her luxury townhouse in Hermosa Beach, where the median value of a home exceeds $1.5 million, and dodged the human feces that lined the sidewalk as she walked to the store. Hermosa Beach is a part of Los Angeles, America's most densely built region. There, alongside a trail used by children to come home from elementary school, a man set up a tent and began taking off his clothes and screaming about killing people.[1]

Parents quickly became desensitized. While a children's party took place in a park, about twenty addicts lay unconscious just steps away, blanketing the grass. "You truly don't know if they're dead or alive," Silver said. "Elsewhere you might call the police, but you come to a point where you kind of can't care, as horrific as that sounds. That was kind of my breaking point: I will not allow that to be my children's normal," she said.

In 2020, she left LA and moved to a North Carolina neighborhood with one-acre lots. She sat in her spacious kitchen and gazed out the window at her husband raking leaves and her son playing outside. "We wake up every day now to swans, to deer jumping into a lake," she said. None of this was about money. "We paid three times as much to live in debilitative Los Angeles."

Other moms gathered in the neighborhood to chat. Occasionally, vignettes of her old life in LA would come up in conversation. How men masturbated in the street, or how her husband's daily jogs included seeing a man stab a tree with a machete. Her new friends just stared at her blankly. It was so foreign that they could not imagine it.

But Silver's escape was not assured simply by leaving California. The foundations and zealots who were dismantling schools in the name of equity had similar plans for adults. Their goals included abolishing single-family housing zoning: the classic suburban neighborhoods of detached houses, gardens, and green expanses, minus the big crowds, grime, and traffic of high-rises interspersed. They sought a world where your next-door neighbor's house could be replaced with an apartment building. Every suburb, in other words, could become a city.

As with schools, this was the kind of policy that affected your life more than most things politicians generally talked about. A pleasant life in the suburbs was the ultimate inequity: it highlighted the failure of the cities and showed it was possible to live so much better. As with schools, social engineers' solution amounted to equalizing everyone by bringing down what worked.[2]

This is such a politically disastrous position that the media did not believe it could be true. After a speaker at the 2020 Republican National Convention said that Democrats "want to abolish the suburbs altogether by ending single-family home zoning," CNN published a "fact check." "This is false. Democrats are not seeking to abolish suburbs or end single-family home zoning. An Obama-era housing rule meant to address racial segregation does not abolish suburbs in any way."[3]

CNN appeared not to have checked then-presidential candidate Joe Biden's website. His housing platform said he would require any state, as a condition for receiving existing federal funding, "to develop a strategy for inclusionary zoning, as proposed in the HOME Act of 2019 by [House] Majority Whip [James] Clyburn and Senator

Cory Booker." As explained on Senator Booker's website, that bill would make towns' "surface transportation funding and community development block grants contingent on" the absence of policies such as "ordinances that ban apartment buildings from certain residential areas or set a minimum lot size for a single-family home."[4]

This would dramatically increase the population density of the suburbs in two ways. First, it would require jurisdictions to allow apartment buildings, townhouses, and duplexes (essentially traditional houses carved up into apartment units) to be built in the middle of any traditional suburban neighborhood. One of the most visible tasks of local government is zoning, through which some areas are set aside to isolate noisy industry; others are planned as neighborhoods of apartments and townhouses for those who want a walkable lifestyle; and still others are reserved exclusively for detached, single-family homes, where a quiet ambiance is guarded by rules that prevent real estate developers from erecting buildings for large numbers of people. But after this change, your home could soon be surrounded by townhouses or apartments whose activities would overshadow your private space.

Second, within the category of *single-family neighborhood*, localities had always established an assortment of aesthetics. Some neighborhoods had village feels, where houses sat only a few feet apart, adults could walk to stores, and children played in the street together. Other people preferred to trade longer drives for more spacious lots, where every yard in the neighborhood had to be at least a certain size—say, half an acre or an acre—and you might not see your neighbors at all unless you wanted to. Booker's bill would override local planning and set off a bonanza for real estate developers to subdivide lots to accommodate as many McMansions as could fit. The proposal stood to turn the various residential neighborhoods into a uniform blanket of undefined mush. It could become hard for the average family to buy a spacious lot, since it would have to compete with real estate developers who would be putting far more housing in the same space, and would therefore be willing to pay more.

Both components would significantly change the daily lives of suburban residents in ways that they did not sign up for. By tying it to federal funding, backers could make the pedantic claim that no one was forcing this. Indeed, zoning was so clearly a local concern that the federal government had no right to *require* such a thing whether it wanted to or not. But by making it a condition for federal funds, the effect was not much different: all but the richest of towns would likely be unable to turn down that money.

Though Biden's support for the HOME Act was indisputably a promise to end single-family-home-only zoning, it was only a portion of what he had in store for suburbs, and CNN apparently assumed that the "abolish the suburbs" remark was a reference to Biden's support for a slightly better-known initiative, the Department of Housing and Urban Development's Affirmatively Furthering Fair Housing (AFFH) rule, which posed a similar threat.

AFFH was enacted near the end of the Obama administration but was suspended before it got off the ground.[5] Under AFFH, unequal statistics automatically pointed toward racism. If fewer people of a certain race or ethnicity lived in a particular neighborhood, that implied the presence of racism, even if no one had done anything to discriminate against those individuals—and even if it was simply because they did not want to live there. It generally defined "segregation" as "a high concentration of persons according to protected class status regardless of the cause."[6] The rule effectively meant that every town had to take steps to attract roughly the same percentage of each race as the "region" at large to avoid "disparities in the jurisdiction's area." So, if a majority-black city were surrounded by small, whiter suburbs, the city's black residents would have to be spread among the towns, and some of the white suburbanites would have to be moved to the city.[7]

An early version of this took place in Dubuque, Iowa, in 2011. Dubuque had a waiting list of poor, elderly, and disabled residents who wanted to get into government-subsidized housing. As was to be expected given the demographics of the community, many were white. HUD said that Dubuque was in the same region as Chicago, which is about four hours away, and citing racial disparities, forced Dubuque to begin recruiting Chicago residents to apply for its vouchers, even if they had no connection to the state. By 2015, the percentage of subsidized housing residents in Dubuque who were black was greater than the percentage of Chicago residents who were black.[8]

AFFH did not apply only to subsidized housing; it applied to everyone. Of course, towns had no control over where people wanted to live, such as many blacks' preference for living in urban areas. The solution was that towns had to *become* cities by densifying. "Elevating communities out of segregation revitalizes the dignity of residents who felt suppressed under previous housing and zoning regimes," the AFFH final rule said. HUD's view implied that zoning laws that required single-family houses kept black people out. Further, because areas on septic systems necessitated low density, even municipal sewer lines could be considered a civil right, the rule suggested. "While zoning and land use are generally local matters . . . when local zoning or land use practices violate the Fair Housing Act or other Federal civil rights laws . . . they become a Federal concern," HUD said.[9]

The now-familiar network of foundations, academics, and activists pushed over the course of decades to turn suburbs into de facto urban areas, or outright consolidate them with the governments of nearby cities, on the premise of equity. They laid the groundwork secretly, with one of their most important leaders, onetime PolicyLink board member and University of Southern California professor Manuel Pastor, saying that they relied on what he called an "optimal level of fog" in which they used deliberately vague language. Some of the groups, he said, were "rooted in the relational organizing techniques laid down by Saul Alinsky and also implemented in other networks such as ACORN."[10]

One metropolis had already implemented many of these policies aimed at creating an equitable society where racism would be a thing of the past. The only problem was that, in 2020, it was on fire and at the center of the nation's race riots.

THE TWIN CITIES AND MYRON ORFIELD

In the early 1990s, Myron Orfield, a white lawyer who served as a Democratic Minnesota state legislator, began a quest to combine Minneapolis, St. Paul, and their suburbs into a single mega-jurisdiction in order to dilute cities' poverty by spreading it into the suburbs.

Minnesota had already implemented a novel revenue-sharing scheme that transferred a portion of suburbs' budgets to the cities. But Orfield saw that money was not working.[11] He came to believe that the best hope was to surround inner-city blacks with whites so that whites' behaviors would rub off on them. To do this, officials did not need big government in terms of spending; they needed government *geographically* big enough to move people around.

"Physical rehabilitation programs . . . cannot unravel the tangle of pathology," Orfield said. "In the social isolation of concentrated poverty, distinctive speech patterns develop, making interaction with mainstream society difficult and complicating education and job searches. An 'oppositional culture' emerges that appears to reject many closely held middle-class mores. . . . Tightly knit gangs replace nonexistent family structures. . . . Individuals who attempt to succeed through steady work at modest employment are often singled out and derided by communities where failure dominates. Ridiculed by peers, children can soon lose their desire to achieve academic success at school."[12]

He also saw that when a city enacted "equitable" policies, such as busing or high taxes, people often did not like them, and moved away to a nearby town. The solution that he came up with involved having a city absorb its suburbs into a mega-government.[13] This meant that residents could not so easily escape. The new government would particularly focus on changing land use policies to stop suburban "sprawl" and create an entire region that was more like the urban core: architecturally dense and with poverty spread throughout.

While in the legislature and in his later career as an activist professor, Orfield spent much of his time on a quest to bus schoolchildren. But efforts at solving problems through social engineering had a terrible track record, and if busing was a solution to uneven racial distribution, it was also a cause. Minneapolis began large-scale busing programs in the early 1970s to shrink the racial achievement gap. Over the next two decades the gap only grew wider, and whites moved out of the city to avoid the detested plan, leaving cities more heavily minority than ever. There simply were not enough white people to bus. By 1995, Minneapolis's black mayor, Sharon Sayles Belton, called for an end to busing, and the school board complied.[14]

In 2000, Minneapolis and its suburbs set up a voluntary metropolitan busing program where poor urban students could go to school in suburban districts if they wanted. But urban students who took part in the busing program scored worse on state exams than city kids who stayed in their neighborhoods.[15]

Orfield appeared to embrace the idea that social engineers simply needed greater power over people's lives in order for the same programs to work. As decades of evidence revealed that such policies only made things worse, he resorted to increasingly aggressive measures to get his way. He began publishing academic papers on purported "segregation" that earned him a reputation as a sloppy scholar who was not above brazenly manipulating data to achieve ideological goals.[16]

When Hopkins, Minnesota, closed a heavily minority school called Curren, he blasted the district for refusing to use the moment as an opportunity to engineer more diversity. He said that Hopkins sent the transplants to Eisenhower, another school that already had many minorities, instead of a school like Glen Lake, which he said was too white, because "vocal" Glen Lake parents "opposed an influx of minority students." An official in charge of the move said almost every element of Orfield's study was false: none of the Curren kids were moved to Eisenhower, and some *were* moved to Glen Lake. There was no evidence of racist parents. And the data that Orfield employed to show that schools were not diverse after the move actually *preceded* Curren's closure, making his analysis wrong even if he had gotten the schools right. When administrators in another district asked for corrections after Orfield subjected them to a similarly flawed treatment, they were repeatedly ignored.[17]

In a 2009 paper, Orfield proposed larger-scale, metropolitan-wide busing of up to twenty thousand students.[18] But what he really wanted was the abolition of local governments in order to allow for something akin to busing for adults.

For a politician, forcing suburbs to become more like a city by adding dense and low-income housing was one of the worst ideas imaginable. *Most* people across America—including majorities of blacks and new immigrants—chose to live in the suburbs. Between 2010 and 2017, more than 92 percent of population growth occurred in the suburbs—a clear sign that most Americans simply preferred the low-density lifestyle.[19] In a struggle between suburbs and cities, the suburbs would win every time.

But Orfield had a plan. Roughly one-third of people lived in the city, one-third lived in older suburbs, and one-third lived in newer suburbs. If he could pit older, relatively poorer suburbs against newer, more affluent ones, the math could work. He sounded the alarm on the urban pathology: "This cancer has broken the central-city membrane, and its early stages are established in the inner suburbs. Virtually every older metropolitan region in the United States has experienced what Minneapolis and Saint Paul are just discovering— left unchecked, the cancer spreads relentlessly outward from the city core."[20]

Few doctors would treat cancer by deliberately spreading it to more parts of the body, but that was Orfield's plan. After "constant cajoling," inner suburbs reluctantly agreed to side with the city and against the outer suburbs—not because they thought moving the urban poor was a good idea, but because it promised to move them to outer suburbs instead of to their own communities. "Regionalism," as he called it, was no kumbaya moment: "Though the notion of building a total win-win regional consensus is appealing in theory, in practice sustained regional reform clearly demands the formation of enduring coalitions that can weather intense opposition and controversy," he wrote.[21]

This was not a minority-driven plan. By his own contention, blacks thought that the "ideal" neighborhood was 50 percent black, something that was impossible to achieve by spreading out racial groups geographically, since blacks have made up some 12 percent of the United States population for decades. But in 1993, Orfield found a minority face for the project, convincing a nascent urban poverty network called the Gamaliel Foundation that it was the suburbs that were to blame for the ailments of the city.[22]

Gamaliel was a Ford Foundation–funded, Chicago-based group that counted a young Barack Obama as one of its community organizers. Its modus operandi was embedding itself in associations of churches whose credibility and infrastructure it could harness for political aims, even if its members were not necessarily asking for what they were pushing. In 1992, pastors and church members protested Mike Kruglik, a Gamaliel leader who trained Obama, calling him "crooked" and alleging in a press release that he was using their churches "to build power for himself and the Gamaliel Foundation." One of Gamaliel's two Minneapolis church-based affiliates (which Orfield described as "a liberal Saul Alinsky–type organizing entity") sprang into action in 1994 to push Orfield's proposals into the legislature. "The lead witnesses in each hearing were religious officials in clerical garb," Orfield wrote.[23]

That year, Minnesota passed the Metropolitan Reorganization Act, which transformed a relatively minor administrative board, the Metropolitan Council of the Twin Cities, "from a $40-million-a-year planning agency to a $600-million-a-year regional government" that eventually expanded into seven counties and 186 jurisdictions.[24]

The metropolitan government, though not as powerful as Orfield hoped it would eventually become, pushed sleepy villages to build apartments. For single-family structures, it recommended that no yard should have to be more than 7,500 square feet—just big enough for a large house and a small strip of grass.[25]

Sure, it brought suburbanites joy to watch their kids play soccer out back; serenity to sit on their deck and hear nothing but birds; and security to live somewhere that it would be unusual to find strangers lurking a few feet outside their door or litter blowing across their yard. Sure, many of the vilified suburbanites were the same individuals who had previously lived in the city or inner suburbs, and had chosen to trade decades of savings and often longer commutes for more space. But to social engineers, they were characters in a version of the game *SimCity* where the challenge was to stack worker bees as efficiently as possible. Smaller lots "would save an average of $3,600 dollars [*sic*] per unit in land costs and $3,750 in utility fees. Smaller lots would also reduce costs of street maintenance, snow plowing, garbage pickup, and other municipal services," Orfield wrote.[26]

While "urbanists"—the political faction of affluent white people who were adamant that everyone should bike to work and live in an apartment—held that cities were the superior way of life, evidence on the ground said otherwise. Suburbs had less crime, better schools, and better-run governments. For this, social engineers blamed city residents. They would need to send them to the suburbs. Then they could lure suburban residents back to the city—and deal with hold-outs by eventually bringing the city's dense buildings to them.[27]

On one hand, urbanists argued that mass transit and walkable communities were key to a modern lifestyle and that city residents found it challenging to travel to work because of "sprawl." On the other hand, city-dwelling minorities must be relocated to suburbs, where the nearest grocery store might be miles away. To get around this, Orfield simply waved away one of his central premises by acknowledging what every suburbanite already knew: "As for transit, an employed person can usually afford some sort of car for travel to whatever services are needed."[28]

INSIDE-OUTSIDE GAME

With Minneapolis as his proof of concept, Manuel Pastor, the PolicyLink board member and University of Southern California professor, picked up the torch, working with Orfield and a handful of others on a crusade for metropolitan governments. As a whole, the plan worked incrementally, but its ultimate goal was to consolidate a city and its suburbs into a mega-jurisdiction in which individual citizens and even towns would have only the tiniest voice when it came to their own local affairs.

As Pastor admits, minorities had no desire for this and "have long been suspicious of regionalism." Consolidation that watered down the influence of individual suburbanites would also deprive minorities in the cities of the ability to elect their own leaders. Majority-black cities meant black mayors. In 2003, the city of Louisville, Kentucky, merged with its surrounding county over the strong opposition of the city's African American community, most local officials, and the local chapter of the NAACP, among others. Minneapolis–St. Paul, where a form of consolidation succeeded, was among the nation's whitest regions and still is today: the Minneapolis–St. Paul–Bloomington metro area ranked in the top twenty-five nationally, with an 81.3 percent white population in 2019.[29]

But to the activists, fewer but bigger governments make the process of spreading unpopular policies simpler. "In regions with multiple local governments, it is harder to develop political or policy strategies that build from city to city within the region," Pastor wrote. "Los Angeles has a population of nearly 3.7 million and a single city government; the Pittsburgh metro area has a population of only 2.3 million but a total of 418 municipalities," he lamented in 2009.[30] Just as important, large local governments had such complexity that only savvy and well-funded political groups knew how to navigate them—groups like PolicyLink.

As PolicyLink and the Government Alliance for Racial Equity (GARE) spread throughout the schools and suburbs, they targeted hub groups that acted as force multipliers by influencing their constituent jurisdictions. In the Washington, D.C., region, for example, GARE embedded into the Metropolitan Washington Council of Governments—the type of body that could eventually morph into a regional government—which encouraged its members to adopt "sweeping racial equity" reforms. Southern states like Virginia typically have strong county governments rather than smaller townships, creating the environment that equity groups colonize most successfully. Minnesota was the opposite, with many small townships, but with the assistance of inter-jurisdictional hub groups the state proved to be one of PolicyLink's and GARE's most extensive and successful conquests. GARE captured the League of Minnesota Cities, the Metropolitan Council, the state government, and even the Minneapolis Park and Recreation Board. Before long, it included among its member cities Red Wing, a city of about 16,000 people, just 312 of whom are black, according to the 2010 census.[31]

The quest continued through multiple front groups. As Maya Wiley's GARE worked Minnesota one piece at a time, the Center for Popular Democracy (CPD) created a density-demanding subsidiary, Local Progress, to play what it called the "inside/outside" strategy and Pastor called the "inside" and "outside" games. Local Progress brought together unions, activists, and more than one thousand elected officials from local governments across the country. In this manner, activists had a mole inside local governments, and local politicians could coordinate policy with each other, causing programs adopted by one jurisdiction to be quickly copied in others.[32]

Wiley and Randi Weingarten, the AFT union national president, were past CPD board members. Chairing its "project," Local Progress, was Brad Lander, a New York City councilman central to the push for equity initiatives in its schools. Rounding out the board is the executive vice president of the AFL-CIO, which represents laborers who benefit from construction projects.[33]

In December 2018, Minneapolis eliminated single-family zoning regulations citywide. Its city council president, Lisa Bender, was a member of Local Progress. Lander and Bender wrote that Minneapolis was only the first in a national push: "Getting rid of exclusionary zoning (long deployed by white homeowners to hoard the benefits of high property values and segregated schools) and building more housing is necessary."[34]

SUSTAINABLE COMMUNITIES

These groups had been working the federal government level at the same time. Less than a year after President Obama took office in 2009, HUD developed the "Sustainable Communities Initiative" (SCI), which gave grants "to improve regional planning efforts." This set the stage for regional governments, and primed those entities to be focused on increasing density. In 2010, forty-five regions, encompassing nearly a quarter of all Americans, applied as "consortiums" of local governments that received a combined $98 million from HUD. In exchange, they committed themselves to plans whose repercussions over the ensuing decades could make that money seem like a pittance.[35]

PolicyLink successfully lobbied HUD to make grants contingent on recipients working with "an organization with a demonstrated commitment and track record of addressing the needs of low-income people and people of color neighborhoods (hereafter referred to as social equity groups) as either a lead applicant or in a strong governance role in the planning process." PolicyLink was describing itself.[36]

HUD's website pointed applicants to a PolicyLink-drafted document that explained how recipients would be more likely to receive the money if their proposals focused on equity.[37]

Activists had played the inside-outside game so successfully that they now had control of every stage of a federal program. While PolicyLink influenced the application criteria, helped regional coalitions write their proposals, and angled to become part of the coalitions, it and two other groups, the Minnesota Housing Partnership and the Kirwan Institute for the Study of Race and Ethnicity, were also paid to work for HUD. Kirwan was led by "john powell," one of the fathers of regionalism, a Tides Foundation board member, and Orfield's predecessor as director of the University of Minnesota Law School's Institute on Race and Poverty (which became the Institute on Metropolitan Opportunity in 2012). Both PolicyLink and Kirwan were funded by the Ford Foundation.[38]

A Kirwan Institute employee, Jason Reece, acknowledged: "I have 'insider status' in regards to the HUD SCI. I acted as an official capacity builder on behalf of the agency, with funding support from HUD and philanthropic entities, including the W. K. Kellogg Foundation, Open Society Foundation and Ford Foundation. . . . I assisted HUD in reviewing grantee materials, and developing and presenting best practices in equity planning. Finally, I acted as a primary capacity builder for the Fair Housing Equity Assessment, in partnership with PolicyLink and Minnesota Housing Partnership."[39]

In the San Francisco area, 101 municipalities came together under a consortium called "Plan Bay Area" or "One Bay Area" and accepted an SCI grant for fiscal 2011. Fear of climate change was the justification for overriding the area's time-honored preference for local control. Plan Bay Area focused squarely on turning San Francisco's suburbs into places that looked more like San Francisco. Forcing the existing suburbs to become dense cities, and blocking low-density development in open spaces in Northern California, ostensibly would mean less driving and therefore less climate change. Yet race, and a new interpretation of the law, were key to enabling this extraordinarily controversial move: activist groups could now sue towns whose zoning blocked real estate developers from building massive apartment buildings, citing federal fair housing standards.[40]

Residents of those towns never got to vote on whether they should cede power to a mega-jurisdiction. The Association of Bay Area Governments and the Metropolitan Transportation Commission, since they were existing regional bodies, played the lead role in this proto-regional government.[41]

But, as it turns out, those bodies turned to foundation and activist groups that were eager to do their work for them. For one Plan Bay Area report supposedly written by the Association of Bay Area Governments, research was "conducted by" Kirwan. Reece's team also wrote an earlier report found on Plan Bay Area's website that was based on "stakeholder engagement meetings" hosted by PolicyLink.[42]

A Tides Foundation "project" also popped up, working with the Gamaliel Foundation, to explain to California regional bodies why the powers being granted in the name of climate change should instead focus on race and equity. It produced a "toolkit" to help form climate change plans that quickly pivoted to race and density, with chapters like "Saying No to Racial, Economic and Health Inequities Caused by Transportation and Land Use." It showed a picture of a highway exit ramp with one arrow pointing to "Poor People / Smog / Asthma / Unemployment" and the other to "Rich People / Trees." Its solution, it seemed, was to cut down the trees.[43]

This blatant use of federal funds to pay activist groups to contort how towns would use funds was a *feature*, not a bug. HUD showered praise on Seattle and Minneapolis because they funneled the largest portions of their grants to activist nonprofit groups. The Metropolitan Council of the Twin Cities, Minneapolis's regional government, spent $750,000 of its $5 million grant paying activist groups to tell them how to spend the remainder.[44]

HUD employees approvingly documented the ways in which its

"capacity builders," purportedly paid to gauge public opinion, instead dismissed the concerns of local residents who opposed density and regionalism. HUD huffed that East-West Gateway, a council of Missouri governments tasked with creating "OneSTL" (or "One St. Louis"), was helmed by "a conservative body composed of elected officials." Once local elected officials could be sidelined, PolicyLink and other intermediaries were more effective in steering the regional plans. In Kentucky, HUD wrote, "the grantee resisted but then did complete a fair housing and equity assessment, with substantial help from the HUD capacity building intermediaries." The Piedmont Authority, an inter-jurisdictional council in North Carolina, lacked "a strong focus on equity" until it got "the help of (capacity builder) PolicyLink's [staffer]." In Des Moines, Iowa, after "disruptions" by citizens who voiced their opposition, the regional consortium "altered the format of our outreach events to prevent this from happening," the consortium wrote.[45]

All of this was set into motion by the philanthropic foundations. In 2010, the Ford Foundation paid PolicyLink $300,000 to "conduct research, produce policy briefs & develop a media strategy promoting economic & social equity as a superior model for sustainable economic growth." It added more than $2.4 million to that amount over the ensuing years. In 2012, George Soros's foundation paid PolicyLink $1.3 million, in part for "research and communications related to the equity as the superior growth model framing project."[46]

Multiple SCI grantees cited PolicyLink's research to justify their proposals, even though at times they did not know what they were repeating: "Some grantees struggled in defining the concept of equity," Reece wrote.[47]

By then, they were on their way to creating regional governments. And fringe activists were essentially in charge.

AFFH

SCI soon led to AFFH, the policy aimed at densifying suburbs. And the process repeated.

Orfield was hired by HUD as a "special consultant," where he "assisted in the development" of the AFFH rule, while PolicyLink "contributed to developing the framework of the rule and led technical assistance and capacity-building efforts."[48]

In 2015, the year the rule was finalized, $1.6 million in grants from the Ford Foundation tasked CPD with "a place based fair housing campaign." By the next year, this initiative was working from within the government. In 2016 and 2017, the Soros foundation paid CPD more than $1.2 million for "AFFH technical assistance" and the activities of Local Progress.[49]

The reaction from people who would actually have to live with AFFH was overwhelmingly negative, including poverty officials from liberal localities. The Public Housing Authorities Directors Association objected that their members were being set up for failure because they have no control over where people choose to live. The National Association of Housing and Redevelopment Officials called the policy "a deeply-flawed [proposal]." The Council of State Community Development Agencies pointed out other unintended consequences. In particular, this agency believed that the rule's command to "take no action that is materially inconsistent with" the obligation to meet racial benchmarks could be interpreted to mean that grantees should not spend money where poor people live, but should instead disinvest in those neighborhoods and build low-income housing in white neighborhoods to lure them there.[50]

New York City pointed out that asking every jurisdiction to have the same percentage of whites as the region as a whole would require it to displace a large portion of its eight million residents. "The Proposed Rule does not anticipate the issues facing localities comprised of majority minority populations," it wrote. "To consult with adjacent local governments, and by implication, request that such localities use their limited entitlement grant funds to assist the central city to meet its fair housing goals, may not be practical or financially feasible."[51]

The rule was finalized anyway, before it was suspended by the incoming Trump administration. In July 2021, the Biden administration announced its intent to revive it.[52] The social engineers played the long game.

REAL ESTATE AND VOTERS

Equity campaigns are formidable because multiple constituencies essentially use each other in alliances of convenience. This strategy is effective from a political standpoint, but disastrous from a policy standpoint. The groups' common ground is a desire to tear down the status quo. But they often have diametrically opposed beliefs about what to do afterward. This means that it is impossible to appease them. It also means that if the activists get their way, it will only lead to chaos and more acrimony.

Orfield is an old-school "champagne liberal," a white professor in his late fifties who made $188,000 in 2018 and chose to live in a neighborhood that was 90 percent white and 2 percent black.[53] He believed that the primary purpose of "regionalism" was to move blacks out of inner cities so they could adopt "middle-class mores." However, by 2020, critical race theory–fueled activists were completely against that sort of thing.

The public schools of Cambridge, Massachusetts, lamented that "many structures and practices are based on white, middle-class norms that do not support equity."[54] Equity trainers in Illinois schools were teaching that the notion of the United States as a melting pot was "antiquated," because assimilation "requires marginalized groups to lose their distinctive identities." Whether Orfield realized it or not, his quest to move inner-city minorities to the suburbs to help them break out of a dysfunctional culture could succeed politically only if it gave up its policy purpose and settled for simply spreading dysfunction.

As for the flip side—bringing more whites to inner-city neighborhoods and revitalizing them by building mass transit and other amenities that would raise property values—racial activists routinely protested that sort of thing as "gentrification."[55]

A love of the environment as a reason to force everyone to live in concrete jungles was also a dubious proposition. Cities were hardly environmental beacons; in San Francisco, residents reported nearly twenty-one thousand instances of human feces on the sidewalk or on the street in 2017 alone. Meanwhile, much of the development taking place was in the exurbs on wooded, multi-acre lots. Those properties *were* nature sanctuaries, and their owners got to actually see it. It could hardly be said that the United States was running out of room—vast tracts were nothing but open space. If anything, the reason that cities like San Francisco were so expensive was that too many people were trying to live in the same place instead of spreading out.[56]

In any case, there was no reason to believe that government policies designed to force every neighborhood to have certain racial percentages would decrease racism. Well-off suburbs were already filled with many races and ethnicities, people who earned enough money to live in those communities and were likely to make a good impression on their white neighbors. Deliberately taking people from the inner cities and placing them in the suburbs while highlighting their race was more likely to *harm* white suburbanites' opinion of minorities. A Brown University study published in November 2020 found that when white students interacted with black students as part of the type of forced busing initiatives that Orfield supports, it "negatively impacted their racial attitudes towards Blacks, and decreased their support for policies promoting racial equity."[57]

So what was this all about? Pastor is up-front: politics. With "regional" governments, moderate and conservative suburbs will be subsumed into their more populous and liberal city cores. This will result in large jurisdictions controlled by Democrats. Entire towns might disagree, but their voices will be drowned out. Regionalism is "a way to create a new political balance that would split the suburbs from the Republican Party," Pastor's book says.[58]

Density, meanwhile, was the surest route to turning every area blue. Of the hundred most densely populated congressional districts in 2017, all but eleven were held by Democrats. Of the hundred most sparsely populated, all but nineteen were held by Republicans.[59]

The average Democratic voter who lives in the suburbs might be tempted to celebrate this partisan strategy—except that it could be only a pyrrhic victory. He likely moved there for a reason, and wants to keep things the way they are.

Equity is best thought of as a virus that embeds within unrelated hosts, hijacks its reproductive mechanisms, then uses the resources of its host to spread even further, leaving wreckage behind on a never-ending quest for power. But in 2020, it was a real virus that dealt a serious blow to the urbanists.

When the coronavirus pandemic hit, it highlighted the many downsides of living in densely populated housing with hundreds of thousands of other people. City dwellers who could afford it decamped to the suburbs or, better yet, the exurbs. A city's notable feature, a cluster of office buildings, suddenly became irrelevant. People could work from anywhere, including nature-filled enclaves across the country. Many of San Francisco's employers saw that this arrangement worked just fine, and allowed their employees to work from home permanently.[60] Social engineers had been wrong again.

This significant increase in remote work reduced pollution more than Plan Bay Area ever could.[61] But to consider it a win, you had to make the mistake of thinking that the plan was ever about the environment.

16

BOOTLEGGERS AND BAPTISTS

Howard County, Maryland, is a quiet suburb where upper-middle-class residents found refuge from the crowding of D.C. and the violence of Baltimore. It has a median household income of $121,600 and only a 4 percent childhood poverty rate.[1] Its highly rated schools made it one of Maryland's fastest-growing counties, with tracts of former farmland sprouting cookie-cutter housing developments on an annual basis.

But in 2019, a handful of local officials, real estate developers, and nonprofit activists decided to plunge the county into turmoil. The school board proposed bringing back 1970s-style busing, tearing thousands of students away from their friends and plummeting home values in some neighborhoods. The initiative was premised on the assertion that the county's remarkably diverse schools were actually "segregated." A prime example was River Hill High School, supposedly elite at the expense of other schools. It is 44 percent white, compared to the school system overall at 35 percent.[2]

The board's public input process garnered only 150 comments supporting the busing policy and 6,650 opposing it. The measure passed anyway. Nothing residents said or did seemed to matter.

If progressive board members were not knowingly taking their cues from self-serving corporations, they were convenient puppets. Real estate developers who stood to profit off the busing scheme had been pulling the strings. The goal was to urbanize Howard County, filling it with densely built townhouses and apartments, sold at massive profit. They worked through altruistic-sounding nonprofits claiming to help the poor and fight racism, but which amounted to fronts for the same clique of developers and power brokers.

Economist Bruce Yandle called this dynamic, in which idealists' moral hectoring functions as the tip of the spear for profiteers, "Bootleggers and Baptists," after the way underground whiskey makers purportedly backed campaigns of churches who pushed Prohibition in the 1920s and 1930s.[3]

Hiruy Hadgu, an Ethiopian immigrant, decided to run for Howard's county council in 2018 to challenge the status quo after realizing that America's local politics are composed of three groups. First, entrenched interests who "control the political parties, the media, elected officials, many of the nonprofits, and the county government, as they accomplish goals in direct conflict to the public interest." Second, community activists, who in rare cases can overcome special interests but only if they can "directly reach the electorate." More often, they will find an uphill battle and give up, or make a deal with the devil by working through the entrenched apparatus, which will bend their concerns to its own desires. Last and least, there are the voters, who have "very little access to useful information" and are "susceptible to relying on political party identification or the endorsement of powerful local organizations (mostly entrenched too)."[4] In other words, when most people cast a ballot in local elections, they have no idea for whom they have voted. Politicians and special interests take advantage of this vacuum.

Hadgu is a nuclear scientist, but voters in the Democratic primary rejected him in favor of a thirty-four-year-old professional "community organizer," a white woman named Christiana Rigby. Buoyed by connections gained as an employee of political and nonprofit groups, and trained by a union-funded national program called Emerge that recruits female Democratic activists to run for office, Rigby secured endorsements from professional progressive circles, including the teachers union. Though views on abortion were unlikely to be relevant to the duties of county council members, she touted a seal of approval from pro-choice group NARAL.[5]

Council members each represent approximately 57,000 people, but local primary elections are virtually ignored by everyone but activists. The votes of only about 3,600 people, or less than 6 percent of her would-be constituents, secured Rigby a substantial majority in the primary, which amounted to a coronation since most in the Democratic-leaning county would select their choice for the general election based on party label alone. The other 94 percent would soon face the consequences.[6]

HHC

Howard County was not named after the Howard Hughes Corporation, but it might as well have been.

The Howard Hughes Corporation (HHC) is a Texas-based real estate company valued at more than $5 billion. It owns several "master-planned cities and communities" and a chunk of Manhattan. It also has a multibillion-dollar development project in Howard County's largest community of Columbia. In 2016, HHC's regional executive, Greg Fitchitt, convinced the county council to provide a $90 million subsidy for that project, the largest "developer giveaway" in county history. It was unclear why an incentive was necessary since, as one resident testified, "downtown is growing at a rapid pace," and development was "clearly in the pipeline" already.[7]

Though local politicians theoretically represent only the interests of existing residents, they kept making plans with real estate developers to crowd the county with new people. So much dense housing was built that schools were overflowing. Columbia's schools, in particular, were so crowded that the granting of building permits within their boundaries was halted. If those kids could be moved to other schools, freeing up capacity, the floodgates would reopen to developers.[8]

A small coalition of progressives began talking about how over-crowding could be the perfect pretext to spread socioeconomic and racial groups equally among each school, a social engineering program they called equity.

Incidentally, this would make land in the county's urban core of Columbia more valuable. Impoverished kids, who were more likely to live in apartments there, would be replaced in schools with rich kids brought in from the newer suburbs. Those kids earned higher test scores, which would boost the schools' rankings without needing to actually help the existing students score better. These rankings were frequently touted by developers since the quality of the local school is a prime determinant of home values. In other words, developers had already sold all the exorbitantly priced houses they could around top-ranked schools like River Hill. But if they could change which schools were highly ranked, they could sell high-priced homes in a new area, while earlier customers potentially went underwater on their mortgages thanks to losing a prime selling point. Additionally, the notion that there were not enough minorities in current top-ranked schools could be used to justify building dense housing like apartments in those areas.

The activists behind the equity push were tied to both county officials and developers. In short, a cabal of obscure regional influence peddlers were taking developer money and using pseudo-grassroots groups to impose a preordained plan on the public. And anyone who stood between real estate developers and a cash cow would be painted as a racist.

The most prominent forum for progressive county politics is a podcast called *Elevate Maryland*. Tom Coale, an attorney for developers, runs it, and HHC has sponsored the podcast.[9] A decade prior, Coale had been a registered Republican who wrote to the *Baltimore Sun* lamenting that if voters had not elected a Democratic governor, the state would be more friendly to business.[10] But by 2019, he had adopted the language of far-left activists and constantly invoked the term *equity*, which he said necessitated both dense housing and school redistricting.[11]

Zoning law, he said, "arose around the turn of the century to separate commercial from residential zones but was then co-opted in the 1920s for the purposes of racial segregation." Equity in schools could only be attained if each school had the appropriate number of minorities, and this could only be achieved by building huge quantities of dense housing throughout the county. He questioned why "dormitory living" should only be for people of college age. Eventually, he wrote a new opinion column arguing that Maryland's next governor should be someone in the mold of Senators Elizabeth Warren and Bernie Sanders, and who would enact policies that "are often cast as 'abolishing the suburbs.'"[12]

"We will need a governor focused on expanding access to housing in high opportunity areas, reexamining local rule as an obstacle to housing growth, and committed to the construction of new units funded by the state," he wrote. It so happens that all of this could also profit his clients handsomely.

In March 2019, articles of incorporation for an activist nonprofit called Howard County for All were signed. Its mission was "advocating for more inclusive policies with regard to education, diversity, housing, and economic development." Its website gave no sign of who composed the group. But state records show that board members include Coale and his podcast cohost Candace Dodson Reed. Each had a close relationship with the most powerful official in the county, having chaired committees on the transition team of County Executive Calvin Ball.[13]

Their wishes came true unusually quickly. In April, the school board solicited consultants to come up with a "redistricting plan," and in May, it hired a for-profit Ohio-based firm called Cooperative Strategies. It was paid at least $326,000 for the work.[14]

In June, the Howard County Public School System (HCPSS) produced a report called "Equity: Responding to Performance and Opportunity Gaps in HCPSS," which found that the 2018 graduation rate for blacks was 89 percent. This rate was the same as the nationwide graduation rate for whites and was higher than the graduation rate for all American public school students, regardless of race. Equity, though, is based not on positive outcomes but on jealousy, and the report took a negative tone because the stellar black graduation rate was 6 percent lower than the rate for whites in Howard, which was a nearly unheard-of 95 percent.[15]

Days later, an advocacy Facebook page called HoCo School Equity was created. The group ran paid ads focused on "segregation" and the need to implement redistricting. It was managed by Tina Horn, who works for an affiliate of Enterprise Community Development, which has a portfolio of more than $1 billion in real estate, mostly multifamily units in Maryland. Its president of the Communities Division, a private equity mogul, is on Howard's Housing Opportunities Master Plan Task Force.[16]

In June and July, an "Attendance Area Committee" of citizens was convened to guide the redistricting consultant's priorities. More than a third of the members were not so much citizens as political cronies: they, too, had served on the transition team of County Executive Ball. Most vocal was Larry Walker, pastor of a church where Ball and school board chair Mavis Ellis have worshipped. Ellis is a retired school system employee who was the consummate entrenched insider. She served on the board of the NEA chairing the teachers union's black caucus. And she served on the board of a statewide association of school board members, through which policies spread from jurisdiction to jurisdiction. Walker's committee agreed to, as it wrote in its minutes, "Prioritize needs of disatvanced stidsnt That s what equity is about. Priority nedd over compfrt [sic]." That meant busing.[17]

Cooperative Strategies then solicited feedback from everyday parents, who said the opposite. The vast majority prioritized "keeping . . . students together" and "maintaining contiguous communities." Fewer than 20 percent placed "consideration of demographic factors" in their top three priorities.[18] Would the consultant listen to the people?

On July 17, HHC president Fitchitt wrote to county officials from his real estate company email: "Please consider supporting a boundary adjustment plan which addresses educational equity and segregation here in Howard County."[19]

He cited an analysis by Richard Kohn, who had sent the same study to Opel Jones, a member of the county council, two days before. Kohn's analysis was imbued with his authority as a "scientist and educator." But this might have had more weight if he were assessing the feces of pigeons for signs of disease: it came from a professor of "Animal and Avian Sciences." And it stemmed more from seething ideology than from training. "Desegregation," the bird scientist wrote in another email to officials, "will expose the cruel policies of this school system. Eventually, even the icy hearts of western Howard County's white supremacists could melt." Kohn, too, was a member of Ball's transition team.[20]

POLITICAL COVER

Rigby, Jones, and another member of the county council decided to intervene in the matter—the exclusive domain of the school board—to tip the scales toward busing. They planned a resolution saying the school system should use redistricting to solve racial segregation. The purpose was to allow the school board to implement an unpopular plan while claiming that it was out of their hands.

The resolution called for halting what it said was the growing number of segregated schools "(defined as schools where less than 40 percent of the student population is white)." In reality, what was happening was that Howard County was getting more diverse. By 2019, the school system had dipped to 36 percent white, meaning that by their definition, if every school in Howard mirrored the county student population, every school would be officially "segregated"—while simultaneously having large populations of every racial group.[21]

Under this standard, it could only achieve its aim of eliminating segregated schools by bringing more white people into the county or getting rid of some minorities. But the resolution's authors seemed more interested in grievance than in practicality. They invoked *Plessy v. Ferguson, Brown v. Board of Education*—and of course, slavery.[22]

On August 13, the resolution was announced via press release. "We are providing them political cover," Councilwoman Rigby, the community organizer, texted a council colleague. "They will know we have their backs and have something they can point to when/if haters come for them."[23]

"Are they asking for this cover, or are we foisting it upon them?" the colleague replied.

It was a curious way to help the school system since the school board was unaware. Jones met with Superintendent Michael Martirano as the press release went out, but never mentioned it to him. "To say I was surprised to see the press release right after my meeting is an understatement," Martirano wrote.[24]

Kirsten Coombs, the school board's vice chair, was told nothing about the resolution. Board member Vicky Cutroneo wrote that she received a call from Councilwoman Rigby about three hours before the press release and "responded that I did not need nor desire political coverage for my decisions."

Sabina Taj, who would later emerge as one of the school board's most vocal busing proponents, denied knowing about the press release to the *Baltimore Sun*. But records suggest that was untrue: on August 12, Jones's aide texted that Rigby "and Sabina discussed putting together a press release [for] the School Segregation [resolution] . . . Sabina said she believes Dr. M. will address Desegregation via his plan, but is unsure if it is going to be watered down or not."

The intervention seemed to have the desired result. Under the eventual Cooperative Strategies plan—which the superintendent endorsed—7,400 students were to be moved.[25] Computer software divvied up children based on demographics with such granularity that some elementary school students were moved to go to the sixth-closest school to their homes.

The same day the press release went out, *Center Maryland*, a website that is one of the few sources of suburban news in the region, began its own pro-busing push, spending $6,400 on Facebook ads. *Center Maryland* purports to serve "news straight down the middle," but is actually an arm of KO Public Affairs, an advocacy-for-hire firm helmed by real estate honchos and lobbyists. A *Baltimore Sun* column called KO the "vampire squid of Maryland politics," saying,

"Their business model relies on getting their friends in government to take more dollars from taxpayers to give to their corporate clients." KO received more than $400,000 from casino interests in return for pushing a measure to expand gambling in Maryland. When a manufacturer of speed cameras was paying lobbyists linked to KO, it created a group giving the impression that residents wanted the ticket-generating devices, which are widely detested by drivers.[26]

The "O" in KO, Damian O'Doherty, is a lobbyist for HHC.[27] HHC also pays KO through a holding company, American City Building Trust, board member Vicky Cutroneo alleged. O'Doherty was the single largest donor to Taj's campaign.

Soon after, the 2019–20 school year began and the proverbial kettle was on the boil. In September, residents attended a public meeting to express their displeasure about the redistricting plan to the county school board. Notably, a state lawmaker cut in line to speak in favor of the plan. That same week, a distraught resident wrote an op-ed criticizing the school system by saying, "Basically, they could care less what the parents think."[28]

By October, residents organized protests and a rainbow of families spilled into the streets. "I want to stay with my friends," a black fourth grader pleaded. At an October 7 school board hearing, more than eighty people spoke, and not one was in favor of the busing plan.[29]

Three days later, with no sign that they had been heard, residents testified at another public hearing. The mother of a black student who worked as an assistant director at the Equal Employment Opportunity Commission warned that the plan was almost certainly illegal. A resident told the board that opponents outnumbered supporters by a ratio of 100 to 1 and that "[a]s far as I can tell, the only proponents of this plan are the politicians."[30]

Though busing proponents attempted to cast the battle as wealthy whites opposing the interests of blacks, they were keenly aware that in fact, average black residents were not asking for busing. Pastor Walker said at a September 8 service at his church: "We have a partnership with the school system and the superintendent is looking for brown people to show up and put our voices behind this plan that he came out with—it's a bold plan and the community is hatin' on it right now—they're hatin' on it . . . he needs some allies, folks."

The protests spawned news coverage, which county officials quickly appeared to try to squelch. On September 5, a political re- porter at WBAL-TV, Kate Amara, emailed county council and school board members noting she was contacting them as a parent, not in her professional capacity. "Please answer the following ques- tions for this howard county [*sic*] mom . . . Why is it important to take up CR112–2019 at this moment in time? Do you believe it is eth- ical for the County Council to insert itself into an already explosive public debate?" The school district published a redacted version of her email online because the day after it was sent, someone submitted a public records request for it. Only the officials who received the let- ter would have had the information necessary to make that request, which appeared to be made using a fake name, as there was no record of any such Maryland resident. The exposure of the reporter's email ensured that her station sidelined her from covering the topic and increased the odds that TV did not cover it at all.[31]

Meanwhile, when parents got an inkling of how Tom Coale, the obscure developers' attorney turned progressive activist, seemed to play an outsize role in county affairs, they submitted their own pub- lic records requests about his interactions with decision makers. The county acknowledged that there were 761 emails from, to, or about Coale in the accounts of top county staff during a time period rele- vant to redistricting, but refused to release all but two, without spe- cifically explaining why.[32]

Coale was not used to anyone noticing his influence on local pol- itics, and he did not like the scrutiny. "The abuse of the Maryland Public Information Act in Howard County merits review by the [*Bal- timore Sun*]," he demanded. That he thought a major newspaper—a foremost advocate of public records laws—would write an editorial lambasting citizens for using the tool on a topic of public concern shows the audacity of the sort of small-time power broker that has shaped many towns for years. Coale does not represent many real people: in 2018, his podcast had a typical audience of 150. Instead, he knows just the right people.[33]

"EXCELLENT DEMOGRAPHICS"

None of the opposition mattered because of the intractability of two new and ultra-progressive school board members.[34]

An elementary school PTA leader explained how Sabina Taj wound up on the school board. "In June 2017, I received a message from Sabina and our PTA president stating that she wanted to chair a position on the Diversity Outreach Committee. . . . This began a disheartening and divisive period where Sabina suggested in meetings that there are too many white women in the PTA, that they must be racist, and that they excluded people of color since she thought too few were represented despite the fact that these are volunteer positions." Taj could not produce any minority parents who wanted the positions. Six months later, she filed to run for school board, citing PTA leadership experience as a qualification.[35]

Taj excelled in grandstanding about racism, but exhibited little grasp of substantive issues. She took her cues from others, such as the board's other flame-throwing newcomer, a white woman named Jen Mallo. Mallo did not have children in the school system, and her campaign website did not seem to give much credence to the Supreme Court ruling prohibiting assigning students to schools based on their race: "We must approach [redistricting] with consideration to racial and socio-economic concerns," it said. During a key vote on the redistricting, Mallo sent Taj text messages midmeeting telling her what to do. "Go ahead and second," one said. "It's fine to vote yes," said another. These secret conversations violated a Maryland law known as the Open Meetings Act.[36]

All the while, what seemed like an "astroturf," or fake grassroots, public relations campaign continued. Broadcasting from HHC headquarters, Coale's podcast hosted a guest from the Century Foundation, a nonprofit pushing busing throughout the country. In September, *Center Maryland* sponsored "Building Equity: An Educational Equity & Housing Affordability Conference." Taj was a keynote speaker.[37]

There, HHC president Fitchitt discussed the role of developers in reducing inequity. "I don't want to cast aspersions on people who live in River Hill . . . but it was built without any affordable housing. And the largest outcry that we hear now with the redistricting plan is from River Hill," Fitchitt said. "They didn't have a right to go into that particular school," he added. "Partnering with developers is how you're going to get the change that you want."[38]

At the time, Fitchitt's company was using a brochure touting River Hill's affluence to attract lucrative retail tenants for its commercial properties. It drew a circle around the area annotated "Average Household Income $223,323."

"Excellent demographics," it said.

PRIVILEGE

After the public comment period had closed, parents packed board meetings anyway, even if all they could do was watch and hold signs signaling their displeasure. On November 7, Mallo issued an epic four-minute lecture to parents. "We have chosen to support each other as board members," she said. "We do not call each other names. We don't intimidate each other and we don't bully each other. Unfortunately, our community has chosen to do the opposite. . . . That will stop today. . . . The Open Meetings Act allows you to be here. We expect you to take that privilege and respect your fellow audience members. From here on out, all signs may be displayed no higher than your chin," she continued. "If they are above your chin, if the conversations continue, you will be asked to leave. . . . On social media, please stop attacking us."[39]

The night of November 21, the plan came to a vote. The three school board members who had spearheaded the initiative from the beginning—Mallo, Taj, and Ellis—had been unmoved by public opinion and data in the months since. And they had a swing vote, Kirsten Coombs, on their side, giving them a four-to-three margin. In a series of rapid-fire votes, groups of students were transferred from one school to another.[40]

Parents said many of these moves amounted to sloppy mistakes— essentially clerical errors or a failure to understand geography. On one vote, Coombs seemed to agree and sided with anti-busing members. The room burst into applause. "I move that we go into recess," Mallo said. When they returned from a back room, Coombs was crying. She said the board should redo the vote. Her voice cracking, she switched her vote to a feeble "yes."[41]

Taking the meeting behind closed doors to hide deliberations from the public violated the Open Meetings Act. Chair Ellis later issued a statement on behalf of the board saying, "There was no intent to evade our obligation to deliberate on these important decisions in public or to violate the Open Meetings Act," adding they went to the back room to look at data "and/or figure out what to do."[42]

Board members' notes spelled out precisely what happened: Mallo "slams her stuff down" and is "screaming at" Coombs. Coombs asks a question. Taj does not fully grasp what has occurred, but after Mallo tells her, Taj "joins [Mallo in] yelling at" Coombs. Coombs bursts into tears. Another member says, "Stop bullying her, don't let them bully you." As Coombs continues to cry, she agrees to change her vote.[43]

So much for "we don't intimidate each other" and the "privilege" of the Open Meetings Act.

AFTERMATH

For all of HHC's preening about how empowering developers is the way to help the poor, there was not much evidence of it putting its money where its mouth is. It "does not have a history as a developer of affordable housing," the *Baltimore Sun* reported in 2015, and none of its existing downtown Columbia housing was "affordable." In 2017, it agreed to begin building some affordable units, but those units were largely paid for with federal tax credits and vouchers, did not count toward the cap that otherwise limited how many apartment units would be permitted, and came as part of a deal in which the county footed the bill for other infrastructure that would help HHC's high-end projects.[44]

Though developers' rampant construction of new homes had lined their pockets and created the school crowding, builders of new homes only paid $1.32 per square foot toward schools. That amounts to a one-time payment of about $5,300 for a 4,000-square-foot house, hardly enough to pay for the new facilities necessary for several children. On November 6, the county council finally voted to raise that rate. Of course, the move was opposed by developers, led by the Maryland Building Industry Association, of which the HHC is a member. HHC said it would lose millions.[45]

More persuasively, the raising of fees on wealthy corporations to fund services for children was opposed by do-gooder nonprofits ostensibly dedicated to the plight of the poor. The Association of Community Services, the Howard County Housing Commission, and the Howard County Housing Affordability Coalition all opposed the measure. In reality, the parade of seemingly disparate nonprofits amounted to fronts for the same clique—more Baptists to HHC's bootleggers. HHC is a member of a coalition called Bridges to Housing Stability, which is associated with all three groups. The Howard County Housing Affordability Coalition includes Tom Coale and Paul Revelle, a builder/developer who was named as a Maryland Building Industry Association's "legislative award winner" days after meeting with officials about school funding.[46]

Jones, one of the council members behind the busing resolution, introduced an amendment to lower the fees for developers operating in the Downtown Columbia Development District, where HHC is active. That amendment failed. Another council member found that developers were sometimes allowed to build in overcrowded school districts even when the rule supposedly forbade it. She introduced a bill tightening the rules. Rigby had claimed that if the school board passed redistricting, she would agree to that, but after the redistricting, she and Jones opposed it anyway. The measure failed as a result.[47]

When HHC delivered its quarterly presentation to investors not long after, it did not say anything about integrated schools. Instead, it opened with the tagline "HHC: The Opportunity to Control Cities." It described its business as being the "dominant residential land owner in markets with superior demographics," where it could exert "monopoly-like control." When it did discuss equity, it was in a different context: "Profits from condominium sales = equity for future developments."[48]

It told investors that its communities are defined by their "exclusive nature" and the fact that HHC has "*substantial* control over planning, zoning, property sales and development." It ensures that "land appreciates in value," as Tom Coale noted occurs when rules are changed to allow increased density. Its presentation summarized the dream of the new confluence of social engineers and cutthroat capitalists: a "real life 'SimCity'" with the "opportunity for *generational* wealth creation."[49]

As for the school board, Mallo ran for reelection despite being a central villain of the most widely detested political move in recent county history. On March 10, 2020, she canceled an appearance at River Hill, the epicenter of the redistricting fury, claiming that she had a contagious "illness." The illness had not stopped her from attending a board meeting the day before or holding a meet-and-greet the day after. Nor did it stop her from holding her campaign kickoff two days earlier. It was held at HHC's office.[50]

The activists and special interests who push schools to adopt a mission that is ideological, not educational, are single-minded and without any sense of balance, and things got even worse for Howard's families. The coronavirus pandemic hit soon after and closed school for the rest of the 2019–20 school year and almost all of the 2020–21 one. Nonetheless, Mallo's school board refused to postpone the new school boundaries even though it meant that when the plan went into effect in September 2020, students had the cruel and lonely fate of going to school online with people that they had never met.[51]

Even when policies are clearly nonsensical, ineffective, or unpopular among those who know about them, many of us view local politics as obscure and local elections as insignificant, an opportunity to signal allegiance to a political tribe or to serve as a referendum on unrelated national issues, if not something to sit out entirely and leave to insiders who we imagine are better qualified.

In Howard County, school board elections are officially nonpartisan and candidates do not appear on the ballot with a party signifier next to their name. The rules say, "Candidates are expected to run nonpartisan campaigns and, when serving as a member of the Board of Education must work in a nonpartisan manner with all elected officials in the best interests of the public school students."[52]

But when the November 2020 election rolled around, the unpopular Mallo knew how to secure victory among a voting base that was largely tuned out to school board races. She sent a mailer to voters implying that if they did not vote for her, it would be like "supporting the reelection of President Trump." She stood outside of a voting location on Election Day—apparently crossing over the "No Electioneering Zone" prohibiting political advertising too close to voting booths—with a sign spouting non-education-related liberal platitudes like "Women's Rights Are Human Rights." She handed out a blue "Democratic Sample Ballot" that instructed voters, many of whom otherwise could not have named down-ballot candidates, to select her if they were the sort of person who wanted Joe Biden to be president.[53]

She was reelected to the board by a margin of 1,382 votes.[54]

Just as in communities all across America, Howard County's version of "Bootleggers and Baptists" was strident and unrelenting as they hijacked schools in ordinary residents' backyards.

Yet just as in communities across the country, some of it was right out in the open; it is just that few of us took the time to look.

Massive, secret forces are undermining American education in ways that will have devastating consequences in all of our daily lives. But the truth is that there is also another group who, whether due to apathy, mistaken priorities, or blind partisanship, bears fault for an educational collapse that has been decades in the making.

It is us.

EPILOGUE

The long journey of this book began with its ending.

After writing a few news articles about the Howard County busing fiasco in 2019, I was contacted by dozens of Howard residents, an unusual level of response. They were begging me—someone who did not even live in the county—for help. They felt like their lives were on the brink of catastrophic disruption. They were lifelong Democratic voters, whereas my articles appeared in the conservative *Daily Caller*. But what was happening was not something they remotely agreed with, and they did not know where else to turn. Even in an area containing many lawyers and D.C. consultant types, most did not know the first thing about how to engage in local policy affairs, which seemed to have been captured by a tight, tiny network that did not particularly care what residents thought. Local media had atrophied to the point of virtual nonexistence.

As a D.C.-based investigative reporter for national outlets, I've written stories that have gotten federal officials fired, spurred congressional hearings, and uncovered millions of dollars in wasted funds. And here I was writing about, of all things, the local school board of a sleepy suburb. Yet I was struck by the sheer emotion and vulnerability of these callers.

I had a revelation that everything I thought I knew was wrong: local politics are more important than national ones. How often does your family feel the impact of whatever it is that Congress does? Local politics routinely have such a personal effect in our daily lives.

My interest was cemented when I began to see the exact things that occurred in Howard, mostly defined by a myopic focus on race, play out in neighboring school districts, including my own, to the point where I was reliably able to predict what would happen next at any given turn. It was clear that to some extent, local governments, so important in their own right, had been co-opted by powerful, coordinated national interests.

In late 2019, I began pitching a book whose "hook" was an offbeat paradox: What if the most boring thing imaginable—local suburban school boards—was actually super-important? At the time, it was an idea so counterintuitive that the Government Accountability Institute and HarperCollins were intrigued.

My biggest challenge was convincing people that I wasn't crazy when I told them that schools were so broken that systems in places like Seattle were saying things like math is racist and that tests were not a valid way to measure accomplishment, and that these ideas were spreading rapidly through well-defined patterns. It understandably seemed like far-fetched fearmongering: surely no sizeable portion of America would permit such a thing.

Before the book even headed to print, everything I had predicted had come true to the point where few needed to be told, much less convinced. The coronavirus pandemic and school shutdown began several months into the writing process, and parents saw the political indoctrination and low level of academics with their own eyes, streamed to the laptops of their children.

They also had no choice, if they wanted their kids out of their living rooms and back in school, to become acquainted with their local school boards. Many school board members went from obscure to reviled for their incompetence, overriding ideology, and hostility to transparency.

What people still did not understand was that none of this was new. What they saw in 2020 and 2021 was just an impossible-to-ignore glimpse into how schools have long operated. It was not an aberration or an isolated incident but a long-overdue wake-up call.

When I began writing this book, I believed that ordinary, politically centrist Americans had made an egregious error by failing to scrutinize the nuts and bolts of their K–12 school systems. Conservative politicians almost never delved into the details of how schools operated—which is where the devil resides. If they were asked about the issue, they'd mumble something about "school choice," which seemed to me an acknowledgment that they were not just losing a war, but not even fighting it.

After two years of immersion in the issue, I may have been too quick to criticize those whose instinct was just to walk away. I am no longer sure America's public school system can be saved.

It is difficult to reform the schools because policy makers deal with high-level changes, while implementation falls to entrenched insiders who will ignore or subvert them. Their record of manipulating data, lying, and keeping the public at bay means we cannot trust whether they have actually implemented reforms. The rot is too deep.

As a natural consequence of their race to the bottom in which they insist that no student in their care do better or have more opportunities than the most fringe, "disadvantaged" one, public schools may become the new public housing: an obviously failing den of dysfunction populated solely by those with no other options. Many may seek "pod" homeschooling co-ops or found a new wave of budget private schools that provide a better education, tailored to that family's preference, for a fraction of what taxpayers spend. I live in Fairfax County, where I moved for the schools and had planned on sending my kids to public school, but now believe that doing so would amount to child abuse. I am convinced that finding virtually any alternative will be worth it, even if making it happen requires major life changes.

Still, my original concerns remain. Paying for a failed system via taxes, and not even using it, is a grossly inefficient policy solution. As long as there is a public school system, a large portion of the country's children will presumably enroll in it. Say I save my own children. When they grow up, they will live among those people, vote with them, and—given the academic results of today's public schools—likely be forced to financially support many of them. What happens in K–12 schools happens to America—and in a relatively short time period.

That's why indoctrinators target schools in the first place, of course. It is effective. But it is also a shocking betrayal of trust. Someone who believes that if Democrats win 51 percent of the votes in a jurisdiction, government-run facilities for children can be turned into hard-core organs of the Democratic Party is someone who cares more about political power than ethics—to say nothing of minority rights and disproportionality. No stable society will tolerate it. But the irony is that even liberals who convince themselves indoctrination is okay as long as they agree with its slant are being conned. As any parent who delves deeply enough will see, the ideology that youth are being inculcated with consists of half-baked ideas far outside the mainstream of either party, with no record of success. To state what should have been obvious to everyone from the beginning: the best way to help the poor is to ensure that they are smart and employable by competently providing an education and demanding a rigorous grasp of the fundamentals.

The consequences of schools' failures—from which the recent focus on race is merely the latest technique for distracting—will be cataclysmic for society. The lack of proficiency in math and science, the poor reading skills, and the abysmal teaching of civics threaten every technological and societal advance we have made. Progress will stagnate. The economy will collapse.

But here's the bigger thing. Perhaps I could make peace with all that as long as my children are happy. It's all any parent wants, at the end of the day.

By now, I hope you have seen that the deliberate goal of indoctrinators is that they are not happy. The indoctrinators are miserable people, desperate for innocent children to be like them. They take children who are joyous, carefree, and effortlessly living in a society that is more multicultural than any of these adults has ever known, and convince them that they are actually living in the midst of horrid oppression—an oppression that can, conveniently, be alleviated only by joining what is essentially a cult that the vast majority of adults would reject as ridiculous.

They will say things like "of course we need to identify the negative, because how else will we work to change for the better?" Yet step back and study the bigger picture, as I have for two years, and it is indisputable that these people simply haphazardly flail in discontent at whatever the status quo happens to be, in a way that can never be satisfied at scale.

While equity activists in one district complained that black children were overrepresented in special ed, claiming it meant they were being stereotyped as mentally challenged, equity activists in another decried that black children there were underrepresented, noting that a special-ed designation means a student gets significantly more resources, of which blacks therefore were being shortchanged.

Within a district, some demand racially segregated schools in which to conduct "culturally responsive teaching," and complain if minorities are, unsurprisingly, a minority in the classroom. Others complain for opposite reasons, having a conniption if each school and classroom does not have the same percentages of each race as the jurisdiction at large.

Of course, if the assorted statistics of every school in a county are balanced in this manner, they will simply complain that there are disparities among counties in the state. But why stop this entirely relative measurement there—once those are dealt with, why not insist that each state in the country looks, earns, and performs exactly the same? For that matter, why not each area of the world?

And if we do that, aren't the children of inner-city Baltimore actually privileged?

Teachers' shakedown of America in 2020–21 was astonishingly lucrative for them. The amount of supplementary funding allocated to schools through one coronavirus bill alone was greater than the amount spent under the Marshall Plan to reconstruct Europe, even adjusted for inflation[1]—for reasons totally unexplained, considering many schools were not even open. But it came at a cost of lasting damage to our children. Just as World War II is seared into the memories of people who lived through it, the experience of being betrayed and abandoned by people you once trusted is likely to be as well.

Still, life has a way of making us tuck away past pain and return to routines. If we weren't wired that way, what woman would go through childbirth a second time?

So I'll end the way this project began: with the call that local politics matter. That residents who treat school board elections as referendums on national elections, expressions of tribal loyalty, or the domain of school employees are making a mistake they cannot afford.

As you have seen, the educational issues illuminated during the coronavirus pandemic were manifestations of problems that were there all along. We were simply woken up to them.

For the sake of our kids' happiness, for the sake of our constitutional republic, for the sake of a modern world fueled by scientific and technological advancement, we can never, ever go back to sleep.

ACKNOWLEDGMENTS

You can find out what's going on in your school district, and warn your neighbors by submitting tips, at www.whataretheylearning .com.

The author is solely responsible for the contents of this book, but it would not have been possible without the brilliant minds of the Government Accountability Institute (GAI), including Peter Schweizer, Peter Boyer, Joe Duffus, and Tarik Noriega. GAI, which has generated some of the most important, rigorous, nonpartisan research on special interest influence in numerous spheres, saw earlier than most that national political forces were creeping into our backyards and classrooms, and enabled me to write a book that required significant research thanks to its GAI Fellowship.

Thanks also to HarperCollins and Eric Nelson; Jerry Seper, Mark Tapscott, Chris Bedford, and John Bickley; and Tucker Carlson and Ben Shapiro.

A growing number of people are fighting against the illiberal ideology of critical race theory in K–12 education, including Nicole Neily of Parents Defending Education; Elana Fishbein and No Left Turn in Education; James Lindsay of New Discourses; Annie and Ethan Keller of the Locke Society; and Chris Rufo.

Respect and condolences to those who have suffered through hundreds of hours of school board and local government meetings—a job that is as important as national politics but comes with none of the glamour—including Elizabeth Schultz, Paul Galletta, Rosie Oakley, and Steven Keller.

And to local journalists who have done the same, such as A. P. Dillon.

Thanks to those of Asian heritage leading the fight to preserve our race-blind meritocracy, including Asra Nomani, Yiatin Chu, Cliff Li, and Kenny Xu.

Capital Research Center's Influence Watch and the Heritage Foundation's Mike Gonzalez have done excellent work on the role of philanthropic foundations. Max Eden of the American Enterprise Institute is one of the few who have studied the nuances of the education policy world without being part of its ideological bubble. Stanley Kurtz and Katherine Kersten have an eye for the policies that do not get much attention but have the potential to dramatically change our lives for the worse.

Though I hope this book will do its small part to prevent children from being taken from their parents by incoherent, unhappy ideologues, the writing of it took me away from my own family for too many hours over the course of more than a year. My undying love to my wife, Eleanor, and my mother-in-law, who sacrificed to make it happen.

NOTES

INTRODUCTION

1. https://go.boarddocs.com/vsba/fairfax/Board.nsf/files/BN442M097615/$file
    /DLP_School%20Board_March27.pdf, pp. 8–10.
2. https://www.theatlantic.com/ideas/archive/2021/01/just-open-schools
    -already/617849/; https://www.cnbc.com/2020/11/08/coronavirus-why-families
    -are-jumping-to-private-schools.html. "As of mid-October, 6 in 10 independent
    schools were operating in-person and just 5% were fully online, according to a
    survey by the National Association of Independent Schools." As of November
    2020, 38 percent of schools were open full-time and nearly 25 percent were in
    hybrid: https://info.burbio.com/school-tracker-update-nov-2-2020/.
3. https://data.virginia.gov/Government/VDH-COVID-19-PublicUseDataset
    -Cases_By-Age-Group/uktn-mwig.
4. https://www.dailywire.com/news/cdc-director-schools-among-safest-places
    -kids-can-be-closing-schools-an-emotional-response-not-backed-by-data.
5. https://www.facebook.com/1400731176895575/posts/2398481980453818/.
6. https://www.insidenova.com/headlines/child-sized-coffins-in-prince
    -william-teachers-protest-caravan-spark-outrage/article_3ceeef7c-0986
    -11eb-9e3d-bbb4f4044b3a.html; https://actionnetwork.org/petitions/keep-fairfax
    -county-public-schools-virtual-for-the-2020-21-school-year; https://www.fox5dc
    .com/news/fairfax-county-educators-union-wants-schools-to-stay-closed-for
    -remainder-of-school-year.
7. https://www.frontpagemag.com/fpm/2020/09/teachers-union-wont-go
    -back-school-will-go-daniel-greenfield/; https://gothamist.com/news/teachers
    -and-parents-march-against-nycs-plan-reopen-schools; https://www.usatoday
    .com/story/news/nation/2020/08/28/march-washington-2020-thousands
    -gather-sharpton-nan-rally/3442726001.
8. https://www.localdvm.com/news/fairfax-county-launches-a-new-childcare
    -program-during-the-virtual-school-year/; https://www.fairfaxcounty.gov/office
    -for-children/sacc/about/#WorkforSACC, "Working for SACC"; https://www
    .fairfaxcounty.gov/office-for-children/supporting-return-school-program.

9. https://go.boarddocs.com/vsba/fairfax/Board.nsf/files/BV3PVV66833A/$file /citizen%20participation-%207-1-19%20PEC.pdf.

10. School board documents; https://nrtwc.org/official-time-in-right-to-work -virginia/; https://www.fcps.edu/staff/kimberly-adams.

11. https://wtop.com/fairfax-county/2020/07/fairfax-co-teachers-advocate -to-stay-out-of-the-classroom-this-fall/; https://www.dailywire.com/news/flash back-media-said-a-vaccine-by-end-of-year-was-impossible-even-fact-checked -trump-making-claim; https://www.foxnews.com/media/laura-ingraham-dem ocrats-teachers-unions-ludicrous-reckless; https://www.wric.com/news/local -news/today-northam-to-give-an-update-on-covid-19-outbreak-in-virginia/; https://www.bbc.com/news/health-54873105.

12. https://www.youtube.com/watch?v=LJxkdOqPYzM&feature=youtu.be, 23:45.

13. https://go.boarddocs.com/vsba/fairfax/Board.nsf/files/BXL2CS019289/$ file/01-07-21_PH_and_ERM_FINAL%5B1%5D.pdf, p. 2; https://www.washington post.com/opinions/2021/01/25/fairfax-county-should-open-schools-or-stop -vaccinating-teachers/; https://data.virginia.gov/Government/VDH-COVID-19 -PublicUseDataset-Cases_By-Age-Group/uktn-mwig.

14. https://www.youtube.com/watch?v=6zIADZdVEsw&feature=youtu.be, 11:00 and 12:26.

15. https://www.youtube.com/watch?v=6zIADZdVEsw&feature=youtu.be, 11:30; https://www.dailywire.com/news/cdc-director-threat-of-suicide-drugs-flu-to -youth-far-greater-than-covid; https://reason.com/2021/01/25/chicago-teachers -union-vote-strike-school-reopen-covid-19/; https://reason.com/2021/01/22/ore gons-plan-to-vaccinate-teachers-before-the-elderly-is-terribly-misguided/; https://twitter.com/FEA_Fairfax/status/1349147319023804417; https://www.de mandsafeschools.org/wp-content/uploads/2020/09/Jan_12_day_of_resistance -1.pdf; https://www.wbaltv.com/article/call-for-regional-school-leaders-to-draw -up-in-person-reopening-plan-for-students/35196161#.

16. https://www.fox5dc.com/news/thousands-of-fairfax-county-teachers-to-work -from-home-despite-districts-plan-to-send-students-back; school board docu ments; https://www.fcps.edu/sites/default/files/media/pdf/FY21-hourly-bands .pdf.

17. School board documents.

18. https://www.youtube.com/watch?v=xlFSNkW2mGU&feature=youtu.be, 1:08:15, 1:08:58, 1:09:17.

19. https://www.washingtonpost.com/local/education/to-keep-bus-drivers-on -the-payroll-fairfax-county-public-schools-directs-some-to-drive-empty-buses -along-old-routes/2020/09/10/983494e2-f386-11ea-bc45-e5d48ab44b9f_story .html; https://www.fcps.edu/blog/message-all-employees-virtual-start; https:// web.archive.org/web/20201028113309/https://www.fairfaxcounty.gov/news2 /the-wheels-on-1630-school-buses-go-round-and-round/; https://www.fcps.edu /sites/default/files/media/pdf/FY-2020-Approved-Budget.pdf, p. 31.

20. https://www.facebook.com/FCPSHunterMill/posts/183440340022898; school board documents.

21. https://www.cdc.gov/coronavirus/2019-ncov/science/science-briefs/transmission _k_12_schools.html CDC: "A study of private schools that reopened for in-

person instruction in Chicago revealed that implementation of layered prevention found minimal in-school transmission." Citing M. J. Fricchione, J. Y. Seo, and M. A. Arwady, "Data-Driven Reopening of Urban Public Education Through Chicago's Tracking of COVID-19 School Transmission," *Journal of Public Health Management and Practice* 27, no. 3 (2020), published online ahead of print December 30, 2020, doi:10.1097/PHH.0000000000001334; https://www.southwestjournal.com/news/schools/2020/10/a-few-cases-no-outbreaks-at-private-schools/.

22. https://www.washingtonpost.com/local/md-politics/hogan-montgomery-private--schools-/2020/08/07/e2c6bdb2-d7fe-11ea-9c3b-dfc394c03988_story.html; https://www.baltimoresun.com/coronavirus/bs-md-elrich-hogan-schools-20200805-2k6mwqglknf7rhqfxecf2id64e-story.html; https://www.washingtonexaminer.com/opinion/vaccination-discrimination-d-c-suburb-appears-to-put-at-home-public-school-teachers-ahead-of-in-class-private-school-teachers.

23. https://wtop.com/fairfax-county/2020/10/fairfax-school-enrollment-drops-nearly-5-taxpayers-unlikely-to-get-a-break.

24. https://www.fcps.edu/blog/message-parents-tutoring-pods.

25. https://reason.com/2020/10/07/alexandria-public-schools-superintendent-gregory-hutchings/; https://twitter.com/ArlParentsforEd/status/1294798413436006403.

26. https://wtop.com/fairfax-county/2020/10/fairfax-school-enrollment-drops-nearly-5-taxpayers-unlikely-to-get-a-break/; https://www.fcps.edu/sites/default/files/media/pdf/FY-2021-Approved-Budget.pdf, pp. 26, 33; school board documents.

27. https://www.fcps.edu/sites/default/files/media/pdf/FY-2020-Approved-Budget.pdf, pp. 21, 30–31; https://web.archive.org/web/20201125030310/https://www.fairfaxcounty.gov/news2/12557-2/.

28. School board documents.

29. https://www.cnbc.com/2020/11/10/nearly-2point2-million-women-left-workforce-between-february-and-october.html; https://www.cnn.com/2021/01/08/economy/women-job-losses-pandemic/index.html.

30. https://reason.com/2020/08/19/school-reopenings-linked-to-union-influence-and-politics-not-safety/.

31. https://www.chalkbeat.org/2020/9/11/21431146/hispanic-and-black-students-more-likely-than-white-students-to-start-the-school-year-online.

32. https://www.newyorker.com/news/news-desk/how-police-union-power-helped-increase-abuses; https://www.rollingstone.com/politics/politics-features/police-unions-politics-george-floyd-breonna-taylor-1024473/; https://www.washingtonpost.com/opinions/interactive/2021/reimagine-safety/.

33. https://www.utla.net/sites/default/files/samestormdiffboats_final.pdf; https://www.latimes.com/california/story/2020-07-09/los-angeles-teachers-union-calls-for-delay-reopening; https://www.dailynews.com/2020/07/10/teachers-union-calls-for-lausd-schools-to-remain-closed-with-classes-100-online/; https://laist.com/2020/07/11/utla-teachers-union-schools-reopening-poll.php; https://www.dailywire.com/news/audio-los-angeles-county-health-director-says-she-expects-schools-to-reopen-after-the-election.

34. https://www.utla.net/sites/default/files/samestormdiffboats_final.pdf; https://

www.apha.org/policies-and-advocacy/public-health-policy-statements/policy
-database/2019/01/29/law-enforcement-violence. Two hundred and fifty-one
blacks were killed by police in 2019, of whom twelve were unarmed: https://
www.washingtonpost.com/graphics/investigations/police-shootings-database/
(last viewed on August 16, 2021). Three hundred and forty thousand blacks
died in 2017. Cancer killed seventy thousand, followed by a long list of the
other expected causes: https://www.cdc.gov/nchs/data/nvsr/nvsr68/nvsr68_09
_tables-508.pdf, pp. 25, 35.

35. https://www.chalkbeat.org/2019/5/14/21121062/new-democratic-divide-on
-charter-schools-emerges-as-support-plummets-among-white-democrats;
https://www.utla.net/sites/default/files/samestormdiffboats_final.pdf, p. 11.

36. https://www.chicagotribune.com/coronavirus/ct-covid-19-cps-union-unfair
-labor-charge-20201024-hh7xwlx6nrbe5d2urtrsbsy32y-story.html.

37. https://chicago.suntimes.com/2020/12/29/22204984/chicago-medical-experts
-in-person-learning-optimal-safe-opinion.

38. https://www.chicagotribune.com/coronavirus/ct-chicago-teachers-union-no
-return-to-school-20210103-d23hjrgpcrhnrgi3oe7xan6jku-story.html; https://
wgntv.com/news/wgn-investigates/ctu-board-member-facing-criticism-for
-vacationing-in-caribbean-while-pushing-remote-learning/; https://www.chicago
tribune.com/news/breaking/ct-chicago-teachers-union-venezuela-trip-20190819
-tbpa3lhjifduxgupdxfs3mosr4-story.html; https://radicaledcollective.wordpress
.com/2019/07/09/introduction-to-ctu-delegation-to-venezuela/.

39. https://www.illinoispolicy.org/ctu-supports-use-of-mock-guillotine-wherever
-it-was-headed/.

40. https://www.cps.edu/globalassets/cps-pages/about/district-data/demo
graphics/demographics_racialethnic_2021_v10072020.xls; https://www.illinois
reportcard.com/district.aspx?source=trends&source2=iar.details&Districtid
=15016299025; https://reason.com/2020/12/06/chicago-teachers-union-reopen
-schools-sexism-racism-misogyny/; https://nypost.com/2020/12/07/chicago
-teachers-union-deletes-tweet-claiming-school-reopening-push-rooted-in-sexism
-racism/. The tweet was deleted, but CTU retweeted a reply in support of the
original tweet.

1: CHEATING MATH

1. https://obamawhitehouse.archives.gov/the-press-office/2016/10/17/fact
-sheet-president-obama-announces-high-school-graduation-rate-has; https://
georgewbush-whitehouse.archives.gov/infocus/education/; https://nces.ed.gov
/programs/digest/d18/tables/dt18_219.46.asp.

2. https://obamawhitehouse.archives.gov/the-press-office/2016/10/17/fact-sheet
-president-obama-announces-high-school-graduation-rate-has.

3. https://www.npr.org/sections/ed/2017/06/29/524357071/every-senior-at-this
-struggling-high-school-was-accepted-to-college.

4. https://www.news-journalonline.com/news/20180615/b-cu-slapped-with
-probation-hubert-grimes-blames-media-lawsuits.

5. https://www.npr.org/sections/ed/2017/11/28/564054556/what-really-happened
-at-the-school-where-every-senior-got-into-college.

6. Ibid.

7. https://osse.dc.gov/page/2016-17-results-and-resources, 2016–17 PARCC results, p. 9 of PDF.
8. https://www.npr.org/sections/ed/2017/11/28/564054556/what-really-happened -at-the-school-where-every-senior-got-into-college.
9. https://atlantablackstar.com/2014/01/03/10-richest-black-communities-amer ica/4/; https://www.washingtonpost.com/local/education/how-high-can-gradua tion-rates-go-the-story-of-one-school-rocked-by-scandal/2018/07/27/98a3c34e -3ab0-11e8-8fd2-49fe3c675a89_story.html.
10. https://www.washingtonpost.com/local/education/how-high-can-graduation -rates-go-the-story-of-one-school-rocked-by-scandal/2018/07/27/98a3c34e -3ab0-11e8-8fd2-49fe3c675a89_story.html.
11. https://www.washingtonpost.com/local/education/four-board-members -in-maryland-school-system-allege-fraud-in-graduation-rates/2017/06/19/391 dbf68-54f3-11e7-b38e-35fd8e0c288f_story.html; https://www.washingtonpost .com/local/education/graduation-rate-falls-in-maryland-school-system-hit-by -diploma-scandal/2019/02/26/8aba25dc-3a02-11e9-a06c-3ec8ed509d15_story .html; https://www.washingtonpost.com/local/education/report-60-percent-of -graduates-sampled-in-md-school-system-excessively-absent/2018/12/04 /c4df0ecc-f7e9-11e8-8d64-4e79db33382f_story.html.
12. https://www.washingtonpost.com/local/education/maryland-investigates -claim-of-inappropriate-help-on-diploma-related-projects/2020/01/20/6df0cb c2-322c-11ea-a053-dc6d944ba776_story.html.
13. https://www.chalkbeat.org/2019/9/23/21109347/this-company-ran-schools-for -dropouts-across-the-country-chicago-is-the-latest-district-to-cut-ties.
14. https://www.propublica.org/article/for-profit-schools-get-state-dollars-for -dropouts-who-rarely-drop-in.
15. Ibid.
16. https://nypost.com/2015/03/23/high-school-accused-of-massive-grade-fixing -scheme/; https://nypost.com/2018/03/24/audit-slams-city-over-troubling-grade -fixing-fallout/; https://nypost.com/2016/04/17/doe-whitewashed-wrongdoing -at-grade-fixing-high-school/; https://nypost.com/2016/05/14/grade-fixing-ex -principal-lands-157k-job-as-doe-administrator/; https://nypost.com/2019/11 /09/queens-lawmaker-calls-for-federal-probe-of-grade-fraud-in-nyc-schools/.
17. http://www.denverpost.com/2015/02/07/colorado-considering-lowering-the -bar-for-high-school-graduation/; https://www.cde.state.co.us/postsecondary /graduationguidelines; https://www.scpr.org/news/2015/06/11/52344/d-grade -may-get-lausd-students-out-of-high-school/.
18. https://www.apsva.us/assessment-2/; https://slate.com/human-interest/2013/05 /the-case-against-grades-they-lower-self-esteem-discourage-creativity-and -reinforce-the-class-divide.html.
19. https://nypost.com/2019/06/29/critics-cry-grade-inflation-at-nyc-schools-as -students-pass-without-meeting-standards/.
20. https://blog.prepscholar.com/complete-guide-to-the-new-sat-in-2016.
21. https://www.usatoday.com/story/news/2015/10/28/naep-math-scores-down /74696238/.
22. https://nces.ed.gov/surveys/pisa/pisa2018/#/math/intlcompare; https://nces.ed .gov/surveys/pisa/idepisa/.

23. https://nces.ed.gov/surveys/pisa/idepisa/.
24. https://nces.ed.gov/surveys/pisa/pisa2018/#/math/intlcompare; https://nces.ed .gov/surveys/pisa/pisa2018/pdf/PISA2018_compiled.pdf, pp. 20–22.
25. https://www.nea.org/sites/default/files/2020-11/NEA%20Policy%20Playbook %202020.pdf.
26. https://www.edweek.org/education/few-states-require-promotion-exams /2008/01; http://www.ascd.org/ASCD/pdf/siteASCD/publications/policypoints /Testing-Time-Mar-15.pdf, p. 1.
27. https://www.cnsnews.com/blog/mary-grabar/who-fair-test; http://fairtest.org /k-12/high%20stake; https://www.washingtonpost.com/blogs/answer-sheet/post /2011/08/16/gIQABKu4JJ_blog.html.
28. https://www.washingtonpost.com/news/answer-sheet/wp/2015/03/10/no-child -left-behind-what-standardized-test-scores-reveal-about-its-legacy/.
29. https://www.linkedin.com/in/bob-schaeffer-3469724; https://www.cnsnews.com /blog/mary-grabar/who-fair-test.
30. https://www.fairtest.org/get-involved/opting-out; https://www.tampabay.com /news/education/2020/05/22/florida-canceled-student-exams-this-spring-is -testing-on-its-way-out.
31. https://nces.ed.gov/programs/statereform/tab5_4.asp; https://www.fairtest.org /sites/default/files/FairTest-TestReformVictoriesReport2017.pdf; https://www .fairtest.org/fairtest-report-test-reform-victories-surge-in-2017.
32. https://www.fairtest.org/university.
33. https://www.fairtest.org/sites/default/files/Optional-Growth-Chronology.pdf; https://www.nytimes.com/2020/05/21/us/university-california-sat-act.html; https://senate.universityofcalifornia.edu/_files/underreview/sttf-report.pdf; https://www.usatoday.com/story/news/education/2020/09/02/university-cali fornia-colleges-barred-using-sat-act-results/5689307002.
34. https://nces.ed.gov/fastfacts/display.asp?id=40; https://collegereadiness.college board.org/sat/scores/understanding-scores/structure; https://collegscorecard.ed .gov/school/?198862-Livingstone-College; https://collegescorecard.ed.gov/search /?id=206491&search=Wilberforce%20University&page=0&sort=completion _rate:desc&toggle=institutions.
35. https://www.detroitnews.com/story/news/local/michigan/2018/06/06/michigan -state-university-math-competency-classes/35751021/; https://admissions.msu .edu/apply/freshman/before-you-apply/admission-standards.aspx.
36. https://detroit.chalkbeat.org/2019/11/15/21109414/i-just-have-to-work-hard-for -it-as-detroit-students-settle-into-their-first-semester-of-college-thes; https:// www.insidehighered.com/news/2016/07/06/michigan-state-drops-college -algebra-requirement.
37. https://docs.google.com/spreadsheets/d/1rNxaH2Z6ljysUdPjVSs9EA2fxs RKd_Od8DcjtWs1K0I/edit#gid=1232320728; https://collegereadiness.college board.org/sat/scores/understanding-scores/structure; https://collegescorecard .ed.gov/school/?198862-Livingstone-College.
38. https://www.nytimes.com/2020/05/21/us/university-california-sat-act.html; https://old.post-gazette.com/nation/20020815tests0815p3.asp; https://www.amer icanprogress.org/issues/education-postsecondary/news/2017/10/16/440711/new -federal-data-show-student-loan-crisis-african-american-borrowers.

39. https://collegescorecard.ed.gov/school/?102270-Stillman-College; https://www
.wsj.com/articles/the-student-debt-crisis-hits-hardest-at-historically-black
-colleges-11555511327; https://www.wsj.com/articles/which-schools-leave-parents
-with-the-most-college-loan-debt-11606936947; https://collegescorecard.ed.gov
/school/?141060-Spelman-College.

40. https://www.forbes.com/sites/zackfriedman/2020/02/03/student-loan-debt
-statistics/?sh=2d44ebd2281f; https://pearsonaccelerated.com/blog/student-loan
-debt-ruins-your-life; https://www.forbes.com/sites/zackfriedman/2020/09/13
/student-loan-forgiveness-free-college/?sh=7173e3563349; https://www.usnews
.com/news/education-news/articles/2019-07-26/kamala-harris-proposes-60
-billion-in-assistance-to-historically-black-colleges-and-universities; https://
business.time.com/2012/02/09/why-cant-you-discharge-student-loans-in
-bankruptcy/.

41. https://web.archive.org/web/20210108081906/https://www.whitehouse.gov
/sites/whitehouse.gov/files/images/MBK-2016-Progress-Report.pdf, pp. 13, 17;
https://www2.ed.gov/about/offices/list/ocr/letters/colleague-201401-title-vi
.html; http://www.justicepolicy.org/news/8775.

42. https://www2.ed.gov/about/offices/list/ocr/letters/colleague-201401-title-vi
.html; https://www.washingtontimes.com/news/2018/mar/5/nikolas-cruz-avoided
-police-scrutiny-help-obama-po/.

43. https://web.archive.org/web/20210108081906/https://www.whitehouse.gov
/sites/whitehouse.gov/files/images/MBK-2016-Progress-Report.pdf, p. 26.

44. http://www.latimes.com/local/education/la-me-school-discipline-20151108
-story.html.

45. https://www.washingtontimes.com/news/2018/mar/5/nikolas-cruz-avoided
-police-scrutiny-help-obama-po/; https://web.archive.org/web/202101080819
06/https://www.whitehouse.gov/sites/whitehouse.gov/files/images/MBK-2016
-Progress-Report.pdf, p. 26.

46. Andrew Pollack and Max Eden, *Why Meadow Died* (New York: Post Hill Press,
2019), Kindle loc. 178; https://www.sun-sentinel.com/local/broward/park
land/florida-school-shooting/fl-florida-school-shooting-discipline-20180510
-story.html.

47. https://www.washingtontimes.com/news/2018/mar/5/nikolas-cruz
-avoided-police-scrutiny-help-obama-po/; https://www.sun-sentinel.com/local
/broward/parkland/florida-school-shooting/fl-school-shooting-cruz-20180
214-story.html; https://www.history.com/this-day-in-history/parkland-marjory
-stoneman-douglas-school-shooting; https://apnews.com/article/4f4f38edddf
b4d34954201bf50b44dbf; Pollack and Eden, *Why Meadow Died*, Kindle locs.
125–26, 129–31.

2: THE MATHEMATICIAN

1. https://loudounnow.com/2018/06/08/with-outspoken-school-critic-as-new
-president-leap-moves-on-without-lcps/; court records; interview.

2. https://www.the74million.org/article/arne-duncans-wrong-turn-on-reform
-how-federal-dollars-fueled-the-testing-backlash/#2; https://www2.ed.gov
/policy/gen/leg/recovery/factsheet/stabilization-fund.html; court records.

3. https://www.brookings.edu/wp-content/uploads/2020/02/Is-the-Rise-in-High

-School-Graduation-Rates-Real-FINAL.pdf; https://www.americanbar.org/groups /crsj/publications/human_rights_magazine_home/human_rights_vol38_2011 /fall2011/a_past_present_and_future_look_at_no_child_left_behind/; https:// www.edglossary.org/student-subgroup/.

4. https://www2.ed.gov/policy/eseaflex/esea-flexibility-faqs.doc, pp. 1, 3.
5. https://www2.ed.gov/programs/racetothetop/executive-summary.pdf, p. 9.
6. https://biz.loudoun.gov/2018/12/11/loudoun-median-income-2018.
7. https://caselaw.findlaw.com/va-supreme-court/1872647.html.
8. Court records.
9. https://loudounnow.com/2019/07/09/trump-twitter-ruling-cites-loudoun-case/; https://loudounnow.com/2017/08/01/court-rules-randall-violated-first-amendment-on-facebook/; https://cases.justia.com/federal/appellate-courts/ca4/17 -2002/17-2002-2019-01-09.pdf?ts=1547062258.
10. https://caselaw.findlaw.com/va-supreme-court/1872647.html.
11. https://calaf.org/?p=1364.
12. https://drive.google.com/file/d/0B5nQmOh4yk4MckNuc1h0ZEliMTQ/view, pp. 18, 20.
13. https://pubs.aeaweb.org/doi/pdfplus/10.1257/aer.104.9.2593, pp. 2, 10; https:// docs.google.com/presentation/d/0B5nQmOh4yk4MOW5DRkxzWUVt QzQ/edit?resourcekey=0-lHFqYv9h1EbyieT2ugEGwA, pp. 20–21; https://docs .google.com/presentation/d/0B5nQmOh4yk4McWoxWXZHeUZFbHM /edit?resourcekey=0-EwUyoHwRsgduvoSFUaQP2A#slide=id.p1, p. 7.
14. https://www.nytimes.com/roomfordebate/2012/01/16/can-a-few-years-data -reveal-bad-teachers/the-value-of-data-in-teacher-evaluations; http://www.raj chetty.com/chettyfiles/value_added.pdf.
15. https://www.brookings.edu/research/scrutinizing-equal-pay-for-equal-work -among-teachers/; https://tntp.org/assets/documents/TNTP-Mirage_2015.pdf, pp. 14–15.
16. https://www.nctq.org/blog/You-dont-get-what-you-pay-for:-paying-teachers-more-for-masters-degrees; C. T. Clotfelter, H. F. Ladd, and J. L. Vigdor, "Teacher-Student Matching and the Assessment of Teacher Effectiveness," *Journal of Human Resources* 41, no. 4 (2006): 778–820, via https://www.brookings .edu/research/scrutinizing-equal-pay-for-equal-work-among-teachers/; https:// tntp.org/assets/documents/TNTP-Mirage_2015.pdf, pp. 18–19, 24; https:// www.brookings.edu/wp-content/uploads/2016/07/Download-the-paper-2 .pdf.
17. https://www.loudountimes.com/news/loudoun-county-administrator -presents-3-02-billion-budget-for-fiscal-2021/article_908c2e3e-4e19-11ea-8f3a -17e09fddb118.html.
18. https://www.dailywire.com/news/teachers-unions-infiltrate-pta.
19. PTA emails, PTA minutes, court records.
20. Court records.
21. https://loudounnow.com/2018/06/08/with-outspoken-school-critic-as-new -president-leap-moves-on-without-lcps.
22. https://www.theatlantic.com/education/archive/2017/06/the-elusive-teacher -next-door/531990/; https://www.cft.org/california-teacher/when-educators

-cant-afford-live-where-they-work; https://jezebel.com/an-increasing-number
-of-teachers-cant-afford-to-live-wh-1766829312.

23. Teacher contract at 197 days: https://www.lcps.org/cms/lib/VA01000195/Cen
tricity/Domain/27243/2020%20-%202021%20LCPS%20Employee%20Hand
book.pdf, p. 9.

24. https://drive.google.com/file/d/1lpRhNdo_SvmoTSazSL41CaMrelYWcHQL
/view, p. 3; https://drive.google.com/file/d/1tlmZQcCIjFdxOaunaPLWuXIzS2
jwu2dy/view, final tab; https://drive.google.com/file/d/1t4sXSuoxpLIGlKHagq
5yGLBU6g87SugY/view.

25. https://drive.google.com/file/d/1tlmZQcCIjFdxOaunaPLWuXIzS2jwu2dy/,
chart at bottom of last tab; https://www.nctq.org/dmsView/Virginia_Pensions
_NCTQ; https://www.vaco.org/vrs-certifies-employer-contribution-rates-for
-teachers/; https://www.lcps.org/cms/lib/VA01000195/Centricity/Domain/74/LC
PS_Active_2021_Health_Insurance_Rates_Biweekly.pdf.

26. https://www.politico.com/story/2019/03/26/kamala-harris-teacher-pay
-1236033; https://www.epi.org/publication/teacher-pay-gap-2018/; https://nces
.ed.gov/fastfacts/display.asp?id=58.

27. https://www.ets.org/s/gre/pdf/gre_table4A.pdf; https://www.ets.org/gre/revised
_general/about/fairness/.

28. https://www.nea.org/sites/default/files/2020–11/NEA%20Policy%20Play
book%202020.pdf,p.4;https://www.chalkbeat.org/2020/11/17/21571346/teachers
-unions-influence-biden-administration.

29. https://ra.nea.org/business-item/2019-nbi-002/; https://ra.nea.org/business-item
/2019-nbi-025/; https://ra.nea.org/business-item/2019-nbi-118/; https://ra.nea
.org/business-item/2019-nbi-011/.

30. http://web.archive.org/web/20161109071712/http://www.newsday.com/opinion
/oped/ed-fix-clouded-by-the-fog-of-protest-andrew-cuomo-1.10027408.

31. https://nces.ed.gov/programs/digest/d19/tables/dt19_236.55.asp?current=yes.

32. https://web.archive.org/web/20210325105601/https://www.edchoice.org/wp
-content/uploads/2020/12/2020-SIA-Wave-2-Final.pdf, pp. 9, 61.

33. https://www.nea.org/sites/default/files/2020-11/2020%20NEA%20Policy%20
Playbook.pdf, p. 9.

34. https://sandera.ucsd.edu/publications/DISC%20PAPER%20Betts%20Tang%20
Charter%20Lit%20Review%202018%2001.pdf,p.7;https://ies.ed.gov/ncee/pubs
/20104029/pdf/20104031.pdf, p. 2; https://cpb-us-e1.wpmucdn.com/wordpressua
.uark.edu/dist/9/544/files/2018/10/making-it-count-in-7-us-cities.pdf,p.13;https://
www.nytimes.com/2010/08/01/education/01schools.html;https://ny.chalkbeat
.org/2012/10/9/21089608/opened-to-prove-a-point-uft-s-charter-school-could
-be-closed; https://nypost.com/2012/10/10/labor-pain-for-school/; https://casetext
.com/case/weinstein-v-city-of-new-york-2.

35. https://www.brookings.edu/blog/brown-center-chalkboard/2016/03/21
/reading-the-tea-leaves-essa-and-the-use-of-test-scores-in-teacher-evaluation/;
https://www.edweek.org/ew/articles/2016/01/06/essa-loosens-reins-on-teacher
-evaluations-qualifications.html; https://www.edweek.org/policy-politics/national
-teachers-unions-step-up-lobbying-efforts-on-nclb-rewrite/2015/02; https://www
.aft.org/sites/default/files/essa_ppt_121115.pdf.

3: SCHOOL BOARD

1. https://www.trendrr.net/3197/top-10-richest-counties-in-usa-america-highest -income/#2_Fairfax_County; https://uselectionatlas.org/RESULTS/state.php? year=2000&fips=51&off=0&elect=0&f=0; https://uselectionatlas.org/RESULTS /state.php?year=2008&fips=51&f=0&off=0&elect=0; https://www.usnews.com /education/best-high-schools/virginia/districts/fairfax-county-public-schools /thomas-jefferson-high-school-for-science-and-technology-20461.

2. https://www.fcps.edu/school-board/school-board-members; https://www.fcps .edu/about-fcps; http://www.fairfaxtimes.com/articles/fairfax-county-stays -blue-in-2019-local-elections/article_73cccc7e-0092–11ea-beab-2b25107a5079 .html.

3. https://www.fcps.edu/sites/default/files/media/pdf/FY21-school-board.pdf.

4. https://web.archive.org/web/20140907015533/http://www.linkedin.com/in/karl frisch; https://www.youtube.com/watch?v=REiWMnOgXBY&feature=emb _title,21:00;https://censusreporter.org/profiles/05000US51059-fairfax-county-va; https://web.archive.org/web/20140907015533/http://www.linkedin.com/in /karlfrisch; http://www.studentsreview.com/CA/COTC_comments.html; https:// www.fcps.edu/staff/karl-frisch; https://www.washingtonpost.com/local/educa tion/fairfax-county-weighs-protections-for-transgender-students-and-teach ers/2015/05/06/71b3cb76-f3cd-11e4-84a6-6d7c67c50db0_story.html.

5. https://dailycaller.com/2012/02/13/media-matters-memo-called-for-hiring -private-investigators-to-look-into-the-personal-lives-of-fox-employees.

6. https://alliedprogress.org/research/its-pay-to-play-for-some-members-of -congress-regarding-the-payday-rule/; https://web.archive.org/web/2020042215 2958/https://www.accountable.us/about/; tax lien per Nexis; https://web.archive .org/web/20160818060225/https://alliedprogress.org/about/.

7. https://historical.elections.virginia.gov/elections/search/year_from:2019 /year_to:2019/office_id:549/district_id:32545; https://www.vpap.org/committees /332492/frisch-for-school-board-karl/; https://www.vpap.org/committees/329216 /bayer-for-fairfax-county-school-board-andrea.

8. https://twitter.com/AbrarOmeish/status/1303302214337859584; https://www.the star.com/news/world/2009/11/08/alleged_shooter_tied_to_mosque_of_911 _hijackers.html; https://www.washingtonpost.com/world/national-security/nidal -hasan-sentenced-to-death-for-fort-hood-shooting-rampage/2013/08/28/aad 28de2-0ffa-11e3-bdf6-e4fc677d94a1_story.html; https://abcnews.go.com/Blotter /anwar-al-awlaki-inspired-terror/story?id=14643383; https://archive.today/201 20707111453/http://archive.frontpagemag.com/readArticle.aspx?ARTID =26058; https://www.israelnationalnews.com/News/News.aspx/215483; https:// www.washingtonpost.com/archive/politics/2004/09/12/facing-new-realities-as -islamic-americans/0f2cc52b-1fc5-44ce-a8d2-68629f533302.

9. https://hijrah.org/board-of-directors/; https://www.phillyvoice.com/philadelphia -muslim-american-society-video-children-beheading-torture-disturbing.

10. https://web.archive.org/web/20210117181651/https://clarionproject.org/next -generation-islamist-abrar-omeish-wins-virginia-election/; https://www.wash ingtonpost.com/wp-dyn/content/article/2007/09/27/AR2007092701244.html.

11. https://www.vpap.org/candidates/109248-esam-s-omeish/; http://voices.washing tonpost.com/rawfisher/2009/04/from_fairfax_to_richmond_the_j.html.

12. https://results.elections.virginia.gov/vaelections/2019%20November%20Gen eral/Site/Locality/FAIRFAX%20COUNTY/Index.html.

13. www.linkedin.com/in/abraromeish-2b561147.

14. https://almarsad.co/en/2019/09/25/senior-mb-leader-esam-omeish-reveals-de tails-of-meeting-with-erdogan/; https://dawnmena.org/about/who-we-are-2/dr -esam-omeish/.

15. www.linkedin.com/in/abraromeish-2b561147;https://yaleherald.com/melting -pot-boils-over-3c88b30eb285; https://yaledailynews.com/blog/2014/09/10/groups -embroiled-in-controversy-over-speaker/; https://hijrah.org/board-of-directors/; https://www.nifusa.org/event-2/libyas-transitional-government-and-the-lead-up -to-december-elections/.

16. https://www.youtube.com/watch?v=uaDwefdXE9w; https://apnews.com/article /arrests-lawsuits-school-boards-virginia-93ec815f81a70f86c352b86a014977df; https://projects.propublica.org/nonprofits/display_990/770646756/2016_01 _EO%2F13–142825_20003_770646756, p. 8; https://www.washingtonpost.com /local/education/a-northern-va-school-board-candidate-was-pepper-sprayed -during-a-traffic-stop-she-decried-it-as-police-brutality-police-say-she-resisted -arrest/2019/06/03/508ac84e-7e45-11e9-8bb7-0fc796cf2ec0_story.html.

17. https://twitter.com/AbrarOmeish/status/1146895150691639296.

18. https://elainetholen.com/meetelaine.

19. https://www.fairfaxcounty.gov/boardofsupervisors/sites/boardofsupervisors /files/assets/meeting-materials/2020/march04-jet-2-19-20-meeting-summary.pdf.

20. https://anastasia4kids.com/about/; https://elainetholen.com/endorsements; https:// www.insidenova.com/news/election/candidates-serve-up-differing-visions-in -quest-to-lead-fcps/article_775ec152-f4f9-11e9-8241-43962a007ab5.html.

21. School board documents.

22. https://theaapc.org/awards/40-under-40/40-under-40-winners-class-of-2017 /karl-frisch/; https://www.huffpost.com/entry/romney-outsourcing_b_1972569; https://www.fairfaxdemocrats.org/event/proud-dems-celebrating-equality-with -karl-frisch-gerry-connolly-danica-roem-nina-west-from-rupauls-drag-race-and -more/.

23. https://www.washingtonexaminer.com/herrity-has-harsh-words-for-school -board; https://www.washingtonexaminer.com/clifton-parents-file-suit-against -school-board; https://historical.elections.virginia.gov/elections/search/year_from: 2011/year_to:2011/office_id:549/district_id:32119; https://www.washingtonpost .com/local/education/the-outspoken-conservative-riling-the-fairfax-county -school-board/2015/07/06/096e3fe8-20e0-11e5-aeb9-a411a84c9d55_story.html; http://connectionarchives.com/PDF/2010/112410/Lorton.pdf.

24. https://www.washingtonpost.com/wp-dyn/content/article/2011/02/06/AR 2011020603710.html.

25. School board documents.

26. School board documents; https://go.boarddocs.com/vsba/fairfax/Board.nsf/files /874MAZ5A5E90/$file/SB+BOS+Presentation+Support+to+Schools +7-06-10.pdf.

27. https://www.washingtonpost.com/local/politics/clifton-fears-closing-towns -only-school-means-end-of-communitys-identity/2011/05/24/AG9IBYBH_story .html.

28. https://www.washingtonpost.com/local/education/the-outspoken-con
servative-riling-the-fairfax-county-school-board/2015/07/06/096e3fe8-20e0
-11e5-aeb9-a411a84c9d55_story.html; http://www.washingtonpost.com/local
/education/no-more-half-day-mondays-in-fairfax-elementary-schools
/2014/06/27/3a86c522-fe14-11e3-8176-f2c941cf35f1_story.html.

29. https://dailycaller.com/2015/05/09/virginia-school-board-member-compares
-transgender-rights-to-desegregation-amid-chaotic-meeting-video/; https://www
.fox5dc.com/news/fairfax-co-school-board-approves-change-to-policy
-to-protect-transgender-students-staff; https://twitter.com/LJ4fcps/status/125245
7606649708544; https://www.dobetterfcps.com/s/Do-Better-FCPS-2nd-FOIA-Re
sponse-Pgs-1-to-283.pdf, pp. 57–58; https://blueviewfairfax.com/2019/04/27/laura
-jane-cohen-victorious-in-springfield-dems-school-board-endorsement-vote/.

30. https://bluevirginia.us/2019/04/fairfax-republican-pat-herrity-continues
-his-anti-immigrant-demagoguery-is-voted-down-7-3; https://twitter.com/LJ4
fcps/status/1257473059436597255; https://twitter.com/MelanieSriv/status/12855
96898951299073; https://twitter.com/SEIUVA512/status/1189334513677156353.

31. https://www.washingtonpost.com/local/education/democratic-backed
-candidates-take-full-control-of-fairfax-county-va-school-board/2019/11/05/9
2a246fa-0002-11ea-8501-2a7123a38c58_story.html.

32. http://www.fairfaxtimes.com/articles/fairfax-county-swears-in-historically
-diverse-school-board/article_6a05bb64-2366-11ea-93a7-bbbe59307aec.html;
https://twitter.com/LJ4fcps/status/1205370878764163072.

33. https://twitter.com/SEIUVA512/status/1230667129365712898.

34. https://twitter.com/BryanScrafford/status/1230672327265918976; https://twitter
.com/LJ4fcps/status/1222729962714816512.

35. https://www.edweek.org/leadership/map-coronavirus-and-school-closures
-in-2019-2020/2020/03.

36. https://www.washingtonpost.com/local/education/fairfax-schools-on
line-learning-blackboard/2020/04/18/3db6b19c-80b5-11ea-9040-68981f4
88eed_story.html; https://thefederalist.com/2020/04/23/highly-ranked-wealthy
-virginia-school-district-still-cant-teach-kids-online-after-six-weeks/; https://
wtop.com/coronavirus/2020/04/fairfax-co-students-encounter-more-problems
-with-online-classes/.

37. https://www.dobetterfcps.com/s/Do-Better-FCPS-2nd-FOIA-Response-Pgs
-1-to-283.pdf, pp. 57–58.

38. https://www.washingtonpost.com/local/education/top-technology-of
ficial-out-at-fairfax-schools-as-fallout-continues-from-online-learning-dis
aster/2020/04/22/ad22f84a-84fe-11ea-ae26-989cfce1c7c7_story.html; https://www
.fcps.edu/news/fcps-names-new-chief-information-officer.

39. https://go.boarddocs.com/vsba/fairfax/Board.nsf/files/BT5MAQ5881B3/$
file/03-27-20%20ERM%20final.pdf, p. 2; https://go.boarddocs.com/vsba/fairfax
/Board.nsf/files/BN442M097615/$file/DLP_School%20Board_March27.pdf,
pp. 8–9; https://law.lis.virginia.gov/vacode/title22.1/chapter8/section22.1–98/;
https://www.youtube.com/watch?v=QqC92xgvc_c&feature=youtu.be,
4:28:00.

40. School board documents; https://go.boarddocs.com/vsba/fairfax/Board.nsf
/files/BQUSYT74FBFC/$file/LJC%20Racism%20and%20bias-2020.pdf.

41. https://www.foxnews.com/media/laura-ingraham-democrats-teachers-unions -ludicrous-reckless.

42. https://twitter.com/RachnaHeizer/status/1281278081827844097.

43. https://twitter.com/LJ4fcps/status/1285405487048151040.

44. https://bluevirginia.us/2020/07/fairfax-county-school-board-member-i-want -kids-to-learn-and-i-dont-want-people-to-die-during-covid-19-pandemic.

45. https://www.bellejardesign.com/pages/frontpage.

46. School board documents.

47. https://thefederalist.com/2020/09/30/fairfax-va-school-district-spent-24000 -on-ibram-kendi-books-for-u-s-history-classes/.

48. Laura Ramirez Drain in Fairfax County and Hunter Mill and Priscilla Magdalena Destefano in Fairfax County had Republican endorsements: https://fairfaxgop.org/fairfax-gop-announces-slate-of-school-board-candidates/.

49. https://www.infosecurity-magazine.com/news/maze-claims-attack-on-us -school/.

50. https://go.boarddocs.com/vsba/fairfax/Board.nsf/files/BPD4M50C2B1F/$file /FCPS%20final%20report%2005.05.20.pdf, pp. 6, 26–28, 30, 32, 40.

51. https://go.boarddocs.com/vsba/fairfax/Board.nsf/files/BUZSBQ719311/$ file/MembershipPresentation_SY2020_v6.pdf, p. 5; https://twitter.com/Karl Frisch/status/1324712595543261185; https://twitter.com/KarlFrisch/status/1325 114781561446402; https://twitter.com/KarlFrisch/status/1325218495236337664; https://karlfrisch.medium.com/board-approves-granting-new-diplomas-re quested-by-alumni-from-renamed-schools-trans-students-c8a60a66cd 48.

52. https://go.boarddocs.com/vsba/fairfax/Board.nsf/files/BY5JH34D3388/$file /12–17–20%20ERM%20FINAL.pdf, pp. 3–8; https://www.usnews.com/educa tion/best-high-schools/national-rankings; https://asrainvestigates.substack.com/p /breaking-analysis-tj-lottery-would; https://go.boarddocs.com/vsba/fairfax/Board .nsf/files/BWDM3959011C/$file/2020%20Superintendent%20Contract.pdf.

53. https://covid-relief-data.ed.gov/profile/entity/144992856; https://www.governor .virginia.gov/newsroom/all-releases/2020/october/headline-860767-en.html; https://www.fairfaxcounty.gov/budget/sites/budget/files/assets/documents /cares/cares-act-stimulus-funding-update-2021-01-22.pdf, p. 1; https://www.you tube.com/watch?v=bBcSzhobxDE.

54. https://www.youtube.com/watch?v=bBcSzhobxDE&feature=youtu.be.

55. https://secure.actblue.com/donate/byebyebetsy; https://keyt.com/politics/2021/02 /04/10-gop-senators-respond-to-white-house-but-underscore-deep-divide-on -covid-19-relief-package/; https://www.npr.org/2021/02/24/970708820/not-all -covid-19-aid-is-spent-but-schools-cities-and-states-say-they-need-more.

56. https://www.youtube.com/watch?v=bBcSzhobxDE&feature=youtu.be, 2:30:20; https://twitter.com/FEA_Fairfax/status/1349153253636907009.

57. https://www.cnbc.com/2021/02/03/cdc-director-says-schools-can-safely-re open-without-vaccinating-teachers.html.

58. https://www.cdc.gov/media/releases/2021/t0212-cdc-update-covid-19.html.

59. https://www.msn.com/en-us/health/medical/cdc-s-classroom-guidance-would -keep-90-of-schools-at-least-partially-closed/ar-BB1dNPQP.

60. https://www.cdc.gov/media/releases/2021/t0212-cdc-update-covid-19.html;

https://nypost.com/2021/05/01/teachers-union-collaborated-with-cdc-on
-school-reopening-emails/.

61. https://www.cdc.gov/media/releases/2021/t0212-cdc-update-covid-19.html.

62. https://www.cbo.gov/system/files/2021–02/hEdandLaborreconciliationestimate
.pdf, pp. 3, 13 (emphasis added).

63. https://thehill.com/homenews/sunday-talk-shows/538804-cdc-head-i-think-we
-need-a-lot-more-resources-in-order-to-get-the.

64. https://lasvegassun.com/news/2021/feb/18/muddled-promises-on-schools-pose
-political-problem/.

65. https://twitter.com/LJ4fcps/status/1362236648545800198.

4: RIOTS

1. https://www.foxnews.com/politics/george-floyd-protests-expensive-civil-dis
turbance-us-history; https://www.theguardian.com/us-news/2020/jun/22/seattle
-dismantle-chaz-protest-zone; https://apnews.com/article/virus-outbreak-race
-and-ethnicity-suburbs-health-racial-injustice-7edf9027af1878283f3818d96c54
f748; Andy Ngo, *Unmasked* (New York: Hachette, 2021), Kindle locs. 514,
548, 794.

2. https://www.washingtonpost.com/graphics/investigations/police-shootings
-database/ (last viewed on August 9, 2021); https://www.indexmundi.com/facts
/united-states/quick-facts/cities/rank/percent-of-people-of-all-ages-in-poverty;
https://censusreporter.org/profiles/16000US5363000-seattle-wa/; https://www
indexmundi.com/facts/united-states/quick-facts/cities/rank/black-population
-percentage.

3. https://www.k12.wa.us/sites/default/files/public/ossi/k12supports/pubdocs
/GATE%20Data%20Tools%20101%2012-9-2020.pptx; https://msbaadvocate
.com/2020/04/01/minnesota-of-department-of-education-provides-equity-lens
-reflection-resource.

4. https://www.eagnews.org/2016/02/school-districts-spending-millions-on
-white-privilege-training-for-teachers/; https://firstschool.fpg.unc.edu/sites/first
school.fpg.unc.edu/files/resources/documents/courageous%20conversations
.pdf, pp. 3, 24, 40–42, 50–51.

5. https://2lffqo2moysixpyb349z0bj6-wpengine.netdna-ssl.com/wp-content
/uploads/2017/03/12.2-Our-Immense-Achievement-Gap-WEB.pdf, pp. 120–21;
https://censusreporter.org/profiles/16000US2718116-eden-prairie-mn.

6. Ibid., pp. 62–63.

7. https://www.twincities.com/2016/01/04/st-paul-school-disciplinary-problems
-increase-as-it-falls-elsewhere/; Glenn Singleton, *More Courageous Conversations* (Thousand Oaks, CA: Corwin, 2013), Kindle loc. 4191.

8. Glenn Singleton, *Courageous Conversations* (Thousand Oaks, CA: Corwin,
2005), Kindle loc. 1447; https://www.linkedin.com/in/gesingleton/; Singleton,
More Courageous Conversations, Kindle locs. 2252, 3707, 4726, 7565; Nexis;
https://censusreporter.org/profiles/15000US060750218001-block-group-1-san
-francisco-ca/.

9. Singleton, *More Courageous Conversations*, Kindle loc. 1729.

10. Ibid., Kindle loc. 2255; Singleton, *Courageous Conversations*, Kindle locs.
1411, 1431, 1440, 4285.

11. Singleton, *Courageous Conversations*, Kindle loc. 2205; Singleton, *More Courageous Conversations*, Kindle loc. 6604.

12. Singleton, *Courageous Conversations*, Kindle loc. 2223; Singleton, *More Courageous Conversations*, Kindle loc. 1022.

13. Singleton, *More Courageous Conversations*, Kindle loc. 4610; https://www.thecut.com/2015/05/can-fieldston-un-teach-racism.html; https://nypost.com/2021/01/30/dalton-school-parents-fight-anti-racism-agenda-in-open-letter/.

14. Singleton, *More Courageous Conversations*, Kindle loc. 4554.

15. Ibid., Kindle loc. 4601.

16. https://www.washingtonpost.com/magazine/2019/10/14/anti-racist-revelations-ibram-x-kendi/; http://www.oregonlive.com/opinion/index.ssf/2009/01/two_faces_of_the_black_america.html.

17. Singleton, *More Courageous Conversations*, Kindle loc. 7420.

18. http://eagnews.org/school-districts-spending-millions-on-white-privilege-training-for-teachers/; https://www.thecut.com/2015/05/can-fieldston-un-teach-racism.html; https://www.baltimorecityschools.org/district-overview; Singleton, *Courageous Conversations*, Kindle loc. 3933; Singleton, *More Courageous Conversations*, Kindle loc. 4160.

19. Singleton, *More Courageous Conversations*, Kindle locs. 3591, 6188; https://conservancy.umn.edu/bitstream/handle/11299/156010/1/Palmer_umn_0130E_13780.pdf, p. 206; Singleton, *Courageous Conversations*, Kindle loc. 1926.

20. Singleton, *More Courageous Conversations*, Kindle loc. 2332.

21. Ibid., Kindle loc. 7595; https://pd.santarosa.edu/sites/pd.santarosa.edu/files/courageous%20conversation%20course%20packet.pdf, p. 36.

22. Singleton, *More Courageous Conversations*, Kindle locs. 3693, 3710, 3728, 3739, 3761, 3800, 3820, 3838, 3844, 6074.

23. https://conservancy.umn.edu/bitstream/handle/11299/156010/1/Palmer_umn_0130E_13780.pdf, p. 194.

24. https://courageousconversation.com/courageous-conversation-certification/; https://us.corwin.com/en-us/nam/product; https://www.thenewamerican.com/culture/education/item/34002-new-curriculum-deep-equity-deeply-racist-demonizes-whites; https://arizonadailyindependent.com/2019/10/30/chandler-unifieds-deep-equity-program-came-with-shocking-price-tag/; https://www.thecollegefix.com/social-justice-program-says-teachers-should-reject-and-resist-parents-who-disagree-with-it.

25. https://web.archive.org/web/20100811123052/http://www.seattleschools.org:80/area/equityandrace/history.html; https://web.archive.org/web/20090912151636/http://www.seattleschools.org:80/area/instructserv/courageousconversations/ccindex.dxml; https://www.fourmilab.ch/fourmilog/archives/seattle_schools_racism_2006-05-29/searace.htm; https://www.law.cornell.edu/supct/html/05-908.ZS.html; https://www.law.cornell.edu/supct/html/05-908.ZO.html; https://www.law.cornell.edu/supct/html/05-908.ZC.html; http://www.greenwichschools.org/uploaded/district/pdfs/Budget/0708_Budget/0708BdgtQ&A120706.pdf; https://www.greenwichschools.org/uploaded/district/pdfs/RISE/Meetings/5_1_07_TF_Meeting/CPlan_RISE_V.pdf, p. 3.

26. https://www.city-journal.org/html/no-thug-left-behind-14951.html.

27. Data as of October 2011. https://www.spps.org/domain/1237; https://www

.twincities.com/2016/01/04/st-paul-school-disciplinary-problems-increase
-as-it-falls-elsewhere/; https://www.city-journal.org/html/no-thug-left-behind
-14951.html.

28. https://www.startribune.com/former-st-paul-teacher-settles-retaliation-suit
-against-district-for-525–000/560627812/; https://www.city-journal.org/html/no
-thug-left-behind-14951.html.

29. https://censusreporter.org/profiles/16000US2718188-edina-mn/; https://www
.publicschoolreview.com/minnesota/edina-public-school-district/2711250
-school-district.

30. https://www.eagnews.org/2015/06/after-critique-white-privilege-training
-company-hides-school-district-client-list-from-public/; https://www.twincities
.com/2016/01/04/st-paul-school-disciplinary-problems-increase-as-it-falls
-elsewhere/; https://files.americanexperiment.org/wp-content/uploads/2019/04
/TM_Winter2018_Edina.pdf, pp. 5–6, 8; https://www.washingtonexaminer.com
/weekly-standard/inside-a-public-school-social-justice-factory.

31. https://www.edinaschools.org/cms/lib07/MN01909547/Centricity/shared/pdfs
/BG5VisionFramework_FINAL-%20Approved%20July%202014%20-%20
PUBLIC-all.pdf, p. 11; https://censusreporter.org/profiles/16000US2718188-edina
-mn.

32. https://www.washingtonexaminer.com/weekly-standard/inside-a-public
-school-social-justice-factory.

33. https://sites.google.com/a/apps.edina.k12.mn.us/mrs-reiling-s-classroom
/student-links/sylabus-for-course-2; https://files.americanexperiment.org/wp
-content/uploads/2019/04/TM_Winter2018_Edina.pdf, p. 4.

34. https://files.americanexperiment.org/wp-content/uploads/2019/04/TM
_Winter2018_Edina.pdf, p. 4.

35. https://web.archive.org/web/20191013034301/https://2lffqo2moysixpyb349z
0bj6-wpengine.netdna-ssl.com/wp-content/uploads/2017/10/Roehl_Voices
FromTheInside.pdf, pp. 1–2; Singleton, *More Courageous Conversations*, Kindle
loc. 6222.

36. https://edinamag.com/article/schools/edina-high-schools-jackie-roehl-named
-minnesota-teacher-year.

37. https://web.archive.org/web/20191013034301/https://2lffqo2moysixpyb349z
0bj6-wpengine.netdna-ssl.com/wp-content/uploads/2017/10/Roehl_Voices
FromTheInside.pdf, p. 4.

38. Ibid., pp. 1, 3–4.

39. https://www.chicagotribune.com/suburbs/skokie/ct-skr-district-219-diversity
-training-tl-0225-20160222-story.html; https://www.deplorablehousewives.news
/edina-school-sarah-patzloff/.

40. https://files.americanexperiment.org/wp-content/uploads/2019/04/TM
_Winter2018_Edina.pdf, p. 6.

41. https://theconversation.com/the-mental-health-crisis-among-americas-youth
-is-real-and-staggering-113239.

42. https://nypost.com/2020/08/27/police-release-video-of-suicide-that-sparked
-minneapolis-looting-riots/; https://thehill.com/homenews/state-watch/503685
-protesters-tear-down-statues-of-union-general-ulysses-s-grant-national;

https://reason.com/2020/08/28/rand-paul-breonna-taylor-rnc-protesters-say-her-name/.

43. https://www.spps.org/cms/lib/MN01910242/Centricity/Domain/10855/digital_suitcase_-_7th_grade_-_civil_rights_1_of_2.docx; https://www.spps.org/cms/lib/MN01910242/Centricity/Domain/10855/digital_suitcase_-_7th_grade_-_civil_rights_2_of_2_ppt.pptx.

44. https://www.spps.org/cms/lib/MN01910242/Centricity/Domain/10855/digital_suitcase_-_7th_grade_-_civil_rights_1_of_2.docx; https://www.spps.org/cms/lib/MN01910242/Centricity/Domain/10855/digital_suitcase_-_7th_grade_-_civil_rights_2_of_2_ppt.pptx; https://www.dol.gov/agencies/ofccp/about/executive-order-11246-history.

45. https://reason.com/2019/11/04/latinx-poll-think-now-hispanics-2020-woke/.

46. https://www.census.gov/library/stories/2020/09/poverty-rates-for-blacks-and-hispanics-reached-historic-lows-in-2019.html.

47. https://www.cnbc.com/2019/10/04/black-and-hispanic-unemployment-is-at-a-record-low.html.

48. https://www.washingtonexaminer.com/washington-secrets/under-trump-black-prison-rate-lowest-in-31-years-hispanics-down-24.

49. https://fas.org/sgp/crs/misc/R45236.pdf.

50. https://www.eagnews.org/2015/06/after-critique-white-privilege-training-company-hides-school-district-client-list-from-public/.

51. https://www1.nyc.gov/assets/nypd/downloads/pdf/use-of-force/use-of-force-2018.pdf, Appendix E; https://scholarlycommons.law.northwestern.edu/cgi/viewcontent.cgi?article=6298&context=jclc, p. 28; https://cwbchicago.com/2020/03/after-years-of-steady-declines-officer-involved-shootings-rise-again-in-chicago.html; https://www.washingtonpost.com/graphics/2019/national/police-shootings-2019/; https://censusreporter.org/profiles/01000US-united-states/.

52. https://theconversation.com/the-mental-health-crisis-among-americas-youth-is-real-and-staggering-113239.

53. https://www.washingtonexaminer.com/washington-secrets/kids-today-4-in-10-call-constitution-outdated-ok-with-silencing-speech.

5: DON QUIXOTE

1. Court and prison records; interview with Ron Hammond; https://southseattleemerald.com/2020/12/02/tracy-castro-gill-is-insuppressible-and-so-is-ethnic-studies/.

2. Castro-Gill divorce records.

3. https://www.seattletimes.com/seattle-news/data/federal-way-to-vashon-island-here-are-the-most-and-least-diverse-places-in-king-county/; https://www.veranda.com/luxury-lifestyle/g28666999/richest-cities-usa/; https://www.indexmundi.com/facts/united-states/quick-facts/cities/rank/percent-of-people-of-all-ages-in-poverty.

4. https://web.archive.org/web/20201201201922/; https://teacheractivist.com/2020/03/03/the-fight-for-ethnic-studies-and-educators-of-color-in-seattle-public-schools/.

5. https://www.facebook.com/tracy.gill.942/posts/10212384878310699.
6. https://southseattleemerald.com/2020/12/02/tracy-castro-gill-is-insup pressible-and-so-is-ethnic-studies/.
7. Interview with Rick Castro.
8. Data from FOIA request.
9. https://web.archive.org/web/20210225154321/https://teacheractivist.com /2019/06/02/pride-in-my-child/.
10. https://www.k12.wa.us/sites/default/files/public/socialstudies/pubdocs /Math%20SDS%20ES%20Framework.pdf; https://www.king5.com/article/news /education/seattle-schools-math-ethnic-studies/281-168fafda-6bf6-4ec1-ba0d -2a47c5030de3.
11. https://web.archive.org/web/20210227040329/https://www.seattleschools.org /families_communities/committees/ethnic_studies_task_force; https://web.ar chive.org/web/20210626140550/https://www.seattleschools.org/UserFiles/Ser vers/Server_543/File/District/Departments/task_forces/ethnic-studies/Ap proved-Board-Action-Report-20170705-Ethnic-studies.pdf, p. 6.
12. https://washingtonstatereportcard.ospi.k12.wa.us/ReportCard/ViewSchool OrDistrict/101058; https://washingtonstatereportcard.ospi.k12.wa.us/Report Card/ViewSchoolOrDistrict/101013.
13. https://waethnicstudies.com/2020/05/29/the-failures-of-ethnic-studies-and -how-to-fix-them-5/.
14. https://www.seattleschools.org/district/calendars/news/what_s_new/ethnic _studies_update.
15. https://southseattleemerald.com/2020/07/21/ethnic-studies-educator-shrad dha-shirude-on-giving-math-purpose/.
16. Castro-Gill divorce records; https://waethnicstudies.com/learn/; https://web .archive.org/web/20210225154321/; https://teacheractivist.com/2019/06/02/pride -in-my-child/.
17. Ron Hammond interview.
18. Rick Castro interview.
19. https://www.seattleschools.org/district/district_quick_facts; https://twitter.com /TCastroGill/status/1185696060548603904.
20. https://www.k12.wa.us/award/2018-2019-regional-teacher-year-tracy-castro -gill.
21. https://www.youtube.com/watch?v=Fs5wgg-zF1I; https://twitter.com/Steven Welliever/status/1315138283622461440.
22. https://waethnicstudies.com/2019/08/10/how-to-start-an-anti-racist-student -group-in-your-school/; https://southseattleemerald.com/2020/10/04/meet-the -naacp-youth-council-and-their-plan-for-a-school-year-of-racial-justice/.
23. https://southseattleemerald.com/2020/12/02/tracy-castro-gill-is-insup pressible-and-so-is-ethnic-studies/; https://waethnicstudies.com/2019/08/10/how -to-start-an-anti-racist-student-group-in-your-school/; https://www.kingcounty .gov/depts/community-human-services/initiatives/best-starts-for-kids/programs /awards.aspx.
24. https://southseattleemerald.com/2020/12/02/tracy-castro-gill-is-insup pressible-and-so-is-ethnic-studies/; emails obtained under FOIA.

25. https://waethnicstudies.com/2020/02/07/what-gives-you-the-white-of-way
-how-seattle-public-schools-educators-of-color-are-fighting-back/.

26. Seattle Public Schools documents.

27. https://web.archive.org/web/20210101174807/https://teacheractivist.com
/2020/05/21/ayudame-ethnic-studies-in-seattle-needs-you/.

28. Facebook.

29. https://web.archive.org/web/20201201202823/https://teacheractivist.com
/2019/12/04/seattle-public-schools-does-not-like-educators-of-color/.

30. Seattle Public Schools documents.

31. https://www.washingtonpost.com/local/md-politics/local-governments-are
-trying-to-fix-racial-inequity-but-the-path-forward-isnt-clear/2019/08/18/4a7d
93ee-beb6-11e9-9b73-fd3c65ef8f9c_story.html; https://www.seattletimes.com
/education-lab/racial-equity-in-seattle-schools-has-a-long-frustrating-history
-and-its-getting-worse/.

32. https://nces.ed.gov/programs/digest/d18/tables/dt18_219.46.asp (omitting Hawaii because of its unusual racial makeup); https://educationpost.org/network
/chris-stewart/; https://brightbeamnetwork.org/wp-content/uploads/2020/01
/The-Secret-Shame_v4.pdf.

33. https://brightbeamnetwork.org/wp-content/uploads/2020/01/The-Secret
-Shame_v4.pdf.

34. https://www.vbschools.com/common/pages/DisplayFile.aspx?itemId=
28275155; https://www.vbschools.com/common/pages/DisplayFile.aspx?item
Id=28235569, pp. 5–6; https://web.archive.org/web/20200910050445/https://
www.vbschools.com/about_us/DEI/resources; https://crtandthebrain.com/four
-tools-for-interrupting-implicit-bias/; https://www.vbschools.com/about_us/DEI
/resources.

35. https://www.nytimes.com/1987/05/30/us/genteel-chicago-suburb-rages-over
-mr-t-s-tree-massacre.html; https://www.chicagotribune.com/news/ct-xpm-1998
-10-15-9810150170-story.html; https://www.illinoisreportcard.com/School.aspx
?source=studentcharacteristics&Schoolid=340491150160001; https://patch
.com/illinois/lakeforest/chala-holland-named-lake-region-high-school
-principal-year; https://patch.com/illinois/lakeforest/controversy-surrounds-pos
sible-lfhs-principal-pick; https://jwcdaily.com/2015/06/09/why-this-candidate-for
-lfhs/.

36. https://evanstonroundtable.com/2008/12/23/eths-to-engage-in-courageous
-conversations/; https://www.illinoisreportcard.com/school.aspx?source=profile
&Schoolid=050162020170001; 11th Grade PSAE black/white achievement
gap math (54 percent in 2010, 59 percent in 2012, and 57 percent in 2014);
https://www.illinoisreportcard.com/school.aspx?source=retiredtests&source
2=achievementgapret&Schoolid=050162020170001; 62 percent in 2017: https://
www.illinoisreportcard.com/school.aspx?source=trends&source2=achieve
mentgapsat&Schoolid=050162020170001; https://evanstonroundtable.com/2013
/12/04/district-202-school-board-discusses-controversial-consulting-group/.

37. https://www.illinoisreportcard.com/School.aspx?source=retiredtests&
source2=achievementgapret&Schoolid=060162000130001; https://intranet.oprfhs
.org/board-of-education/board_meetings/Regular_Meetings/Packets/2011-12

/August_2011/Finance/PEG_Contract_2011-12.pdf; https://campussuite-storage
.s3.amazonaws.com/prod/1558748/bd01c7ae-765f-11e9-9402-0a56f
8be964e/1933684/f29fc81e-806b-11e9-a15c-1214fa4bbf7c/file/082511ab.pdf,
p. 12; https://www.illinoisreportcard.com/School.aspx?source=retiredtests&
source2=achievementgapret&Schoolid=060162000130001, Grade 11 black/
white; https://theundefeated.com/features/america-to-me-shows-why-all-the
-black-kids-sit-together-in-the-cafeteria/; https://slate.com/culture/2018/08/amer
ica-to-me-review-steve-james-starz-documentary-series-is-a-worthy-follow
-up-to-hoop-dreams.html.

38. https://web.archive.org/web/20130225083738/http://www.hollanded.com
/academic-tracking; https://www.westsiderag.com/2019/04/15/tuesday-panel-with
-chancellor-carranza-will-talk-race-and-education-on-uws.

39. https://www.rockdalenewtoncitizen.com/news/lindsey-sends-former-ahs
-employee-cease-and-desist-notice/article_9268ac6c-bf48-5ef9-a28c-4efc
ca054b09.html.

40. https://www.covnews.com/news/boe-member-named-in-ahs-lawsuit/; https://
www.rockdalenewtoncitizen.com/news/lindsey-sends-former-ahs-employee
-cease-and-desist-notice/article_9268ac6c-bf48-5ef9-a28c-4efcca054b09
.html.

41. https://www.covnews.com/news/education/carpenters-claim-continued
-harassment/.

42. http://northeastnews.net/pages/hope-academy-draws-concern/; https://www.ks
hb.com/news/local-news/missouri-sues-closed-kansas-city-charter-school
-hope-academy-for-37m.

43. https://www.kansascity.com/news/local/article125369789.html.

44. Ibid.; https://www.kansascity.com/news/local/article231309088.html.

45. https://www.kansascity.com/news/local/article220194435.html.

46. https://www.kansascity.com/news/local/article231309088.html.

47. https://www.kansascity.com/news/local/article230491129.html.

48. https://www.kansascity.com/news/local/article233059232.html.

49. https://twitter.com/EquitySupt1/status/1288637930420961280.

50. https://www.aspirationalinsights.com/; https://www.kansascity.com/article239
080048.html; https://www.facebook.com/fox4kc/posts/its-not-ok-to-interfere
-with-any-individuals-right-to-make-a-living-and-be-a-pro/101573717682586
45/.

51. https://twitter.com/EquitySupt1/status/1293584236285505538.

52. https://waethnicstudies.com/wp-content/uploads/2020/07/WAESN-Services
-Catalog-1.pdf.

53. https://southseattleemerald.com/2020/12/02/tracy-castro-gill-is-insup
pressible-and-so-is-ethnic-studies/.

54. https://www.seattletimes.com/education-lab/washington-ethnic-studies
-graduation-requirement-gains-support-from-board-of-education/.

6: CRITICAL RACE THEORY

1. https://biz.loudoun.gov/2018/12/11/loudoun-median-income-2018/; https://www
.washingtonpost.com/local/loudoun-incumbents-lead-the-way-in
-fundraising-for-nov-3-election/2015/09/04/4c47b366-50d4-11e5-8c19-0b6825a

a4a3a_story.html; https://data.census.gov/cedsci/table?q=Table%20S0201%20&t=Income%20and%20Poverty%3ARace%20and%20Ethnicity&g=0500000US51107&tid=ACSDT1Y2019.B19013B&hidePreview=false; https://censusreporter.org/profiles/05000US51107-loudoun-county-va/.

2. https://www.lcps.org/Page/219268.

3. https://theequitycollaborative.com/about/who-we-are/; https://s3.amazonaws.com/jnswire/jns-media/db/cb/11474280/loudouncontract.pdf; https://theequitycollaborative.com/wp-content/uploads/2020/05/Intro-To-Critical-Race-Theory.pdf, p. 11.

4. https://mtsu.edu/first-amendment/article/1254/critical-race-theory; https://www.tandfonline.com/doi/abs/10.1080/095183998236863, p. 17.

5. https://www.americanbar.org/groups/crsj/publications/human_rights_magazine_home/human_rights_vol38_2011/fall2011/a_past_present_and_future_look_at_no_child_left_behind/; https://www2.ed.gov/policy/eseaflex/esea-flexibility-faqs.doc, p. 1.

6. https://theequitycollaborative.com/wp-content/uploads/2020/05/Intro-To-Critical-Race-Theory.pdf, p. 14.

7. https://acresofancestry.org/wp-content/uploads/2021/01/Harris_Whiteness-as-Property_1993.pdf, pp. 30–31; https://www.foxnews.com/media/nikole-hannah-jones-politically-racially-black; http://socialistreview.org.uk/415/politically-black-back; James Lindsay and Helen Pluckrose, *Cynical Theories* (Durham, NC: Pitchstone, 2020), Kindle loc. 832.

8. https://theequitycollaborative.com/wp-content/uploads/2020/05/Intro-To-Critical-Race-Theory.pdf, p. 13.

9. Dolores Delgado Bernal and Octavio Villalpando, "An Apartheid of Knowledge in Academia: The Struggle over the 'Legitimate' Knowledge of Faculty of Color," *Equity & Excellence in Education* 35, 2 (2002): 169–80, DOI: 10.1080/713845282, pp. 2, 10.

10. Ibid., p. 5.

11. Ibid., pp. 5–6, 9, 11; https://www.calstatela.edu/academic/cls/faculty-staff; https://www.jstor.org/stable/3347168?seq=1.

12. Bernal and Villalpando, "An Apartheid of Knowledge in Academia."

13. https://theequitycollaborative.com/wp-content/uploads/2020/05/Intro-To-Critical-Race-Theory.pdf, p. 21.

14. Ibid., pp. 23, 26.

15. Ibid.

16. https://loudounnow.com/2020/11/11/count-complete-2020-election-turnout-neared-80-in-loudoun/.

17. https://www.loudountimes.com/news/prominent-pastor-elected-loudoun-naacp-president/article_b7b7ba28-ed9e-11e8-9925-5f388f9ee908.html.

18. https://web.archive.org/web/20200924141456/https://www.americanmusliminstitution.org/sisteract.

19. https://loudounnow.com/2020/11/20/ag-finds-racial-discriminatory-impact-in-academies-admissions-policies/; https://www.wusa9.com/embeds/video/65-34e0902a-37fe-4ec9-9c76-f30f37fb2706/iframe?jwsource=fb&fbclid=IwAR10BvoMwAsz0Xj57mIVVv78Wt43gorsOLwsAucmdrsCEkxZFoBtTCRqh00; https://www.loudountimes.com/news/toll-brothers-to-transfer-belmont

-slave-cemetery-property-to-loudoun/article_ba674dda-3824-5e11-9439-2fe
8fb9cb1de.html; https://www.npr.org/local/305/2020/08/28/907003159/in-virginia
-a-family-tragedy-stirs-new-life-in-a-burial-ground-for-the-enslaved.

20. https://drive.google.com/file/d/1EXqSe-1XrZxJwjHMtTev6lm1hqV0NZuB
/view.

21. www.linkedin.com/in/michellecthomspmp; https://www.facebook.com/Holy
andWhole/.

22. https://www.americanmusliminstitution.org/sisteract.

23. https://www.everycrsreport.com/reports/RL33284.html; https://web.archive.org
/web/20161029004801/http://mcacg.com/gpage.html; www.linkedin.com/in
/michellecthomspmp.

24. https://fcw.com/articles/2003/01/28/unisys-moving-on-tsa-systems.aspx;
https://web.archive.org/web/20170625195702/http://mcacg.com/.

25. https://www.oig.dhs.gov/assets/TM/OIGtm_JLT_091708.pdf, p. 3.

26. https://patch.com/virginia/ashburn/loudoun-county-public-schools-among
-best-va; https://loudounnow.com/2017/07/06/40-loudoun-schools-rank-top-in
-state/.

27. https://scholar.google.com/scholar?q=%22critical+race+theory%22+dis
rupt&hl=en&as_sdt=0&as_vis=1&oi=scholart (last viewed on August 9,
2021).

28. https://drive.google.com/file/d/1BVpQC9Unf6WSvuebFixSK5_fAHDCpbN9
/view?usp=sharing, pp. 3–4, 8, 10.

29. https://drive.google.com/file/d/16WeFPlZjtt8icDULu2SrKrHdtFsNH1sp
/view?usp=sharing, pp. 15, 18.

30. https://s3.amazonaws.com/jnswire/jns-media/db/cb/11474280/loudoun
contract.pdf.

31. https://www.lcps.org/cms/lib/VA01000195/Centricity/domain/60/equity
_initiative_documents/LCPS_Equity_Report_FINALReport12_2_19.pdf, pp.
13, 25.

32. Ibid., p. 8.

33. Ibid., pp. 11, 18; https://www.nytimes.com/2020/12/26/us/mimi-groves-jimmy
-galligan-racial-slurs.html.

34. https://www.lcps.org/cms/lib/VA01000195/Centricity/domain/60/equity
_initiative_documents/LCPS_Equity_Report_FINALReport12_2_19.pdf, pp.
11–12; https://s3.amazonaws.com/jnswire/jns-media/d2/95/11474279/addendum
.pdf; https://www.foxnews.com/us/virginia-county-spends-nearly-500g-on
-critical-race-theory-programs-for-schools.

35. https://www.lcps.org/cms/lib/VA01000195/Centricity/domain/60/equity
_initiative_documents/LCPS_Equity_Report_FINALReport12_2_19.pdf, p. 13.

36. https://www.loudountimes.com/news/loudoun-county-school-board
-extends-equity-committee-indefinitely/article_a9c4ca7c-42ad-11ea-9407
-37e339a05f84.html; https://www.lcps.org/cms/lib/VA01000195/Centricity/domain
/60/voag/LCPS_Nov_26_2019_Letter_to_Attorney_General.pdf, p. 79; https://
loudounnow.com/2021/01/05/loudoun-schools-equity-committee-expanded
-not-dissolved/; Equity Committee documents; https://www.newsbreak.com
/news/1499014130207/loudoun-county-school-board-extends-equity-com
mittee-indefinitely.

37. https://s3.amazonaws.com/jnswire/jns-media/d2/95/11474279/addendum.pdf; https://player.vimeo.com/video/386944572 @ 2:10.

38. http://www.kapaxsolutions.com/about.html; https://www.usaspending.gov /recipient/d31f6390-1dad-6a31-eb60-8ccba8626fd0-C/latest; https://player.vimeo .com/video/386944572 @ 9:40, 2:04:20.

39. https://www.trilloquy.org/opuses; Equity Committee documents.

40. https://ethicalsociety.org/welcoming-our-new-director-of-lifelong-learning/; www.linkedin.com/in/laraprofitt.

41. Equity Committee documents.

42. https://s3.amazonaws.com/jnswire/jns-media/0e/61/11477272/policydraft.pdf; https://go.boarddocs.com/vsba/loudoun/Board.nsf/files/BQUPY2663CC6/$ file/LCPS%20Action%20Plans%20to%20Combat%20Systemic%20Racism _062320%20Presentation.pdf, p. 9.

43. https://s3.amazonaws.com/jnswire/jns-media/0e/61/11477272/policydraft.pdf; https://thenewamerican.com/virginia-school-board-pauses-plan-to-punish -teachers-who-criticize-critical-race-theory/.

44. https://www.lcps.org/cms/lib/VA01000195/Centricity/domain/60/equity _initiative_documents/Detailed_Plan_to_Combat_Systemic_Racism_August _2020.pdf, p. 5.

45. https://newdiscourses.com/2020/06/do-better-than-critical-race-theory/; https://www.foxnews.com/media/nikole-hannah-jones-politically-racially -black; http://socialistreview.org.uk/415/politically-black-back; https://nces.ed .gov/programs/coe/indicator_cge.asp, Table 203.50.

46. https://censusreporter.org/profiles/05000US51107-loudoun-county-va/; https://www.loudoun.gov/86/Board-of-Supervisors; https://player.vimeo.com /video/386944572, Introductions @ 8:00.

47. https://wjla.com/news/local/lcps-parents-raise-concerns-about-6-figure -equity-contract.

48. https://www.lcps.org/cms/lib/VA01000195/Centricity/domain/60/voag/FINAL _DETERMINATION_2020-11-18_NAACP_Loudoun_Branch_v_Loudoun _County_Public_Schools.pdf.

49. https://www.lcps.org/page/8; https://www.wusa9.com/embeds/video/65-34e0902 a-37fe-4ec9-9c76-f30f37fb2706/iframe?jwsource=fb&fbclid=IwAR10BvoM wAsz0Xj57mIVVv78Wt43gorsOLwsAucmdrsCEkxZFoBtTCRqh00.

50. https://censusreporter.org/profiles/05000US51107-loudoun-county-va/.

51. https://www.lcps.org/cms/lib/VA01000195/Centricity/domain/60/voag/FINAL _DETERMINATION_2020-11-18_NAACP_Loudoun_Branch_v_Loudoun _County_Public_Schools.pdf, p. 32.

52. https://www.baconsrebellion.com/wp/a-threat-to-due-process-comes-from -drum-roll-virginias-division-of-human-rights/.

53. https://www.lcps.org/cms/lib/VA01000195/Centricity/domain/60/voag/FINAL _DETERMINATION_2020-11-18_NAACP_Loudoun_Branch_v_Loudoun _County_Public_Schools.pdf, pp. 1–2.

54. https://loudounnow.com/2020/11/20/ag-finds-racial-discriminatory-impact -in-academies-admissions-policies/; https://www.wusa9.com/embeds/video/65 -34e0902a-37fe-4ec9-9c76-f30f37fb2706/iframe?jwsource=fb&fbclid=IwAR 10BvoMwAsz0Xj57mIVVv78Wt43gorsOLwsAucmdrsCEkxZFoBtTCRqh00.

55. https://www.lcps.org/cms/lib/VA01000195/Centricity/domain/60/voag/FINAL _DETERMINATION_2020-11-18_NAACP_Loudoun_Branch_v_Loudoun _County_Public_Schools.pdf, pp. 13, 38, 45.

56. Ibid., pp. 11–12, 18 (#4).

57. https://stoplcpscrt.com/wp-content/uploads/2020/10/NAACP-Terms-of -Conciliation_9-30-2020.pdf, #1aii; https://go.boarddocs.com/vsba/loudoun /Board.nsf/files/BSCJSG4E8AE0/$file/Academies%20Admissions%20 Changes%20Presentation%20081120.pdf, p. 21; https://www.loudountimes .com/news/more-school-board-approves-inequity-combating-changes-to -academies-of-loudoun-admissions-process/article_abf519f2-dc39-11ea-988b -d7e7bbca120c.html.

58. https://www.lcps.org/cms/lib/VA01000195/Centricity/domain/60/voag/FINAL _DETERMINATION_2020-11-18_NAACP_Loudoun_Branch_v_Loudoun _County_Public_Schools.pdf, p. 18.

59. Ibid., pp. 19, 57–61; https://stoplcpscrt.com/wp-content/uploads/2020/10/NAACP -Terms-of-Conciliation_9-30-2020.pdf.

60. https://www.lcps.org/cms/lib/VA01000195/Centricity/domain/60/voag/FINAL _DETERMINATION_2020-11-18_NAACP_Loudoun_Branch_v_Loudoun _County_Public_Schools.pdf, p. 59.

61. Ibid., p. 58.

62. Ibid., p. 61.

63. Ibid., pp. 57–61.

64. https://www.lcps.org/cms/lib/VA01000195/Centricity/domain/60/equity _initiative_documents/An_Apology_to_the_Black_Community.pdf.

65. https://loudounnow.com/2020/10/05/loudoun-naacp-leaders-find-school -divisions-segregation-apology-lacking/.

66. https://www.houstonchronicle.com/news/houston-texas/education/article /Clear-Creek-ISD-superintendent-racist-incidents-15716184.php; https://loud ounnow.com/2020/11/11/texas-school-district-defends-decision-to-hire -williams/; https://communityimpact.com/houston/bay-area/education/2021/02 /04/clear-creek-isd-modifies-policy-to-address-concerns-surrounding-critical -race-theory/.

67. https://www.insidenova.com/news/education/loudoun-county-schools -superintendent-leaving-for-houston/article_5c22b5fe-2308-11eb-9298 -f328e8cb4ccd.html; https://www.galvnews.com/news/article_076926a7-4bdc -59a4-8fd2-5e447a748358.html.

7: RACE TO THE BOTTOM

1. https://nypost.com/2019/05/20/richard-carranza-held-doe-white-supremacy -culture-training/.

2. https://www.k12.wa.us/sites/default/files/public/socialstudies/pubdocs /Math%20SDS%20ES%20Framework.pdf; https://www.edweek.org/ew/articles /2019/10/11/seattle-schools-lead-controversial-push-to-rehumanize.html.

3. https://projects.propublica.org/nonprofits/display_990/526078980/10_2020 _prefixes_52-55%2F526078980_201908_990_2020102117396330, p. 1, line 20; http://www.ascd.org/about-ascd.aspx; http://www.ascd.org/publications

/educational-leadership/sept20/vol78/num01/%C2%A3Antiracist%C2%A3
-Grading-Starts-with-You.aspx.

4. https://www.sandiegouniontribune.com/news/education/story/2020-10-15/san
-diego-unified-changes-grading-protocols-to-be-more-equitable; https://www
.nbcsandiego.com/news/local/san-diego-unified-school-district-changes
-grading-system-to-combat-racism/2425346/; https://go.boarddocs.com/ca/sandi
/Board.nsf/files/BU8VCU802554/$file/AR%205121%20Grades-Evalua
tion%20of%20Student%20Achievement%20-%20Redline.pdf.

5. https://www.brookings.edu/blog/brown-center-chalkboard/2017/08/10/ana
lyzing-the-homework-gap-among-high-school-students/.

6. https://blogs.edweek.org/edweek/DigitalEducation/2015/01/is_grit_racist
.html.

7. https://www.insidehighered.com/blogs/technology-and-learning/could-grit
-thinking-drive-inequality.

8. https://crescendoedgroup.org/services/grading/why-grading/; http://crescendo
edgroup.org/wp-content/uploads/2014/03/Equitable-grading-Leadership-Mag
_NovDec.pdf.

9. https://www.kippnyc.org/results/; https://www.kipp.org/news/weekly-thought
s-turning-words-into-action/.

10. https://www.heraldtribune.com/story/news/education/2020/09/02/sarasota
-schools-table-race-discussion/5691277002/.

11. https://pd.santarosa.edu/sites/pd.santarosa.edu/files/courageous%20conver
sation%20course%20packet.pdf, p. 62.

12. https://www.latimes.com/archives/la-xpm-2007-nov-18-me-gap18-story.html.

13. https://www.imsa.edu/imsa-ranks-as-a-best-stem-school-by-newsweek/;
https://digitalcommons.imsa.edu/cgi/viewcontent.cgi?article=1057&context
=pres_pr, p. 34.

14. https://digitalcommons.imsa.edu/cgi/viewcontent.cgi?article=1057&context
=pres_pr, p. 34.

15. https://digitalcommons.imsa.edu/cgi/viewcontent.cgi?article=1001&context
=dei_ianarai, pp. 2–4; https://vimeo.com/126890109 8:50; https://www.eddie
moorejr.com/.

16. https://alphanewsmn.com/chaska-school-district-tries-to-stay-woke-instead
-associates-with-anti-semites/.

17. Muhammad Khalifa, *Culturally Responsive School Leadership* (Cambridge,
MA: Harvard Education Press, 2018), p. 8, https://www.amazon.com/gp
/product/1682532070/ref=dbs_a_def_rwt_bibl_vppi_i3.

18. https://digitalcommons.imsa.edu/cgi/viewcontent.cgi?article=1057&context
=pres_pr.

19. https://www.maa.org/sites/default/files/pdf/AMC/usamo/2020/MO%20List
.pdf.

20. https://www.wsj.com/articles/new-york-city-set-to-adopt-culturally-respon
sive-education-in-schools-11564606684; http://www.nysed.gov/common/nysed
/files/programs/crs/culturally-responsive-sustaining-education-framework.pdf,
pp. 8, 33–34, 53.

21. https://research.steinhardt.nyu.edu/scmsAdmin/media/users/atn293/pdf/CRE

_Brief_2017_PrintBooklet_170817.pdf; https://www.wsj.com/articles/new-york-city-set-to-adopt-culturally-responsive-education-in-schools-11564606684.

22. https://ethicalschools.org/2019/10/prioritizing-mindsets-what-new-york-states-culturally-responsive-sustaining-education-framework-gets-right/; https://research.steinhardt.nyu.edu/scmsAdmin/media/users/atn293/pdf/CRE_Brief_2017_PrintBooklet_170817.pdf.

23. https://ethicalschools.org/2019/10/prioritizing-mindsets-what-new-york-states-culturally-responsive-sustaining-education-framework-gets-right/.

24. https://research.steinhardt.nyu.edu/scmsAdmin/media/users/atn293/pdf/CRE_Brief_2017_PrintBooklet_170817.pdf, p. 15.

25. https://ethicalschools.org/2019/10/prioritizing-mindsets-what-new-york-states-culturally-responsive-sustaining-education-framework-gets-right/.

26. https://research.steinhardt.nyu.edu/scmsAdmin/media/users/atn293/pdf/CRE_Brief_2017_PrintBooklet_170817.pdf, p. 23.

27. Ibid., p. 53.

28. Ibid., p. 56.

29. https://rossieronline.usc.edu/blog/praxis-core-teaching-credential/; https://www.ets.org/Media/Research/pdf/ETS-NEA-2011-01.pdf, p. 9; https://www.ets.org/praxis/about/subject/; https://www.mometrix.com/academy/praxis-ii/elementary-education-content/.

30. https://www.nea.org/sites/default/files/2020–05/ETS_NEAteacherdiversity11.pdf, pp. 7, 14; https://www.nctq.org/dmsView/A_Fair_Chance, p. 4; https://www.nea.org/professional-excellence/professional-learning/teacher-licensure/praxis.

31. https://www.nea.org/sites/default/files/2020-05/ETS_NEAteacherdiversity11.pdf, pp. 13–14; https://www.chalkbeat.org/2017/9/12/21100902/certification-rules-and-tests-are-keeping-would-be-teachers-of-color-out-of-america-s-classrooms-her.

32. https://www.seattletimes.com/education-lab/many-are-interested-in-washington-states-hardest-to-fill-teacher-jobs-they-just-need-support-to-get-there-survey-finds/; https://edsource.org/2020/california-may-soon-require-fewer-tests-to-become-a-teacher-at-least-temporarily/631186; https://leginfo.legislature.ca.gov/faces/billTextClient.xhtml?bill_id=201920200AB1982; https://abc7news.com/archive/7339426/; https://chalkbeat.org/posts/ny/2017/03/13/new-york-officials-vote-to-eliminate-controversial-literacy-exam-for-prospective-teachers/; https://www.poughkeepsiejournal.com/story/news/education/2017/03/11/test-meant-screen-teachers-instead-weeded-out-minorities/99050796/.

33. https://www.nationsreportcard.gov/ndecore/xplore/NDE; https://infohub.nyced.org/docs/default-source/default-document-library/school-ela-results-2013-2019-(public).xlsx; https://www.sciencedirect.com/science/article/abs/pii/S0272775715000084.

34. https://reports.collegeboard.org/pdf/2020-total-group-sat-suite-assessments-annual-report.pdf; http://i.bnet.com/blogs/education-major-study.pdf.

35. https://www.ets.org/Media/Research/pdf/RR-11-08.pdf, p. 24.

36. https://www.aera.net/About-AERA/Who-We-Are.

37. http://www.aera19.net/uploads/7/6/6/4/76643089/06_indices_final.pdf.

8: FUNDING

1. https://foxbaltimore.com/news/project-baltimore/13-baltimore-city-high
    -schools-zero-students-proficient-in-math.
2. https://www.educationnext.org/new-york-times-lets-senator-spread-misinfor
    mation-again-kamala-harris-schools/; https://www.theatlantic.com/education
    /archive/2019/05/kamala-harris-america-needs-fix-public-k-12-funding
    /589207/.
3. https://elizabethwarren.com/plans/public-education.
4. https://berniesanders.com/issues/reinvest-in-public-education/.
5. https://nces.ed.gov/pubs2020/2020308.pdf, p. 7, https://handbook.fas.harvard
    .edu/book/tuition-and-fees; https://oir.harvard.edu/fact-book/undergraduate
    _package; https://censusreporter.org/profiles/05000US24510-baltimore-city-md/.
6. "Table 215.30. Enrollment, Poverty, and Federal Funds for the 120 Largest School
    Districts," Department of Education, accessed September 2, 2021, https://nces
    .ed.gov/programs/digest/d19/tables/dt19_215.30.asp; https://baltimore.cbslocal
    .com/2015/02/18/baltimore-ranked-one-of-americas-poorest-cities/; ttps://www
    .baltimoresun.com/news/investigations/bs-md-baltimore-schools-funding-2018
    0601-story.html; https://www.educationnext.org/progressive-school-funding
    -united-states/.
7. https://www.brookings.edu/blog/brown-center-chalkboard/2017/05/25/do
    -school-districts-spend-less-money-on-poor-and-minority-students/; https://
    www2.ed.gov/programs/titleiparta/index.html;https://eric.ed.gov/?id=ED0421
    10; http://www.urban.org/sites/default/files/publication/90586/school_funding
    _brief.pdf, pp. 1–2.
8. https://www.urban.org/sites/default/files/publication/32136/411785-Racial
    -Disparities-in-Education-Finance-Going-Beyond-Equal-Revenues.PDF, p. 9.
9. https://www.fairus.org/sites/default/files/2017-08/Cost_in_translation_DC
    Metro_Feb2015.pdf; https://news.mit.edu/2018/cognitive-scientists-define-crit
    ical-period-learning-language-0501.
10. https://www.justfacts.com/education#k12_spend; https://nces.ed.gov/programs
    /digest/d19/tables/dt19_236.55.asp?current=yes.
11. https://nces.ed.gov/programs/digest/d19/tables/dt19_211.60.asp; https://www
    .edchoice.org/wp-content/uploads/2017/06/Back-to-the-Staffing-Surge-by
    -Ben-Scafidi.pdf, pp. 6, 22.
12. https://www.baltimoresun.com/opinion/editorial/bs-ed-0306-kirwan-taxes
    -20200305-ivzfhnwoqvexhg5mrrwfq6wa4y-story.html; https://www.wbal.com
    /article/419367/2/gov-hogan-kirwan-proposal-to-add-to-state-deficit-cost-tax
    -payers-thousands; https://baltimore.cbslocal.com/2020/01/20/baltimore-city
    -school-educators-students-urge-lawmakers-to-adopt-kirwan-plan/.
13. https://censusreporter.org/profiles/05000US24510-baltimore-city-md/; https://er
    pextapps.bcps.k12.md.us/pls/sec5/f?p=109:2:2726896750490.
14. https://www.marylandmatters.org/2020/07/09/pro-kirwan-forces-spent-most-on
    -session-37-lobbyists-cleared-250k/; https://www.mabe.org/adequacy-funding/.
15. https://www.cato.org/sites/cato.org/files/pubs/pdf/pa-298.pdf, pp. 1–3, 7, 9;
    https://www.chicagotribune.com/news/ct-xpm-1995-06-22-9506220051-story
    .html.

16. https://twitter.com/KamalaHarris/status/1322963321994289154.

17. https://www.washingtonpost.com/education/study-finds-black-and-latino-students-face-significant-funding-gap/2020/07/21/712f376a-caca-11ea-b0e3-d55bda07d66a_story.html; https://tcf.org/content/report/closing-americas-education-funding/.

18. https://docs.google.com/spreadsheets/d/1sADaSq-zzAo1bQIA0AICN2dsPrLAmRgJ7dUccy9VY-c/edit#gid=1578744110;https://censusreporter.org/profiles/04000US35-new-mexico/.

19. https://www.losalamosnm.us/government/departments/economic_development/doing_business_here_demographics; https://docs.google.com/spreadsheets/d/1sADaSq-zzAo1bQIA0AICN2dsPrLAmRgJ7dUccy9VY-c/edit#gid=1578744110; https://tcf.org/content/report/closing-americas-education-funding/?agreed=1&agreed=1#methodology.

20. https://tcf.org/content/report/closing-americas-education-funding/?agreed=1&agreed=1#methodology.

21. https://www.gse.harvard.edu/news/ed/17/05/battle-over-charter-schools.

22. For example, Myron Orfield, a professor in Minneapolis who has spent his career pushing equity, was paid by three Illinois teachers unions and the Ford Foundation to write the report that ultimately "recommended that the Chicago Public School District institute a three-year moratorium on new charter schools." Orfield compared charter schools unfavorably to public schools through what charter school representatives said was a combination of factual errors and manipulating the data in the name of equity, with Orfield conducting statistical manipulations that "adjusted" charter school students' performance downward since they were less likely to be truant. https://www.law.umn.edu/sites/law.umn.edu/files/newsfiles/8a690b58/Chicago-Charters-FINAL.pdf; https://web.archive.org/web/20160422092649/https://www.incschools.org/five-reasons-im-taking-professor-orfields-research-seriously.

23. https://www.privateschoolreview.com/tuition-stats/private-school-cost-by-state.

24. https://nces.ed.gov/programs/digest/d20/tables/dt20_236.75.asp.

25. https://www.nationsreportcard.gov/reading/states/achievement/?grade=8.

26. https://www.glassdoor.com/Salaries/phd-student-salary-SRCH_KO0,11.htm.

27. https://www.the74million.org/article/how-minnesotas-push-for-integrated-schools-is-sparking-a-war-against-charters-serving-minority-families.

28. Total spent on public K–12, 2018–19: $752.3 billion; https://www.census.gov/library/stories/2021/05/united-states-spending-on-public-schools-in-2019-highest-since-2008.html. This increased significantly more recently thanks to coronavirus-justified funds, such as $128.6 billion, here: https://www.cbo.gov/system/files/2021-02/hEdandLaborreconciliationestimate.pdf, p. 3.

9: BRAINWASHED

1. Greta Thunberg, Svante Thunberg, Malena Ernman, and Beata Ernman, *Our House Is on Fire: Scenes of a Family and Planet in Crisis* (New York: Penguin Books, 2018), Kindle locs. 398, 924; https://ladyliberty1885.com/2019/10/04/wcpss-says-no-complaints-over-school-mural-of-controversial-climate-kid-thunberg-and-rapper-lil-nas-x/.

2. Department of Education Table 215.30, "Enrollment, Poverty, and Federal Funds for the 120 Largest School Districts" (available at https://nces.ed.gov/programs /digest/d19/tables/dt19_215.30.asp).

3. https://drive.google.com/drive/folders/1k0sqquiRa2m6NdbbgFitXTN2pz 88pHlC?usp=sharing2020SessionNotes/WhitenessinEdSpaces-SessionNotes .docx.

4. Ibid.

5. https://debbyirving.com/schedule/.

6. Debby Irving, *Waking Up White* (Plano, TX: Elephant Room Press, 2014), Kindle locs. 283, 363; https://censusreporter.org/profiles/15000US250173543003 -block-group-3-middlesex-ma/.

7. https://censusreporter.org/profiles/14000US23003952600-census-tract-9526 -aroostook-me/.

8. Irving, *Waking Up White*, Kindle locs. 2688, 3999, 4076; https://education.uw .edu/people/rjd.

9. https://drive.google.com/drive/folders/1k0sqquiRa2m6NdbbgFitXTN2pz 88pHlC?usp=sharing.

10. https://drive.google.com/drive/folders/1k0sqquiRa2m6NdbbgFitXTN2pz 88pHlC?usp=sharing 2020SessionNotes/PrisonPipeline-Sessionnotes.docx.

11. https://drive.google.com/drive/folders/1k0sqquiRa2m6NdbbgFitXTN2pz 88pHlC?usp=sharing2020SessionNotes/WhitenessinEdSpaces-SessionNotes .docx, p. 5; https://drive.google.com/drive/folders/1k0sqquiRa2m6NdbbgFit XTN2pz88pHlC?usp=sharing2020SessionNotes/TeachingRealHistory -Sessionnotes.docx, p. 1.

12. https://nces.ed.gov/programs/edge/Geographic/DistrictBoundaries.

13. https://redstate.com/brandon_morse/2018/06/20/southern-poverty-law-center -faces-dozens-lawsuits-organizations-falsely-labeled-hate-groups-n91296.

14. http://www.tolerance.org/sites/default/files/general/TT_Lets_Talk_web.pdf; https://www.tolerance.org/magazine/subscribe.

15. https://www.montgomeryadvertiser.com/story/news/2019/03/16/morris-dees -splc-southern-poverty-law-center-martin-luther-king-jr-levin-hatewatch-klan -tracy-larkin/3173039002/.

16. https://www.fbi.gov/history/famous-cases/kkk-series; https://freebeacon.com /issues/southern-poverty-surpasses-half-billion-in-assets-121-million-now -offshore/.

17. https://www.learningforjustice.org/educator-grants.

18. http://www.corestandards.org/standards-in-your-state/.

19. http://www.learningforjustice.org/sites/default/files/Perspectives%20User %20Guide.pdf, p. 2; https://www.learningforjustice.org/frameworks/national -standards; https://www.learningforjustice.org/classroom-resources/learning -plans; http://www.corestandards.org/ELA-Literacy/RF/3/; https://www.toler ance.org/classroom-resources/tolerance-lessons/the-color-of-law-developing -the-white-middle-class.

20. https://www.learningforjustice.org/magazine/fall-2019/teaching-hard-his tory-from-the-beginning; https://www.learningforjustice.org/classroom-resources /lessons/white-antiracist-biographies-early-grades; https://lockesociety.org /destroying-the-us-one-student-at-a-time-part-1-teaching-tolerance/; https://

web.archive.org/web/20170529151953/https://www.nea.org/assets/docs/18
141%20DR%20NEA%20HCR%20Lesson%20Introduction_12-29-15.pdf;
https://www.tolerance.org/sites/default/files/2017-06/TT_Social_Justice_Stan
dards_0.pdf; https://www.doe.in.gov/sites/default/files/news/ias-and-sjs-ana
lysis-social-justicedocx.pdf.

21. https://www.tolerance.org/magazine/spring-2011/ten-myths-about-im
migration.

22. https://www.tolerance.org/magazine/fall-2018/this-is-not-a-drill; https://www
.tolerance.org/magazine/spring-2011/ten-myths-about-immigration.

23. https://www.learningforjustice.org/sites/default/files/2018-11/TT-Social
-Justice-Standards-Facilitator-Guide-WEB_0.pdf, p. 7, https://ladyliberty1885
.com/2019/04/24/wcpss-office-of-diversity-affairs-openly-promotes-splc-tied
-social-justice-standards/; https://www.city-journal.org/html/demagogic-bully
-15370.html; https://www.tolerance.org/magazine/spring-1998/an-unconditional
-embrace.

24. https://ethics.house.gov/campaign/general-prohibition-against-using-official
-resources-campaign-or-political-purposes; https://gai.georgetown.edu/changes
-to-both-hatch-act-and-anti-lobbying-act-you-should-be-aware-of/.

25. https://web.archive.org/web/20210703150326/https://futureforlearning.org
/who-we-are/; https://www.zinnedproject.org/about/.

26. https://www.wcpss.net/equity; https://www.wcpss.net/cms/lib/NC01911451/Cen
tricity/Domain/4/wcpss-letterhead-OCR%20Resolution%20Agreement%20
Summary%20.pdf; https://ladyliberty1885.com/2019/07/01/wcpss-office-of-eq
uity-affairs-taxpayer-price-tag/; https://www.washingtonpost.com/education
/2018/11/21/controversy-over-teaching-thanksgiving-kids-edition/.

27. https://ladyliberty1885.com/2019/07/09/wcpss-equity-affairs-we-will-leverage
-student-voices-to-advance-equity-framework/; https://ladyliberty1885.com
/2019/08/29/diversity-inventory-worksheet-given-to-heritage-high-students
-yanked-after-parents-push-back/.

28. https://simbli.eboardsolutions.com/AboutUs/AboutUs.aspx?S=10399
&TID=1; https://www.newsobserver.com/news/local/education/article210451
41.html; https://ladyliberty1885.com/2020/07/10/state-board-of-ed-social-studies
-changes-racial-social-justice/.

29. https://sites.google.com/wcpss.net/edcamp-equity/who-we-are.

30. https://www.eventbrite.com/e/edcamp-equity-2020-tickets-83628104913.

31. https://sites.google.com/view/equity4wake/join-us; https://ladyliberty1885.com
/2020/02/23/wcpss-updates-enrollment-edcamp-equity-board-member-lie
-green-hope-dance/.

32. https://ladyliberty1885.com/2020/09/05/records-whiteness-in-ed-spaces-wcpss
-edcamp-equity-2020/.

33. https://k12database.unc.edu/lesson/.

34. https://k12database.unc.edu/wp-content/uploads/sites/31/2016/11/Ideas-for
-Teaching-about-Terrorism.pdf.

35. https://k12database.unc.edu/wp-content/uploads/sites/31/2012/05/Other
Victims.pdf.

36. https://k12database.unc.edu/wp-content/uploads/sites/31/2012/04/American
Dream.pdf.

37. https://lockesociety.org/the-people-behind-the-current-curriculum/; https://locke society.org/zinns-america-rewriting-history/.

38. Mary Grabar, *Debunking Howard Zinn* (Washington, DC: Regnery History, 2019), Kindle locs. 558, 1150, 1226, 1237, 1283, 1317.

39. Ibid., Kindle locs. 1079, 72.

40. https://www.zinnedproject.org/materials/; https://www.zinnedproject.org/about /faq/; https://www.zinnedproject.org/news/zep-articles-at-newsela/; https://news ela.com/about/press-releases/newsela-launches-new-content-solutions-to -strengthen-ela-social-studies-and-science-instruction/.

41. https://www.zinnedproject.org/if-we-knew-our-history/teaching-more-civics.

42. https://www.zinnedproject.org/materials/coronavirus-pandemic-tribunal/.

43. https://www.hardyms.org/m/pages/index.jsp?uREC_ID=874712&type=u; 2017 PARCC results; https://m.facebook.com/watch/?v=691290431646414&_rdr.

44. http://www.oregonlive.com/opinion/index.ssf/2009/01/two_faces_of_the _black_america.html; https://news.yale.edu/2018/04/02/writer-hannah-jones -discusses-black-education-desegregation-and-privilege; https://nikolehannah jones.com/about/; https://thefederalist.com/2020/06/25/in-racist-screed-nyts-16 19-project-founder-calls-white-race-barbaric-devils-bloodsuckers-no-dif ferent-than-hitler/.

45. https://www.nytimes.com/2019/12/20/magazine/we-respond-to-the-historians -who-critiqued-the-1619-project.html; https://www.politico.com/news/magazine /2020/03/06/1619-project-new-york-times-mistake-122248; https://www.wsws .org/en/articles/2019/09/03/proj-a03.html.

46. https://www.realclearinvestigations.com/articles/2020/01/31/disputed_ny _times_1619_project_is_already_shaping_kids_minds_on_race_bias_122192 .html.

47. https://pulitzercenter.shorthandstories.com/2019-annual-report/index.html; https://www.nytimes.com/interactive/2019/12/20/magazine/1619-intro.html; https://blog.cps.edu/2019/09/17/the-1619-project-and-chicago-public-schools/; https://www.wbfo.org/education/2020-01-17/your-story-is-in-the-textbooks -ours-isnt-buffalo-schools-adopt-the-1619-project; https://www.buffaloschools .org/cms/lib/NY01913551/Centricity/Domain/9000/1619-BPS-Curriculum -Infusion-Standards-Alignment_2020-2021.pdf.

48. https://quillette.com/2020/09/19/down-the-1619-projects-memory-hole/; https://www.washingtonpost.com/lifestyle/style/1619-project-took-over-2020 -inside-story/2020/10/13/af537092-00df-11eb-897d-3a6201d6643f_story.html; https://www.washingtonexaminer.com/opinion/the-1619-project-is-a-fraud; https://pulitzercenter.org/sites/default/files/printable_pdf_exploring_the_idea _of_america_by_nikole_hannah-jones_1.pdf. As of November 18, 2020: "chal lenges us to reframe U.S. history by marking the year when the first enslaved Africans arrived on Virginia soil as its foundational date."

49. https://web.archive.org/web/20210205082459/https://pulitzercenter.org/blog /announcing-1619-project-education-network; https://pulitzercenter.shorthand stories.com/2019-annual-report/index.html; IRS Form 990; https://pulitzercenter .org/blog/media-coverage-1619-project; https://www.nationalreview.com/news /chicago-public-schools-ceo-says-nyt-1619-project-to-be-taught-in-all-city -high-schools/.

50. https://pulitzercenter.org/builder/lesson/lesson-plan-exploring-idea-america -nikole-hannah-jones-26503.

51. https://pulitzercenter.org/builder/lesson/activities-extend-student-engage ment-26505.

52. https://whataretheylearning.com/detail/21/; https://www.learningforjustice.org /author/rebecca-coven.

53. https://web.archive.org/web/20100823105309/http://www.nea.org/tools/17231 .htm; https://web.archive.org/web/20210704090803/https://ra.nea.org/business -item/2021-nbi-039/; https://www.nationalreview.com/2021/07/reading-writing -and-racism-the-neas-campaign-to-gaslight-parents/.

54. https://www.blacklivesmatteratschool.com/endorsements.html; https://www .blacklivesmatteratschool.com/partnerships.html; https://neaedjustice.org/black -lives-matter-school-resources/; https://www.blacklivesmatteratschool.com/the -demands.html; https://www.blacklivesmatteratschool.com/contact.html; https:// ra.nea.org/business-item/2019-nbi-019/.

55. https://web.archive.org/web/20060317212535/http://www.essence.com/essence /lifestyle/voices/0%2C16109%2C1081943%2C00.html; https://www.brooklynron .com/2013/05/assata_shakur.html#:~:text=The%20conversations%20with %20Newsday%20are,of%20the%20Black%20Liberation%20Army.&text =In%201977%2C%20when%20Shakur%20got,in%20the%20law%2Den forcement%20community; https://www.google.com/books/edition/Forced_Pass ages/ss6WP-Y7wooC?hl=en&gbpv=1&pg=PA1&printsec=frontcover.

56. https://www.blacklivesmatteratschool.com/.

57. BLM 2020 Curriculum Resource Guide/High School/BLM High School_The Black Panther Party/BPP 10-point program Qs.doc, via https://www.blacklives matteratschool.com/curriculum.html; http://www.blacklivesmattersyllabus.com /wp-content/uploads/2016/07/BPP_Ten_Point_Program.pdf.

58. BLM 2020 Curriculum Resource Guide/Middle school/LESSON PLANS.docx, p. 6, accessed October 18, 2020, via https://www.blacklivesmatteratschool.com /curriculum.html.

59. https://www.ajc.com/blog/get-schooled/students-from-two-parent-families -achieve-grade-level-higher-than-children-single-parents/OR3uPiQPk22b DgN6FGqbBJ/.

60. https://nypost.com/2020/09/24/blm-removes-website-language-blasting-nuclear -family-structure/.

10: CHILD ACTIVISTS

1. https://nces.ed.gov/fastfacts/display.asp?id=372; https://www.cnn.com/2016/12 /21/politics/donald-trump-hillary-clinton-popular-vote-final-count/index .html; https://www.nationsreportcard.gov/.

2. https://files.texaspolicy.com/uploads/2020/09/01100711/Lindsay-Meckler -Action-Civics.pdf, p. 1.

3. http://actioncivicscollaborative.org/about-us/action-civics-declaration/; https:// files.texaspolicy.com/uploads/2020/09/01100711/Lindsay-Meckler-Action -Civics.pdf, p. 5.

4. https://woodrow.org/news/national-survey-finds-just-1-in-3-americans-would

-pass-citizenship-test/; https://citizenpath.com/us-citizenship-test-interview-prep aration.

5. https://files.texaspolicy.com/uploads/2020/09/01100711/Lindsay-Meckler -Action-Civics.pdf, pp. 13–14.

6. http://webserver.rilin.state.ri.us/BillText/BillText21/HouseText21/H6070.pdf.

7. https://defendinged.org/incidents/barrington-high-school-teacher-promises -bonus-points-for-students-who-testify-on-crt-bill/.

8. https://www.educationnext.org/kids-political-props/.

9. https://www.dailywire.com/news/dem-tells-high-school-grads-theyre-enter ing-capitalism-white-supremacy-remember-jihad-reject-objectivity; https://onem oco.org/stop-attacking-students-who-speak-out-for-equity/.

10. https://www.educationnext.org/kids-political-props/.

11. https://twitter.com/davidhogg111/status/1221645982187823110; https://twitter .com/davidhogg111/status/1225139236506042371; https://twitter.com/davidhogg 111/status/1225183660481163266.

12. https://www.washingtontimes.com/news/2018/mar/29/only-10-march-our -lives-student-protesters-were-un/.

13. https://www.influencewatch.org/non-profit/march-for-our-lives-action-fund/; https://freebeacon.com/issues/march-lives-now-operating-dark-money-non profit-advocacy-group/; https://www.philanthropy.com/article/march-for-our -lives-movement-sparks-broader-foundation-response-to-gun-violence.

14. https://www.everytown.org/press/everytown-continues-to-support-student -organizers-following-march-for-our-lives/; https://www.everytown.org/press /everytown-for-gun-safety-announces-2-5-million-grant-program-to-support -march-for-our-lives-sibling-marches-around-the-country.

15. https://www.fox5dc.com/news/montgomery-county-student-member-of-the -board-matt-post-addresses-crowd-at-march-for-our-lives.

16. https://www.cnn.com/2019/11/06/politics/bloomberg-everytown-for-gun-safety -virginia-elections/index.html; https://www.instagram.com/p/B3uuT9_JIwM/; https://www.everytown.org/about-everytown/history/.

17. https://web.archive.org/web/20200806170451/https://www.mocoforchange .org/voter-registration-drive; https://cuahmcmd.org/about-ycc; https://cuahmcmd .org/agents-of-change.

18. https://twitter.com/DA_Osorio/status/1318202968689311745; https://local12 .com/news/local/longer-video-paints-picture-of-cov-cath-confrontation-in-dc; https://www.nytimes.com/2019/01/20/us/nathan-phillips-covington.html.

19. https://www.youtube.com/watch?v=1f6rscSnooE&feature=youtu.be& list=PLk16vCS0BfPd8Gm5x4uguLztAGBFq9aUF&t=195; https://www.washing tonpost.com/local/public-safety/during-his-own-bachelor-party-teacher-sent -nude-photo-of-himself-to-eighth-grader-police-say/2020/08/27/45490ea4 -e8a8-11ea-bc79-834454439a44_story.html; https://bethesdamagazine.com/beth esda-beat/courts/mcps-teacher-congressional-candidate-pleads-guilty-to -sexually-abusing-student.

20. Stacey M. Childress, Denis P. Doyle, and David A. Thomas, *Leading for Equity: The Pursuit of Excellence in the Montgomery County Public Schools* (Cambridge, MA: Harvard Education Press, 2009); https://www.washingtonpost

.com/lifestyle/magazine/exit-interview-moco-superintendent-jerry-d-weast
-on-lessons-learned/2011/03/07/AFh6RxvC_story.html; https://www.montgom
eryschoolsmd.org/departments/budget/citizens/pdf/Citizens_BudgetFY03
.pdf, p. 26; https://www.montgomeryschoolsmd.org/uploadedFiles/learning
-journey/Board%20Report%20-%20All%20sections%20v28%209%2030.pdf,
p. 49.

21. https://www.montgomeryschoolsmd.org/uploadedFiles/learning-journey
/Board%20Report%20-%20All%20sections%20v28%209%2030.pdf, p. 29;
https://www.montgomerycountymd.gov/OLO/Resources/Files/2019%20Re
ports/OLOReport2019–14.pdf, p. 93.

22. https://www.montgomeryschoolsmd.org/uploadedFiles/learning-journey
/Board%20Report%20-%20All%20sections%20v28%209%2030.pdf, pp. 7, 29.

23. https://docs.google.com/spreadsheets/d/1cL1nXHpokPF22i_8yRQiCFjWlpET
-lhjE3iRdXwNe8E/edit?usp=sharing.

24. https://www.montgomeryschoolsmd.org/uploadedFiles/about/homepage/At
%20a%20Glance%20%2001.24.19.pdf, p. 1; https://docs.google.com/spread
sheets/d/1cL1nXHpokPF22i_8yRQiCFjWlpET-lhjE3iRdXwNe8E/edit?usp
=sharing.

25. https://mcpsmd.new.swagit.com/videos/20578, Item #5: 35:50; https://mcpsmd
.new.swagit.com/videos/20644, Item #10: 1:04:00; https://www.boarddocs.com
/mabe/mcpsmd/Board.nsf/files/AT6RL36C41F5/$file/Jennifer%20Young
.pdf, November 2017, pp. 2–3; https://www.montgomeryschoolsmd.org/uploaded
Files/departments/publicinfo/Boundary_Analysis/BoundaryAnalysis_Final
%20Report.pdf, p. 112.

26. https://www.washingtonpost.com/local/education/legislation-would-expand
-student-voting-rights-on-maryland-school-board/2016/03/30/1c5578c6-f6a8-1
1e5-8b23-538270a1ca31_story.html; http://mgahouse.maryland.gov/mga/play
/bc09bc49-8c30-4d13-ba53-f88733ebd5f9/?catalog%2F03e481c7-8a42-4438
-a7da-93ff74bdaa4c& https://www.montgomeryschoolsmd.org/press/index
.aspx?page=showrelease&id=6075.

27. https://www.mymcmedia.org/matt-post-elected-as-next-student-member-of
-the-board-of-education-video/; https://d3n8a8pro7vhmx.cloudfront.net/moco
forlocalschools/pages/21/attachments/original/1580314314/Lawsuit_-_Admin
istrative_Appeal.pdf?1580314314, pp. 6–7.

28. Emails obtained under FOIA; https://www.learningforjustice.org/author/me
linda-anderson; https://d3n8a8pro7vhmx.cloudfront.net/mocoforlocalschools
/pages/21/attachments/original/1580314314/Lawsuit_-_Administrative_Appeal
.pdf?1580314314, pp. 6–7.

29. https://www.mymcmedia.org/ananya-tadikonda-sworn-new-student-member
-board/; https://d3n8a8pro7vhmx.cloudfront.net/mocoforlocalschools/pages/21
/attachments/original/1580314314/Lawsuit_-_Administrative_Appeal.pdf
?1580314314, p. 7.

30. https://mcpsmd.new.swagit.com/videos/20578, Item#5; https://www.boarddocs
.com/mabe/mcpsmd/Board.nsf/files/B4DJU64CE644/$file/bfa%20draft%20
3%20rev.pdf.

31. https://www.montgomeryschoolsmd.org/boe/members/district1.aspx.

32. https://mcpsmd.new.swagit.com/videos/20644, Item #5.
33. https://www.montgomeryschoolsmd.org/uploadedFiles/about/homepage/At%20a%20Glance%20%2001.24.19.pdf.
34. https://poolesvillepulse.org/1782/current-events/mcps-board-of-education-takes-a-step-towards-increased-diversity/.
35. https://docs.google.com/spreadsheets/d/1cL1nXHpokPF22i_8yRQiCFjWlpET-lhjE3iRdXwNe8E/edit?usp=sharing.
36. https://mcpsmd.new.swagit.com/videos/20578, Item #5: 44:00.
37. https://mcpsmd.new.swagit.com/videos/20644, Item #5: 32:50.
38. https://www.washingtonpost.com/archive/politics/1978/09/25/prince-georges-white-flight-seen-linked-to-busing-order/13a8381f-9173-4ad9-9a24-4ffbf66b24b2/.
39. https://web.archive.org/web/20200806163442/https://www.mocoforchange.org/countywide-integration-project-1-1; https://www.youtube.com/watch?v=0DqlbHOtchQ.
40. https://www.youtube.com/watch?v=oqm36RlqM6o&feature=youtu.be, 1:30.
41. https://www.montgomeryschoolsmd.org/departments/regulatoryaccountability/glance/currentyear/schools/04201.pdf.
42. https://bethesdamagazine.com/bethesda-beat/schools/racial-equity-concerns-surface-at-boundary-meeting/.
43. https://diversity.unc.edu/data/ (last viewed on July 29, 2021); https://www.montgomeryschoolsmd.org/boe/smob/history.aspx; https://bethesdamagazine.com/bethesda-beat/opinion/opinion-repairing-progress-on-racial-economic-justice-must-be-priority-in-new-year/; https://bethesdamagazine.com/bethesda-beat/schools/student-school-board-finalists-share-common-views-on-reforms/; https://censusreporter.org/profiles/05000US24031-montgomery-county-md/; https://www.montgomeryschoolsmd.org/boe/members/.
44. https://www.fox5dc.com/news/montgomery-county-student-member-of-the-board-matt-post-addresses-crowd-at-march-for-our-lives; https://bethesdamagazine.com/bethesda-beat/schools/mcps-student-leaders-to-take-stage-at-march-for-our-lives-in-dc/; https://www.cia.gov/library/publications/the-world-factbook/geos/et.html.
45. https://montgomerycountymd.gov/boards/Resources/Files/sites/becc/minutes/2019/BECC-Minutes-11-18-19.pdf, p. 4; https://bethesdamagazine.com/bethesda-beat/government/proposed-raise-for-school-members-cut-from-140-to-40/.

11: FOUNDATIONS

1. https://www.sfgate.com/lifestyle/article/The-Rich-Kids-Who-Want-to-Tear-Down-Capitalism-15759903.php; https://medium.com/delapierced/how-i-became-a-patriotic-millionaire-8d3ba645b3e1; https://medium.com/delapierced/sel4sj-9ababbc6f5ab.
2. https://medium.com/delapierced/how-i-became-a-patriotic-millionaire-8d3ba645b3e1; https://www.sfgate.com/lifestyle/article/The-Rich-Kids-Who-Want-to-Tear-Down-Capitalism-15759903.php.
3. https://medium.com/delapierced/about-e1770f9f8577.

4. https://www.sfgate.com/lifestyle/article/The-Rich-Kids-Who-Want-to-Tear -Down-Capitalism-15759903.php; https://resourcegeneration.org/who-we-are /history/; https://resourcegeneration.org/frequently-asked-questions/.

5. https://www.fordfoundation.org/the-latest/news/ford-foundation-announces -180-million-in-new-funding-for-us-racial-justice-efforts/; https://www.new yorker.com/magazine/2016/01/04/what-money-can-buy-profiles-larissa-mac farquhar.

6. https://www.opensecrets.org/pres16/candidate?id=N00000019; http://data.foun dationcenter.org/#/foundations/all/nationwide/top:giving/list/2015.

7. https://www.macfound.org/grantee/propublica-41271/; https://www.propublica .org/series/segregation-now/p2; https://www.nytco.com/press/nikole-hannah-jones -joins-the-new-york-times-magazine/; https://www.macfound.org/videos/551/; https://www.nytimes.com/2019/08/18/reader-center/1619-project-slavery-james town.html; https://www.macfound.org/fellows/933/; https://www.nytimes.com /interactive/2019/08/14/magazine/slavery-capitalism.html; https://pulitzercenter .org/blog/pulitzer-center-named-education-partner-new-york-times-maga zines-1619-project; https://pulitzercenter.org/donors.

8. https://newsroom.howard.edu/newsroom/article/14641/two-iconic-writers -join-howard-university.

9. https://www.teachingforchange.org/zinnedproject; IRS Form 990 and foundation disclosures; https://www.zinnedproject.org/search/?_keywords=capitalism; https:// www.zinnedproject.org/search/?_keywords=imperialism.

10. https://steinhardt.nyu.edu/news/metro-center-wins-wk-kellogg-foundation -grant-racial-equity-work-among-parent-leadership; https://steinhardt.nyu.edu /news/nyu-metro-center-wins-bill-melinda-gates-grant-crse-research.

11. https://twitter.com/jbrownedianis/status/1247591896786120706; https://advance mentproject.org/staff/judith-browne-dianis/; https://projects.propublica.org/non profits/organizations/222653502/201800099349301420/full, p. 7; IRS Form 990 and foundation disclosures.

12. https://obamawhitehouse.archives.gov/sites/whitehouse.gov/files/images /MBK-2016-Progress-Report.pdf, pp. 12–13.

13. https://www.osibaltimore.org/wp-content/uploads/RP-plan-and-appendix .pdf, p. 4; https://www.osibaltimore.org/wp-content/uploads/2020/09/RP-Report -2020-FINAL.pdf, p. 6. A 2018 study in Pittsburgh found that suspension and arrest rates in restorative justice schools were essentially the same as others, and that academic performance worsened. Math scores for black students especially went down. A 2019 study in Maine "found that middle-school students who received the Restorative Practices Intervention did not report more school connectedness, better school climate, more positive peer relationships and developmental outcomes, or less victimization." https://www.baltimoresun.com/education /bs-md-restorative-practices-20201001-2quav5634zdnjpahbcx46w6m6e-story .html.

14. https://www.osibaltimore.org/wp-content/uploads/2020/09/RP-Report-2020 -FINAL.pdf, pp. 14, 28.

15. https://equityinthecenter.org/our-partners-and-advisors/; https://equityinthe center.org/eics-next-chapter/; https://equityinthecenter.org/so-you-want-to-be-a

-white-ally-healing-from-white-supremacy/; https://adawaygroup.com/wp-content /uploads/2020/06/Awake-to-Woke-to-Work.pdf.

16. https://equityinthecenter.org/services/working-sessions/awake-to-woke-to-work -building-a-race-equity-culture-open-enrollment-workshops/; https://community actionpartnership.com/wp-content/uploads/2020/11/Community-Action -Partnership-Leading-in-Crisis-20200820-1.pdf, pp. 6–8, 41–42.

17. https://ncee.org/2015/01/gene-wilhoit-on-the-common-core-part-1/; https://www .educationviews.org/common-core-architect-david-coleman/; Joe Clement and Matt Miles, *Screen Schooled* (Chicago: Chicago Review Press, 2017), Kindle loc. 2803; https://www.kentuckyteacher.org/news/2012/06/gene-wilhoit-announ ces-retirement/; IRS Form 990 and foundation disclosures; https://about.college board.org/leadership/david-coleman.

18. Clement and Miles, *Screen Schooled*, Kindle loc. 2803.

19. IRS Form 990 records.

20. https://hechingerreport.org/about/; https://hechingerreport.org/opinion-white -men-run-social-media/.

21. https://www.the74million.org/about/; https://www.the74million.org/supporters/; https://www.the74million.org/?s=equity; https://educationpost.org/about/; https:// educationpost.org/if-you-really-want-to-make-a-difference-in-black-lives -change-how-you-teach-white-kids/.

22. https://www.spencer.org/grant-archive/leading-while-black-and-female-ex ploring-microaggressions-lived-experiences-black-female-school; https://www .spencer.org/grant_types/journalism-program.

23. https://allianceforyouthorganizing.org/about/; https://www.fordfoundation .org/work/our-grants/grants-database/grants-all?minyear=2006&maxyea r=2020&page=0&minamount=0&maxamount=30000000&originating offices=&thematicareas=&search=%26SearchText%3Dalliance%20for%20 youth%20organizing; https://www.forbes.com/sites/michaeltnietzel/2019/11 /19/mtv-revs-up-its-1-thevote-campaign-for-the-2020-election/#537c 64ed1d44; https://yppg.org/; https://www.nysenate.gov/legislation/bills/2019/s2 273.

24. https://allianceforyouthorganizing.org/our-network/.

25. Ibid.

26. https://www.fordfoundation.org/work/our-grants/grants-database/grants-all ?search=%26SearchText%3Dsunrise&page=0; https://www.vox.com/the-high light/2019/9/10/20847401/sunrise-movement-climate-change-activist-mill ennials-global-warming; https://www.politico.com/magazine/story/2019/06/16 /sunrise-movement-boot-camp-227109.

27. https://www.youtube.com/watch?v=2EfHOAZg3xc.

28. https://www.theatlantic.com/ideas/archive/2019/02/dianne-feinstein-video -climate-change-sunrise-movement/583501/.

29. https://www.fordfoundation.org/just-matters/just-matters/posts/the-fight-for -equality-at-the-center-of-the-george-floyd-case/#:~:text=Law%20for%20 Black%20Lives%3A%20Law,social%20services%20in%20black%20communi ties; https://southernersonnewground.org/wp-content/uploads/2019/07/Until -Freedom-Comes-A-Comprehensive-Bailout-Toolkit.pdf; http://www.law4black

lives.org/values; https://drive.google.com/file/d/1o9UyprQgHsaNo-zDmsJTaU PgrOJDLBK_/view, p. 33.

30. https://www.politico.com/story/2019/06/07/kamala-harris-maya-1356591; https://thefederalist.com/2020/08/31/foundation-with-biden-campaign-ties -funding-leftist-agitators-on-u-s-streets/; https://www.independent.co.uk/news /people/news/untold-story-obama-s-mother-1787979.html.

31. https://www.fordfoundation.org/work/our-grants/grants-database/grants-all ?minyear=2006&maxyear=2020&page=0&search=%26SearchText%3Ddr eam%20defenders; https://web.archive.org/web/20180217092927/https:/dream defenders.org/about; https://dreamdefenders.org/stateattorneys/; https://dream defenders.org/ideology/; https://www.adl.org/blog/phillip-agnew-and-the-dream -defenders.

32. https://twitter.com/NorthStarFund/status/1351944940935385089.

33. For example, the congresswoman whose district includes all of Loudoun, plus part of a neighboring county, raised thirty-two times more than the nine-person Loudoun school board combined, while her district is only twice as big as Loudoun in population. https://dailycaller.com/2019/11/13/soros-prosecutors -virginia/.

34. https://worldpopulationreview.com/us-counties; https://www.worldatlas.com /articles/us-states-by-population.html; https://www.governing.com/archive/gov -voter-turnout-municipal-elections.html; https://www.niemanlab.org/2019/11 /damaged-newspapers-damaged-civic-life-how-the-gutting-of-local-news rooms-has-led-to-a-less-informed-public/.

35. https://empoweryouthnc.org/freedom-school/.

36. https://southernvision.org/sponsoredprojects/; https://projects.propublica.org /nonprofits/organizations/611639641/201902249349302260/full, part III, 4b, p. 2; https://www.fordfoundation.org/work/our-grants/grants-database/grants-all ?minyear=2006&maxyear=2020&page=0&minamount=0&maxamount =30000000&originatingoffices=&thematicareas=&search=%26SearchText %3Dsouthern%20vision%20alliance.

12: ARABELLA INC.

1. https://www.history.com/topics/us-presidents/theodore-roosevelt.

2. Karen Ferguson, *Top Down: The Ford Foundation, Black Power, and the Reinvention of Racial Liberalism* (Philadelphia: University of Pennsylvania Press, 2013), p. 25. The foundation existed before his death, but in a vastly smaller form.

3. Rene A. Wormser, *Foundations: Their Power and Influence* (South Carolina: Covenent House Books, 1993).

4. https://www.newyorker.com/magazine/2016/01/04/what-money-can-buy-profiles -larissa-macfarquhar.

5. https://rockfound.rockarch.org/precursors-to-a-new-philanthropy.

6. http://library.cshl.edu/special-collections/eugenics; https://www.battlecreeken quirer.com/story/news/2019/03/21/john-harvey-kellogg-battle-creek-michigan -eugenics-race-nazis/3202628002/.

7. http://thirdworldtraveler.com/Engdahl_F_William/Rockefeller_Plan_SOD

.html; https://dimes.rockarch.org/objects/EKVEPQLSDZ4B2PwYzX9ecp/view, p. 24; https://dimes.rockarch.org/collections/MBSHfZUUxYSMc2egA4MLAP? category=&limit=40&query=mary%20beard.

8. https://www.influencewatch.org/non-profit/population-council/; https://third worldtraveler.com/Engdahl_F_William/Rockefeller_Plan_SOD.html; https:// www.ourbodiesourselves.org/book-excerpts/health-article/forced-steriliza tion/; https://www.cwluherstory.org/health/35-of-puerto-rican-women-sterilized ?rq=Puerto%20rico.

9. Wormser, *Foundations*.

10. https://fordhaminstitute.org/national/commentary/power-people-part-2-historys -lessons-community-control; Ferguson, *Top Down*, pp. 1, 159.

11. Ferguson, *Top Down*, pp. 137–41, 162–63.

12. https://www.city-journal.org/html/race-and-americas-soul-15548.html; https:// www.jta.org/1969/01/17/archive/teachers-union-protests-anti-semitic-poem -broadcast-over-new-york-radio-to-fcc.

13. https://fordhaminstitute.org/national/commentary/power-people-part-2-historys -lessons-community-control; Ferguson, *Top Down*, pp. 145–46.

14. Ferguson, *Top Down*, p. 162.

15. Ibid., pp. 77, 109, 158, 164–65.

16. Rockefeller Archives, "Communications Consortium Media Center 1991–1993," via https://dimes.rockarch.org/, p. 30.

17. https://surdna.org/our-organization/our-history/.

18. https://philanthropynewsdigest.org/news/surdna-foundation-names-don-chen -as-new-president; https://philanthropynewsdigest.org/news/surdna-foundation -in-dispute-over-founder-s-intent; https://democracycollaborative.org/learn/collec tions/theory-and-policy-next-system; https://philanthropynewsdigest.org/news /surdna-foundation-in-dispute-over-founder-s-intent.

19. https://philanthropynewsdigest.org/news/surdna-foundation-announces-new -mission-grantmaking-areas;https://mellon.org/news-blog/articles/mellon-found ation-announces-transformation-its-strategic-direction-and-new-focus-social -justice/; https://news.yale.edu/2018/02/07/elizabeth-alexander-84-named-pres ident-mellon-foundation.

20. https://capitalresearch.org/article/foundation-adrift-part-1/.

21. https://capitalresearch.org/article/foundation-adrift-part-2/.

22. For example, https://www.detroitnews.com/story/news/local/wayne-county/2014 /11/11/detroitbankruptcyphilanthropykresgekellogggfordfoundation/188954 17/; https://www.fordfoundation.org/the-latest/news/five-major-foundations-to -increase-support-with-over-17-billion-to-assist-nonprofit-organizations-in -wake-of-global-pandemic/; IRS Form 990 and foundation disclosures.

23. https://drive.google.com/file/d/1G9RnGimM8ajtWQWntVhXRxJ3u16zD439 /view?usp=sharing, pp. 18, 21–29, 47–48.

24. https://capitalresearch.org/app/uploads/CRC_Arabella-Advisors-Dark-Money .pdf, pp. 5–10.

25. https://wikileaks.org/podesta-emails/emailid/21958.

26. https://www.usatoday.com/story/news/politics/2017/01/01/progressive-cam paigns-nationwide-get-silent-partner/96004224/.

27. https://wikileaks.org/podesta-emails/emailid/15393.

28. https://projects.propublica.org/nonprofits/organizations/205806345/201843 169349302864/full, p. 7; https://projects.propublica.org/nonprofits/organizati ons/205806345/20190316934930248O/full, pp. 1, 8; IRS Form 990 and founda- tion disclosures.

29. https://capitalresearch.org/app/uploads/CRC_Arabella-Advisors-Dark-Money .pdf, pp. 4, 8; https://www.influencewatch.org/app/uploads/2019/11/Sixteen -Thirty-Fund-Form-1024-Applicaton-for-Recognition-of-Exemption-Under-5 01a.pdf, p. 16; IRS Form 990 and foundation disclosures.

30. https://capitalresearch.org/app/uploads/CRC_Arabella-Advisors-Dark-Money .pdf, pp. 4–5, 10.

31. https://www.opensecrets.org/federal-lobbying/clients/summary?cycle=2020 &id=D000064955; https://www.opensecrets.org/federal-lobbying/clients/lobby ists?cycle=2020&id=D000070975; https://www.wusa9.com/article/news/local /virginia/arlington-man-wins-lottery/65-2fc4ce9f-2b61-4418-b8f7-171fb63 bbaea.

32. https://cdn1.opensecrets.org/news/wp-content/uploads/2020/06/01192922 /ChartUpdatesJune1.png.

33. https://www.opensecrets.org/news/2020/05/dark-money-networks-fake-news -sites/.

34. https://www.marylandmatters.org/2020/05/01/opinion-fomenting-fear-and -division-in-montgomery-county/.

35. https://twitter.com/EricLuedtke/status/1256199834954010625; https://twitter .com/GabrielAcevero/status/1256995259034341377; https://twitter.com/Delegate Reznik/status/1256938951803371525; https://www.marylandmatters.org/2020 /05/25/montgomery-co-elected-officials-warn-voters-about-school-board-can didate/; https://elections.maryland.gov/elections/2020/election_data/index.html; https://assets.documentcloud.org/documents/6827837/States-Newsroom-1023 -Application-Materials.pdf, pp. 5–6; https://cdn1.opensecrets.org/news/wp-con tent/uploads/2020/06/01192922/ChartUpdatesJune1.png.

36. https://www.gatesfoundation.org/about/committed-grants?q=national%20 network%20of%20State%20teachers%20of%20the%20year; https://www.gates foundation.org/about/committed-grants/2012/04/opp1058401; https://www .gatesfoundation.org/about/committed-grants/2015/06/opp1111876; https:// www.gatesfoundation.org/about/committed-grants/2016/10/opp1156107; NN STOY has recently spun off from New Venture by establishing its own nonprofit; https://www.gatesfoundation.org/about/committed-grants/2018/04/opp1192734.

37. http://www.nnstoy.org/wp-content/uploads/2018/01/Discussion-Guide-Cour ageous-Conversations-about-Race-in-Schools-1.pdf, pp. 1, 4.

38. https://www2.ed.gov/about/bdscomm/list/eec/equity-excellence-commission -report.pdf, p. 6; https://www.fordfoundation.org/work/our-grants/grants-data base/grants-all?search=%26SearchText%3Dequity%20and%20excellence %20commission&page=0&minyear=2006&maxyear=2021; https://www.gates foundation.org/about/committed-grants/2011/11/opp1045447; https://hewlett .org/grants/new-venture-fund-for-the-equity-and-excellence-commission-pro ject/; https://www.wkkf.org/grants/grant/2011/12/education-equity-and-excellence -commission-p3020365; https://www2.ed.gov/about/bdscomm/list/eec/index.html;

https://www.govinfo.gov/content/pkg/FR-2010-08-11/html/2010-19800.htm; https://www2.ed.gov/about/bdscomm/list/eec/meeting-transcript-02222011 .pdf; https://www.phillyvoice.com/former-congressman-chaka-fattah-sentenced -prison-fraud-schemes/.

39. https://www2.ed.gov/about/bdscomm/list/eec/equity-excellence-commission -report.pdf, pp. 35–36.
40. https://web.archive.org/web/20210608041722/http://archive.discoverthenet works.org/Articles/Buying%20Reform2.html.
41. https://www.battlecreekenquirer.com/story/news/2019/03/21/john-harvey -kellogg-battle-creek-michigan-eugenics-race-nazis/3202628002/.

13: THE CRISIS

1. https://www.cdc.gov/polio/what-is-polio/polio-us.html; https://www.discover magazine.com/health/the-deadly-polio-epidemic-and-why-it-matters-for -coronavirus.
2. David M.Oshinsky, *Polio: An American Story* (Oxford: Oxford University Press, 2005), p. 96.
3. https://www.notablebiographies.com/news/Ge-La/Greene-Brian.html; https:// www.justice.gov/ag/bio/attorney-general-eric-h-holder-jr.
4. https://www.stuyspec.com/undercurrents/diversity-in-depth-an-analysis-of -stuyvesant-s-demographics; https://data.nysed.gov/enrollment.php?year=2019 &instid=800000046741.
5. https://www.gothamgazette.com/city/8406-where-top-city-officials-stand-on -the-shsat-and-specialized-high-school-admissions.
6. https://data.nysed.gov/enrollment.php?year=2019&instid=800000046741; https://ny.chalkbeat.org/2018/6/5/21105142/de-blasio-s-specialized-school -proposal-spurs-outrage-in-asian-communities.
7. https://ny.chalkbeat.org/2019/3/28/21107180/i-wish-i-had-done-it-better-de -blasio-reflects-on-the-rollout-of-his-specialized-high-school-plan; https://www1 .nyc.gov/office-of-the-mayor/news/281-18/mayor-de-blasio-chancellor-car ranza-plan-improve-diversity-specialized-high/#/0; https://infohub.nyced.org /docs/default-source/default-document-library/school-math-results-2013 -2019-(public).xlsx.
8. https://ny.chalkbeat.org/2017/3/10/21099620/new-york-city-expanded-its -efforts-to-boost-diversity-at-elite-specialized-high-schools-so-why-hasn.
9. https://www.realclearinvestigations.com/articles/2018/06/21/asian_study_art .html; https://ny.chalkbeat.org/2018/6/2/21105076/mayor-bill-de-blasio-our-spec ialized-schools-have-a-diversity-problem-let-s-fix-it; https://nextshark.com/asian -americans-poorest-minority-group-new-york-city; https://www.fox5ny.com/news /students-across-nyc-prepping-for-shsat-exam; https://www.schools.nyc.gov /learning/programs/dream-program; https://www.bklynlibrary.org/calendar/free -shsat-prep-class-mckinley-park-meeting-20190713; https://web.archive.org/web /20210224140100/https://www.schools.nyc.gov/learning/student-journey /grade-by-grade/testing/specialized-high-school-admissions-test.
10. https://www.nbcnews.com/news/latino/unconscionable-latino-black-student -numbers-nyc-elite-public-high-schools-n1166741; https://docs.wixstatic.com /ugd/1c478c_63318392e5074e87bf6a934bbc7b3b56.pdf; https://cdn-blob-prd

.azureedge.net/prd-pws/docs/default-source/default-document-library/sample
-test-a-explanations.pdf?sfvrsn=831f566_4, pp. 4, 42.

11. https://nypost.com/2019/01/06/the-hypocrisy-behind-bill-de-blasio-and-rich
ard-carranzas-quota-drive/; https://www.nydailynews.com/opinion/ny-oped-my
-problem-with-shsat-20180614-story.html; https://www.nytimes.com/interactive
/2019/06/03/nyregion/nyc-public-schools-black-hispanic-students.html.

12. https://www.nytimes.com/2018/08/03/nyregion/admissions-test-shsat-high
-school-study.html.

13. https://www.nydailynews.com/opinion/ny-edit-save-these-schools-20201206
-zetx2p33bzbfvpwfhbiltu3gvq-story.html; https://nypost.com/2020/02/11/state
-sen-john-liu-clashes-with-richard-carranza-over-doe-treatment-of-asian-new
-yorkers/.

14. https://academic.oup.com/qje/article/135/2/711/5687353, Table I; https://data
.census.gov/cedsci/table?q=Table%20S0201%20&t=002%20-%20White%20
alone%3AIncome%20and%20Poverty&tid=ACSSPP1Y2019.S0201&hidePre
view=truecensus/ACSSPP1Y2019.S0201_data_with_overlays_2020–11–20T1
35121.xlsx.

15. https://centerracialjustice.org/our-supporters/; https://nypost.com/2019/05/26
/doe-may-have-claimed-asian-students-benefit-from-white-supremacy/; https://
www.nydailynews.com/new-york/education/ny-metro-city-officials-shutdown
-critics-of-desegregation-plan-20181025-story.html; https://www.wsj.com/articles
/new-york-city-set-to-adopt-culturally-responsive-education-in-schools-1156
4606684; https://nypost.com/2020/02/05/asian-protesters-temporarily-barred
-from-carranza-town-hall/.

16. https://www.pix11.com/2019/03/19/few-black-hispanic-students-receive
-offers-to-nycs-specialized-high-schools/; https://data.nysed.gov/profile.php?in
stid=7889678368.

17. Department of Education, Table 215.30, "Enrollment, Poverty, and Federal
Funds for the 120 Largest School Districts" (available at https://nces.ed.gov/pro
grams/digest/d19/tables/dt19_215.30.asp).

18. https://ny.chalkbeat.org/2017/11/20/21103783/five-months-in-crucial-part-of
-new-york-city-s-school-diversity-plan-begins-to-take-shape; https://projects.pro
publica.org/nonprofits/display_990/133297197/06_2019_prefixes_06–16%
2F133297197_201806_990_2019062116434222, p. 21; https://www.nydailynews
.com/opinion/ny-oped-mayas-choices-20201219-xixzzew55rd67div7eugnj
wadq-story.html; https://www.yourtango.com/2020335847/who-maya-wiley-hus
band-harlan-mandel; https://www.nytimes.com/2020/12/09/nyregion/scott
-stringer-schools-reopening.html; https://www.cityandstateny.com/articles/person
ality/interviews-profiles/maya-wiley-woman-nyc.html.

19. https://twitter.com/MATTtheG/status/1179760353317703680; https://nypost
.com/2019/11/24/quit-the-racial-demagoguery-and-start-working-for-better
-schools/; https://docs.wixstatic.com/ugd/1c478c_63318392e5074e87bf6a934b
bc7b3b56.pdf, p. 22.

20. https://www.nytimes.com/1970/09/27/archives/now-its-welfare-lib-now-its
-welfare-lib-welfare-has-come-to-be.html; https://www.nytimes.com/1973/08
/10/archives/dr-george-wiley-feared-drowned-civil-rights-leader-42-who
-headed.html.

21. https://www.nytimes.com/1970/09/27/archives/now-its-welfare-lib-now-its
-welfare-lib-welfare-has-come-to-be.html; David Horowitz, *The Shadow Party*
(Nashville: Thomas Nelson, 2010), Kindle locs. 1581, 1598, pp. 108–10; https://
www.nytimes.com/1973/08/10/archives/dr-george-wiley-feared-drowned-civil
-rights-leader-42-who-headed.html.

22. Horowitz, *The Shadow Party*, Kindle locs. 1638, 1647, 1669, pp. 111–12, 114.

23. https://www.thenation.com/article/archive/weight-poor-strategy-end-poverty/;
https://www.nytimes.com/1970/09/27/archives/now-its-welfare-lib-now-its
-welfare-lib-welfare-has-come-to-be.html; Horowitz, *The Shadow Party*, p. 106.

24. Horowitz, *The Shadow Party*, Kindle loc. 1638, p. 113; https://encyclopediaof
arkansas.net/entries/volunteers-in-service-to-america-4257/; https://www.nytimes
.com/1970/09/27/archives/now-its-welfare-lib-now-its-welfare-lib-welfare-has
-come-to-be.html.

25. https://www.nytimes.com/1973/08/10/archives/dr-george-wiley-feared-drowned
-civil-rights-leader-42-who-headed.html; Horowitz, *The Shadow Party*, p. 113.

26. Horowitz, *The Shadow Party*, pp. 123–24; https://www.foxnews.com/politics
/acorn-pleads-guilty-to-voter-registration-fraud-in-nevada; https://www.foxnews
.com/politics/18-former-acorn-workers-have-been-convicted-or-admitted
-guilt-in-election-fraud; https://chieforganizer.org/2004/04/01/different-days-on
-park-avenue-with-citibank/.

27. https://www.postandcourier.com/aikenstandard/news/acorn-embezzlement
-totaled-5m-not-1m/article_77905c42-646d-5fc1-8b24-38637324ac0a.html;
https://oag.ca.gov/system/files/attachments/press_releases/n1888_acorn_report
.pdf, pp. 6, 26; Horowitz, *The Shadow Party*, Kindle loc. 1787, pp. 124–25; Ron
Arnold, *Undue Influence* (Bellevue, WA: Merril Press, 2010), pp. 76–78.

28. https://www1.nyc.gov/site/ccrb/about/board/maya-wiley.page; www.linkedin
.com/in/mayawiley; Horowitz, *The Shadow Party*, Kindle loc. 1787, pp. 125–
26; https://projects.propublica.org/nonprofits/display_990/203395198/2007_12
_EO%2F20-3395198_990_200612, p. 22; https://projects.propublica.org/non
profits/display_990/203395198/2012_12_EO%2F20-3395198_990EZ_201112,
pp. 14–15; https://projects.propublica.org/nonprofits/organizations/943213100;
https://projects.propublica.org/nonprofits/organizations/510198509; https://
www.nytimes.com/2014/03/01/nyregion/de-blasio-picks-more-liberal-activists
-than-managers-for-city-posts.html.

29. https://docs.wixstatic.com/ugd/1c478c_1d5659bd05494f6d8cb2bbf03fcc95dd
.pdf, pp. 32–33.

30. https://placenyc.org/2020/05/06/parent-survey-middle-and-high-school-ad
missions/; https://pix11.com/news/panel-recommends-getting-rid-of-gifted-pro
grams-in-nyc-schools/.

31. https://www.nationalservice.gov/programs/americorps/americorps-programs
/americorps-vista.

32. https://twitter.com/realSEEnyc/status/1320830380904189953/photo/4;
https://twitter.com/realSEEnyc/status/1321098641050927122; https://votefwd
.org/impact2020; https://twitter.com/realSEEnyc/status/1212736910776524800;
https://twitter.com/JaspreetVinayak/status/1129431898084847616/photo/1;
https://docs.wixstatic.com/ugd/1c478c_1d5659bd05494f6d8cb2bbf03fcc95dd
.pdf, p. 2.

33. https://www.seenycdoe.com/disproportionality/data; https://www.seenycdoe .com/disproportionality/definition; https://www.teenstakecharge.com/.

34. https://nypost.com/2020/05/16/carranzas-claim-he-cant-cut-34b-budget-a-lie -advocates/; https://nycimplicitbias-workshop.com/; https://nycimplicitbias-work shop.com/meet-our-team/; https://twitter.com/JChanKraushar/status/12679931 81871890432.

35. https://www.crainsnewyork.com/article/20180725/OPINION/180729955/asian -americans-should-embrace-reform-of-specialized-high-school-admissions.

36. https://nypost.com/2020/05/26/nyc-doe-wants-competitive-school-admissions -opposers-to-get-louder/.

37. https://studentequitysolutions.com/equity-consulting-services; https://integrated schools.org/nice-white-parents-in-nashville/; https://medium.com/teens-take -charge/im-one-of-the-lucky-ones-8bcbfd80185.

38. https://nypost.com/2019/12/31/top-doe-official-busted-on-child-sex-charge -was-never-vetted-by-agency/; https://nypost.com/2019/10/01/fourth-white-doe -executive-sues-over-racial-discrimination/.

39. https://ny.chalkbeat.org/2019/5/28/21108199/calling-all-educators-help-us -understand-new-york-city-s-implicit-bias-training; https://nypost.com/2020/05 /16/carranzas-claim-he-cant-cut-34b-budget-a-lie-advocates/; https://twitter.com /PaulForbesNYC/status/1262428971171536898.

40. https://www.thecut.com/2017/01/psychologys-racism-measuring-tool-isnt-up -to-the-job.html.

41. https://www.wsj.com/articles/new-york-city-education-official-charged-with -facilitating-a-child-sex-crime-11577752317; https://nypost.com/2019/12/31/top -doe-official-busted-on-child-sex-charge-was-never-vetted-by-agency/; https:// nypost.com/2020/02/24/city-investigators-say-doe-official-accused-of-sex -crime-lied-on-application/.

42. https://www1.nyc.gov/site/planning/planning-level/nyc-population/ population-facts.page.

43. https://nypost.com/2020/05/05/richard-carranza-calls-for-nyc-doe-overhaul- amid-coronavirus-crisis/.

44. https://nypost.com/2020/04/11/nyc-public-schools-will-remain-closed-for-rest -of-the-year/; https://nypost.com/2020/10/24/doe-gives-widely-differing-attend ance-data-for-nyc-schools/; https://nypost.com/2020/05/23/principal-caught-on -tape-pass-students-who-dont-learn-but-try/.

45. https://www.politico.com/states/new-york/city-hall/story/2020/04/15/remote -learning-exacerbates-longstanding-hurdles-for-low-income-families-1276811.

46. https://nypost.com/2020/04/28/de-blasio-unveils-new-school-grading-policy -due-to-pandemic/.

47. https://nypost.com/2019/12/17/over-140-nyc-schools-have-grades-with-90 -percent-state-exam-failure-rate/; https://www.ny1.com/nyc/all-boroughs/edu cation/2021/03/30/for-second-straight-year-students-will-be-exempt-from -regents-requirements; https://www.nea.org/advocating-for-change/new-from-nea /survey-70-percent-educators-say-state-assessments-not; https://www.nea.org /advocating-for-change/new-from-nea/racist-beginnings-standardized-testing; https://www.nea.org/advocating-for-change/new-from-nea/how-advocate-stand ardized-test-opt-out-policy.

48. https://nypost.com/2020/04/11/nyc-trying-to-graduate-as-many-kids-as-pos sible-amid-coronavirus/.

49. https://nypost.com/2020/10/26/new-doe-policy-wont-penalize-students-for -late-work-attendance/.

50. https://ny.chalkbeat.org/2020/5/5/21247484/coronavirus-screens-school-diver sity; https://nypost.com/2020/12/19/lawsuit-demands-doe-give-the-test-for-top -schools-in-30-days/.

51. https://projects.propublica.org/nonprofits/display_990/362481232/09_2020 _prefixes_35-37%2F362481232_201906_990_2020090417283414; https://www .sfchronicle.com/bayarea/article/S-F-school-board-strips-Lowell-High-of-its -15938565.php; https://www.cgcs.org/domain/57; https://www.bostonglobe.com /2020/10/21/metro/school-committee-debates-dropping-admissions-tests-citys -exam-schools-one-year/.

52. https://www.sfchronicle.com/education/article/Elite-Lowell-High-School-ad missions-would-become-15635273.php.

53. https://twitter.com/AliMCollins/status/1315789057654321152; https://www.daily wire.com/news/sf-board-of-education-commissioner-merit-is-an-inherently -racist-construct-designed-and-centered-on-white-supremacist-framing.

54. https://nypost.com/2020/05/07/de-blasio-dodges-questions-on-using-corona virus-to-overhaul-schools/.

55. https://placenyc.org/2020/05/06/parent-survey-middle-and-high-school-ad missions/; https://www.bloomberg.com/news/articles/2020-06-23/school-children -don-t-spread-coronavirus-french-study-shows; https://nypost.com/2020/05/17 /nypd-will-stop-people-from-partying-outside-nyc-bars-de-blasio/; https://www .msn.com/en-us/news/us/the-results-are-in-for-remote-learning-it-didnt-work /ar-BB155PAl.

56. https://www.demandsafeschools.org/wp-content/uploads/2020/07/Flyer-for -August-3-with-endorsers.pdf; https://www.demandsafeschools.org/demands/.

57. https://web.archive.org/web/20200817222150/https://www.demandsafeschools .org/action/.

58. https://web.archive.org/web/20200807203700/https://www.demandsafeschools .org/wp-content/uploads/2020/07/August-3-one-pager.pdf; https://www.demand safeschools.org/action/.

59. https://web.archive.org/web/20160317004743/http://populardemocracy .org/about-us/board; https://web.archive.org/web/20170824234844/http://pop ulardemocracy.org/about-us/board; https://www.whois.com/whois/demand safeschools.org; https://www.populardemocracy.org/brian-kettenring; https:// carnegieendowment.org/2015/06/19/dear-democrats-populism-will-not -save-you-pub-61788; https://www.foxnews.com/politics/acorn-pleads-guilty-to -voter-registration-fraud-in-nevada; https://www.populardemocracy.org/dir ector-base-engagement-0; https://www.populardemocracy.org/our-work/issues /all.

60. Department of Labor data.

61. IRS Form 990 and foundation disclosures.

62. https://projects.propublica.org/nonprofits/organizations/453813436; https://pop ulardemocracy.org/our-partners; https://www.opensocietypolicycenter.org/pdfs /ospc-summary_of_lobbying_activities-2019-q3.pdf, p. 9; https://www.nvm-ed

ucationfund.org; https://www.nvm-educationfund.org/ace-collaborative; IRS Form 990 and foundation disclosures.

63. https://web.archive.org/web/20170427225501/https://www.centerforsocial inclusion.org/about/our-history/.

14: ONE FAIRFAX

1. https://www.portlandoregon.gov/oehr/article/482467; https://cssp.org/wp-content /uploads/2019/01/One-Fairfax-FINAL.pdf, pp. 10–11.

2. https://cssp.org/wp-content/uploads/2019/01/One-Fairfax-FINAL.pdf, pp. 2, 10.

3. https://www.racialequityalliance.org/about/who-we-are/leadership-and-staff/.

4. https://www.racialequityalliance.org/wp-content/uploads/2015/02/GARE-Re source_Guide.pdf, p. 32.

5. https://cssp.org/wp-content/uploads/2019/01/One-Fairfax-FINAL.pdf, p. 11.

6. https://www.policylink.org/equity-in-action/webinars/job-guarantee-now -campaign; https://www.policylink.org/covid19-and-race/reparations; https:// allincities.org/where-we-work/chief-equity-officers-policy-network; https://us10 .campaign-archive.com/?u=e9543a56e4b46dff477f54e7e&id=1cbea3f448; https://cssp.org/wp-content/uploads/2019/01/One-Fairfax-FINAL.pdf, p. 12.

7. https://www.racialequityalliance.org/2018/03/14/gare-awards-innovation-im plementation-fund-three-core-member-cities/.

8. https://www.fairfaxcounty.gov/topics/sites/topics/files/assets/documents/pdf /equitable-growth-profile-summary.pdf; https://www.fairfaxcounty.gov/topics /one-fairfax.

9. https://cssp.org/wp-content/uploads/2019/01/One-Fairfax-FINAL.pdf, pp. 3, 13; https://nvaha.org/wp-content/uploads/2014/09/BECOMING-ONE-FAIR FAX-NVAHA-Community-Forum-1.pptx, p. 4; https://www.fairfaxcounty .gov/topics/sites/topics/files/assets/documents/pdf/one-fairfax-policy.pdf, p. 1; https://www.racialequityalliance.org/wp-content/uploads/2017/09/GARE _GettingtoEquity_July2017_PUBLISH.pdf, p. 20; https://www.fairfaxcounty .gov/topics/sites/topics/files/Assets/images/one-fairfax-equity-lens-info graphic.png; https://www.fairfaxcounty.gov/topics/sites/topics/files/assets/doc uments/pdf/one-fairfax-policy.pdf; https://www.fairfaxcounty.gov/housing/sites /housing/files/Assets/documents/One%20Fairfax/One%20Fairfax%20Resolu tion.pdf.

10. https://www.insidenova.com/opinion/editorials/sun-gazette-editorial-try -using-plain-english-fairfax-officials/article_79177812-4e72-11e6-96a1-83c2a 48ce6b1.html.

11. Renamed in 2020: https://dornsife.usc.edu/pere/about-pere/; https://cssp.org/wp -content/uploads/2019/01/One-Fairfax-FINAL.pdf p. 12; https://www.fairfax county.gov/topics/one-fairfax; https://projects.propublica.org/nonprofits/organi zations/943297479/201913189349312821/full; https://projects.propublica.org/non profits/organizations/943297479/201803199349318135/full; https://dornsife.usc .edu/eri/staff-directory.

12. https://www.fairfaxcounty.gov/topics/sites/topics/files/assets/documents/pdf /equitable-growth-profile-report.pdf, p. 45.

13. https://www.fairfaxcounty.gov/housing/sites/housing/files/Assets/documents /One%20Fairfax/One%20Fairfax%20Resolution.pdf, p. 2; https://www.fairfax

county.gov/topics/sites/topics/files/assets/documents/pdf/equitable-growth
-profile-report.pdf; https://dailycaller.com/2019/10/08/liberal-network-racial-eq
uity-policies/.

14. https://dailycaller.com/2019/11/04/school-busing-achievement-gap-data/.
15. https://www.youtube.com/watch?v=lanLp0XQ93U&feature=youtu.be, 53:38;
    http://www.connectionnewspapers.com/news/2019/jun/25/great-falls-res
    idents-fired-school-issues/.
16. https://www.youtube.com/watch?v=f2gs4kR-hAU; https://www.youtube.com
    /watch?v=SppzehDD7K4&feature=emb_imp_woyt.
17. https://twitter.com/Keys_Gamarra/status/1192152539321577472; https://twitter
    .com/PatHynes2020/status/1192247775028826112; https://twitter.com/KarlFrisch
    /status/1192162548004655105; https://www.secondwavemedia.com/concentrate
    /features/equityinitiative0485.aspx and https://www.racialequityalliance.org/wp
    -content/uploads/2017/09/GARE_GettingtoEquity_July2017_PUBLISH.pdf;
    Bernabei contract.
18. Bernabei contract; https://www.equityandresults.com/testimonials-1.
19. https://web.archive.org/web/20210118063500/http://www.pisab.org/programs/;
    https://pisab.org/our-history/; https://pisab.org/press-inquiries/.
20. https://www.pisab.org/our-principles/.
21. https://cssp.org/wp-content/uploads/2019/01/One-Fairfax-FINAL.pdf, p. 10.
22. https://www.racialequityalliance.org/wp-content/uploads/2015/02/GARE
    -Resource_Guide.pdf, p. 3, "Spotlights on Best Practices."
23. https://www.racialequityalliance.org/where-we-work/jurisdictions/.
24. https://allincities.org/where-we-work.
25. https://www.theatlantavoice.com/articles/atlanta-mayor-keisha-lance-bottoms
    -announces-opening-of-one-atlanta-the-citys-first-office-of-equity-diversity-and
    -inclusion/.
26. https://wisconsinexaminer.com/brief/a-closer-look-at-the-one-milwaukee
    -task-force/.
27. https://www.tampabay.com/health/report-with-population-shifts-on-the-way
    -pinellas-needs-to-change-20190418/.
28. https://www.policylink.org/sites/default/files/ABQ-Fact-Sheet-final.pdf.
29. https://allincities.org/where-we-work/economic-inclusion-southern-cities.
30. https://racialequitybuffalo.org/files/documents/report/theequitydividend
    finaljune2018.pdf, p. 83; https://racialequitybuffalo.org/our-work/roundtable
    -members/profile:dr-kriner-cash/; https://www.buffaloschools.org/domain/26;
    https://racialequitybuffalo.org/our-work/about-us/p:1/; https://www.wkkf.org
    /grants#pp=10&p=1&q=Greater%20Buffalo%20Racial%20Equity%20
    Roundtable.
31. https://racialequitybuffalo.org/files/documents/report/theequitydividendfinal
    june2018.pdf, pp. 1, 51; http://www.nationalcivicleague.org/wp-content/uploads
    /2017/11/Kimbrough-2017-National_Civic_Review-1.pdf, p. 2.
32. Manuel Pastor, *This Could Be the Start of Something Big: How Social Move-
    ments for Regional Equity Are Reshaping Metropolitan America* (Ithaca, NY:
    Cornell University Press, 2009), Kindle loc. 314.
33. https://twitter.com/Prof_MPastor/status/1276957024023019520; https://nonprofit
    quarterly.org/scaling-economic-solidarity-the-pandemic-nonprofits-and-power/.

34. https://dornsife.usc.edu/eri/about/.
35. https://dornsife.usc.edu/eri/manuel-pastor/; https://nonprofitquarterly.org/scaling-economic-solidarity-the-pandemic-nonprofits-and-power/.
36. https://twitter.com/Prof_MPastor/status/1277280882420641794.
37. https://prospect.org/civil-rights/latinos-future-american-politics/.
38. Pastor, *This Could Be the Start of Something Big*, Kindle loc. 3813.
39. https://www.ashevillenc.gov/department/equity-inclusion/https://www.racial equityalliance.org/jurisdictions/asheville-north-carolina-2/; https://allincities.org /where-we-work; https://kimberleearchie.com/about; https://www.ashevillenc .gov/news/asheville-reparations-resolution-is-designed-to-help-black-com munity-access-to-the-opportunity-to-build-wealth/.

15: SOCIAL ENGINEERS

1. Interview with Carol Silver; https://censusreporter.org/profiles/16000US0633 364-hermosa-beach-ca/; https://www.census.gov/newsroom/releases/archives /2010_census/cb12-50.html.
2. https://www.usatoday.com/in-depth/news/nation/2021/04/14/zoning-biden-in frastructure-bill-would-curb-single-family-housing/7097434002/.
3. https://www.cnn.com/politics/live-news/rnc-2020-day-1/h_ca56ac2d425e49 59d6ce5c94b84c6d7e.
4. https://joebiden.com/housing/; https://www.booker.senate.gov/news/press/booker -clyburn-take-innovative-two-pronged-approach-to-tackling-affordable-hous ing-crisis.
5. https://nlihc.org/sites/default/files/AG-2019/07-06_AFFH-Suspended-2015 -Final-Rule.pdf, pp. 1–2.
6. https://beta.regulations.gov/document/HUD-2013-0066-0889/; https://nlihc.org /sites/default/files/AG-2019/07-06_AFFH-Suspended-2015-Final-Rule.pdf, p. 5.
7. https://web.archive.org/web/20200722163631/https://www.huduser.gov/portal /sites/default/files/pdf/AFFH_Final_Rule.pdf, p. 305; https://beta.regulations .gov/document/HUD-2013-0066-0001.
8. https://web.archive.org/web/20170226034840/http://www.limitedgovernment .org/publications/pubs/studies/ps-15-6.pdf, pp. 3, 10–12, 14.
9. https://beta.regulations.gov/document/HUD-2013-0066-0889/.
10. Pastor, *This Could Be the Start of Something Big*, Kindle locs. 376, 258.
11. Myron Orfield, *Metropolitics* (Washington, DC: Brookings Institution Press, 1997), p. 12.
12. Ibid., pp. 18–19, 28.
13. Ibid., pp. 9, 118, 124.
14. https://web.archive.org/web/20191013031550/https://2lffqo2moysixpyb349z0bj6 -wpengine.netdna-ssl.com/wp-content/uploads/2017/03/12.2-Our-Immense -Achievement-Gap-WEB.pdf, pp. 17–18, 65, 87.
15. Ibid., pp. 12, 19, 47.
16. https://www.the74million.org/article/how-minnesotas-push-for-integrated -schools-is-sparking-a-war-against-charters-serving-minority-families/.
17. https://open.mitchellhamline.edu/cgi/viewcontent.cgi?referer=&httpsredir =1&article=1365&context=wmlrpp, pp. 50–54, 60; https://open.mitchellham

line.edu/cgi/viewcontent.cgi?referer=&httpsredir=1&article=1296&context
=wmlr.

18. https://web.archive.org/web/20191013031550/https://2lffqo2moysixpyb349
z0bj6-wpengine.netdna-ssl.com/wp-content/uploads/2017/03/12.2-Our
-Immense-Achievement-Gap-WEB.pdf, pp. 13, 87–89.

19. https://www.politico.com/news/magazine/2020/08/06/suburbs-history-race
-politics-391966; https://www.newgeography.com/content/006882-latest-data
-shows-pre-pandemic-suburbanexurban-population-gains.

20. Orfield, *Metropolitics*, pp. 12–15.

21. Ibid., pp. 13, 109–11, 115, 12, 15, 37.

22. Ibid., p. 83; https://censusreporter.org/profiles/01000US-united-states/; https://
www.census.gov/prod/cen1990/wepeople/we-1.pdf p. 3; Stanley Kurtz, *Spreading the Wealth* (New York: Sentinel, 2012), Kindle loc. 903.

23. https://www.influencewatch.org/non-profit/gamaliel-foundation/; Kurtz, *Spreading the Wealth*, Kindle locs. 175, 875; St. Paul Ecumenical Alliance of Congre-
gations; https://shelterforce.org/1998/03/01/leveling-the-playing-field/; Orfield,
Metropolitics, pp. 131, 139–41.

24. Orfield, *Metropolitics*, pp. 13, 133; https://metrocouncil.org/Planning/Pub
lications-And-Resources/Thrive-MSP-2040-Plan-(1)/ThriveMSP2040.aspx, p. 7.

25. Orfield, *Metropolitics*, pp. 127, 141, 152–53, 59.

26. Ibid., p. 59.

27. https://www.city-journal.org/rise-of-new-left-urbanists; https://www.planetizen
.com/features/95189–100-most-influential-urbanists; https://www.national
review.com/corner/meet-tod-way-obama-wants-you-live-stanley-kurtz/.

28. Orfield, *Metropolitics*, pp. 3, 140, 86, 84.

29. Pastor, *This Could Be the Start of Something Big*, Kindle locs. 3102, 2852;
https://abell.org/sites/default/files/publications/cd-louisvillemerger1013.pdf;
https://www.statista.com/statistics/432599/us-metropolitan-areas-with-the
-highest-percentage-of-white-population/.

30. Pastor, *This Could Be the Start of Something Big*, Kindle locs. 2689, 2701.

31. https://www.mwcog.org/newsroom/racialequitycohort/; https://wamu.org/story
/19/11/20/sweeping-racial-equity-bill-passed-unanimously-by-montgomery
-county/; https://www.racialequityalliance.org/where-we-work/jurisdictions/.

32. https://localprogress.org/wp-content/uploads/2019/01/Livable-Cities.pdf; https://
localprogress.org/wp-content/uploads/2019/01/Equitable-Infrastructure.pdf;
https://localprogress.org/wp-content/uploads/2019/01/Funding-Public-Transit
-and-Improving-Service.pdf; https://localprogress.org/who-we-are/about-us/;
Pastor, *This Could Be the Start of Something Big*, Kindle loc. 1877; https://
localprogress.org/who-we-are/network/; https://localprogress.org/who-we-are
/staff/; https://localprogress.org/who-we-are/board-members/.

33. https://web.archive.org/web/20160317004743/http://populardemocracy.org
/about-us/board; https://web.archive.org/web/20170824234844/http://popular
democracy.org/about-us/board; nydailynews.com/opinion/ny-oped-this-virus
-should-finally-kill-school-screens-20201009-itgnpuark5b3xbgzl4wgmeuaxi
-story.html; https://localprogress.org/who-we-are/board-members/ (last viewed
on August 4, 2021); https://www.liuna.org/liuna-structure.

34. https://tcf.org/content/report/minneapolis-ended-single-family-zoning/; https://www.nytimes.com/2018/12/13/us/minneapolis-single-family-zoning.html; https://www.bloomberg.com/news/articles/2019-10-11/how-cities-tackle-the-affordable-housing-crisis; https://www.minneapolismn.gov/government/city-council/ward-10/about-lisa-bender/.

35. https://beta.regulations.gov/document/HUD-2011-0061-0001; Jason Reece, *In Pursuit of a Just Region: The Vision, Reality and Implications of the Sustainable Communities Initiative*, Ph.D. diss., The Ohio State University, 2016, pp. 125, 20, 21, http://rave.ohiolink.edu/etdc/view?acc_num=osu1468971589.

36. https://www.policylink.org/sites/default/files/policylink-sci-comments 3-12-10.pdf.

37. https://www.hudexchange.info/resource/4601/the-2011-sustainable-communities-regional-planning-grant-equity-guide/; https://www.policylink.org/sites/default/files/2011-sc-regional-planning-grant-equity-guide.pdf.

38. john powell chooses not to capitalize his name; https://beta.regulations.gov/document/HUD-2011-0061-0005; https://kirwaninstitute.osu.edu/article/milestone-hud-sustainable-communities-initiative; https://www.mhponline.org/images/stories/docs/research/Report_Fair-Housing-in-Rural-Regions-MHP-Kirwan-2015.pdf, p. 4; https://www.policylink.org/sites/default/files/PNIBMA resourceguide_6%2B24%2B13.pdf, p. 3; Pastor, *This Could Be the Start of Something Big*, Kindle loc. 2346; https://www.law.umn.edu/institute-metropolitan-opportunity/about-institute-metropolitan-opportunity; https://projects.propublica.org/nonprofits/display_990/510198509/2011_07_EO%2F51-0198509_990_201012, p. 8.

39. Reece, *In Pursuit of a Just Region*, pp. 6, 121, 127.

40. https://www.hud.gov/sites/documents/2017PSS_POC.PDF; https://www.lwvlamv.org/glossary/plan-bay-area/; https://www.bizjournals.com/sanfrancisco/print-edition/2013/05/31/new-housing-targets-spur-a-bay-area.html?page=all.

41. https://www.planbayarea.org/2040-plan/quick-facts/faq-page.

42. https://www.planbayarea.org/sites/default/files/pdf/prosperity/research/FHEA_BAY_AREA_and_Appendices.pdf, pp. 2, 179.

43. http://breakthroughcommunities.info/pdf/breakthrough-communities-resource-kit-2012-04-05-revision-b.pdf, pp. 2, 8, 22–23.

44. Reece, *In Pursuit of a Just Region*, pp. 192, 195–96, 124.

45. Ibid., pp. 126, 138, 175, 182–83, 163; https://www.ewgateway.org/community-planning/sustainability-planning/.

46. IRS Form 990 and foundation disclosures.

47. Reece, *In Pursuit of a Just Region*, p. 250.

48. https://www.law.umn.edu/profiles/myron-orfield; https://www.policylink.org/our-work/community/housing.

49. https://projects.propublica.org/nonprofits/organizations/131684331/2016 13139349100776/IRS990PF; https://www.opensocietyfoundations.org/grants/past?filter_keyword=center+for+popular+democracy.

50. https://beta.regulations.gov/comment/HUD-2013-0066-0768, Attachment 1, pp. 1, 11–12; https://beta.regulations.gov/comment/HUD-2015-0009-0024; https://beta.regulations.gov/comment/HUD-2013-0066-0691, Attachment, p. 8.

51. https://www.regulations.gov/comment/HUD-2013-0066-0822, Attachment, pp. 2, 6.
52. https://www.federalregister.gov/documents/2021/06/10/2021-12114/restoring -affirmatively-furthering-fair-housing-definitions-and-certifications; https://www .hud.gov/press/press_releases_media_advisories/HUD_No_21_098.
53. https://govsalaries.com/orfield-jr-myron-w-30630292.
54. https://www.cpsd.us/cms/one.aspx?portalId=3042869&pageId=69206927.
55. Orfield, *Metropolitics*, pp. 88–89; https://www.nytimes.com/2020/12/10/us/port land-eviction-protests.html; https://www.usnews.com/news/cities/articles/2020 -06-18/how-gentrification-is-displacing-black-people-from-george-floyds -childhood-neighborhood-in-houston; https://www.jstor.org/stable/27894698; https://www.newsweek.com/seattle-capitol-hill-protesters-gentrification -black-lives-matter-1511192.
56. https://www.sfgate.com/local-donotuse/article/map-street-sidewalk-poop- feces-311-report-waste-13278828.php; Robert Bruegmann, *Sprawl: A Compact History* (Chicago: University of Chicago Press, 2006), Kindle locs. 83, 943; https://www.nytimes.com/2021/05/04/upshot/census-new-results-county.html; https://www.forbes.com/sites/joelkotkin/2015/11/03/so-much-for-the-death-of -sprawl-americas-exurbs-are-booming. There are 3,000 counties in the United States, but half of the population lives in 146 of them. https://www.business insider.com/half-of-the-united-states-lives-in-these-counties-2013-9.
57. https://www.edworkingpapers.com/sites/default/files/ai20-318.pdf, p. 5.
58. Pastor, *This Could Be the Start of Something Big*, Kindle loc. 570.
59. https://overflow.solutions/special-projects/each-congressional-district-ranked -by-population-density-colored-by-political-party-of-the-representative/.
60. https://www.nytimes.com/2020/05/05/business/coronavirus-live-leave.html; https://www.wsj.com/articles/the-great-reshuffling-is-shifting-wealth-to-the -exurbs-11624636827; https://www.wsj.com/articles/remote-work-is-reshaping -san-francisco-as-tech-workers-flee-and-rents-fall-11597413602; https://www.sf weekly.com/news/remote-work-is-here-to-stay/; https://www.cnbc.com/2020/10 /13/dropbox-latest-san-francisco-tech-company-making-remote-work-per manent.html; https://www.vox.com/recode/2020/5/21/21266570/facebook-re mote-work-from-home-mark-zuckerberg-twitter-covid-19-coronavirus.
61. https://www.bloomberg.com/news/articles/2020-12-08/san-francisco -apartment-rents-drop-35-as-tech-embraces-remote-work-during-covid.

16: BOOTLEGGERS AND BAPTISTS

1. https://censusreporter.org/profiles/05000US24027-howard-county-md/.
2. https://www.hcpss.org/f/schools/profiles/prof_hs_riverhill.pdf; https://www.hc pss.org/f/aboutus/profile.pdf.
3. https://ppe.mercatus.org/system/files/the_legacy_of_bruce_yandle_sample .pdf, p. 16.
4. https://www.hiruyhadgu.com/news/2019/9/27/the-circle-of-influence-hurting -affordable-housing-in-howard-county.
5. https://elections2018.news.baltimoresun.com/primary/howard-county/county -council/district-3/hiruy-hadgu/; https://elections2018.news.baltimoresun.com

/howard-county/county-council/district-3/christiana-rigby/; https://cc.howard countymd.gov/Districts/District-3/Biography; https://emergeamerica.org/about/; https://emergeamerica.org/about/frequently-asked-questions/; https://www .opensecrets.org/527s/527cmtedetail_contribs.php?ein=464904157&cycle =2018; https://emergeamerica.org/alumnae-in-office/; https://web.archive.org /web/20190421211854/https://christianarigby.com/endorsed-by-the-balti more-sun/.

6. https://elections.maryland.gov/elections/2018/results/primary/gen_results _2018_1_by_county_140.html; https://jameshoward.us/2018/11/13/the-size-and -structure-of-the-howard-county-council/.

7. https://finance.yahoo.com/news/howard-hughes-announces-management -reshuffle-202005358.html; https://apnews.com/press-release/pr-newswire/new -york-houston-north-america-government-regulations-government-and-politics -38af6b344cf92cf300679b97a5791474; https://www.baltimoresun.com/maryland /howard/columbia/ph-ho-cf-downtown-hearing-july-0721-20160719-story .html; https://www.bizmonthly.com/fitchitt-named-region-president/; https:// apps.howardcountymd.gov/olis/GetFile.aspx?id=13914, p. 7.

8. https://web.archive.org/web/20210505113359/https://www.howardcountymd .gov/About-HoCo/County-Executive/Adequate-public-facilities-ordinance -task-force; https://www.mdspe.org/page/Newlaws; https://www.baltimoresun .com/maryland/howard/columbia/ph-ho-cf-council-legislative-session-0208 -story.html.

9. http://talkin-oh.com/index.php/our-attorneys-and-staff/thomas-g-coale; https://thedailyrecord.com/2018/12/03/thomas-g-coale-talkin-oh/; https://twit ter.com/PodcastElevate/status/1204131850257489920; http://elevatemdpodcast .com/.

10. https://patch.com/maryland/columbia/blogger-to-resign-from-ca-board-to -run-for-public-office; https://www.baltimoresun.com/news/bs-xpm-2009-04-19 -0904170112-story.html.

11. https://twitter.com/hocorising/status/1134584421640749062; https://twitter.com /hocorising/status/1138115393040650243; https://twitter.com/hocorising/status /1192178000059682823.

12. https://www.marylandmatters.org/2021/05/26/opinion-ending-single-family -detached-zoning-benefits-everyone/; https://twitter.com/hocorising/status/14 18911394712391684; https://www.marylandmatters.org/2021/08/02/opinion -maryland-needs-a-housing-governor/.

13. https://egov.maryland.gov/businessexpress/EntitySearch/BusinessInformation /D19769033?ImageError=error&ErrorCode=1&FilingNumber=5000 000002687217, pp. 1–2; hocoforall.com; https://mpia.hcpss.org/sites/default /files/2020-03/MPIA%202020-172%20S2%20Emails_REDACTED.pdf, pp. 41, 43.

14. https://mpia.hcpss.org/sites/default/files/2019-09/060.19.B1School.Boundary -RFP.pdf; https://mpia.hcpss.org/sites/default/files/2019-06/Cooperative%20 Strategies%20Response%20REDACTED.pdf; https://mpia.hcpss.org/sites/de fault/files/2019-09/Coop.%20Strategies%20Signed%20Agreement.pdf,p.1;https:// mpia.hcpss.org/sites/default/files/2019-11/MPIA%202020-214%20Supplier _Invoices%20CoopStrategies.pdf.

15. https://apps.howardcountymd.gov/olis/GetFile.aspx?id=25598, pp. 1–5; https://nces.ed.gov/programs/coe/pdf/coe_coi.pdf.

16. https://www.facebook.com/ads/library/?active_status=all&ad_type=all&country=US&view_all_page_id=440606919827309&search_type=page&media_type=all; https://www.enterprisecommunity.org/financing-and-development/community-development; https://www.enterprisecommunity.org/about/our-people/brian-mclaughlin; https://www.howardcountymd.gov/News/ArticleID/1730/News103019c.

17. https://mpia.hcpss.org/sites/default/files/2020–03/MPIA%202020-172%20S2%20Emails_REDACTED.pdf; https://twitter.com/mavisellisboe/status/747107723444092928; https://www.youtube.com/watch?v=3vwuRN_kGwM 0:27; https://mavisellisblog.wordpress.com/about/; https://www.mabe.org/advocacy/legislative-committee-2/; https://www.hcpss.org/school-planning/boundary-review/process/; https://mpia.hcpss.org/sites/default/files/2019-10/MPIA%202020-146%20Unofficial%20Draft%20Notes.pdf, p. 8; https://www.hcpss.org/f/schoolplanning/2019/aac-report-draft.pdf.

18. https://go.boarddocs.com/mabe/hcpssmd/Board.nsf/files/BFATU378FF8A/%24file/08%2020%202019%20Attendance%20Area%20Adjustment%20BR.pdf, p. 8.

19. https://mpia.hcpss.org/sites/default/files/2020-03/1%20Pages%20from%20MPIA%202020-163%20Emails%20REDACTED.pdf, pp. 22–23.

20. Ibid., p. 24; https://twitter.com/richardakohn; https://web.archive.org/web/20190830052109/https://www.ansc.umd.edu/people/rick-kohn; https://mpia.hcpss.org/sites/default/files/2020-03/1%20Pages%20from%20MPIA%202020,163%20Emails%20REDACTED.pdf, pp. 4–5; https://www.howardcountymd.gov/News/ArticleID/1378/News012819.

21. https://apps.howardcountymd.gov/olis/LegislationDetail.aspx?LegislationID=12323; https://www.yumpu.com/en/document/read/24087382/pdf-report-howard-county-public-schools, p. 3; https://web.archive.org/web/20191228210628/https://www.hcpss.org/f/aboutus/profile.pdf.

22. https://apps.howardcountymd.gov/olis/LegislationDetail.aspx?LegislationID=12323.

23. https://cc.howardcountymd.gov/Portals/0/Documents/CouncilMain/Press%20Releases/2019/CMR_OJ_DJ%20Desegregation%20Press%20Release.pdf.

24. https://www.baltimoresun.com/maryland/howard/cng-ho-school-board-resolution-emails-0821-20190822-ua36brcubbc3lhjtu7agbviuiy-story.html.

25. https://foxbaltimore.com/news/local/mass-protests-howard-county-parents-furious-over-redistricting-plans; https://baltimore.cbslocal.com/2019/10/07/i-want-to-stay-with-my-friends-protests-continue-against-howard-county-school-redistricting-plan-at-hearings/; https://www.baltimoresun.com/opinion/columnists/zurawik/bs-ed-zontv-amara-wbal-schools-20190926-4vpmc7vjyrgureartygedin7t4-story.html.

26. https://www.facebook.com/ads/library/?id=2384538068290298; http://www.centermaryland.org/; https://www.kopublicaffairs.com/leadership; https://www.baltimoresun.com/opinion/op-ed/bs-ed-ko-20131205-story.html.

27. https://www.howardcountymd.gov/LinkClick.aspx?fileticket=z1eeYd4cA98%3d&portalid=0.

28. https://scotteblog.com/2019/09/18/apparently-there-are-different-rules
-for-elected-officials-and-the-public-when-it-comes-to-testifying-about
-hcpss-redistricting/; https://www.baltimoresun.com/opinion/readers-respond
/bs-ed-rr-parents-howard-county-redistricting-letter-20190919-p7b7
cggqyjcgtfbjtn66goo6ru-story.html.

29. https://baltimore.cbslocal.com/2019/10/07/i-want-to-stay-with-my-friends
-protests-continue-against-howard-county-school-redistricting-plan-at-hear
ings.

30. https://www.youtube.com/watch?v=TvbDWcfDdG0; https://dailycaller.com
/2019/10/31/honors-classes-math-racist-activists/.

31. https://mpia.hcpss.org/requests/2020-070; https://mpia.hcpss.org/sites/default
/files/2020-02/MPIA%202020-336%20Emails_REDACTED.pdf; https://www
.baltimoresun.com/opinion/columnists/zurawik/bs-ed-zontv-amara-wbal
-schools-20190926-4vpmc7vjyrgureartygedin7t4-story.html.

32. Unpublished FOIA communication; https://mpia.hcpss.org/requests/2020-
172; https://mpia.hcpss.org/requests/2020-265; https://mpia.hcpss.org/requests
/2020-160.

33. https://twitter.com/hocorising/status/1210579696905310208; https://mpia.hc
pss.org/sites/default/files/2020-03/MPIA%202020-172%20S2%20Emails
_REDACTED.pdf, p. 50.

34. https://www.baltimoresun.com/maryland/howard/ph-ho-cf-school-board
-election-1108-story.html.

35. https://rocoinhoco.com/september-11th-2018-sabina-taj-board-of-education
-candidate-on-kids-communities-and-pancakes/.

36. https://www.baltimoresun.com/maryland/howard/cng-ho-first-redistricting
-work-session-1017-20191018-stkwdrfofvcerpb26jtiv4432a-story.html; https://
www.law.cornell.edu/supct/html/05-908.ZC1.html; https://votejenmallo.com
/issues/; https://mpia.hcpss.org/requests/2020-217, p. 3; https://scotteblog.com
/2020/03/28/the-howard-county-board-of-education-violated-the-open-meet
ings-act-when-two-of-its-members-exchanged-electronic-messages-during-a
-public-meeting/.

37. https://www.eventbrite.com/e/episode-74-with-dana-goldstein-michelle
-burris-tickets-80128328989;https://web.centralmarylandchamber.org/Real-Estate
-Developers/The-Howard-Hughes-Corporation-1972; https://tcf.org/bridges
-collaborative/; https://www.eventbrite.com/e/building-equity-an-educational
-equity-housing-affordability-conference-tickets-65261667404#;https://www
.facebook.com/CenterMaryland/videos/478256539681116/; https://www.face
book.com/marylandbuilders/posts/2038858056214945; https://baltimorepositive
.com/odoherty-explains-significance-of-sept-10-educational-equity-and
-housing-affordability-conference-for-future-of-baltimore/.

38. https://www.facebook.com/CenterMaryland/videos/859600721123677/Uzpf
STc4NDM2NDEzMDpWSzoyNTUyMTU0MTQxNjc1Mjk0/.

39. https://www.facebook.com/groups/2481593048731404/permalink/254
5275365696505/.

40. https://hcpsstv.new.swagit.com/videos/38244?fbclid=IwAR2PvDunUPOK
WrL4DWBpqXtpcrASRZ0OM9pCW5zhTr0MixLt9JZtgzaUM84.

41. https://mpia.hcpss.org/sites/default/files/2020-01/MPIA%202020-259%20 KC%2011.21%20Notes_0.pdf.

42. https://www.baltimoresun.com/maryland/howard/cng-ho-redistricting -ratification-vote-1217-20191217-kke43vo5mvasdhjwhyd33ymd6i-story .html.

43. https://mpia.hcpss.org/sites/default/files/2020-01/MPIA%202020-272%20 VC%20Notes%2011_21.pdf; https://mpia.hcpss.org/sites/default/files/2020-01 /MPIA%202020-259%20KC%2011.21%20Notes_0.pdf; https://mpia.hcpss.org /sites/default/files/2020-01/MPIA%202020-260%20JM%2011_21%20Notes .pdf.

44. https://www.baltimoresun.com/maryland/howard/columbia/ph-ho-cf-hous ing-follow-0709-20150702-story.html; https://www.baltimoresun.com/maryland /howard/columbia/ph-ho-cf-tif-suit-0420-20170418-story.html; https://www .baltimoresun.com/maryland/howard/columbia/ph-ho-cf-council-votes -november-delay-1117-20161109-story.html; https://www.baltimoresun.com /maryland/howard/columbia/ph-ho-cf-drra-signing-0209-20170206-story.html.

45. https://www.baltimoresun.com/maryland/howard/cng-ho-school-surcharge -fee-1108-20191108-fbzsz65it5bm7jateuawkoy2vq-story.html; https://apps.how ardcountymd.gov/olis/GetFile.aspx?id=26307, pp. 18, 141.

46. https://apps.howardcountymd.gov/olis/GetFile.aspx?id=26307, pp. 1–3, 12, 18; https://bridges2hs.org/our-partners/; https://www.househoward.org/history.html; https://www.acshoco.org/programs/community-partnerships/housing-afford ability-coalition/; https://marylandbuildingindustrymdassoc.wliinc34.com/news /newsarticledisplay.aspx?ArticleID=36; https://web.marylandbuilders.org/news /newsarticledisplay.aspx?ArticleID=43; https://mpia.hcpss.org/sites/default/files /2019-12/MPIA%202020-239%20Emails_REDACTED.pdf, p. 13.

47. https://apps.howardcountymd.gov/olis/PrintSummary.aspx?Legislation ID=12334, pp. 5–6; https://www.baltimoresun.com/maryland/howard/cng-ho -apfo-bill-fails-20200409-2ciazibuzne3tcdj6omxh2indm-story.html.

48. http://www.snl.com/Interactive/newlookandfeel/4265772/pdf/Q3_2019_in vestor_deck.pdf, pp. 3–4.

49. Ibid., pp. 11, 13, 15, 20; https://twitter.com/hocorising/status/1410641148 960460802.

50. https://www.facebook.com/jenmallo4boe/posts/608843923179778; https://www .facebook.com/events/2545138838947725/; https://scotteblog.com/wp-content /uploads/2020/04/Mallo.pdf; https://scotteblog.com/2020/04/28/howard-hughes -corporation-provides-an-in-kind-contribution-to-a-howard-county-board-of -education-candidates-campaign/.

51. Interview with Dennis Kenez.

52. https://www.boarddocs.com/mabe/hcpssmd/Board.nsf/files/9XEKVT 4C268E/$file/02%2026%202015%20Approved%20Board%20Handbook.pdf, p. 16.

53. https://www.baltimoresun.com/opinion/op-ed/bs-ed-mcdaniels-1106-election -racial-divide-20201105-k67vpl3f6fbahichhp3hscheoa-story.html; https://codes .findlaw.com/md/election-law/md-code-elec-law-sect-16-206.html; https://case text.com/regulation/maryland-administrative-code/title-33-state-board-of

-elections/subtitle-17-early-voting/chapter-331706-early-voting-activities/sec
tion-33170610-electioneering.

54. https://www.msn.com/en-us/news/politics/howard-election-school-board
-seats-go-to-delmont-small-watts-mosley-mallo-and-lu-coleman-wins-judge
-race/ar-BB1b0cEF.

EPILOGUE

1. https://www.sigar.mil/pdf/quarterlyreports/2014-07-30qr.pdf, p. 12; https://
www.cbo.gov/system/files/2021-02/hEdandLaborreconciliationestimate.pdf,
p. 3.

ABOUT THE AUTHOR

LUKE ROSIAK is an investigative reporter with *The Daily Wire* who broke nationally known stories about the school system in Loudoun County, Virginia. He previously worked as a journalist at *The Daily Caller* and the *Washington Post* and is the author of the congressional-scandal true thriller *Obstruction of Justice*. He lives with his wife and children outside Washington, DC, in Fairfax County, Virginia.